ORDER AND HISTORY

VOLUMES IN THE SERIES

Volume Two - The World of the Polis

ERIC VOEGELIN

ORDER AND HISTORY

VOLUME TWO

The World of the Polis

LOUISIANA STATE UNIVERSITY PRESS

Coniugi Dilectissimae

In consideratione creaturarum non est vana
et peritura curiositas exercenda; sed gradus
ad immortalia et semper manentia faciendus.

(In the study of creature one
should not exercise a vain and perishing curiosity, but ascend toward
what is immortal and everlasting.)

St. Augustine, *De Vera Religione*

Preface

Order and History is a philosophical inquiry concerning the principal types of order of human existence in society and history as well as the corresponding symbolic forms.

The oldest civilizational societies were the empires of the ancient Near East in the form of the cosmological myth. And from this oldest stratum of order emerged, through the Mosaic and Sinaitic revelations, the Chosen People with its historical form in the present under God. The two types of order, together with their symbolic forms, were the subject matter of Volume I, *Israel and Revelation.*

In the Aegean area emerged, from the stratum of order in cosmological form, the Hellenic polis with the symbolic form of philosophy. The study of Polis and Philosophy matches, in the organization of *Order and History,* the earlier one on Israel and Revelation. Because of its size this second study had to be divided into the present Volumes II, *The World of the Polis,* and III, *Plato and Aristotle.* The two volumes, though each stands for itself in the treatment of its respective subject matter, form a unit of study.

Brief sections of the two volumes have been previously published as "The World of Homer" (*The Review of Politics,* Vol. 15, 1953, 491–523), "The Philosophy of Existence: Plato's *Gorgias*" (*The Review of Politics,* Vol. 11, 477–98), and "Plato's Egyptian Myth" (*The Journal of Politics,* Vol. 9, 307–24).

As in the earlier volume I want to say my thanks for the material aid, which facilitates the final work on this study, to the institution that wishes to remain unnamed.

ERIC VOEGELIN

1957

Table of Contents

Analytical Table of Contents

INTRODUCTION

Mankind and History

As our study of *Order and History* moves from Israel to Hellas, it does not move onward in time. In fact, the Hellenic experience of God as the unseen measure of man is neither a sequel to the Israelite experience of the God who reveals himself from the thornbush to Moses and from Sinai to his people, nor even an intelligible advance beyond it in the sense in which both of these experiences differentiate a new truth about the order of being beyond the compact truth of the myth. The leap in being, the epochal event that breaks the compactness of the early cosmological myth and establishes the order of man in his immediacy under God—it must be recognized—occurs twice in the history of mankind, at roughly the same time, in the Near Eastern and the neighboring Aegean civilizations. The two occurrences, while they run parallel in time and have in common their opposition to the Myth, are independent of each other; and the two experiences differ so profoundly in content that they become articulate in the two different symbolisms of Revelation and Philosophy. Moreover, comparable breaks with the myth, again of widely different complexions, occur contemporaneously in the India of the Buddha and the China of Confucius and Laotse.

These multiple and parallel occurrences complicate the problems of the relation between the orders of concrete societies and the order of mankind, which arise on occasion of every one of the leaps taken singly; and they add new ones that will not come into focus in the separate studies of the Israelite and Hellenic orders. A few reflections on this class of problems will be appropriate at this juncture, as an introduction to the Hellenic break with the myth.

The primary field of order is the single society of human beings, organized for action to maintain itself in existence. If, however, the human species were nothing but a manifold of such agglomerations, all of them displaying the same type of order under the compulsion of in-

stinct as do insect societies, there would be no history. Human existence
in society has history because it has a dimension of spirit and freedom
beyond mere animal existence, because social order is an attunement of
man with the order of being, and because this order can be understood
by man and realized in society with increasing approximations to its
truth. Every society is organized for survival in the world and, at the
same time, for partnership in the order of being that has its origin in
world-transcendent divine Being; it has to cope with the problems of its
pragmatic existence and, at the same time, it is concerned with the truth
of its order. This struggle for the truth of order is the very substance of
history; and in so far as advances toward the truth are achieved by the
societies indeed as they succeed one another in time, the single society
transcends itself and becomes a partner in the common endeavor of mankind. Beyond the primary field of order there extends a secondary field,
open toward the future, in which mankind is constituted as the subject
of order in history. Hence, neither is mankind a mere species in the
biological sense, nor are the single societies mere individuals of the genus
human society. While the societies and their orders have generic qualities
by which they are recognizable as such, these qualities are inextricably
interwoven with the unique qualities which the societies have by virtue
of their status in the process of history, by virtue of their participation
in the unfolding of an order that reveals mankind as something more
than a species. The nature of man is both generic and unique.

The generic-unique nature of man is not accessible to analysis in the
same manner as the essence of a finite plant or animal species. For, in the
first place, the history of mankind in which this nature unfolds extends
unknowably into an indefinite future. History has no knowable meaning
(eidos, or essence), and by the same token there remains a core of the
unknowable in the nature of man. And second, even what is knowable
about human nature is not explicitly known at all times to all men. For
history is the process in which man articulates his own nature; and neither the dimensions nor the limitations of man are explicitly known
before they have been experienced and the experience has articulated the
order of human existence. This is especially true of the historical dimension
of human nature. Though it is an essential component of man, its presence rises to the level of consciousness only through the leap in being.
Only when man advances from the truth of cosmic-divine order to the
differentiated experience of transcendent-divine order, does the order

of human existence in society acquire the luminosity of conscious historical form—as it does through the Mosaic response to revelation in the case of the Chosen People.

The anthropological and epistemological situation just adumbrated is the abysmal source of difficulties for a philosophy of history. For mankind, which is so blandly assumed to have history, is not an object of finite experience. However much we talk about mankind and history as if they were objects of science, all that is really given are the concrete societies whose members experience themselves in historical form by virtue of the leap in being. When such a center, luminous with truth about the order of being and its origin in God, springs up in the sequence of human societies, the light of the discovery radiates over the sequence and transforms it into the history of mankind in which the leap in being has occurred. The truth, to be sure, is not an illusion; and neither is the discovery in retrospect of a history of mankind. But if the philosopher accepts the truth, as he does when he makes history and its order the subject of his inquiry, he must also face the spiritual mysteries and theoretical problems which originate with the phenomenal manifestations of the generic-unique nature of man. And above all, he must face the phenomena themselves.

The principal phenomena which cause the difficulties are four in number:

(1) The leap in being, when it occurs, transforms the succession of societies preceding in time into a past of mankind.

(2) The leap in being, while it gains a new truth about order, neither gains all of the truth, nor establishes an ultimate order of mankind. The struggle for the truth of order continues on the new historical level. Repetitions of the leap in being will correct the initial insight and supplement it with new discoveries; and the order of human existence, however profoundly affected by the new truth, remains the order of a plurality of concrete societies. With the discovery of its past, mankind has not come to the end of its history, but has become conscious of the open horizon of its future.

(3) The initial leap in being, the break with the order of the myth, occurs in a plurality of parallel instances, in Israel and Hellas, in China and India, in each instance followed by its own indigenous history of repetitions on the new level of existence.

(4) The parallel leaps in being differ widely with regard to the radi-

calism of their break with the cosmological myth, as well as with regard to the comprehensiveness and penetration of their advance toward the truth about the order of being. The parallel occurrences are not of equal rank.

The mysteries and problems, which originate in the phenomenal manifestations, can also be reduced to a small number of principal types:

(1) Since the leap in being occurs really, and mankind is thereby discovered as advancing historically toward higher levels of existence in truth, the relation between this meaningful advance of mankind and the meaning of concrete human existence becomes problematic. In the progressivist intoxication of the eighteenth century Kant raised the sober question what interest a generation of man at any given time could have in the progress of mankind toward a cosmopolitan realm of reason. Even if a man should consider the labors of his life a step of mankind toward perfection, the fruit of his labors would be enjoyed by the men of a distant future. Hence, the meaning of history is not the answer to the question of meaning in the life of man. From progress in history we are referred back to the pilgrim's progress toward fulfilment through grace in death. The destiny of man lies not in the future but in eternity. Nevertheless, the raising of the question does not abolish the advances of mankind in the truth of order. Kant did not doubt the reality of progress. The relation between personal fulfilment and the partnership in the fulfilment of mankind is a mystery.

(2) The Kantian question, raised in the position of a man looking from his present toward the future, becomes even more poignant in view of the manner in which the unfortunates of the past, who once upon a time had also a present, are treated by their successors on the higher levels of the historical process. For in the retrospect of the leap in being, the cosmological order of the empires is not merely assigned its place at an earlier point of objective time, but sinks back into a past of substantive untruth, now superseded by the truth of existence in immediacy under God. Egypt becomes Sheol, the underworld of the dead souls, when Israel gains its life through the Berith; the Pharaonic order becomes the house of bondage when Israel wins its freedom in the Kingdom of God. And the same demotion in rank is inflicted on the past by the poets and philosophers of Hellas. From Hesiod to Plato, when the leap in being has gained the *aletheia,* the truth of existence, the old myth becomes the *pseudos,* the falsehood or lie, the untruth of existence in which the for-

bears lived. And the past fares no better at the hands of the moderns: the primitives have a prelogical mentality; the ancients indulge in anthropomorphic representations of the gods without seeing through the fallacies of their own making; and the Middle Ages are plain dark. These depreciations, to be sure, do not exhaust the attitude of man toward the past of mankind; they could well be balanced by praises of the past, by expressions of admiration for classic periods, by generous recognitions of the so-called contribution of earlier societies to the climax of contemporary civilization. The denigrations, however, more clearly than the eulogies, point to the real problem: that the past of mankind is not a spectacle staged to be praised or blamed by a present which at the time was the future. For human nature is constant in spite of its unfolding, in the history of mankind, from compact to differentiated order: the discernible stages of increasing truth of existence are not caused by "changes in the nature of man" that would disrupt the unity of mankind and dissolve it into a series of different species. The very idea of a history of mankind presupposes that constancy of nature; and the reality of that constancy is attested beyond a doubt by the experiences of the leap in being, by the experience of a transition from untruth to truth of existence in which the same man is the "old man" before, and the "new man" after, he has suffered the infusion of divine Being. Hence, the play of order is always enacted, not before the future but before God; the order of human existence is in the present under God even at the times when the consciousness of that present has not yet disengaged itself from the compactness of the myth. And the philosopher of history must, therefore, remain critically aware that the past and future of mankind is a horizon that surrounds every present, even though it becomes conscious only through the leap in being. Though we know, by virtue of our existence in historical form, that the truth about order differentiates in the course of history, we neither know why mankind has a past, nor do we know anything about its goal in the future. The millenniums in which the mystery of history has reached the level of consciousness have not diminished the distance from its eternity. The philosopher must beware of the fallacy of transforming the consciousness of an unfolding mystery into the gnosis of a progress in time. A study of order does not have the purpose of showing up the primitivity, naïveté, logical deficiency, or general benightedness of ages of the past but, on the contrary, to show men of the same nature as ours, wrestling with the same problems as ours, under the conditions of more compact experiences of reality and correspondingly less differentiated instruments of symbolization. This problem of historical interpretation is hardly yet acknowledged; and the task of reinterpreting the materials of history under critical, nonideological principles of relevance has barely begun.

(3) Only when the constancy of human nature and the sameness of its problems of order in every present is theoretically secured against ideological misconstructions, will the problem of a mankind that advances in history toward higher levels of truth reveal its formidable proportions. For precisely because the problem of order is the same for all men at all times, and because nothing less is at stake than the existence in truth under God, does every newly differentiated insight into the truth of order become everyman's concern. The leap in being entails the obligations to communicate and to listen. Revelation and response are not a man's private affair; for the revelation comes to one man for all men, and in his response he is the representative of mankind. And since the response is representative it endows the recipient of revelation, in relation to his fellow men, with the authority of the prophet.

This structure of authority, around which the history of mankind is built, would be a source of difficulties under all circumstances, because it brings the human passions into play. Spiritual fervor is not necessarily accompanied by tact; and men at large do not willingly recognize a new voice of authority when they hear it. The difficulties are infinitely aggravated, however, by the multiplicity of successive and parallel authorities whose rival claims extend into our own present through the historical continuity of the followership which they have found. And the philosopher of order and history cannot escape these passionate conflicts. When we proceed in our study from Israel to Hellas, we must be prepared to answer the pointed but quite legitimate questions that will be immediately raised: Why do we not proceed from Israel to China or India? Why do we proceed laterally in time at all? Why do we not rather follow the Augustinian example and develop a Judaeo-Christian *historia sacra* to the exclusion of Hellenic philosophy? Moreover, one could ask: Why do we not stop with Israel? And most radically: Why did we start with Israel in the first place, and not rather with India or China? Are we not indulging a "Western prejudice" in the choice of the starting point and the mode of procedure?

Whatever the answers to these questions will be—and only the execution of the study on *Order and History* as a whole can give them—it will have become clear that a philosophy of history cannot be an amiable record of memorabilia, in the hope that the passions which have caused phenomena of the past to survive in the memory of mankind were judicious in their choice. It must be a critical study of the authoritative structure in the history of mankind. Neither can the authoritative communications of truth about order, as they have sprung up in the course of history, be sympathetically accepted on an equal footing—for that would submerge us in the evils of historicism, in skepticism and relativism; nor can they be rejected by the standards of an ultimate truth, whether such ultimacy be attributed to a truth of the past or a new one discovered by ourselves—for such absolutism would involve us in the gnostic fallacy of declaring the end of history. A study that wants to be critical must take seriously the fact that the truth about the order of being emerges in the order of history. The Logos of history itself provides the instruments for the critical testing and ranking of the authoritative structure. For, without the leap in being that brings God and man into their mutual presence, without the creation of history as the inner form of existence in opposition to the cosmological form of order, there would be no problem of a history of mankind; and without the discovery of the logos in the psyche and the world, without the creation of philosophical existence, the problem of history would not be a problem of philosophy. Hence, the manifold of authorities must be critically measured, and their relative rank can be determined, by the degrees of approximation to the clarity of historical consciousness and of penetration to the order of the psyche and the world.

The principles which I have just attempted to formulate are supposed to furnish the critical foundation for the study *Order and History*. Since, however, the study moves within the millennial historical and philosophical forms that are its subject matter; and since in the course of this millennial history more than one attempt has been made to explore the essence of the phenomena as well as to formulate the principles of their study, it will be necessary to relate the present attempt with its predecessors. Twice in the history of mankind, the problem of successive and parallel leaps in being has become acute: A first time, in antiquity, through the indigenous histories of the historical and philosophical forms in Israel and Hellas, followed by the absorption of the parallel forms into Christianity; a second time, in the modern period, through the enlargement of the historical horizon to include the parallel histories of the Far East.

In Israel, the problems of history appeared with the formation of the Chosen People in opposition to the Pharaonic order. They continued, within Israel, through the opposition of the Prophets to the Law, and through the leap in being of Deutero-Isaiah, with its climactic symbols of the Suffering Servant and the Exodus of Israel from itself. These successive clarifications of existence under God were conducted with the means of the original symbols: Through revision of the Message from Sinai, through the opposition of a new Berith to the old one, and through the transformation of the symbols of the Anointed and the Servant. Only toward the end, in Deutero-Isaiah, appeared something approaching a theoretical treatment of the problem, that is, the theology of history, in which the world, Israel, and salvation were construed as the successive acts of divine creation and revelation. In Hellas, with its more diversified transitions from myth to philosophy, first the old myth was set off as a falsehood from the new truth of the Hesiodian mythical speculation; then both the old myth and the Hesiodian speculation became falsehood in relation to the truth of philosophy, until Plato finally developed the new concept of types of theology by which the degree of truth or untruth in the expressions of man's relation with God was to be measured. The phases of increasing truth, thus, were clearly distinguished in Hellas; and the transition from myth to philosophy was understood, at the latest in Plato's *Gorgias*, as an historical epoch. Nevertheless, a theology of history comparable to the Deutero-Isaianic appeared only in the Hellenistic period. Panaetius (*c.*180–110) developed the so-called *theologia tripertita*, that is, the classification of divine figures into the physical gods of the philosophers, the political gods of civil theology, and the mythical gods of the poets. And his pupil Poseidonius (*c.*130–50), then, constructed a theology of history in which the original mankind, through the participation of its Logos in the creative divine force, had a pure conception of the one God, invisible and unrepresentable, while the diversification into the impure types of the *theologia tripertita* was the consequence of the diversification of mankind into a multitude of peoples. From this impurity of diversification mankind had yet to recover the pristine understanding of truth, a task representatively executed by the Stoic philosophers. Moreover, in his construction the parallel leaps

in being became a problem for the first time. Poseidonius was a Syrian—
the Maccabaean wars fell in the generation preceding his birth, and the
rule of the Hasmonaean high priests ran parallel with his lifetime. Hence,
he was familiar with Judaism in a "current events" fashion. He knew
about Moses. He assumed him to have been an Egyptian priest and ruler
of the Delta, who emigrated with his followers and conquered Jerusalem
as the place of his new settlement. Moses was dissatisfied with the Egyptians and Hellenes because of their respective theriomorphic and anthropomorphic representation of the gods. The Exodus, thus, was understood
as a conflict between the early, true conception of the one God and the
Egyptian and Hellenic deterioration.[1]

The phenomena in which originate the problems of a history of mankind had become visible, and a good deal of the problems, too. In Israel
it was understood that the Chosen People as constituted by the Sinaitic
Berith would not live in its Canaan happily ever after, but that an arduous process of history had begun on the level of revelation. Of this process, the phases of the law, the prophets, and the salvation from the exile
had been lived through already, and no end was in sight. In Hellas, correspondingly, the phases of the old myth of the people, of the speculative
myth of the poets, and of the truth of the philosophers had already been
lived through and distinguished. Moreover, in both Israel and Hellas, it
was fully understood that these events were not local conflicts in the
competition for social power, but that in the war for the truth of human
existence the affairs of mankind were representatively transacted. Nevertheless, there were factors present which limited the penetration of the
problems. The recency of the discoveries, the resistance of a hostile environment, the regional isolation in relatively small communities, the contrast between the representative importance of the truth and the insignificant social effect, the continued worldly domination of the compactly ordered societies that were a past of untruth in the spirit of
solitary individuals and their small groups of followers—created a situation in which the joy of discovery and the fervor of truth were overcome by the effort of communication, by the struggle against the slug-
gishness of human nature. And in the bitterness of this struggle for
survival the accents would fall more heavily on the character of the past

---

[1] Cf. Max Pohlenz, *Die Stoa*, 2 vols. (Goettingen, 1948), s.v. *theologia tripertita*. For the
theology of Poseidonius and the Moses fragment see Pohlenz, *Stoa und Stoiker* (Zurich, 1950),
266f., 341f.

as an untruth than on its character as a preparation for the emergence of a new, differentiated truth. The conflict between the representative advance of truth and the empirical societies was still so burning that the character of the resisting societies as members of the represented mankind, and their historical function as the matrix of the new truth, could not yet be clearly discerned. A deeper penetration of the problems was furthermore handicapped by the fact that the break with the cosmological order was not quite as radical as the emotional impact of even the partial break was massive. In Israel, it was only slowly realized that the order of human existence under God was indeed a universal order of mankind and, therefore, could not be adequately represented by the constitution of a Chosen People on a definite territory. And when the insight was gained at last, the people broke asunder in the two equally vehement responses of the withdrawal into the shell of Judaism and the explosive expansion of Christianity. In Hellas Plato's understanding of the historical epoch created by philosophy was limited in both his experience and symbolization by the myth of the cosmic cycles. And, finally, the insufficient empirical knowledge of the historical process at large must not be underrated as a limiting factor. In the construction of Poseidonius, for instance, must be noted not only the limitation through the cosmological myth which induced him to place the results of the leap in being into a Golden Age (in the Hesiodian manner, at the beginning of cosmic history), but also the lack of precise knowledge about Egyptian and Israelite history, about the relative time positions of the Egyptian cosmological order and the appearance of Moses, which allowed him to make Moses the representative of a primordial knowledge in rebellion against its deterioration.

A decisive change in this situation was brought about through the appearance of Christ. In the letters of St. Paul, especially in the Epistle to the Romans, we find for the first time a profound understanding of the mutual involvement of man in the advance of mankind toward truth and of mankind in the truth of everyman's existence. The Law of Israel and the Jews is for St. Paul not a mere past now superseded by Faith, but the very condition for the extension of divine grace through Christ. For grace is extended to the sinner; only when man is conscious of his existence in the untruth of sin, only when he is aware of his death, is he on the way toward the life; and this consciousness of death in sin is awakened when man finds himself unable to fulfil the law. "If it had not been for the Law, I should never have learned what sin was: I should not have known what it was to covet if the Law had not said, Thou shalt not covet" (Rom. 7:7). "So the Law has been our schoolmaster [*paidagogos*] on our way to Christ, so that we might be made upright [justified] through faith. But now that faith has come, we are no longer under the schoolmaster" (Gal. 3:24–25). The climax of revelation, the entrance of God into history through the sacrificial assumption of human form, is followed by a sudden luminosity of man's spiritual life. Three stages are distinguished by St. Paul:

(1) The opaque existence before the awakening to the untruth of existence. "I once was alive without law" (*nomos*) (Rom. 7:9).

(2) The consciousness of existence in untruth. "When the command [*entole*] came, sin came to life: and I died" (7:9–10).

(3) The resuscitation through faith. "For the law of the spirit, of the life in Christ Jesus, has freed me from sin and death" (8:2).

These generically human stages of the spiritual process are at the same time the historically unique phases through which mankind grows, by the inscrutable order of creation, toward the illumination of existence through faith (Rom. *passim*; and 1:18–32; 2:14–16; 8:18–25). From the natural order of Hellenes and barbarians, through the old law of the Chosen People, mankind advances toward self-comprehension in the new law of the Christians.[2]

The Pauline insight has corollaries which become visible in the letters but are not pursued into their consequences. The three stages, while they succeeded one another in time, did not abolish one another. Neither the cosmological order of the empires dissolved with the formation of the Chosen People, nor did the Jews dissolve into the Christianity that emerged from them. The societies of the new truth were enclaves, very small ones, in a mankind which showed little inclination to bow to the representative authority. The succession of stages debouched in the co-existence of societies which by their types of order belonged to different periods in the history of mankind. St. Paul responded to this phenomenon by articulating the theologoumena of predestination, but he did not fully explore the historical aspects of the problem. In his analysis of the spiritual process, it is true, he dealt with the motives of persistence in obedi-

---

[2] On the Pauline conception of history and mankind cf. Rudolf Bultmann, *Theologie des Neuen Testaments* (Tuebingen, 1948), 258–66.

ence to the law, and the corresponding resistance to faith. He found the motives in the daemonism of the flesh that believes it can operate its own salvation through works, through conformity with the law, and therefore rejects the salvation through divine grace (*charis*). And against this resistance he declared: "By the works of the law no flesh shall be justified" (Gal. 2:16). Not the violation of the law so much, but the reliance on justification through its fulfilment, is the sin that leads into death. Nevertheless, while we have no quarrel with the profoundness of this insight, we cannot accept it as an answer to the questions raised by the persistence of Judaism. The Pauline method of historical interpretation is defective because it does not take into account the problems of compactness and differentiation. When St. Paul interprets the spiritual process, and especially the relation between law and sin, his insights are achieved through the experience of his faith in Christ. Only in retrospect, from the position of faith achieved, will the old law become visible as the guide to the new law of the spirit; only when the experience of justification through faith has differentiated, will obedience to the law correspondingly acquire the differentiated meaning of a "justification through works" which it has in the letters of St. Paul. However, for the men who live unbroken in the Jewish tradition the problems of this nature do not exist. In the compact order of the Chosen People, the Torah is inseparable from the Berith; and the Berith is the unconditioned act of divine grace, by which Israel is set apart from the nations as the *am Yahweh*, the people of God. The chosenness of Israel does not rest on the observation of the law, but on the act of divine grace which St. Paul apparently did not perceive. The "sons of God" are already "the ransomed of Yahweh" and need no Son of God for their salvation. Judaism has its own theology of sin and salvation which runs parallel, on the level of ethnical compactness, with the universalist theology of Christianity.[3] This recognition of the parallelism, to be sure, does not deny the differences in the levels of truth between Judaism and Christianity. Nevertheless, every order has its own present under God, as we formulated the principle; and this present is not abolished when it becomes a past in retrospect from a differentiated experience of order. Hence, the resistance to representative advances of truth about order, and the continued existence of more compactly ordered societies by the side of more differentiated orders, is in-

---

[3] On the Jewish theology of sin and salvation cf. Hans Joachim Schoeps, *Aus fruehchristlicher Zeit* (Tuebingen, 1950), 184–211.

timately a part of the mystery of the mankind that unfolds in history. This mystery must not be destroyed by progressivist slogans about "backward" peoples, or by inflicting on the survival of Judaism the pseudo-scientific epithet of "fossilization." It must be treated with the utmost caution and respect in a critical philosophy of history.

The Hellenes and Romans displayed greater awareness of, and more sensitiveness for, the problem of coexistent orders than the Prophets, Jews, and Christians. The *theologia tripertita,* in the form developed by Panaetius, must have been infused with a tolerance which did not oblige a philosopher to bear down on everybody who did not follow him in the pursuit of his truth, for the *principes* of republican Rome could accept it as a guide for settling the conflict between their own philosophical inclinations and the cult of the city, and transform it into the Roman theology that was still considered the great opponent of Christianity by St. Augustine when he wrote his *Civitas Dei.* The pontifex maximus Scaevola (d. 82 B.C.), the highest cult official of Rome, agreed with his teacher Panaetius on the relative merits of the types of theology, the philosophical one being the highest, but he thought it unwise to disturb the people and its civic cult by the dissemination of superior knowledge. The civil and philosophical theologies would have to exist side by side in the community; and Scaevola himself apparently found no difficulty in being a philosopher and the pontifex maximus at the same time. Unfortunately, we know practically nothing about the experience of order which made this policy possible. St. Augustine, our principal source, reports neither why Scaevola considered certain parts of the philosophical truth superfluous for the people, nor which these parts were; and his attacks on the deceit practiced by the high priest penetrate the problem no more than the parallel criticisms of St. Paul penetrated the issues of Judaism.[4] We can only recognize the phenomenal pattern of two orders prevailing simultaneously in the same society, held together by a class of philosophical rulers who continue in public to practice the cult of the people. The pattern is unmistakably an alternative solution to the blending of civil theology with the truth of revelation in the experience and symbolism of the Chosen People. The same lack of sources prevents a closer knowledge of the experiences which motivated the *principes* of imperial Rome to extend toleration to Christianity and enabled them to play the double role, from Constantine to Theodosius, of Christian em-

[4] Augustine, *Civitas Dei,* IV, 27.

peror and pagan pontifex maximus. The experiences of the conflict between the orders and the motives of harmonization in the practice of
conduct can be discerned with any certainty only in the literary sources
of the Hellenic period that will be treated in the present volumes on polis
and philosophy.

The question of multiple and parallel leaps in being has become acute
for a second time with the enlargement of the historical horizon—a
period that begins in the eighteenth century and lasts into our own time.
While no fundamentally new problems have appeared in addition to the
ones just treated, the theoretical situation is rather confused for two
reasons. In the first place, the problems that had already arisen in antiquity had never been analyzed conclusively. The premature generaliza-
tions from the phenomena known at the time had been absorbed into
the *Civitas Dei* of St. Augustine and the parallel *History against the
Pagans* of Orosius. This Augustinian conception of mankind and history
had, then, been transmitted through the Middle Ages; and now, in the
eighteenth century, it collapsed under the impact of increased knowledge.
That enormous increase of phenomenal knowledge, second, fell into the
age of the Western intellectual breakdown—with the result of an exuberant, almost vegetative growth of gnostic speculation on history
which rather obscured than illuminated the nature of the problem. Only
during the last generation has a recovery from the theoretical confusion
become distinctly noticeable. This complex period in the history of order
will be extensively treated in the last volume of *Order and History*. In
the present context I shall attempt no more than to list, and to characterize briefly, the problems as they emerged from the breakdown of
the Augustinian-Orosian authority.

The period opened with the Augustinian construction of history still
accepted, in the form in which Bossuet had elaborated it, and brought it
up to date for the last time, in his *Discourse on Universal History* of
1681. The construction had always suffered under the difficulty that the
events of Israelite history, as far as they were known through the Biblical
narrative, followed by the appearance of Christ and the history of the
Church, had been elevated, under the title of an *historia sacra*, to the rank
of the representative history of mankind, while the history of the cosmological empires, Hellas and Rome, had been reduced to a byplay of profane history, uneasily connected with the representative history through

such categories as the *praeparatio evangelica,* the martyrizing tribulations of Jews and Christians, the provision of an imperial peace so that Christian missionaries could travel with safety and spread the gospel throughout the empire, and the edifying spectacle of the rise and fall of mundane power. The problem of the concrete society, whose order is both an organization for pragmatic survival and an attunement with the order of being, had, if not completely disappeared, at least receded into the background of theoretical consciousness. In this respect the Augustinian construction was heir to the defects of the Pauline method of historical interpretation. Even in late antiquity the construction had required a generous overlooking of obstreperous phenomena, such as the existence of a Sassanian by the side of the Roman empire; during the Middle Ages, when the Roman organization of the Mediterranean area had collapsed and given way to the centrifugal, parallel organizations of the Byzantine-Orthodox, Arabic-Islamic, and Western-Christian civilizations, the conflict with reality had worsened; and by the eighteenth century, with the rise of Russia to great-power rank and the beginning familiarity with the size and civilizational rank of China, it had become unbearable. The defectiveness of the prevailing construction, the length of its persistence, the range of conflicts with the phenomena, and the magnitude of adjustment necessary to bring theory and reality again into congruence—all these factors must be taken into account in appraising the reaction against the unsatisfactory state of things. Not all of the intellectual confusion in matters of historical interpretation, and not even all of the dilettantism displayed on the occasion, must be laid at the doorsteps of modern thinkers.

The massive blow against the Augustinian construction, as represented by Bossuet, was delivered by Voltaire in his *Essay on General History* of 1756. The attack was conducted primarily on the phenomenal level—it was easy to show that a europocentric, unilinear construction of history had to omit such phenomena as China, Russia, and the Arab world. But the blow was no sooner delivered than it was clear that even a defective construction, which had at least a grip on the problem, was better than the dilettantic smartness of phenomenal argument. For the problem of mankind and its history, far from coming into view through an increase in the number of civilizations studied, disappears altogether if none of them is recognized as constituting mankind through the consciousness of representative humanity, that is, through its own existence in historical form. And the Gnosis of progress toward the reason of the eighteenth-century bourgeoisie, which Voltaire tried to substitute for the Augustinian *historia sacra*, could be applied to the interpretation of phenomena only under the condition that nobody would raise the fundamental question where and how the symbolism of an historical mankind had originated. For mankind is not constituted through a survey of phenomena by even the most erudite historian, but through the experience of order in the present under God. Hence, the Voltairean attack did not resolve any problems—it could only bring them into the open.

The problems, as they now became topical under the pressure of new phenomena, bore the mark of the Augustinian-Orosian construction from which they were released. Their complexion changed very slowly, and the process has not come to its end even today. It will be appropriate, therefore, to classify the principal attempts at a solution according to their relation with the Augustinian construction.

A first revision, motivated by the experience of parallel histories reaching into the present of the eighteenth century, could isolate the rise and fall of empires in profane history, introduce the neglected phenomena, and try to arrive at type constructions valid for all cases of rising and falling societies. That course was pursued indeed. The empires of the earlier construction became the plurality of civilizational societies; and the morphology of civilizations, the cycle theory of history, became a branch of modern historical science. When the problem was pursued in radical isolation against the *historia sacra*, as it was for instance by Spengler, mankind and its history were eliminated. The unit of study was the civilizational course; the time of history was the inner time of a course; the relation between the phases of the isolated courses was that of "philosophical contemporaneity." The study of history had run into the impasse of self-annihilation—a difficulty that makes itself still strongly felt in the earlier part of Toynbee's work (Volumes I–VI, 1934–1939).

The work of revision could be undertaken, second, from the side of the *historia sacra*. Representative history could be expanded beyond the Judaeo-Christian sacred history by demonstrating the participation of all human societies in the unfolding of the Logos in time. That was done by Hegel. The success of this enormous enterprise was remarkable as far as the inclusion and diagnosis of phenomena was concerned, especially if one considers the limitations of empirical knowledge at the time. For the chronology of ancient history was still rather blurred—the relative time positions of the Egyptian and Chinese imperial orders, for instance, were not too clear; the critical study of the Old Testament was as yet a task for the future; and the principal source of Egyptian history was still Herodotus. In spite of such handicaps, the Hegelian genius for discerning the characteristics of each level of intellectual and spiritual order has achieved feats of insight to which even contemporary historians and philosophers might have recourse with profit more often than they do.

The serious defect of the enterprise, the cause of its ultimate failure, was Hegel's attempt to reduce the Logos of revelation to the logos of philosophy, and the logos of philosophy to the dialectics of consciousness. Philosophy (*Liebe zum Wissen*) was supposed to advance toward Gnosis (*wirkliches Wissen*) [5]—and that could be done only through anaesthetizing the philosopher's sensitiveness for the borderline between the knowable and the unknowable, for the point at which the knowable truth of order is rooted in the Eros of the transcendent Sophon. As the anaesthetic that made the "advance" possible served the famous identifications which reduced the tension between transcendence and immanence: The Incarnation was no longer the mystery of God's entrance into history, but the appearance of the identity of God and man, as the consciousness of a truth, in the world; God and man blended in the *Geist*, revelation and reason in the unfolding of the *Idee*; reason became real and reality, therefore, was reasonable. "The absolute object, the truth, is the *Geist*; and since man himself is *Geist*, he is present to himself in this object, and thus has found in the absolute object not only essence but his essence." [6] By means of the symbol *Geist*, the dialectical Gnosis could slide from God to man, from man to God, and from both to the subject as the substance of the world. The superbly skilful manipulation of the gnostic symbolism could, of course, not abolish the mystery— either of the order of being, or of an historical mankind—but the sheer massiveness of the dialectical work, the vast expansion of the gnostic

---

[5] Hegel, *Phaenomenologie des Geistes*, Hoffmeister, ed. (Hamburg, 1952), 12.
[6] Hegel, *Vorlesungen ueber die Philosophie der Geschichte*, Brunstaed, ed., Leipzig (Reclam), 408, 413.

opus to the limits of the phenomenal world, could push the mystery so far out of sight that the impossible at least appeared to have become possible: the philosopher's Logos in possession of Being.[7]

The ambiguity of this monumental work of modern Gnosis has become the object of controversy between anti-Hegelians who sneer at the conceit of a philosopher who believed that the history of mankind had come to its fulfilment in 1830, in Berlin, in his work; and pro-Hegelians who indignantly reject such slander and can quote the texts which show Hegel's awareness that history had not come to its end. While the controversy attests the existence of the ambiguity, it is otherwise unprofitable. What is critically important is the source of the ambiguity in the experience of consciousness, of the subject, as the substance of being. For under the aspect of this experience, the Hegelian Gnosis is closely related to the speculation of the Upanishads on the identity of the *atman*, the self (consciousness, subject), with the *brahma*, the supra-personal and supra-mundane reality. The operations with the *Geist*, who is ontologically God and man as well as the identity of both, belong to a type of speculation within the medium of the cosmological myth that can appear pre-philosophically in the Indian and post-philosophically in the Hegelian Gnosis, though for the rest, to be sure, the acosmistic direction of the Indian is the exact opposite of the Protestant immanentist direction of Hegel's speculation.[8] Moreover, the similar experiences, with their corresponding speculative articulation, have curiously similar historical sequels: from the late Upanishads the way leads to the atheistic salvation of the Buddha; from Hegel it leads, via Bruno Bauer and Feuerbach, to the atheistic salvation of Marx. Though again, to be sure, in both cases the respective acosmistic and immanentist directions remain untouched by the transition. These atheistic sequels bring more clearly into view the ahistoric character of gnostic speculation. In the case of the Indian experiences of order, both Vedic and Buddhist, their ahistorism is well known and generally accepted. In Hegel's case the recognition of the same character will not be so easily granted because of the apparent absurdity that the most comprehensive and penetrating philosophy of

---

[7] *Ibid.*, 42f.

[8] On the relation between Indian and Hegelian speculation cf. Georg Misch, *The Dawn of Philosophy* (Cambridge, Mass., 1951), *s.v.* Hegel. Hegel himself was aware of the problem of "Oriental" speculation, but preferred to stress the difference between acosmism and immanentism rather than the similarity of Gnosis. Cf. Hegel, *Vorlesungen zur Geschichte der Philosophie*, the chapter on Spinoza.

history should be motivated by an ahistorical experience of order. Nevertheless, I am afraid, the ahistoric motivation must be recognized. Gnosis is a speculative movement within the form of the myth; and modern Gnosis, as the Hegelian identifications show, is a throwback from differentiation into the pre-historic compactness of the myth. And this character is not affected when Gnosis appears in societies which have received their historical form through philosophy and Christianity, or when the speculation is applied to the accumulated subject matter of an historical tradition, or when, under these circumstances, the symbols of God, mankind, and history are left to hover somewhere on the fringes of the dominant gnostic form. Neither Hegel's own protests, nor those of the Hegelians, against the charges of atheism can abolish the fact that in a consistent unfolding of Hegel's work its ambiguity has given way to the unambiguous attack on philosophy and Christianity by Marx. When finite speculation possesses itself of the meaning of history, philosophy and Christianity are destroyed and existence in historical form has ceased. Mankind and history are no less abolished when the abolition assumes the form of a speculation on the concluding scene of the historical drama.

A third line of revision, bringing into play the enlarged phenomenal knowledge, was possible through the construction of parallel sacred histories. The idea suggested itself in the wake of the observation that the Western leaps in being, through the prophets in Israel and the philosophers in Hellas, had their counterparts in the India of the Buddha and the China of Laotse and Confucius. The observation was made early in the nineteenth century by Orientalists, at the time accompanied by the assumption of cultural diffusion; [9] and it penetrated by the middle of the nineteenth century into the work of the philosophers of history.[10] In our own time the construction has gained considerable strength through the work of Jaspers and Toynbee.

The motivations of the new construction were conscientiously articulated by Jaspers. He acknowledges that philosophy of history has its roots in Christian faith. From Augustine to Hegel, the epiphany of the

[9] J.-P. Abel-Remusat, "Mémoire sur la vie et les opinions de Lao-Tseu," *Académie des Inscriptions et Belles-Lettres*, VII (Paris, 1824), 1–54.

[10] First appearance in Lasaulx, *Neuer Versuch einer Philosophie der Geschichte* (Munich, 1856). Cf. Karl Jaspers, *Vom Ursprung und Ziel der Geschichte* (Zurich, 1949), 28.

Son of God is the axis of world history. That conception he considers, however, marred by the fact that Christian faith is one among many. It is not the faith of mankind. The Christian view of world history has validity (*Geltung*) only for faithful Christians. The true axis of world history would have to be found empirically as a fact that is valid for all men, including the Christians; it would have to be the epoch in which was born what ever since man has proved able to be, an overwhelming fertility in the formation of humanity, equally convincing to Orient and Occident, so that for all peoples there would be a common frame of historical self-understanding. This epoch is to be found in the spiritual processes which take place in China and India, in Iran, Israel, and Hellas, between 800 and 200 B.C., with a concentration about 500 B.C. when Confucius, Laotse, the Buddha, Deutero-Isaiah, Pythagoras, and Heraclitus were members of the same generation. In this axis-time "man becomes conscious of the universe, himself, and his limitations. He experiences the awfulness of the world and his own impotence. He asks radical questions. On the edge of the abyss, he strives for liberation and salvation. In the consciousness of his limitations, he sets himself the highest goals. He experiences the absolute in the depth of himself and in the clarity of the transcendent." In this epoch were created the fundamental categories in which we think to this day, and were laid the foundations of the world religions by which men live to this day. In every sense mankind advanced toward the Universal.[11]

Toynbee has misgivings on two counts. In the first place, he wants to extend the "axis-time" so that it will include the full periods of disintegration of the Indic, Syriac, Sinic, and Hellenic civilizations. With that extension it would last from the tenth century B.C. to the thirteenth century A.D. Only by the end of that period could the truly relevant result of universal history, that is, the coexistence of the four higher religions—Mahayana Buddhism, Hinduism, Christianity, and Islam— be considered established. He protests, secondly, against the concentration on the year 500 B.C. For Buddha, Confucius, and Pythagoras, though they lived at the same time, were only chronological, not philosophical contemporaries, since their appearance was conditioned by different phases in the disintegration of their respective civilizations.[12] What is important about these exceptions is less their content, than the fact that

---

[11] Jaspers, *Ursprung*, 18–20.
[12] Arnold J. Toynbee, *A Study of History*, VII (London, 1954), 420–26.

Toynbee can now accept the problem of Jaspers as valid on principle and enter into a debate with him at all. That has become possible because of Toynbee's great reversal which occurred between the earlier and later parts of his work. In the earlier part (Volumes I–VI) history was understood as the humane study of civilizational societies in their internal and external aspects.[13] In the later part (Volumes VII–X) the "history of religion" has become history proper, and the various civilizational societies must now be ranked according to their function in the "progress of Religion."[14] The *Study of History*, which in the earlier part had approached the same impasse of a self-annihilation of history as Spengler's work, has recaptured itself in the later part through an approach to the Augustinian *historia sacra*—though with the recognition of four parallel "higher religions" of equal dignity.

The advantages and limitations of the two constructions are apparent in the brief reports. Both thinkers recognize the phenomenon of parallel leaps in being in the major civilizations; and both are inspired by tolerance toward the variegated ways on which mankind advances in its search of truth. As a result, the history of mankind has gained a lateral dimension, the breadth of movement that is so regrettably lacking in the europocentric, unilinear constructions. Both thinkers have furthermore found the way back from the worst aberrations of the preceding generations. The annihilation of mankind and history through the restriction of historical study to the morphology of civilizations was overcome by Toynbee himself in the course of his gigantic work; and both thinkers, in spite of their differences of emphasis, have placed the substance of history beyond the gnosis of progress.

Against these advantages must be held the theoretical limitations which are all too visible even on the surface of the phenomenal argument. While the parallelisms are duly recognized, neither the problem of the successive leaps in being within the various societies, nor the problem of their differences of rank, have been worked through. As a consequence, the respect for the advances toward truth in parallel societies is mixed with a sometimes surprising disrespect for phenomena which do not easily fit into the constructions on which the two thinkers have settled. Whether Jaspers finds the common humanity authentically constituted in a crosscut of "philosophies" about 500 B.C., or Toynbee finds it in the crosscut of "religions" at a later date, their inclusions and

[13] *Ibid.*, I, 46.　　　　　[14] *Ibid.*, VII, 423, 449.

exclusions bear the signature of willfulness. Toynbee considers Judaism a "fossil" of the Syriac civilization and throws it out of the representative assembly of "higher religions"; Jaspers courteously admits the prophets, but in his turn excludes Christianity from "validity" for all mankind; and neither of them seems to have any use for Moses. I do not intend to rush to the aid of the outcasts—Judaism and Christianity need no defense; in the present context the wilfulness is of interest only as the symptom of a profound misconception of history and its structure. In his conscientious manner Jaspers himself has articulated the misconception, and even formulated the conflict between the objective structure of history and his own construction to which it must inevitably lead. For, on the one hand, he acknowledges that "philosophy of history in the Occident had its root in Christian faith"; while, on the other hand, he finds that "a view of universal history" in which the epiphany of Christ is the central event can be valid only for Christians.[15] Setting aside the fact that Christian faith is by far not the only root of Western philosophy of history—Israel and Hellas also have something to do with it —there still remains the hard fact that philosophy of history has indeed arisen in the West and nowhere *but* in the West. There is no such thing as a non-Western philosophy of history. For a philosophy of history can arise only where mankind has become historical through existence in the present under God. Leaps in being, to be sure, have occurred elsewhere; but a Chinese personal existence under the cosmic *tao,* or an Indian personal existence in acosmistic illumination, is not an Israelite or Christian existence under God. While the Chinese and Indian societies have certainly gained the consciousness of universal humanity, only the Judaeo-Christian response to revelation has achieved historical consciousness. The program of a universal history valid for all men, when it is thought through, can mean only one of two things: the destruction of Western historical form, and the reduction of Western societies to a compact form of order in which the differentiations of truth through philosophy and revelation are forgotten; or, an assimilation of the societies, in which the leap in being has not broken the cosmological order as thoroughly as in the West, to existence in Western historical form. The same inconclusiveness with regard to theoretical issues marks the attitude of Toynbee. In defending his equal ranking of the four "higher religions," he takes shelter in the generically human inability to discern truth in matters

---

[15] Jaspers, *Ursprung*, 19.

spiritual.[16] This is an engaging humility—but intellectual humility is sometimes difficult to distinguish from intellectual evasiveness.

We conclude: The problem of multiple and parallel leaps in being cannot be met theoretically with the eighteenth-century resignation and wisdom of Lessing's Nathan. What is valid in the Nathan wisdom, and remains valid when Jaspers and Toynbee treat a wider and more variegated historical scene in its spirit, is the respect for every order, and every truth about order; for every society, on whatever level of compactness or differentiation its experiences and symbols of order move, strives for attunement with the order of being. This respect, however, must not degenerate into a tolerance which disregards the differences of rank, both in the search of truth and the achievement of insight. The generous thesis of Jaspers, for instance, that in the axis-time were "created the fundamental categories in which we think to this day," will appear doubtful if we consider concretely that the Aristotelian *Analytica Posteriora*, the fundamental work on analytical thinking to this day, was created, not perhaps in China or India, but in Hellas; and that the introduction of the Western modes of thinking in the Asiatic societies, in the twentieth century, requires a formidable effort under the pressure of dire necessity. With regard to the great question of Europocentrism it will be advisable, therefore, to distinguish between its phenomenal and its philosophical aspects. While the phenomenal restriction of the historical horizon to the Near Eastern, Mediterranean, and Western societies must be abandoned in the face of increased historical knowledge, the Europocentrism of position and standards cannot be abandoned by the philosopher of history, because there is nothing he could put in its place. History is made wherever men live, but its philosophy is a Western symbolism.

The philosophy of order and history is a Western symbolism because Western society has received its historical form through Christianity. And the Patres of early Christianity could create the symbolism because they could draw on the resources of Israel and Hellas when they articulated their own mode of existence. As Clement of Alexandria formulated it: "To the barbarians God has given the Law and the Prophets; to the Hellenes he has given philosophy; so that the ears of both might be prepared to hear the Gospel." And on the same relation in retrospect: "To us he gave the New Testament; those of the Judaeans and Hellenes are

[16] Toynbee, *Study*, VII, 494–95.

the Old ones." The scriptures of both Israel and Hellas are the Old Testaments of Christianity.[17] The origin and historical structure of Western order were better understood by the men who created the form than by their late successors who live in it without remembering the conditions of tenancy. It should be clear why our study had to begin with Israel; and why it has to move from Israel to Hellas.

[17] Clement of Alexandria, *Stromateis,* VI.

PART ONE

Cretans, Achaeans, and Hellenes

CHAPTER 1

Hellas and History

§ 1. PRELIMINARY QUESTIONS

A philosophical inquiry into the Greek experiences of order and their symbolization is faced, in our time, with certain difficulties. For several generations now, our empirical knowledge of Greek culture has been steadily increasing, and new horizons are still opening as they have done recently with the decipherment of the Mycenaean Linear B script. Theoretical analysis, however, has not kept pace with the advances of knowledge; it is lagging behind, perhaps inevitably, in its struggle with a hitherto unending stream of new materials and the rapidly shifting perspectives. The difficulties resulting from this situation for our study are indeed so numerous, variegated, and complex, that an introductory survey would bewilder the reader rather than enlighten him. It will, therefore, be preferable to present the theoretical issues as they arise with the unfolding of the subject matter itself.

But we cannot avoid beginning—and the first theoretical issue imposes itself with the very attempt to identify and delimit the subject matter we intend to unfold. The nature of the problem will become apparent as soon as we ask the critical question: To which concrete society, organized for political action in permanent form, does the language of "Greek order," of "Greek experiences of order and their symbolization" refer? Negatively one can answer that in the Greece of the classical period we find neither empires in cosmological form, as in Egypt, Babylonia, or Assyria, nor a society in historical form, as in Israel with its close relationship between political institutions and a revealed truth about order. It is less easy to say positively what we do find. In a first approach, to be sure, there can be no doubt that in Greece, as it emerges into the fuller light of history after 800 B.C., we encounter a manifold of poleis, torn by rivalries and engaged in frequent wars, sometimes in such atrocious form that it is considered a proof of humanity if only half the population of a city is massacred. But this stratum of Greek order, though it is concrete enough, certainly is not the complete structure of Greek society. The history of Greece does not dissolve into the histories of the single poleis and their wars; and a type study of the polis order and its symbolization could not be considered an adequate treatment of Greek order. For above the order of the poleis there rises recognizably the sense of belonging to a larger, common society. This sense is operative in the creation of the name of Hellenes for the peoples of the mainland, the isles, and Ionia, as well as in such pan-Hellenic institutions as the Olympian games, beginning in 776 B.C.; it furthermore motivates the federations of poleis in leagues and it can even inspire, in an emergency, the common effort of organization that was achieved for the defense against the Persian attack. Nobody has theoretically penetrated this stratum of Greek order more deeply than Thucydides, when he recognized in the common name and the common action the proofs of existence of a Greek society. Moreover, he surmised that the sequence of migrations in ancient times, the want of permanent, undisturbed settlement, and the thinness of population had for so long delayed the genesis of a consciousness of belonging together among the ethnically and linguistically closely related local societies. Even when he has reached this level of the sense of belonging together, with its scanty institutional and symbolic expressions, however, the student of Greek order will not yet be satisfied. For the Greek experience of order (barring for the moment the fact that we don't know yet of whose order we are speaking) has its place in the history of mankind neither through its institutionalization in the poleis, nor through the "common action" which, in pragmatic history, averted the Persian conquest of the incipient Europe, but through its articulation in the symbolic form of Philosophy. A symbolism for the expression of true order was found which claimed to be scientifically valid for all men. And only when this last segment is added to the structure of Greek order will the nature of the problem appear in its due proportion: For the order of the concrete societies, of the polis institutions and their polytheistic cult symbolisms, was not formed by philosophy; and the paradigms of true order developed in the works of Plato and Aristotle never formed the institutional order of any concrete polis.

At this juncture the problem can be only formulated. It will require the whole subsequent study to explore the relationship which actually exists between the concrete poleis in nonphilosophical form and the phil-

osophical form without a concrete society. Nevertheless, we can relieve
the suspense somewhat by a few reflections on an obvious fact: Philosophy, as an experience and symbolization of universally valid order, arises
from the orbit of the polis. This phenomenon, now, is reminiscent of the
Deutero-Isaianic "exodus of Israel from itself"; that is, of the process
in which the universalist component in the experience of the Kingdom
of God separates from the attempt to realize the Kingdom in the institutions of a concrete society. The similarity, to be sure, must not induce
rash speculations that would obscure the profound differences between
Israelite and Hellenic phenomena, but it suggests as relevant the further
observation that the two experiences of order that arose from concrete
societies without forming them became ordering forces on a world-
historic scale, in both instances with explosive vehemence. Both Hellenism and Christianity must be understood, it seems, as the continued operation, on the imperial scale, of ordering forces for which Israel and Hellas,
the concrete societies of their origin, had proved too narrow. And if the
parallelism of imperial expansion should indeed be essentially connected
with the similarity first observed, the suspicion may prove justified that
the Hellenic tension and explosion has roots as deeply burrowed in time
as the corresponding Israelite phenomenon. As in the case of Israel the
problems of the prophets have their origin in the age of Moses, and even
of Abraham, so in the case of Hellas it may prove necessary to ascend
beyond the eighth century B.C., toward the pre-Hellenic phases of Greek
history, in order to arrive at some clarity about the origin of the problems
which mark the classic period.

Before the problem can be advanced any further, certain questions
of terminology must be clarified. Our contemporary political and historical science has a vocabulary to designate several types of concrete
societies in organized form—such as empire, kingdom, state, city state,
federation; and it has a vocabulary for at least some types of governmental organization—such as monarchy, republic, democracy, and tyranny. These vocabularies, while they are quite insufficient to cover the
historical manifold of institutional types, will at least serve as instruments of rough reference. But we have no technical vocabulary at all
by which we could briefly refer to phenomena of the just adumbrated
Hellenic type; and as these phenomena are of world-historic importance,
and hence one must talk about them a good deal, semantic vacillation and
confusion is the inevitable result. While the problems arising from this

source cannot be resolved here and now, a few terminological decisions must be made in order to avoid misunderstandings.

The term most commonly used for the historical complex in question (as we shall say cautiously) is *civilization*. And since the concept of a civilizational society (for our present interests, fortunately) is poorly theorized, we shall not prejudice our own analysis if we continue to use the term as a convenience. More critical care is indicated, however, with regard to the choice of adjectives. One frequently speaks of Greek or Hellenic civilization, using the two terms synonymously. This usage is not only wasteful, since we badly need a larger number of distinguishing terms in order to meet the complexities of the phenomenon, but it also appears unsuitable in the present state of our empirical knowledge. For the study of Greek order must extend, as we shall see presently, over a historical complex which comprises three so-called civilizations, that is, not only the Hellenic, but the Minoan and Mycenaean civilizations as well. And since the decipherment of Linear B has revealed the Mycenaean language to be Greek, a decisive argument has been added in support of the view that the Mycenaean and Hellenic civilizations must be considered two phases of Greek history. It will be advisable, therefore, to reserve the term *Greek* for the historical complex in question as a whole, however far back we may have to extend it, and for the rest to accept the conventional language of Minoan, Mycenaean, and Hellenic civilizations. This decision is far from satisfactory, but it will permit us to embark on our study with a minimum of deviation from established usage and without extensive methodological explanations.

We cannot dispense, however, with a critical supplement that will bring the theoretical issue, now blotted out by the conventional terminology, again into focus. The names of the three civilizations, as they stand, are formed according to three different principles. The Minoan civilization derives its name from the royal style of the ruler of Cnossus; the Mycenaean civilization from the palace and settlement of Mycenae; and the Hellenic civilization from the post-Homeric self-designation of the people as *Hellenes*. Only the last one of these names makes theoretical sense in a study of order in as much as it derives from a self-designation, that is, from a symbolic form developed by the society itself. The names of the other two civilizations make no sense of this kind; and the pertinent question might be raised whether the terms refer to anything at all relevant in our context. It must be stressed, therefore, that the Minoan and Mycenaean civilizations have as their carriers societies about whose names we know at least something. If we let Homer be our guide, the carrier of the Mycenaean civilization was a society which had developed the self-designation of *Achaeans*.[1] And while, in the absence of sources, we do not know whether the society behind the Minoan civilization had developed a comparable self-designation or not, we are at least informed about the name by which this society was known in Hellenic times. For Homer speaks of the people of the island as Cretans and, furthermore, distinguishes, on linguistic grounds, between Eteocretans (original or true Cretans) and population groups which speak other languages. And the account of Herodotus suggests that the name *Cretans* applied to the inhabitants of the island from the time of Minos and did not change with their re-composition through migrations, so that the name, in his own time, referred already to the third "Cretans."[2] Scanty as these indications are, they assure us of the existence of societies with names somewhat closer to their own time than the terminological conventions of modern archaeologists and historians. Hence we shall speak of Cretans, Achaeans, and Hellenes in the sense of the societies which are the subjects of order in the corresponding Minoan, Mycenaean, and Hellenic civilizations.

The terminological digression has advanced the problem of delimitation to the point where it can be formulated with precision: A study of Greek order needs, for the identification of its subject matter, a set of criteria which have their origin in the symbolism of Greek order itself. Moreover, there can be no doubt that the search for such criteria must concentrate on the time when the dangers to freedom and survival of society made the problem of its order a topic of general discussion, and on the literary sources in which the problem was made the object of

[1] This probability is supported by the appearance of a Western power under the name of *Akhijava* in the Hittite archives—though some authorities have their doubts about the identification. The identification is favored by Sir John L. Myres, "Kleinasien," *Historia Mundi II* (Bern, 1953) 463ff.; it is treated as a piece of fancy by Albrecht Goetze, *Hethiter, Churriter und Assyrer* (Oslo, 1936), 58. In the Cnossos tablets, the name occurs in a form which philologically could be the basis for the Hittite form, but the evidence is inconclusive. Cf. Michael Ventris and John Chadwick, *Documents in Mycenaean Greek* (Cambridge, 1956), 138 and 209.

[2] Homer, *Odyssey* XIX, 172ff. Herodotus VII, 171. In this connection the Ugaritic legend of Krt is of interest. If the vocalization of the name as Keret should prove correct, it possibly designates the Cretan founder of a Ugaritic dynasty. Cyrus H. Gordon, *Homer and Bible. The Origin and Character of East Mediterranean Literature* (Off-print from Hebrew Union College Annual, 26, 1955), 53, feels sure of the Cretan derivation of the name and even ventures to speak of the legend of Krt as an "Ur-Ilias." Others are more cautious. Cf. G. R. Driver, *Canaanite Myths and Legends* (Edinburgh, 1956), 5 n. 3.

philosophical investigation with a maximum of articulation. Hence, in order to conduct the search with reasonable expectation of success, we must consult the philosophers and historians of the classic period.

Again, however, an obstacle must be removed before the search itself can get under way. For philosophy as the science of order has become a universal symbolism indeed, accepted beyond the spatial and temporal confines of Greek society, and it has retained this status through the course of Western civilization to this day. It is still a living force in the exploration and articulation of our contemporary problems of order. As a consequence, modern thinkers are inclined to be selective in their interpretation of classic philosophy, and especially so where political questions in the narrower sense, with their emotional charge, are concerned. The temptation is great to ignore the very problem that is our primary concern, that is, the order of Greek society in its geographical extension and in its depth in time, and to concentrate on those sectors of the classic literature which contain what seems to be the Greek "contribution" to political science—political science defined in terms of order which preoccupy the moderns. Moreover, such selective interpretation is possible with an appearance of legitimacy; for in the work of Plato and Aristotle one can indeed find the origins, for instance, of constitutionalism if one is careful enough to omit what does not fit into the picture. Hence, the Platonic-Aristotelian constructions of a best polis tend to become the primary object of investigation, while other thinkers and their problems will be admitted only in as much as they can be intelligibly connected as "predecessors" with the supposedly central issues of a "theory of the polis." A convention has been established, especially in the historiography of "political ideas," to ignore the far-flung concerns of the classic philosophy of order and to replace them with the restricted interests of modern constitutionalism.

In a critical study of order and history we must break with this convention for two reasons. In the first place, the selective interpretation is empirically inadequate as an account of the classic science of order; and second, if we accept its restrictions we shall never find the criteria we are looking for.

The Greek science of order was in fact much more than a theory of the best polis. The very conception of a paradigmatic polis was, in the hands of Plato and Aristotle, an instrument of critique to be used against the not at all paradigmatic reality of the surrounding political scene.

Their elaboration of a science of order was a conscious political act, undertaken in a concrete situation of disorder. Moreover, the necessity of laying the empirical foundations for the diagnosis of disorder, as well as the self-understanding of their own act of opposition, forced the philosophers to analyse the situation in terms of its historical genesis. The creation of a paradigm of order, held up as a model of action in opposition to the established order of society, would have indeed been a strange, and perhaps unintelligible, enterprise unless a philosophy of historical decline and regeneration of order had come to its support and endowed it with meaning. Hence, the integral science of order comprised both a science of paradigmatic order and a science of the non-paradigmatic, actual course of society in history. And the paradigmatic constructions had to make sense in terms of the remembered past that had entered into the present in which they were created. Consciousness of the historical situation, thus, was an essential part of the Greek experience of order; and the range of order that is properly to be designated as Greek must be determined, therefore, by the memory of continuous history which the thinkers of the classic period brought to bear on their situation as well as on the understanding of their own place in it.

§ 2. THE HELLENIC CONSCIOUSNESS OF HISTORY

The historical consciousness of Hellenic society will be, first, described with regard to its extension in time, its geographical location and civilizational diversification, and the nature of its sources. The brief account of general characteristics will, then, be followed by three sections on the specific forms which the historical consciousness assumed in Herodotus, Thucydides, and Plato. These sections intend to characterize the actual range of knowledge and the principal motives of recollection; and they will furthermore adumbrate some problems of the Hellenic symbolic form. A last section will, finally, summarize the conclusions.

1. General Characteristics

With regard to depth in time, the classic memory of continuous history went back for more than a thousand years beyond the Hellenic civilization proper. Hesiod was aware of a dark Iron Age, extending from the migration storms of the twelfth century B.C. into his own time, as well as of a preceding Bronze Age. The classic memory knew, furthermore, about the invasions, and especially the Doric one, and about the emigration of mainland and island Greeks to Ionia, as the events which marked the end of Hesiod's Heroic Age with its expedition against Troy. It included the Mycenaean and Minoan civilizations. And it was even aware of the ancient populations on the mainland, the Archipelago, and in Anatolia which had been replaced or conquered by migratory movements, back to the Achaean immigration of c.1950 B.C. Hence, if memory be accepted as a guide, the history of Greek society extended over approximately the same period as the parallel history of Israel with its memory of Abraham's exodus from Ur of the Chaldaeans.

The memory of a society is not an indifferent collection of knowledge, but the experience of certain events as factors which constitute the society as it exists in history at the time of the remembering historian and philosopher. Nevertheless, not every item of knowledge, even though it has a bearing on the civilizational order, will indiscriminately extend the limits of Greek society. When, for instance, Herodotus remembers that practically all the names of the gods came to Hellas from Egypt (II, 50), or that the alphabet came to Hellas from the Phoenicians (V, 58), neither Egypt nor Phoenicia are thereby included in the history of Greece. The observation may sound trivial, but its methodological importance is considerable in view of the fact that the rough criteria for the identification of a society, which in other instances are provided by the power organization, are not given in the Greek case. In the absence of a permanent political organization with dominion over a definite, though perhaps expanding or contracting territory, Greek society is indeed constituted through a consciousness of civilizational unity with fluid boundaries and varying intenseness of participation. The content of the Hellenic memory is, therefore, inseparable from the historical process of its growth. A brief recollection of the dynamics of this process will be in place.

In the wake of the invasion of the twelfth century something like a cultural vacuum formed on the Greek mainland, when the carriers of Mycenaean civilization were forced in large groups, presumably including the socially and culturally ruling stratum, to emigrate to the islands and the Anatolian coastal area. In the ninth century B.C. a new Greece began to rise. The rebirth started in the poleis of Asia Minor where the "Sons of Yavan" had become the neighbors of the "Sons of Ashkenaz" (Gen. 10). In this border area of the emigration originated the Homeric epics, and from here they began to diffuse their influence over the islands and the mainland, furnishing the recovering Greeks with the consciousness of a common past. The pan-Achaean federative enterprise against Troy became the living symbol of a pan-Hellenic cultural and precariously even political bond. Moreover, since the war of men was at the same time a war of the gods, the epics furnished a common mythology wherever they spread, thus creating a counterweight to the diversification of local divinities and their cults. The function of the Homeric gods—though not the gods themselves—may be compared in this respect with the Egyptian summodeism, with its interpretation of the various sun gods of Egypt as aspects of the one god who had become politically supreme. And, finally, the language of the epics was a unifying factor in as much as it balanced the dialectic diversification. From the eastern Aegean area, then, the Greek recovery expanded over the Hellenic world and, through the expansion, created it. Homer was an Anatolian or island Greek, the first of a brilliant line. The Ionian coastal cities and the neighboring islands were the meeting place of the surviving pre-Hellenic culture with Asiatic culture; and from this focal region, the vital mixture spread over the southern semicircle of isles to the west of the Greek mainland and further to Sicily and southern Italy. From the outside this vast semicircle was hemmed in by the Lydians, Persians, and Phoenicians to the east, by the Egyptians in the south, and by the Carthaginians and Etruscans in the southwest and west. In this border circle appeared, besides Homer, the travellers and historians Hecataeus and Herodotus; the poets Alcaeus, Sappho, Callinus, and Alcman; the philosophers Thales, Anaximander, Anaximenes, Heraclitus, Xenophanes, Parmenides, Pythagoras, and Anaxagoras. Here was the frontier of contacts and conflicts with Asiatic forces which dominated Hellenic pragmatic history; and here also must the *Iliad* have received the pointed interpretation, that was taken for granted by Herodotus, as the epic of the great struggle between Europe and Asia. The mainland Greeks were the last to enter this growing consciousness of the common Hellenic society in articulate form, though they were destined to have the most important role in mastering the Asiatic threat—Lacedaemon through its military strength, Athens through the outburst of intellectual and spiritual vitality which made it the Hellas in Hellas. On the margin, in time and space, moved the northern Greeks who, through Macedonia, became the hegemonic power in the conquest of Asia and the carriers of imperial Hellenism.

The content of the Hellenic memory, as we have said, is inseparable from the process of its growth. Whatever could be understood as a constituent factor of Hellenic society and its order in the present of the classic period became historically memorable: The populations of the geographical area, with their origins, migrations, languages, and myths; the great civilizational enterprises, such as the Minoan and Mycenaean, in which these populations had participated; the power organizations of the Cretan thalassocracy and of the Achaean federation against Troy; the antecedents of the present poleis; the pragmatic events of the great migrations as well as of the conflicts with Asia; and the genesis of symbolic forms, such as the gods, their names, and functions. These variegated contents, however, were not at the disposition of historians in the form of official records or monographic studies, but existed only in the form of traditions—if we may use a neutral term that will have to embrace the epic literature, heroic ballads, hymns, the myths of the gods, and local traditions concerning pragmatic events. From this complex manifold of sources, once they had collected it, the historians of the fifth century had to extricate a course of pragmatic events. The attempt, to be sure, could not avail itself of our contemporary critical methods, but had to rely on comparison of conflicting traditions, shrewd guesses concerning the pragmatic core of a legend or myth, and common sense in the reconstruction of a probable course of events. Especially for the earlier periods it could produce, therefore, no more than a skeleton history, thin with regard to facts and vague in chronology. Nevertheless, while our modern knowledge surpasses the ancient by far in quantity and accuracy of detail, the Hellenic construction of the course of Greek history has been proven substantially correct by the discoveries of modern archaeology. And even with regard to the specific date of the expedition against Troy, c.1184 B.C., the modern methods can only confirm the ancient calculation.

No strand of pragmatic history would ever have been pulled from the fabric of traditions unless there had been men who conceived the project and were able to execute it. From the problems of content we are, thus, referred back to the growth of the Hellenic consciousness of history. The consciousness was not a body of knowledge mysteriously diffused among the members of Hellenic society, but a symbolism by which historians and philosophers representatively articulated their experience of Hellenic society and the meaning of its order. Hence, before we can explore this creation of a Greek history in Hellenic retrospect any further, we must survey some of the forms which the phenomenon assumed. Our brief survey will properly begin with the *Histories* of Herodotus, the first Hellenic thinker who made the deliberate attempt to preserve the living traditions before time had erased them from the memory of the living.

2. *Herodotus*

The *historiai* were the inquiries undertaken by Herodotus with the purpose of generally preserving *ta genomena*, the recollections or traditions, and of specifically preserving the traditions which had a bearing on the prehistory of the great conflict between Hellenes and barbarians in the Persian Wars (I, 5). At the moment we are concerned, not with the rich detail of the *Histories*, but with the method used by Herodotus for extracting what he considered the truth of events from his sources. Two examples will illustrate the problem.

The most comprehensive source for the prehistory of the European-Asiatic conflict was Homer. But Herodotus distrusted Homer, and on several occasions doubted the correctness of his account, because he was familiar with the Asiatic versions of the same events. And he preferred to lean on the Asiatic versions when he became critical, because they had already transformed the mythical and poetic traditions of the Greeks into the new type of pragmatic account that he wanted to develop himself. The spirit of this transformation can be gathered best from the account of the Trojan War given to Herodotus by Egyptian priests.

The historian questioned the Egyptians concerning their opinion about the reliability of Homer's story in the *Iliad*; and he found them quite willing to set him right and to tell him how it all really happened. This is their story condensed:

> Helen was indeed abducted by Paris; and the Greeks really went with a great host to Troy. They demanded by a mission the return of Helen and the stolen treasure. But the Trojans swore that they had neither the woman nor her possessions but that both were in Egypt in the hands of King Proteus. The Greeks, not believing the Trojans, embarked on the long siege; and when they had conquered the city, they found that the Trojans had spoken the truth. Menelaus, then, was dispatched to Egypt and there he received back Helen and the treasure.

Herodotus was inclined to believe the Egyptians, because the Homeric story violated common sense. If Helen had really been at Troy, she would have been returned to the Achaeans. Neither Priam nor his entourage must be assumed to have been mad, and to have risked their own persons, their children, and their city for the purpose that Paris might keep Helen. Even if at the beginning they had been so minded, they would soon have changed their minds when they saw the losses mounting. Moreover, Paris was not an important personage in Troy; it is inconceivable that Hector, the older and more valiant man, should have consented to the mad policy. The only explanation is that Helen really was not there. If the Greeks did not believe them, it was the will of the gods to punish Troy for her wrongdoing (II, 118–120). On this occasion Herodotus carefully distinguished between the story, which he attributed to the Egyptians, and the argument for his preference, which he claimed as his own.

The Asiatic background of the method becomes even more apparent in the opening chapters of the *Histories* when Herodotus reports his Persian and Phoenician sources concerning the conflict between Europe and Asia. From Persian sages he received the following story about the origin of the conflict (condensed):

> The Phoenicians started the trouble. They came from the Indic Ocean and settled on the Aegean shore. There they engaged in sea trade and, on one occasion, abducted Io, the daughter of the King of Argos, and brought her to Egypt. The Asiatic misdeed was countered by the Greeks, probably Cretans, who abducted Europa, the daughter of the King of Tyre in Phoenicia. The accounts were balanced. Then the Greeks started new trouble by abducting Medea from Colchis. And two generations later it was the turn of the Asiatics, when Paris abducted Helen. Again it was a draw. But now the Greeks did something for which they were greatly to be blamed, when they countered with an armed invasion of Asia.

This time, the rationalistic reasons for the blame are given by the Persians themselves (condensed):

> The Persians admit that it is wrong to abduct women, but to chase after them with serious intention of revenge is foolish. A prudent man will not pursue the matter further; for obviously such women are not abducted against their wishes. The Asiatics did not pay much attention to the abduction of their women; but the Greeks gathered a great host and destroyed the kingdom of Priam. Ever since, the Asiatics have regarded the Hellenes as their enemies.

There can hardly be a doubt that Herodotus is on the side of the Asiatic psychologists, for he points up the argument of his Persian sages by the Phoenician version of the abduction of Io. According to these worldly-wise seafarers the lady had an affair with the captain of the ship and departed with him of her own accord when she perceived herself to be with child (I, 1–5).

The two examples will be sufficient for our purpose. It appears that Herodotus, in order to transform his sources into history, employed and developed a method that was already widely applied in the border area of Greek and Asiatic civilizations. In the report of the Persian sages, a chronology of events was derived from a number of Greek myths; the facts were slanted somewhat in order to serve what today we would call the "national interest"; and a reasonable history emerged through the application of common sense and elementary prudence. In the case of the Helen story which he received from the Egyptians, we see Herodotus proudly taking a hand himself at developing an argument of the Asiatic type in order to justify his preference for the Egyptian story against Homer.

The method is of interest in several respects. When Herodotus took the *mythoi* at their face value as historical sources, a large vista of early Greek history opened, with its relations to Egypt, Phoenicia, and Crete —a vista which, on the whole, was historically true. And while the methods developed by modern historians and archaeologists for the purposes of using the myths and epics as guides to historical reality have become infinitely more cautious, subtle, and complicated, and usually will lead to widely differing results in the detail, the principle of the procedure is still the one followed by Herodotus. We still assume that a concentration of myths on a geographical site indicates historical happenings at this site—and we expect that an excavation will render important results. When Homer chooses the name Phoenix for the educator of Achilles, or the name Aegyptius for the lord who opened the assembly on Ithaca, we assume that Mycenaean civilization had connections with Phoenicia and Egypt which made the choice of such names intelligible to the hearer. And inversely when, according to the report of Herodotus, Egyptian priests had developed a long story about Helen in Egypt and built it into some place in their history, we assume that they had a rather intimate knowledge of various cycles of the Greek epic and must have been duly impressed by them.

The method, second, reveals a far-reaching destruction of the myth through a rationalist psychology. From the Herodotean texts it appears that the new psychology had its origin on the Asiatic frontier; and that would cast an interesting light on at least one of the sources of the rationalism that prevailed in Athens, in the wake of the Persian Wars, at the time when Herodotus temporarily settled in the city. By rationalist destruction is meant the development of the dispassionate co-ordination of means and ends as a standard of right action, inevitably in opposition to the Homeric participation in the order of Zeus and Themis as the standard. The destructiveness appears, therefore, most glaringly in Herodotus' argument against the historical reliability of Homer. The story that the Trojans did not want to surrender Helen could not be true, because nobody would have been so foolish as to ruin a city for such a cause. The profound concern of Homer with the aetiology of disorder, his subtle analysis which tried to explain precisely why such foolishness happened, were apparently lost on Herodotus.

In the light of the preceding reflection, the method is, third, of interest as a symptom of the decay of Hellenic civilization. Herodotus not only knew his Homer well, but was in general one of the most widely informed and cultivated men of his age. If Herodotus could no longer understand Homer, the question imposes itself: Who could? Only one generation earlier, Aeschylus was still moving on the spiritual level of Homer; considering the fact that Herodotus was a greatly admired and popular author in Athens only a few decades later, the spiritual and intellectual decline must have been as rapid as it was terrific. The question is of further interest because of the later Platonic attacks on Homer. If the Herodotean interpretation was representative of a general trend, if more or less everybody read Homer in this manner, one part at least of the Platonic attack would have been directed not so much against Homer as against the manner in which he was misunderstood. The notion of Homer as "the educator of Hellas" will bear some closer study for the fifth and fourth centuries.

3. Thucydides

Herodotus had transformed traditions into history by using a common sense means-end relation as the standard of selection; and he had woven the selected actions into a pattern of history by arranging them as the genesis of the great war between Persians and Hellenes. Thucydides went one step further on the road of mundane rationalism, in so far as he used the rationality of power as the standard of action. The generally common-sensible, worldly-wise, urbane reflections of Herodotus were now replaced by a hard scrutiny of the traditions under the aspect of power politics. The advance from Herodotus to Thucydides, if an advance it can be called, reflects the hardening temper of Athenian democracy. Pragmatic rationality of action, disregarding the participation in right order, is a dangerous indulgence that may grow into an irrational force destructive of order. Ever since the Persian Wars, the danger of which the amiable work of Herodotus was a glaring symptom had grown rapidly and issued into the catastrophe of the Peloponnesian War with its suicidal effect for the whole of Hellas. The strict rationality of a struggle for power, without regard for the order of Hellenic society, had indeed become the standard of action in political practice. In conformity with the temper of his time, Thucydides wanted to interpret Greek history from its earliest times as a process that would lead up to the conflict of his own age.

In carrying out his plan Thucydides went as far back as his traditions would permit, in order to show that at no preceding time in Greek history had there been enough stability, wealth, and firmness of governmental organization to execute great power schemes, or to conduct a major war. Since Homer did not use the term Hellenes for designating Greeks collectively, Thucydides used this argument for the conclusion that Greek communities were rather small and weak, had little intercourse with each other, and certainly no occasion and ability for a collective action that would express itself in a common self-designation. And since this usage, or rather nonusage of the Hellenic name, was still to be found in Homer "who lived long after the Trojan war," the insignificant conditions must have continued well into historical times. The "ancient times" were weak because they were times of migration. Small communities, living in poverty with little equipment and few skills, were at any time ready to abandon their unfortified places under the pressure of superior numbers because they might live off the land at one place as well as at another. Since the soil was good, this policy of evasion was possible, but it also was a dire necessity because the fertility invited ever new invasions. Life at a low nomadic tribal level, without commerce, ships, or governmental organization around defensible places, was all that was possible under such conditions (I, 2–3).

The description would roughly apply to the pre-Mycenaean age on the mainland. The Trojan War proved to Thucydides that a turn for the better must have taken place because the Greeks were now in possession of a navy and capable of a confederate enterprise. The problem of sudden naval power occasioned some reflections on the Minoan empire. Thucydides knew "by tradition" (*akoe*) that Minos was the first ruler to establish a navy. The Cretan king used this instrument of power for the purpose of making himself master of the Hellenic sea. He cleaned the sea of the pirates, who were Hellenes and barbarians indiscriminately, he conquered and colonized the Cyclades and expelled the dangerous Carians. And his naval control of the sea was the preliminary step for securing revenue from the pacified area for himself (I, 4).

Thucydides knew that the Minoan thalassocracy preceded the Mycenaean age and the expedition against Troy. The Cretan abolition of piracy was the precondition for Greek coastal settlements. The Greeks were an inland people, for as long as pirate raids were a permanent danger, villages had to be established sufficiently far inland to be out of easy reach. Only after the pacification of the sea by the Minos were coastal settlements in safety possible, with gradual undisturbed accumulation of wealth, the building of fortifications for its protection, and ultimately the building of ships. With regard to the great expedition against Troy, Thucydides was cautiously skeptical. He admitted that the resources must have become considerable in order to make the expedition possible at all; and he warned doubters that the present, apparently dismal appearance of the famous sites of the *Iliad*, did not permit conclusions with regard to their former power. Nevertheless, the expedition could not have been all that it was believed to be, since it took the Greeks ten years to finish their siege of Troy. The only explanation for such delay was their insufficient equipment. Considerable detachments were engaged in agriculture and piracy to keep the army fed; and the actual fighting contingent was probably so small that it had no chance of storming the city at any time. That is to say, poverty was still the limiting factor that made it impossible to equip a sufficiently large army with enough supplies and foodstuff to engage in a brisk campaign (I, 5–11).

The period after the Trojan War was one of domestic revolutions, new invasions and migrations, and especially of the Doric invasion. Only after this new migratory turmoil had settled down could the present Hellas develop, with rapid population increases that made possible the foundation of numerous colonies (I, 12).

That was as shrewd a reconstruction of Greek history as anybody could give with the limited resources of the age.

4. Plato

While the achievement of Herodotus and Thucydides as the great collectors of traditions and creators of Hellenic historiography must in no way be diminished, the limitations of their achievement should be understood. Both authors reconstructed Greek history in order to give a causal explanation of the wars of their age. It was also possible, however, to study history for the purpose of recovering past insights into the conditions of order, with the view of breaking the apparently inevitable chain of causes that led to one war after another. From the causality of rational action, as it was understood by Thucydides, nothing could result but a power struggle to the death. Restoration of order could only come from the soul that had ordered itself by attunement to the divine measure. This entirely different conception of history was Plato's. With the same range of historical knowledge as Thucydides, he created an idea of order that would bind into a balance the very forces which Thucydides could understand only as factors in a game of war. Plato's gigantic enterprise will be explored at length in Volume III of this study. For the present, a brief indication of his principle as it appears in the *Laws* will be sufficient.

At the time of the rapid decay of the Athenian polis, the old Plato chose Crete as the scene of his last great dialogue on politics. The *dialogi personae* were Megillos of Lacedaemon, Clinias the Cretan, and the Athenian stranger. The choice of the interlocutors expressed the historical structure of Greek political culture. The nameless Athenian, Plato himself speaking, personified the youngest area of Greece that had grown into its intellectual and spiritual center; the Spartan stood for the political virtues and military strength of the older Doric institutions; and the Cretan represented the Minoan period. The Hellenic renaissance since Homer, the savage, primitive, disciplined warrior communities of the Doric centuries, and the mythical golden splendor of the Minoan sea empire gained life in the three venerable elders who discussed the foundation of a rejuvenated, healthy polis on the island that once had been the center of political power.

The three old men met in Cnossus, "the mighty city where Minos was king," the mythical lawgiver who received from Zeus himself the laws which he gave to his city. Every ninth year the king repaired to the cave of Zeus on Mount Ida to converse with the gods, and returned to lay down the law. The Cretan and Lacedaemonian, thus, were chosen as participants in the dialogue not only because they represented earlier Greek institutions, but also because these earlier institutions were closer to the divine origin and, therefore, nearer to perfection. For the Cretan institutions of Plato's day were supposed to have preserved essential features of the divinely instituted Minoan polis; and the Lacedaemonian constitution, according to Aristotle, was supposed to be in a great measure a copy of the Cretan. Hence, the Athenian stranger in the *Laws* started the dialogue by suggesting that the two men "who were brought up in legal institutions of so noble a kind" would have no aversion to discuss the subject of government and laws. And the three men agreed to discuss the topic while they took a walk from the city of Minos up to the temple and cave of Zeus. In this construction Plato reached a high point of his unsurpassed art of embedding the subject matter of his discourse into the form of its presentation. The topic was the foundation of a savior polis in the hour of Greek decay; the solution had to come through the combination of the living forces of Greece, personified by the three men, and through recourse to their fountainhead in the Minoan civilization; and the spiritual recourse to the divine fountainhead took place while the actors of the dialogue repeated the actual recourse from the habitat of the king to the cave of the god. Let us add that the number of three participants was probably not an accident, since the trinity was the sacred symbol of Cretan civilization (*Laws* 624–625).

The *Laws* is the sublime expression of the experiences which connected the order of classic Hellas with its origins. Crete was still the divine omphalos of Greece. And the island as the omphalos was not an antiquarian curiosity cherished by the old Plato, but a rather pervasive idea in Greek thought. The visual impression of this omphalos of a sea dominion may be gathered from the wonderfully sonorous verse in which Homer celebrated Crete as the island "in the mid of the wine dark sea." (*Od.* XIX, 178f). On the level of a dry strategic consideration, the impression recurred in Aristotle's description: "The island seems to be intended by nature for dominion in Hellas, and to be well situated; it extends right across the sea, around which all the Hellenes are settled. Hence Minos acquired the empire of the sea." (*Politics* 1271 b). And we remember the reflections of Thucydides on Crete as the strategically situated pacifier of the area of Greek civilization. The idea was so essential to Hellenic culture that the myth connected the foundation of Apollinian Delphi, the omphalos of the Hellenic world, with the older Cretan center. According to the Hymn to the Pythian Apollo, the god was born on Delos by Latona as the son of the Cretan Zeus. In search of a resting place he came to the rocky Pytho which in Minoan times was a sanctuary of the Great Mother goddess. In order to secure the foundation of a sanctuary of his own at this place he assumed the form of a dolphin, one of the Cretan sacred animals. In such disguise he appeared to a company of Cretans travelling to Pylos and guided them to the Gulf of Corinth. He installed them as a sacerdotal body at Pytho which from then on was called Delphi. Through the myth of its omphalos the new Hellas, thus, was securely linked to the Minoan past.[3]

5. Conclusions

The issues of the Hellenic consciousness of history can now be formulated on the basis of the sources introduced in the preceding survey.

With regard to the spatial and temporal extension of the classic memory the facts are fairly clear—the sources bear out the picture that we have drawn in the section "General Characteristics." The whole extent of the Aegean area that was considered Hellenic at the time became the stage on which Greek history was enacted; and in the drama itself were included the Mycenaean and Minoan civilizations, as well as the migration events back to approximately the turn from the third to the second millennium. One should especially note the manner in which Cretan society, in spite of its apparently non-Greek language, was taken for granted as part of Greek society. Not only was there no hesitation in the matter, but the Minoan order was even accorded the rank of the origin of Greek order, with equal regard to both power and substance. This should be a warning against overrating the importance of archaeological discoveries for the problems that occupy the philosopher of order and

[3] *The Homeric Hymns*, Allen, Halliday and Sikes, eds., 2d ed. (Oxford, 1936), III, 388 to end.

history. That Greek history begins with the Cretans is established by the literary sources of the classic period. Archaeological discoveries can add to our knowledge of that historical course—and they do it magnificently—but the course itself exists by virtue of its creation in the memory of the Hellenic historians and philosophers.

The structural details of the memory are not altogether clear. As soon as one examines the two dominant motifs of the construction, that is, the experiences of institutionalized power and of substantive order, more closely, serious questions will arise.

In the first place, considering the absence of permanent institutions for the whole of Greek society through the whole of its course, it is rather suprising that reflections on power and strategy should be a dominant motif at all. The peoples of the Aegean area apparently experienced themselves as a civilizational society of the same type and rank as the imperially organized societies of Anatolia, Iran, Mesopotamia, Syria, and Egypt. If Greek society had in fact no comparable institutions, it was at least considered a suitable candidate with a potential for having them; hence, the ephemeral or partial organizations of power in the area, as far back in time as they were discernible, became events in the history of Greek order. This motif was indeed strong enough to link such apparently unrelated phenomena as the Hellenic "common effort" of the Persian Wars, and the subsequent Athenian Empire, with the Achaean expedition against Troy, and with the Cretan control of the Aegean as a series of manifestations of Greek power. And the constructive strength of the motif indicates that a Greek society above the level of the polis order was experienced with greater intenseness than one would assume if the judgment were guided only by the lack of permanent institutions, or by the observation that Plato and Aristotle concentrated their efforts on a paradigm of the best polis. In search of a comparably odd structure of experience, institutionalization, and symbolization one can only fall back on that of Israel at the time of the Judges, before the pressure of surrounding powers forced the people to have a king like the other nations. The parallel, to be sure, must not be pressed, because of the lack of information on the Hellenic side—the authors of the classic period did not say all we would like to know, perhaps because their readers knew it already. Still, one should observe the curious vacuum of articulate expression in an otherwise very articulate literature, yawning between the awareness that Hellenic society, in order to exist and survive, needed a common organization of power, and the knowledge that the Hellenes were not an *ethnos* like the Asiatic peoples and, therefore, should not have imperial institutions like the other nations.

The objection must, then, be considered that the identification of Greek society by means of the erratic power organizations back to the Minoan is no more than the wilful notion of a few isolated thinkers and has nothing to do with the real course of Greek history. This argument is hardly tenable. For the Hellenic memory was not based on written records of antiquity, accessible perhaps only to a small group of literati. In this respect we are in the Hellenic case probably on safer ground than in the Israelite, where indeed one may doubt to what extent the population at large in the Kingdoms of Israel and Judah participated in the issues ventilated by the prophets. For the art of writing, which had existed in the Minoan and Mycenaean civilizations, had disappeared, as far as we know, in the dark centuries after the Doric invasion, and was recovered only through contact with the Phoenicians. When Herodotus and Thucydides wrote their histories, without a doubt they had to draw on such oral traditions as were alive in the Hellenic society at large, or on a literature of epics and hymns which had been committed to writing, however old the contents preserved in the literary forms may have been, not earlier than the introduction of the alphabet (presumably after 1000 B.C.). Hence, the classic memory of Greek history is not an archaistic reconstruction of events long forgotten by the people, but the organization of a living memory which, by its very existence, proves the continuum of Greek history to be real.

The reality of the continuum obtrudes itself especially in the Platonic construction of the divine origin of Greek order and the necessity of a return to the first omphalos. Here the second motif, the experience of substantive order and disorder, dominates the identification of Greek society. For Plato is, in the *Laws,* not satisfied with tracing the line of pragmatic power to its beginning, but introduces, as the ultimately decisive criterion, the substance of order and its vicissitudes in the historical course. Greek society is now identified through the epiphany of order in the rule of the Minos, and its course is understood as the exhaustion of the original substance, down to the Hellenic crisis of Plato's own present. This symbolism could never have been developed unless traditions about the Cretan as the oldest Greek order, about the close relation between Doric and Cretan order, and about the transfer of the omphalos from

Crete to Delphi, had been in existence so that Plato could draw on them; and unless they had been so widely diffused and accepted that he could build them into his symbolism without appearing absurd or becoming unintelligible.

The materials used in the constructions, thus, belong to a body of traditions living among the people at large; and quite probably even the dominant motifs were already dominant on the general level of Greek conversations on power and order. Still, there remain the formal constructions themselves, the works of the concrete historians and philosophers. What motivated their creators to organize the Hellenic memory in these specific forms?

With regard to the motive itself, the organizers of the classic memory were quite outspoken: it was the experience of the Hellenic crisis. Herodotus wanted to explore the antecedents of the situation in which the Hellenes found themselves involved in a death struggle with the Persians; Thucydides wanted to explore the causes of the great *kinesis* in which the Athenians and Lacedaemonians fought Hellas to death together with themselves; and Plato wanted to understand the disintegration of substantive order which made Athens unfit to discharge its functions as the hegemonic power of a united Hellas. Beyond this point, however, the issues become more complicated. And since they are the subject matter of the following study, I shall at present reflect only on the central issue, *i.e.*, the conception of the historical course of a society as a cycle with a beginning and an end, as well as on its principal implications.

Before the conception of the historical course itself can be analyzed, however, a preliminary question must be solved. Up to this point we have spoken of Greek history, of the Hellenic consciousness of history, of the historical memory of the classic period, of the historical course of Greek society, of a cycle of order extending from the rule of the Minos to the exhaustion of substance in Plato's time, and so forth, taking it for granted that such language can be legitimately used in a study of Greek phenomena. In a critical study of experiences of order and their symbolization, however, no symbols can be taken for granted, even though they are used in accordance with contemporary conventions. Hence, before proceeding further it must be ascertained whether we can speak of history in the present context at all.

The term *history*, though it derives from the Greek *historia*, does not have in its modern usage the classic meaning. When Herodotus speaks of *historiai* he means his *inquiries* into a subject matter, somewhat arbitrarily accepted today as historical. And Toynbee stresses on occasion that in his title *A Study of History,* the study rather than the history renders the classic *historia.* Thucydides, furthermore, did not give the *History of the Peloponnesian War* the title under which the work is known today. Rather, he was interested, as just indicated, in a type study of the *kinesis,* of the great movement or convulsion of Hellenic society, and whether this study is history in the modern sense is precisely the issue that must be explored. These observations will be sufficient to show that the Hellenic symbolism raises the same problems as the Israelite "historical narrative." In the Israelite case we had to distinguish between the historiographic symbols appearing in the text, on the one hand, and the terminology that had to be employed in the interpretation of the symbolic form, on the other hand. And among the historiographic symbols developed by the creators of the narrative, there was no term that could be considered the Hebrew equivalent of *history.* Our usage had to be justified, therefore, through appeal to the categories of compactness and differentiation; and it proved to be legitimate to speak of history in as much as the Israelite symbolism contained compactly the meanings which later, in the orbit of Christian experiences, were differentiated and expressed by the new symbol.[4] The same argument will apply to the Hellenic case. While the meaning of history that has been created through Christianity is not to be found in the classic memory, the later problems are nevertheless contained in the less differentiated historical consciousness of an Herodotus or Thucydides, or in Plato's conspectus of the historical cycle of order. That the argument is indeed valid in the Hellenic case, to be sure, can be proven only through the analysis of the literary sources itself. For the moment we must anticipate the proof.

Under the assumption that one can speak of history at all in the present context, the main issue, the experience and symbol of the historical cycle, must now be explored.

The symbolism of a cyclical decline and restoration of order is peculiar to societies in cosmological form. In the earlier volume *Israel and Revelation* we studied the symbolism of the New Year Festivals, of the cult acts which annually heal the defections from, and revitalize the order of, society, with the implication of repeating the original cosmogonic

[4] *Order and History,* I, 162ff.

act that has brought forth order from chaos.[5] These periodic acts of restoration also betray a consciousness of history; but far from articulating it, they are rather calculated to prevent the experience of the decline of a society from reaching the level of consciousness. The time of history in which a society experiences the vicissitudes of its order down to exhaustion and ultimate dissolution, is annulled through the magic of cultic repristination.[6] What we call today the historical course of Egyptian society was not a course for the Egyptians, but a rhythmical repetition of cosmogony in the imperially organized humanity which existed at the center of the cosmos. The prolonged disturbances and revolts, for instance between the Old and the Middle Kingdoms, were not epochs of history from which order in new form could arise, but simply disruptions of the cosmological form to be borne with nothing but the hope that the same type of order would ultimately be somehow restored. It required the Mosaic leap in being to break this compact experience of order and to differentiate the new truth of existence in historical form, in the present under God. The new understanding of order, it is true, could not abolish the rise and fall of societies in pragmatic history; and the experience of the decline of order, which in the cosmological form could be expressed and, at the same time, contained and annulled through cultic restorations, now had to search for new modes of adequate articulation. Such new expression was found in Isaiah's metastatic faith in the imminent transfiguration of the world that would abolish the cycle of defection and return; and when the impasse of this faith became clear, the problem of transhistorical, eschatological events began to differentiate from the historical phases of order and disorder which correspondingly became the world-immanent structure of events. With regard to the evolution of symbols we could draw, therefore, the lines from the cosmological rhythms of order to the phases of history,[7] from cosmology to eschatology,[8] and from the cultic restoration to the historical metastasis of order.[9]

The question then arises how the structure of the Hellenic symbolism is related to the problems of order just recalled. And with regard to that issue it must be recognized above all that the Hellenic conception of the

[5] *Ibid.*, 34f., 45, 287ff., 299.

[6] On the annulment of historical time through acts of cultic restoration cf. Mircea Eliade, *Le Mythe de l'Éternel Retour. Archétypes et Répétition,* 3d ed. (Paris, 1949), 128, 184, 209.

[7] *Order and History,* I, 475ff.   [8] *Ibid.*, 298f., 302f.   [9] *Ibid.*, 452.

cycle of history is a new symbolic form. Nothing comparable is to be found either in the Near Eastern societies in cosmological form, or in the Israel in historical form. For the Mesopotamian and Egyptian empires never developed the conception of a society with a beginning and end in historical time, but remained compactly bound in the experience of cosmic divine order and of the participation of the respective societies in its rhythm. And the Israel that existed as the Chosen People under God, while it had a beginning in historical time, could have no end because the divine will, which had created Israel as the omphalos of salvation for all mankind, was irreversible and remained unchanged beyond both the rhythms of the cosmos and the phases of history. While the Hellenic symbolism, thus, belongs neither to the cosmological nor the Israelite historical type, it seems to partake of both of these forms; and this apparently intermediate structure has indeed motivated the divergent opinions that, on the one hand, the Greeks had no genuine idea of history at all but fundamentally expressed themselves in the symbolism of eternal return, and that, on the other hand, the Greeks were the creators of historiography, that in particular Herodotus was the Father of History and the work of Thucydides one of the greatest histories ever written. Such indulgences of opinion can be avoided only if the analysis goes beyond the surface of disparate characteristics and penetrates to the motivating center of the symbolism.

This motivating center can be circumscribed through comparisons with the Israelite motivating experiences and their articulation. The Hellenic consciousness of history is motivated by the experience of a crisis; the society itself, as well as the course of its order, is constituted in retrospect from its end. The Israelite consciousness of history is motivated by the experience of a divine revelation; the society is constituted through the response to revelation, and from this beginning it projects its existence into the open horizon of time. The Hellenic consciousness arrives, through the understanding of disorder, at the understanding of true order—that is the process for which Aeschylus has found the formula of wisdom through suffering; the Israelite consciousness begins, through the Message and Decalogue from Sinai, with the knowledge of true order. The Mosaic and prophetic leap in being creates the society in which it occurs in historical form for the future; the philosophic leap in being discovers the historical form, and with it the past, of the society in which it occurs. Such contrapuntal formulations will bring into focus the essential difference between the historical forms that are developed respectively by Revelation and Philosophy. The word, the *dabar*, immediately and fully reveals the spiritual order of existence, as well as its origin in transcendent-divine being, but leaves it to the prophet to discover the immutability and recalcitrance of the world-immanent structure of being; the philosopher's love of wisdom slowly dissolves the compactness of cosmic order until it has become the order of world-immanent being beyond which is sensed, though never revealed, the unseen transcendent measure.

The reality of the continuum of Greek history, an issue that apparently has been settled, is raised anew by these formulations. If the past of Greek society was indeed constituted through the classic memory and its symbolisms, in what sense was their history ever real to preclassic Greeks? Does the situation not resemble the Egyptian, in which the historical course as understood by us in retrospect of Judaeo-Christian history was never experienced as a course by the members of Egyptian society? The answer to such questions will have to be that the classic memory did not constitute a new society, as did the Mosaic response to revelation, but climaxed with its articulate consciousness the history of the old society from which it emerged. The classic memory refers us back to the order and history in which this phenomenon could occur. Once more we must stress that it occurred nowhere else. And it will be our task, therefore, to trace the growth of the final experiences and symbols through the course of the Greek society which is retrospectively identified as the field of that growth by the historians and philosophers of the Hellenic period. The following inquiry concerning the principal stages through which the final form was reached will move from the cosmological myth of the Cretan society, through the Homeric myth and the Hesiodian speculation, to the philosophers' break with the myth.

CHAPTER 2

The Cretan and Achaean Societies

On the scale of organization, large societies with imperial institutions have been built, without transitional stages, out of a manifold of comparatively primitive nomad tribes, as in the case of the Hiung-nu empires that were formed in opposition to the Chinese Han empire, or of the Mongol empire of Djinghis Khan and his successors. Empires of this type, while they could achieve the stature of great powers and attack high civilizations with destructive effect, proved, however, to be ephemeral; and their role as participants in the search of mankind for the truth of order was no more than peripheral.[1] The growth beyond the tribal level, if it is to reach effective participation in the history of order, requires the intermediate stage of town or city-state cultures. The imperial institutions of the ancient Near East, with their creation of the cosmological form, were erected over a manifold of city-states of fairly homogeneous culture, or over a population with an urban density of settlement as in the special case of the Nile valley. These town cultures, the apparently necessary matrix for high-civilizations, extended from the river valleys of the Euphrates, Tigris, and Nile to the islands of the Aegean and the coastal areas surrounding it. Even in the third millennium B.C., parallel with the flowering of the Near Eastern civilizations, there are distinguishable definite Hellespontic, Cycladic, Cretan, and Greek Mainland areas of this type. And in the formation of an Aegean civilizational area before 2000 B.C., Crete seems to have had a dominant role, probably because of its favorable geographical position. Why neither the Aegean area as a whole nor its subdivisions, at the time, displayed any tendencies towards organization on a larger scale, comparable to the Mesopotamian

---

[1] The symbolisms of the nomadic empires are peripheral, but not devoid of interest. On the symbols of the Hunnish empire in the west cf. Joachim Werner, *Beitraege zur Archaeologie des Attilareiches* [Abhandlungen. Bayerische Akademie der Wissenchaften, Phil.-Hist. Klasse, Neue Folge 38 A (Munich, 1956)], especially the section "Adlersymbolik und Totenkult", 69–81. On the symbolism of the Mongol empire cf. my "The Mongol Orders of Submission to European Powers, 1245–1255," *Byzantion*, XI (1941), 378–413.

and Egyptian, is not known with certainty. With regard to the causes of the time lag one can only surmise that they had something to do with the comparative smallness, poverty, and correspondingly low power potential of the town populations, the more scattered mode of settlement on islands, the geographic divisions into relatively closed landscapes on the mainland, and with mountain and sea barriers difficult to overcome. Anyway, whatever the possibilities of indigenous growth and organization in the area may have been, they were rudely broken, and their unfolding delayed for centuries, by the migration waves which brought the Achaeans to the Greek mainland and the Hittites to Asia Minor after 2000 B.C. From this disturbance of the urban cultures through the non-urban invaders, which extended from Greece to Babylon, only Crete was exempted in the Aegean area. And here we find, at approximately the time of the Achaean occupation of Hellas proper, the great flowering of the indigenous Minoan civilization, attested by the old palaces which must be dated c.2000–1700 B.C.[2]

1. The Cretan Society

The history of the island society must rely on inferences, not always too certain, from archaeological materials.[3] A primary co-existence of tribal societies was followed by the concentration of power in the hands of a number of chieftains who must be assumed as the founders of the Cretan city centers. The first flowering of Cretan society was marked by the building of the older palaces, at the beginning of the second millennium. The largest among the cities and palaces was Cnossus, according to tradition the seat of the Minos. Since no traces of fortifications could be found, the island must be assumed to have been at peace within, as well as secure against attack from the sea. Hence, the internal order of

---

[2] For the history of Cretan society were used, of the older literature, Eugène Cavaignac, *Histoire de l'Antiquité*, I/1 and I/2 (Paris, 1917 and 1919), Gustave Glotz, *The Aegean Civilization* (New York, 1925); Sir William M. Ramsey, *Asianic Elements in Greek Civilization* (New Haven, 1928); Eduard Meyer, *Geschichte des Altertums*, II/1 (2d ed., Stuttgart and Berlin, 1928). Furthermore, the following chapters from the *Cambridge Ancient History* were used: A. J. B. Wace, "Early Aegean Civilization," I/17 (1923); H. R. Hall, "The Keftians, Philistians and Other Peoples of the Levant," II/12 (1924); and A. J. B. Wace, "Crete and Mycenae," II/16 (1924). Of the more recent literature: Albin Lesky, *Thalatta. Der Weg der Griechen zum Meer* (Vienna, 1947); and the article by Fritz Schachermeyr, "Kreta und Mykenae" in *Historia Mundi*, III (Munich, 1954), 42–55.

[3] The archaeology of Crete is principally indebted to the work of A. J. Evans. For the history of Mycenaean and Minoan archaeology cf. the Foreword by A. J. B. Wace in Ventris and Chadwick, *Documents in Mycenaean Greek*.

the island was probably that of a cult league, with the Minos of Cnossus recognized as the cultic hegemon, while the protection against external dangers was assured by the navy that, according to tradition, had been created by the Minos. To what extent the conventional language of a thalassocracy or sea empire can be filled with concrete meaning, is difficult to say. Certainly the navy must have been strong enough to suppress rival seafarers and to prevent their predatory raids; the suppression of piracy in the Aegean, attributed by Thucydides to the Minos, may be safely assumed. Whether the successful operation resulted in a Cretan monopoly of piracy, with ensuing conquests on the islands and the mainland, or the establishment of protectorates and exaction of tribute, is entirely a matter of conjecture. Certainly there has existed a trade empire. For Cretan contacts are known in the west in Italy, Sicily, the Balearic islands, and Iberia; on the Greek mainland as far north as Macedonia, with particular density in the Argolis; in the northeast on the coast of Asia Minor; in the east in Cyprus, Syria, and Egypt.

The first flowering came to an end through a catastrophe, probably an earthquake, which destroyed the older palaces c.1700 B.C. An even richer flowering, marked by the younger palaces, was again terminated catastrophically c.1600 B.C. On occasion of this second catastrophe a substantial part of the navy must have also been destroyed, perhaps through flood waves, for after 1600 the Achaean ascendancy on the sea made itself felt—through plundering raids on the devastated Crete, as well as through direct contacts with Egypt which were intense enough to make the Achaean support in the expulsion of the Hyksos, c.1570, an important factor. Crete recovered and regained her independence, but the domination of the sea was permanently lost. There still were close relations with the Egyptian court at the time of Hatshepsut and Thutmosis the Great, c.1500, but by 1460 an Achaean prince ruled in Cnossus and probably controlled the whole of the island. In 1400 the palace in Cnossus was again destroyed, possibly again by an earthquake, but more probably by a Cretan revolt against the Achaean prince. That was the last disaster. After 1400 Crete became an area of immigration for the Achaeans. The Minoan civilization which had lasted for six hundred years had come to its end.

The Minoan symbols of order cannot be traced with any certainty to their experiential origins, since no literary sources are available. The

Minoan hieroglyphic and Linear A scripts have not yet been deciphered; and their decipherment would probably be of little help for our problems, since the preserved records appear to be inventories and bookkeeping notes.[3a] Such literary creations as may have existed were probably written on papyrus and have perished. Nevertheless, since the Cretan order found its expression in symbols similar to the Near Eastern, we can recognize the general type as cosmological. Making allowance for the probability, not certainty, of the propositions, one can say the following: the Minos was a god-king, and the Labyrinth of Cnossus was the sacred habitat of the god. The divinity was incarnate both as an animal (the sacred bull) and as a man (the Minos). The bull-god received human sacrifice, of which the memory survived in the myth of Theseus and the abolition of the Athenian tribute (suggesting the existence of Athens and its tributary relationship to Cnossus at least in the early second millennium). One phase of the ritual drama was the immolation of the bull-god himself; and those who wished to commune with the gods participated in the sacred meal. The offering was preceded by a *corrida* in honor of the gods; and on this occasion probably slaves and prisoners of war were used as bullfighters and human sacrifices. Some understanding of the meaning of these rituals, in which elements of a totemistic age survived, can be gained from Plato's *Critias* where, based on oral tradition from the Aegean past, the bullfight and the sacrifices form the core of the Atlantian rituals of order.[4]

The bull-god was neither the only nor the highest divinity. The matriarchal Minoan civilization was dominated by a goddess whose functions resemble those of the corresponding figures in the Near Eastern pantheons. She appeared as Dictynna, the Great Mother (the Rhea or Demeter of the later Greeks), and as Britomartis, the virgin daughter who was united with the god in sacred marriage (Kore, Persephone, Artemis, Europa, Pasiphae in the later myth). To the fusion of mother

---

[3a] While reading the proofs I learn that the Linear A script has been deciphered, or at least a beginning of the deciphering has been made, by Professor Cyrus H. Gordon, at Brandeis University. The language is Akkadian. Cf. the report in *The New York Times*, August 29, 1957. The evaluation, given above in the text, of the content of the tablets, as well as of its relevance for the present study, remains unchanged for the time being.

[4] On the Cretan symbolism were used, besides Glotz' *Aegean Civilization*, especially Martin P. Nilsson, *Geschichte der Griechischen Religion* I (Munich, 1941), and the same author's *The Minoan-Mycenaean Religion and Its Survival in Greek Religion* (2d ed., London, 1950). Of interest proved furthermore Karl Pruemm, "Die Religion der Griechen," *Christus und die Religionen der Erde,* ed. by Franz Koenig, II (2d ed. Vienna, 1956).

and daughter corresponded the fusion of the god as son and lover. There was a wealth of myths—of Minos and Britomartis, of Dionysos and Ariadne, of Europa and Zeus in the shape of the bull, of Pasiphae and the bull-god—in which are blended the figures of the Great Mother, of the son and lover, the totemistic and anthropomorphic symbols, the fertility of the earth and the animal world, and the earthly and heavenly powers. What always remains discernible through this veil of not exactly dateable stories of gods, men, and animals is, first, the Labyrinth, the royal palace, and second, the Minotaur, the offspring of Pasiphae and the Bull, the incarnation of the divinity that required human sacrifice.

Every ninth year the Minos had to repair to the seat of the god, that is, to the habitat of the Minotaur in the more totemistic, or to the cave of Zeus in the more anthropomorphic version, in order to render account of his government and to receive ordinances for the future. The myth suggests the institution of a king who received power from the god for nine years and had to be reordained when the power was exhausted, so that he could continue to function. From the nine-year cycle of ordination one may infer the existence of a sacerdotal organization of nobles, perhaps the chieftains of the other cities, to whom the king was accountable in nine-year periods. The reordination was not certain—the king might not return from his visit to the Minotaur. Again it is possible that an echo of this ritual account of the king to the god was caught in Plato's *Critias,* in the nocturnal judgment ceremony for the rulers of Atlantis.

The symbols that link the power of the king with his divine ordination, as well as with the death and rebirth of the god, are obviously related with the corresponding Near Eastern cosmological forms. Nevertheless, one cannot speak of imitative derivation, although there is no doubt that considerable cultural diffusion, especially from Egypt, has occurred. In some respects Minoan symbols may have been as old as, for instance, the Sumerian, so old indeed that even a common origin may be assumed; in other respects they probably represented new developments beyond the common stratum. A few reflections on some symbols of order will illustrate the problem.

In the sacrifice of the sacred bull the double axe (labrys) was used, from which the habitat of the God, the Labyrinth, received its name. The labrys, originally a stone that was supposed to be the male god, belonged to a fetishistic stratum of symbols even older than the totemistic.

This stone axe is found at an early phase in the Asiatic cultures, and since it appears in Crete earlier than with the peoples who settled between Mesopotamia and the Aegean, original connections between Minoan and Mesopotamian cultures are probable. Parallels suggesting such connections, however, occur only on the level of fetishistic and totemistic symbolisms, of animal incarnation of gods, and of the Osiris and Tammuz symbolism of the dying and reborn god. They do not occur on the level of the imperial symbolism proper, and especially not in the form of a rationalization of the pantheon through theogonic speculation in the service of a political summodeism. The absence of such parallels could be explained, to be sure, by the lack of literary sources. Nevertheless, it is rather doubtful that symbolisms of this type ever existed, for the Cretan society never developed the imperial institutions that would have required them—the cultic hegemony of the Minos was not a Pharaonic rule originating in conquest. Beyond the first stratum, on which Cretan parallels to Near Eastern symbolisms can be found, and a second stratum, on which they are missing, there lies a third stratum, on which the Cretan society developed symbols not to be found in the same manner in the Near East. For peculiar to Crete is the development of certain symbols which imply a cult of sacred numbers. One of them, the fleur-de-lis, is of particular interest, because it apparently was an original creation of Minoan civilization. Together with the labrys, this symbol of the trinity has been carried to the farthest reaches of Minoan influence. It is so omnipresent that the Minoan sphere of power has, on occasion, been called the realm of the fleur-de-lis.

An interpretation of the fleur-de-lis must beware of suggestive associations. It is not advisable to speak of the symbol, as has been done, as if it were a mysterious achievement of mankind in the dim past, long before the Christian symbol of the trinity was evolved. For the interest in the number three is a quite ordinary occurrence wherever the problem of origin is expressed in terms of procreation; the symbolization of the origin of being through the trinity of the procreating couple and its offspring is in fact so obvious as to be almost compulsory. Hence, the trinity of father, son, and a female principle is a constant topic of speculation, though in the Near East it never achieved the intenseness of a symbolization of the number in the abstract. What trains of speculation the Cretans associated with the fleur-de-lis we do not know, but its very existence proves that, at least in sacerdotal circles, the elaboration of problems of origin and power must have gone rather far, probably farther than in the Near Eastern anthropomorphic myth.

An approximate idea of the intellectual processes involved in the creation of the symbol can be formed through a comparison with the closely related Pythagorean tetractys. The tetractys consists of the first four integers, adding up to ten, represented by pebbles or dots so that they will form a triangle:

The tetractys was invoked in the Pythagorean oath as containing "the root and fountain of everflowing nature." [5] As far as the meaning of the symbol in detail is concerned, Aristotle has preserved an interpretation of the first three numbers: the even is the Unlimited, the odd the Limited, while the One is even and odd at the same time and, therefore, the origin of the Limited and Unlimited.[6] According to other sources the even was identified as the female principle, an element of unorganized chaos, needing the union with the male principle in order to determine itself to a definite product, while the odd represented the male principle. The monad, in this construction, was the bisexual origin, capable of releasing the even and the odd from its undifferentiated unity. A trinitarian symbol, thus, may express more than one train of speculation. It can symbolize the sex differentiation, representative of Becoming, and the originating unity, representative of Being, but it can also symbolize the two procreating principles and their offspring.[7] Whatever the Minoan meaning may have been, the existence of the symbol indicates that speculations on "the root and fountain of everflowing nature" must have reached a high degree of abstraction.

There are furthermore definite indications that celestial phenomena played an important role in the Minoan symbolization of order. On a gold ring from Mycenae, representing an offering to the Great Mother, the goddess sits under the Tree of Life and among the symbols surrounding her there can be discerned sun, moon, and several stars (perhaps the galaxy) in addition to the labrys and the fleur-de-lis. The aggregate is

[5] Diels-Kranz, *Die Fragmente der Vorsokratiker* (7th ed., Berlin, 1951), 58. Die Pythagoreische Schule, fragm. B 15.

[6] Aristotle, *Metaphysics* I, 987a13–20.

[7] On the interpretation of the tetractys cf. F. M. Cornford, "Mystery Religions and Pre-Socratic Philosophy," *Cambridge Ancient History*, IV (1926), 15.

something like a Minoan pantheon. Moreover, speculative processes must have gone rather far with regard to celestial phenomena, too, for the symbol of the cross, the bars dividing the sun disk into the four quarters of the world, occurs not only as a talisman or amulet as it can be found anywhere between the Aegean and India, but as a sacred symbol attached to the divinity. In pictorial representations it is handed down from the mother goddess to the son, and it is the repository of the serpent goddess of Cnossus. In the absence of literary documents we know as little about the meaning of the cross as about the meaning of other Cretan symbols. Still, the association of such abstract symbols with divine power is peculiar to Minoan civilization; it will be permissible, therefore, to throw out the suggestion for what it is worth that the peculiarity is symptomatic of an inclination toward abstract speculation of the type that found the field for its flowering in the Hellenic phase of Greek civilization.

In the history of Cretan society, though we know so regrettably little about the detail, the rudiments of a form of order can be discerned that later will become the great problem of Hellenic society. The town culture, as we have stressed, is the matrix of civilizational societies which effectively participate in the quest of mankind for true order. If we now recognize, as an advance toward effective participation, the creation of a society in which common humanity beyond membership in a biologically determined group is accepted, as it is clearly done in town cultures, we have touched the level of experience which can motivate more than one type of larger societies with their orders and symbols. On principle, the whole area of town culture from Babylon to Hellas could have developed into one huge society. If, instead, it developed into several smaller societies, the reasons must be sought in the limiting factors of the human condition—in ethnic and linguistic differences, in geopolitical divisions into landscapes with sparsely settled areas separating them, in the limits of governmental organizations which require capable founders, successors, administrators, writing and bookkeeping skills, in the difficulties of building and maintaining communication systems, in disturbances through invasions, in internal rivalries for power, and so forth. Under this aspect, the imperial institutions of the Near Eastern societies in cosmological form both express common humanity and limit it to their subjects. The area of town culture, to be sure, remained conductive for trade relations and cultural diffusion, especially on the court level, from one end to the other; the relations even increased to such a degree that in the Amarna age, in the fourteenth century B.C., one can indeed speak of a common civilization of mankind which embraced the whole area;[8] and this civilizational conductivity was retained even under circumstances that will surprise the moderns, as in the case of continued trade relations between Athens and Persia, by way of the Syrian Alalakh, during the Persian Wars.[9] Nevertheless, the imperial orders were as much an obstacle to the unfolding of a civilizational society on a larger scale as they were an advance toward participation in the history of mankind.

Against the background of these reflections must be set the peculiar structure of Cretan society: its flowering of courtly manners; the elegance of its men and women that still speaks to us from the murals of the palaces and from the vase paintings; its peace among the cities of the island; its absence of any traces of revolt from the lower classes; its receptiveness for Libyan, Egyptian, and Syrian cultural influences; its own dynamism as a transmittor of culture to the Aegean area; and its crowning exploit of Minoizing the Achaeans—and all this without conquest and imposition of empire. In this favored island grew, on a minute scale, the type of order which Plato envisaged as a federation of all Hellas; and from this corner of the area of town culture grew the Greek society which, in the wake of Alexander's conquest, Hellenized the world from the Mediterranean to India.

2. *The Achaean Society*

The civilizational eruption on Crete could not immediately draw the Aegean area into its orbit, because in *c.*1950 B.C. the mainland was overrun by Greek-speaking Indogermanic tribes. During the following centuries, down to *c.*1600, a process of amalgamation took place between conquerors and conquered, comparable in many respects to the amalgamation of the Hebrew tribes with the indigenous population in Canaan from which emerged the new "Israel" that wanted a king like the other nations. On the Greek mainland emerged the "Achaeans," Greek by language, but with a syncretistic culture that becomes especially noticeable in the pantheon composed of divinities of patriarchal and matriarchal origins. With regard to political organization nothing can be discerned but a considerable number of small principalities among which Mycenae

---

[8] Cyrus H. Gordon, *Homer and Bible* (1955), 44ff.
[9] Sir Leonard Woolley, *Spadework* (London, 1953), 112.

in the Argolis achieved some eminence by the seventeenth century B.C. In Mycenae are to be found the oldest traces of contact with Cretan civilization, in the form of Minoan artifacts in the shaft graves of c.1650.

After the Cretan catastrophe of 1600, this relatively quiescent culture acquired civilizational momentum. In the shadow of Minoan power, Achaean sea enterprise had extended only to the Cyclades, the Chalcidice, and the Hellespontic area. Now Cnossus could be raided, its treasures plundered and its skilled workmen deported; moreover direct contacts with Egypt could be established. The few decades from 1600 to 1570 were sufficient to diffuse, among the Achaeans, familiarity with the Minoan court style, the war chariots of the Hyksos, and the fighting technique of the Mariannu. By the middle of the sixteenth century a new civilization with Mycenae as its center had emerged, in possession of naval power, of a new military technique, and of a Minoized way of life. By the fifteenth century the Achaeans had expanded their settlements to Rhodes and Miletus, on a smaller scale to Cyprus and the Cyrenaica, and had become successors to the Minoan trade with Egypt, Cyprus, and Syria. By 1460 an Achaean prince ruled in Cnossus. The great material flowering, the late Mycenaean period, lasted from c.1400 to the twelfth century, when the Achaean society was badly broken through the passing invasion by new primitive tribes, probably Illyrians and Thracians, from the north.[10]

About the pragmatic history of the Achaean society, next to nothing is known in detail with any certainty. Reconstructions, especially for the thirteenth century, have been attempted on the basis of the Greek saga tradition in combination with data from Hittite and Egyptian sources, but they must remain on the level of precarious conjecture. At the utmost one can place the Achaean expedition against Troy in the context of the invasions of the twelfth century and reflect on the fact that the stemming of the tide on the borders of Egypt, by Ramses III in 1193, coincided with the accepted date of the Trojan War c.1194–1184.[11]

The Minoan Linear B script has recently been deciphered by Ventris and Chadwick.[12] It has become possible to read the clay tablets from

---

[10] Fritz Schachermeyr, "Kreta und Mykenae," loc. cit., 42–55.

[11] For such reconstructions cf. Sir John L. Myres, "Kleinasien," loc. cit., 449–83, 464 and 466.

[12] M. G. F. Ventris and J. Chadwick, "Evidence for Greek Dialect in the Mycenaean Archives," Journal of Hellenic Studies 73 (1953), 84–103. M. G. F. Ventris, "King Nestor's

Cnossus, Mycenae, and Pylos; and new source materials concerning the order of Achaean society are available. The enthusiasm about the brilliant feat of decipherment, as well as about the general importance of the fact that a Greek dialect, closely related to the Homeric language, is now established in writing for the fifteenth century B.C., must not deceive, however, about the narrowness of the information offered by the documents. The clay tablets in question, rather perishable in their original state, have been preserved because they were baked hard at the time when the respective palaces and storage rooms went up in fire on occasion of a conquest. And since they contain bookkeeping accounts, and such accounts on clay were probably pulped after a year or two, the preserved tablets almost certainly represent only vouchers of the year immediately preceding the destruction of the site. The tablets from Cnossus, thus, represent a year around 1400, when the palace was destroyed for the last time, never to be rebuilt; while the tablets from Pylos and Mycenae date from the year in which the respective palaces and towns were destroyed, some time after 1200.[13]

About the age of the Achaean language and script nothing is known except what can be inferred from the state of the tablet materials. Certainly both language and script existed in the second half of the fifteenth century B.C. Since the Linear B was derived from the Minoan Linear A, with considerable innovations to make it usable for the Achaean language, some time must be allowed for the development of the script and its standardization. Whether the time of the Achaean rule in Cnossus, c.1460 to 1400, was sufficient for this process is doubtful, especially in view of "the astonishing uniformity which the Knossos tablets show with those of Pylos and Mycenae, in script, spelling, and arrangement." The possibility cannot be rejected that the invention goes back to the critical decades of contact with Crete in 1600–1570. In that case, an Achaean *koine* and script for commercial purposes may have prevailed in the whole area of Mycenaean civilization ever since the middle of the sixteenth century B.C.[14] Whether the script was used for other than commercial purposes is not known, though its forms betray that it was de-

Four-handled Cups: Greek Inventories in the Minoan Script," *Archaeology* 7, 1 (1954), 15–21. M. G. F. Ventris and J. Chadwick, *Documents in Mycenaean Greek. 300 Selected Tablets from Knossos, Pylos and Mycenae with Commentary and Vocabulary* (Cambridge, 1956). For the history of excavation, publication, and decipherment of the tablets, as well as for the bibliography, the reader should refer to the last quoted work.

[13] Ventris and Chadwick, *Documents*, 37f.   [14] *Ibid.*, 38f.

veloped for writing on papyrus or leather rather than for incision on clay; and whether any literary texts, if they ever existed, will come to light is doubtful in view of the perishable character of the writing materials. Still, there are archaeologists who will not be happy before they have found an Achaean *Ur-Ilias,* or at least a personal letter from Agamemnon —and perhaps they will.

While the facts to be derived from the tablets are restricted with regard to time and locality, they are sufficient to prove the existence of an Achaean society of substantially the type that appears in the Homeric epic. The unit of organization was a small territory with a few townships; the absence of an occupational designation for peasants suggests that everybody was still close to the soil and derived his living at least in part from agriculture; no completely urbanized sector of the population had yet formed. These units were organized as monarchies. At the head stood a *wanax,* a lord or master. The term still occurs in Homer (*Il.* 1.442), where Agamemnon is designated as the *anax andron,* the master of men. The administration was feudal in the sense that the functionaries were recompensed by landholdings, the *temene* or preserves. Next in rank to the *wanax* as holder of a *temenos* stood a *lawagetas,* a military commander; but it is not clear whether this office was permanent or only created in time of emergency. The word *lagetas* still appears in classic Greek with the meaning of a leader of men. Then there were a number of fief holders, the *te-re-ta* (Gk. *telestai*) of higher and the *ka-ma-e-u* of lower rank, whose feudal services cannot be determined with certainty. A type of landholder, the *heqetas* (Gk. *hepetes*), must have been of some importance since the names associated with this rank are given with their patronymic. They were probably *comites,* comrades-in-arms, companions of the king, corresponding to the Homeric *hetaroi* (*Il.* 1.179). Of special interest is the title *pa-si-re-u* (Gk. *basileus*) for the minor lord of an outlying district. It corresponds to the Homeric use of *basileus* as feudal lord, and makes more intelligible the ruling clique of *basileis* in Hesiod's small town. Furthermore there appear cultorganizations as landholders, and temples with "slaves of the god" as tenants. About the legal status of the people at large not much can be said except that there were, besides the free population, a considerable number of slaves, especially women slaves acquired by overseas raids. Trades were richly diversified; there are mentioned various types of building and metal workers, carders, spinners, weavers, fullers, unguent boilers, goldsmiths, and even one physician.[15]

More than one half of all the words on the tablets are proper names. Of the names of persons, fifty-eight could be identified with names occurring in the Homeric epic. Since among them are to be found such names as Achilles and Hector, Priamus and Aiax for men in humble positions, the Achaean range of names was apparently limited. That should be a warning against rash identifications of names occurring in Hittite sources with persons that have been made famous by myth or epic. Moreover, twenty of the fifty-eight names are attributed by Homer to Trojans, or to heroes fighting on the Trojan side. This surprisingly high percentage perhaps indicates that the cultural homogeneity between Achaeans and Trojans, as well as the possession of a common pantheon, presupposed by Homer, is not fictitious.[16] And finally, the tablets attest some of the figures of the Homeric pantheon, though the restricted character of the sources does not permit inferences concerning the nature and function of the gods. Among the names appear with certainty Zeus, Hera, Poseidon, Hermes, Athena, Artemis; with probability Ares and Hephaestus. The name of Apollo does not appear, but there is a god with the name of Paiawon, the epithet of Apollo in the classic period; the Potnia, the epithet of Athena, also stands by itself as the name of a divinity. Besides Hera, there is coupled with Zeus a Diwja, presumably a Magna Mater; and in Cnossus, but not on the mainland, appear dedications to All the Gods.[17]

The thirteenth and twelfth centuries B.C. are the period in which the whole area of town culture suffered a severe setback. The kingdom of Mittanni fell to an Assyrian attack. Invaders from the north destroyed the Hittite empire and penetrated to the borders of Egypt. Assyria was weakened commercially by the Hittite breakdown and had to struggle with the reviving Babylonian power. The Peoples of the Sea had to be repelled by the Pharaoh Merneptah in 1221; and a second wave, which met with the invaders fresh from their destruction of the Hittites, could be contained by Ramses III; but Egyptian authority in Asia remained

---

[15] *Ibid.*, the section on "Social Organization," 119–25.
[16] *Ibid.*, the chapter on "The Personal Names," 92–105.
[17] *Ibid.*, the section on "Mycenaean Religion," 125–29.

purely nominal in the wake of that effort. And a further wave of invaders, probably the same which ultimately reached Egypt from the sea, swept through the Mycenaean area, leaving a trail of thorough destruction. The decline and fall of empire was so general a phenomenon that one suspects an internal exhaustion of the area that made it succumb to the attacks. In the Aegean sector of the area, the vacuum of power ensued in which Israel and Hellas could grow and unfold, undisturbed by imperial interventions.[18]

The process of transition from Achaean to Hellenic society is fairly clear in its outlines, but almost completely dark in the detail. The physical destruction through the barbarian invasion must have been terrific. With the settlements and palaces, the economic basis of the higher crafts had perished; and possibly the art of writing was lost, too. Into this shattered territory moved, c.1100, the Dorians, followed by the northwestern Greeks. While the earlier invaders had only moved through the area, leaving no noticeable ethnic traces, the new immigration resulted in massive settlements, of Dorians in the Argolis, Laconia, and Messenia on the Peoloponnesus, on Crete and Rhodus, of northwestern Greeks in Achaea and Elis, in Aetolia and Phocis. Under this pressure the Achaeans emigrated in large numbers over sea to the islands and the Anatolian coast. From these enforcements of the Achaeans by related Greek tribes, from the Ionian migration and the reshuffling of populations resulted the ethnic composition and territorial expanse of the society which, by the eighth century, emerged as the Hellenes. The astonishing feat of these centuries was the maintenance of civilizational continuity with the Mycenaean, and through the Mycenaean with the Minoan phases of Greek society. This was the feat of the Achaean aristocrats who preserved their traditions, however modified by the new situation, through the dark centuries and now, as the Ionians of the islands and Anatolia, became the center of civilizational revival for the whole Hellenic area.

[18] For this and the following paragraph cf. Fritz Schachermeyr, "Geschichte der Hellenen bis 356," *Historia Mundi*, III (1954), 116–215, 118–26.

CHAPTER 3

Homer and Mycenae

The primitive, Greek-speaking invaders of 1950 B.C. had become, through cultural syncretism and amalgamation with the indigenous population, the Achaeans of 1600. They had then through Minoization as well as through contacts with Egypt and Syria, gained their civilizational momentum. And after the demise of Cretan society in 1400, the Mycenaean had become the dominant civilization of the Aegean area. The area as a whole, thus, had been civilizationally penetrated for more than eight hundred years, before substantial parts of the Achaeans moved eastward under the pressure of the Doric migration.

The depth and strength of this past must not be forgotten in any consideration of the problems of order during the dark age that extends from *c.*1100 to the emergence of the Homeric epic in the eighth century B.C. However severe the loss of power and wealth, the fact of the Achaean mass migration as well as the foundation of new towns on the coast of Anatolia and the islands, proves that neither the cohesion of the society nor its spirits were broken; however straitened and precarious the material circumstances of the reorganized communities, the Achaeans were still the carriers of Mycenaean order. The Doric migration had displaced, not a primitive tribe, but the active center of civilization that once before had moved from Crete to Mycenae. From its new geopolitical and reduced material position, the Achaean nobility could recapture its past, if it had the stamina and ability. It could engage in its *recherche du temps perdu* and make the glory of its past the guide for its present and future; and it could even impose its own past as *their* history on the primitive ethnic relatives who now were sitting in Mycenae, Tiryns, and Crete, if a convincing form was found. An Aegean-wide society, in continuity with the earlier civilizational societies, could be formed in spite of the discouraging circumstances of the moment, if the consciousness of a common Aegean order in terms of the Minoan-Mycenaean past was awakened. This feat was indeed performed through the creation of the Homeric epic.

If the problem of transition from the pre-Hellenic to the Hellenic phase of Greek history be formulated in this manner, the connection between the work of Homer and the formation of the classic consciousness of history will become apparent. The symbolism of the historical course was created in retrospect at its end; but the study of the phenomenon, in Chapter 1, had to stress the living traditions which provided the material for the construction of the course and at the same time, by the fact of their existence, attested its reality. The continuum of Greek society back to the Cretans was real, before the experience of its course was expressed by the historians and philosophers of the fifth and fourth centuries B.C. And the critical event in this course was the conversion, by the epic, of Mycenaean civilization into the past of the Aegean-wide society that now was growing from the center in Ionia. From the historical consciousness of the classic period we are, thus, referred back to its origin in the epic consciousness of Homer, from the relation Hellas-and-History to the relation Homer-and-Mycenae.

§ 1. HOMERIC QUESTIONS

The question of Homer and Mycenae in the sense just adumbrated must be disengaged from the great philological controversy concerning genesis, date, and authorship of the epics, that is, from the "Homeric question" in the conventional sense. The controversy, which goes back to Friedrich August Wolf's *Prolegomena* of 1795, closely resembles, with regard to its structure, the controversy concerning the Biblical narrative. Since in *Israel and Revelation* I have devoted a special note to the changing climate of opinion in Pentateuchal criticism, it will not be necessary to furnish a similar digression on the Homeric question.[1] For our purpose, a brief indication of the parallels between the two controversies will be sufficient, followed by an equally brief statement of those points in the Homeric question which are of immediate relevance to the present study.

The Bible critics abolished Moses as the author of the Pentateuch; Wolf abolished Homer as the author of the *Iliad* and *Odyssey*. The fatherless works fell apart into component literary units—the "sources" of the Wellhausen school, the "lays" of Lachmann; and somebody had to be

[1] *Order and History* I, Ch. 6, § 1.

found who assembled the pieces and joined them in the extant literary form—the postexilic redactor for the Biblical narrative, Peisistratus for the epics. In neither of the two cases could the hypotheses find general and ultimate acceptance, as they made inexplicable the literary architecture and spiritual contents of the integral works, so obvious to every reader who does not have a source-critical axe to grind. Nevertheless, one could not return to the unqualified assumption of authorship by a definite person. For in both cases the devoted and competent work of the critics had proven beyond a doubt that sources of variegated origin in space and time had entered the final form. Hence, there remained a formidable problem of genesis and date of the respective literary documents, as a whole and in their parts, even if definite authorship of the final form was assumed. In order to cope with the problems of this type, in both instances theories concerning the genesis of huge literary bodies were developed that would make the architecture and meaning of the works (pointing to a single author) compatible with collective creation in a process extending over centuries: With regard to the Biblical narrative, the "tradition-historical" method which assumes traditionist circles as the collectors, organizers, and transmittors of materials; with regard to the epic, the theory of "oral composition" which assumes an organized succession of rhapsodes in the same function. These theories, while they are plausible and empirically well supported, still are not quite satisfactory. In the Israelite case, definite persons—the author of the David memoirs, and the Yahwist—appeared to be the creators of a nucleus of symbolic form that could be expanded, through the work of traditionalist circles, into the Biblical narrative; and in the case of the epics, the analysis will show that we can hardly dispense with a definite creator of the symbolism, even though we know nothing about him as a historical personality.

The epics have preserved the memory of the late Mycenaean age with such fidelity that they can be used as guidebooks for archaeological discoveries; and the excavations in their turn have confirmed the accuracy of the epics with regard to numerous details of topography and material civilization. This reliability of the poems as historical sources causes the difficulties of assigning authorship and date. On the one hand, the epics as they stand are intricate literary compositions which presuppose a great artist, at some specific time, as their creator. On the other hand, various strata of materials can be distinguished within them. They have, first, absorbed pre-existing stocks of sagas, belonging to more than one cycle, in the case of the *Iliad* perhaps going back to the middle of the second millennium; they furthermore contain inventions by the poet who welded the materials into a literary whole; and they finally betray, in various sections, reworkings of a nuclear composition as well as inter-polations. The internal stratification of the epics will, therefore, support the argument that they have grown over a long period of time and that the date of their ultimate composition must be placed rather late. If, however, the date is assumed to be late, perhaps as late as the eighth or seventh century B.C., the miracle of a cultural tradition which saved the final author from mistakes with regard to details of material civilization becomes somewhat unbelievable. Hence, some scholars want to move the date closer to the time of the events narrated, as high up as the tenth or even the eleventh century. Under that assumption the quality of the poems would have caused the preservation of their material content, while otherwise it would be difficult to explain how a deliberately archaizing poet could achieve the freshness of accurate detail in describing a past that had grown dim by his time. To the reasons for an early date, the advocates of a late one can, however, answer that "heroic poetry" and its tradition by the "oral composition" of rhapsodes has a peculiar strength of survival, as proven by the preservation of south-Slavic epics of even larger size than the Homeric. A late poet would have had sufficient amounts of impeccable, archaic traditions at hand to weld them into his composition.[2]

If the various arguments be taken into account, and especially if the archaeological evidence be weighed, one can arrive at the dates for the

[2] For a balanced brief introduction to the Homeric question cf. Werner Jaeger, *Paideia* I (2d ed., New York, 1945), especially the Notes to Chapter II. A comprehensive survey of recent literature is given in Albin Lesky, *Die Homerforschung in der Gegenwart* (Vienna, 1952). My own views approach most closely those of Albin Lesky, "Muendlichkeit und Schriftlichkeit im Homerischen Epos" (Reprint from *Festschrift fuer Dietrich Kralik,* 1954). Of the older literature the following were especially used: U. von Wilamowitz-Moellendorf, *Die Ilias und Homer* (Berlin, 1920); John A. Scott, *The Unity of Homer* (Berkeley, 1921); J. T. Sheppard, *The Pattern of the Iliad* (London, 1922); T. W. Allen, *Homer* (Oxford, 1923); C. M. Bowra, *Tradition and Design in the Iliad* (Oxford, 1930); S. E. Bassett, *The Poetry of Homer* (Berkeley, 1938); Wolfgang Schadewaldt, *Homer und die Homerische Frage* (Berlin, 1938). Of the more recent literature: Renata von Scheliha, *Patroklos. Gedanken ueber Homers Dichtung und Gestalten* (Basel, 1943); Wolfgang Schadewaldt, *Von Homers Welt und Werk. Aufsaetze und Auslegungen zur Homerischen Frage* (2d ed., Stuttgart, 1944); Heinrich Pestalozzi, *Die Achilleis als Quelle der Ilias* (Zurich, 1945); Ernst Howald, *Der Dichter der Ilias* (Zurich, 1946): H. T. Wade-Gerry, *The Poet of the Iliad* (Cambridge, 1952); C. M. Bowra, *Heroic Poetry* (London, 1952).

epics proposed by Lorimer. As the *terminus ante quem* for the *Iliad* should be considered "the introduction of the hoplite phalanx and the substitution of its tactics for the loose unorganized fighting of the Homeric field." [3] It is not probable that the epic was composed for an audience which had become unfamiliar with the tactics of an Homeric battle. Since Late Geometric vases depict the old armature down to *c*.700, while the first vase-painting of a hoplite shield appears *c*.680, the date of the *Iliad* cannot be moved much below 700. For a *terminus post quem* of the *Iliad* the evidence is scanty, but help can be derived from the *Odyssey*. For the *Odyssey* presupposes relations of Greeks and Phoenicians which hardly existed before 750, and the epic will have been, therefore, composed not earlier than the last third of the eighth century. And since the *Iliad* is somewhat but not much older than the *Odyssey*, the earliest date for the *Iliad* cannot be moved too much upward of 750. The question whether one poet wrote both epics, or whether two authors should be assumed, must remain open.[4]

This should be enough of a bow to the Homeric question. For we are concerned, not with the history of literature, but with the Greek experiences of order and their symbolization. For the purpose of our study it must be retained that the Homeric epics, first, are in existence by 700, but not much earlier than 750; that they, second, are not collections of pre-existent sagas, but weld older materials into a new literary composition; and that, third, they probably have an author, or authors.

In a study on order and history the enigma, for which the name of Homer stands, is not the authorship of a work of literature, but the creation of a symbolism which expresses a new experience of human existence under the gods, of the nature of order and the causes of disorder, and of the historical decline and fall of a society. Who was the man, if it was only one man, who broke with the cosmological myth and created a non-cosmological form of social order? The problem is adumbrated in a passage of Herodotus (II, 53):

> Whence came into being each of the gods, or whether they had all
> for ever existed, and what forms they had, the Hellenes did not
> know until the other day, so to speak. For the age of Hesiod and
> Homer was not more than four hundred years before my own, I
> believe. And they were the first to compose theogonies for the Hel-

---

[3] H. L. Lorimer, *Homer and the Monuments* (London, 1950), 462.
[4] For the whole, extended argument cf. Lorimer, *ibid.*, the "Conclusions," 452–528.

lenes, to give the gods their epithets, to allot them their ranks and functions, and to describe their forms.

From this text two pieces of information can be extracted. In the first place, the Hellenes knew that the order of their gods was of recent origin and could not be traced beyond the age of the epics. The time span surmised by Herodotus places the event, at the earliest, in the ninth century B.C. And second, they were convinced that the myth had not grown anonymously over a long period of time, but had been created by definite persons, the poets. These facts, to be sure, do not illuminate the darkness in which the historical Homer is shrouded, but they come close enough to the enigma to allow its circumscription through the definite questions: What is a poet? What is the source of his knowledge? And by what authority does he create a new symbolism of divine and human order?

The sources that will supply the answers to these questions are surprisingly scarce. Still, they are sufficient to make recognizable a relation between the poet and a divine source of revelation that resembles the relation between the Israelite prophet and the word of Yahweh. The *Iliad* opens with the verse: "The wrath do thou sing, O goddess, of the Pelide Achilles"; and the *Odyssey* with "Tell me, O Muse, of the man of many devices." As in the prophetic texts of the Bible Yahweh and his prophet are interchangeable as the speakers of the word, the *dabar,* so in the epic the Muse and the singer are interchangeable as the speakers of the poem. For the rest, the *Iliad* is uninformative since it invokes the goddess only by the standard formula: "Tell me now, O Muses, housed on Olympus . . .", as an authenticating opening line for a new section of the story. In the *Odyssey,* however, we find an interesting passage. Demodocus is introduced (VIII, 63–64) as "the singer [*aoidos*] whom the Muse loved greatly, and gave him both good and evil; of his sight she deprived him, and gave him sweet song." The passage suggests a connection between blindness to the world and song, since both are given by the Muse. And the theme is resumed in a paean of Pindar (VII, b) where the poet prays for inventive skill to Mnemosyne and her daughters, the Muses. "For the minds of men are blind"; they need help who, without the Muses, "seek the steep path of them that walked it by their wisdom [*sophia*]"; to the poet, Pindar, the Muses have charged this "immortal labor." The terseness of the verses, as well as their fragmentary character, make it impossible to decide whether the immortal labor means Pindar's walking of the "way of wisdom" for himself, or as the helper to his blind fellow men, but the latter seems to be the more probable meaning. The Homeric and Pindaric passages together formulate the great theme of blindness and seeing that recurs in Aeschylus and Plato: Who sees the world is blind and needs the help of the Muses to gain the true sight of wisdom; and who is blind to the world, is seeing in the wisdom of sweet song. The Muses, and through them the poets, are the helpers of man who seeks to ascend from his darkness to light.

More explicit on the subject is Hesiod in the opening pages of the *Theogony*. A tale of the gods must begin with the Muses, for whatever the poet knows about them he has learned from the Heliconian maids. They were begotten, by Zeus on Mnemosyne, to sing to the gods about the things that are, and shall be, and were aforetime; and to praise to men the Olympians. They sing to remember—the world to the gods, and the gods to man—and they remember in order to make forget. They are "a forgetting of ills and a rest from sorrow." For though a man's soul be troubled and his heart be distressed, when "a singer, the servant of the Muses" sings the deeds of the forbears and the blessedness of the gods, he will forget his heaviness, and the gifts of the goddesses will turn him away from his sorrows. This antinomy of remembrance and forgetting corresponds to the previous one of blindness and seeing. The sorrow of "the newly-troubled soul" will be forgotten when the truly memorable is remembered; and the tenaciously held grief and distress is a forgetfulness about the things that are preserved by true memory, by Mnemosyne. The same opposition of true and false reality recurs in the tragedy, in the Aeschylean distinction between true action in conformity with the order of Zeus and the evasive or indifferent conduct which does not even deserve the name of action; and it is ultimately transformed by the philosophers into the tension between true Being and the turgid stream of Becoming.

The Hesiodian text (99–100) refers to the singer as the servant (companion, attendant, *therapon*) of the Muses; the same formula occurs in *Homeric Hymns* XXII, 19–20. More frequently he is the *prophetes*, the interpreter or spokesman of the gods. The term is generally applied to the interpreters of oracles at temples; Herodotus speaks of the prophets at a shrine of Dionysus (VII, 111) and of a prophet at Delphi (VIII, 36–37). The "truthful seer" Teiresias is for Pindar the "prophet of Zeus" (*Nem.* I, 60–61). And Pindar himself, "the holy mouth of the Muses," [5]

[5] *Lyra Graeca*, ed. J. M. Edmonds (Loeb Classical Library), I, 2 (*Anth. Pal.* 9.184).

succinctly enjoins them: "Reveal [*manteueo*], O Muse, and prophesy shall I" (fragm. 150). The parallel with the relation of Israelite prophets to the *dabar* of Yahweh is obvious—with the important difference, however, that in Israel the transcendent God manifests himself through the word, while in Hellas the gods are still present and visible within the world and the "word" spoken is the poet's song. The *logos* has no function yet in the symbolism of the prophetic poets; only with the philosophers does it begin to replace the earlier theophanies.[6]

The poets sing what is memorable; and the life of man reaches its climax, even in suffering, when his action and passion is worthy to be sung. A few texts will illuminate the problem. In *Iliad* VI, 354–58 Helen speaks of the evil fate that Zeus has brought on her and Paris "so that in days to come we shall be a song for men yet to be." In *Odyssey* VIII, 579–80 Alcinous speaks of the ruin which the gods have wrought on men at Troy "that there might be a song for those yet to be." Pindar (*Nem.* VI, 29–31) invokes the Muses to praise the victor; for, when the heroes have passed away, "songs and legends store their noble deeds." And Euripides (*Troiades* 1242–45) lets Hecuba, about to be carried off into slavery, reflect: Had not a god thrown us down, even beneath the earth, "we would have been unfamed, unhymned by lays, and not a song to the mortals to come." The poet himself is not exempt from the hunger for survival through his song. A fragment betrays the proud consciousness of a Sappho: "Happy in truth have made me the golden Muses—when I die I shall not be forgotten." [7]

The Hellenes had no Message and Covenant from Sinai to create them a Chosen People in historical form. They had no Moses to lead them from the bondage of Pharaoh to the freedom of God. But they had the prophetic singers who experienced man in his immediacy under the gods; who articulated the gulf between the misery of the mortal condition and the glory of memorable deeds, between human blindness and divine wisdom; and who created the paradigms of noble action as guides for men who desired to live in Memory. That was less than the Mosaic insight which placed the people in the present under God; but it was more in as much as the singers appealed to the psyche of every man singly. From its very

---

[6] Thorleif Boman, *Das Hebraeische Denken im Vergleich mit dem Griechischen* (2d ed., Goettingen, 1954), 54.

[7] *Lyra Graeca*, I, 192.

beginning the appeal went to the divine essence of order in the soul, to the immortal core. The experience of immortality, to be sure, was still bound by the cosmos as were the gods. Man could not yet, through the sanctification of life and divine grace in death, move toward the beatific vision; but he could place himself before the gods forever by action that entered the stream of Memory through the song of their prophets.[8]

We still know nothing about the historical Homer. But we know that the Hellenes believed him to be the man who first transfigured their past into song.

When the memorable events are transfigured by song, they become the past of the society for which the poet sings. But the events transformed into past by the Homeric epic belong to the Achaean society with its power seat in Mycenae, while the poem is sung for the inchoate Hellenic society with its active center on the Anatolian coast. And the two are separated by the disasters of the Achaean and Ionic migrations. Hence, the question must be asked: What interest could the descendants of the refugees in Ionia have in the exploits of a society which, if the middle of the eighth century be accepted as the date of the epics, had been defunct for more than two hundred years? The answer to this question must be sought in the act of transfiguration which links the two societies into one.

As the subject matter of the *Iliad*, Homer did not choose a splendid enterprise, but an episode of disorder which presaged the catastrophe that was to overcome Mycenaean civilization. In an earlier context we have suggested the internal exhaustion of civilizational societies in the area of town culture by the twelfth century B.C. The *Iliad*, now, furnishes a paradigmatic study of the causes of decline in the Aegean-wide Mycenaean order. For Homer's Achaeans are not Hellenes, and his Trojans are not barbarians; they both belong to the same society and their strife is a civil war. The one Olympian order extends over them all: the Zeus who endows Agamemnon with his royal authority is also the protector of Troy against Hera who sides with the Achaeans. But the gods are divided. The rift among men is a disturbance in the Olympian order of the world; and the division among the gods is a disturbance of human

---

[8] On this section cf. Walter F. Otto, *Theophania* (Hamburg, 1956), 28–33, and in general the same author's *Die Goetter Griechenlands* (4th ed., Frankfurt, 1956).

order. While the war is conducted, on the pragmatic level, as a sanction against a Trojan violation of law, the human disorder reaches into the divine sphere. Something more is at stake than a breach of order that could be repaired by due compensation or by an Achaean victory. For the war itself, destructive for Troy and exhaustive for the Achaeans, is a wanton indulgence; it reveals a universal order—embracing both gods and men, both Trojans and Achaeans—in decline and judgment. The misery of the vanquished will fall back on the victors.

In the fall of Achaean society the poet found more than a political catastrophe. In the action and passion of the heroes he discovered the touch of divinely ordained fate, the element of tragedy which lets the events ascend to the realm of Mnemosyne. From the disaster he wrested his insight into the order of gods and men, from the suffering grew wisdom when the fall became song. In this act of transfiguration the poet transcended Achaean society and created the Hellenic symbolic form. We can speak of it as the style of self-transcendence, corresponding to the Israelite style of exodus from civilization and ultimately from itself. For with its past the new society had acquired its future. The Hellenic society did not have to die as did the Babylonian or Egyptian, the Cretan or Achaean. Hellas could transcend itself into Hellenism; and it could transcend the symbolic form of the Olympian myth, in which it had constituted itself, into philosophy as the symbolic form of mankind.

§ 2. Order and Disorder

The *Iliad* studies an episode of disorder in a society which the poet considers to be Achaean. The formulation must be cautious for two reasons. In the first place, the study extends in fact also to the order and disorder of the Trojans who are, together with the Achaeans in the narrower sense, part of the nameless, Aegean-wide civilizational society. And second, the picture of order drawn by the poet has absorbed materials from more than one phase of Mycenaean civilization; and furthermore there have been added material and ethnic features of post-Mycenaean history down to the poet's own time. We shall accept the Homeric intention and continue to speak of Achaean society; but the reader must remain aware that the following analysis of constitutional order, which must be furnished as the background to the study of disorder, pertains to the specifically Homeric society of the epic. While it certainly closely resembles the historical Achaean society, the exactness of the picture cannot be demonstrated in detail.

1. *The Constitutional Order of Achaean Kingdoms*

The age is in decline. The *Odyssey* is more expansive on the symptoms of constitutional disorder than the *Iliad*. The situation of an army in the field, held together by a military purpose and the tension of effort, does not allow for a weakening of institutions so deep that victory would be endangered. For an understanding of late Achaean political culture, therefore, the two epics most felicitously supplement one another. If only the institutions of the *Iliad* were known, it would be difficult to decide whether they reflect the political order of Achaean kingdoms, or whether they must be considered the specific organization of a federal army in war time; but the *Odyssey* proves that the constitution of the army before Troy roughly corresponds to the constitution of a kingdom. If only the dismal situation of the leaderless kingdom of Ithaca were known through the *Odyssey*, it would be difficult to form an opinion about the functioning of its order under less unfortunate conditions; but the *Iliad* shows such a constitution in operation, at least effective enough for successful conduct of the war. As a consequence we can attempt to draw a composite picture of the constitutional order of the Achaean age, of its operation, and of its decline.

The constitutional order of an Achaean kingdom appears in outline on occasion of the events in Ithaca. A kingdom was a region of moderate extent, settled by a primarily agricultural population. Economically the population was stratified on the scale from small homesteads to large manorial enterprises with dependent (slave?) labor for field work, the tending of herds, and home industry; socially the stratification expressed itself in the distinction of nobles (*aristoi*) and common men. The king (*basileus*) was one of the nobles, a *primus inter pares*, whose position depended on his recognized superiority through noble ancestry, wealth, strength, and intelligence. The political organs of such a region were the king, a council (*boule*) of elders (all or the most distinguished of the nobles) and a popular assembly (*agore*) of the arms-bearing freemen. A region of this type had local subdivisions. The manor of a noble was the center of a local district; and if the district was large and wealthy enough it might contain a village or town. The manor of Odysseus had a town (*asty*) in its neighborhood, and since its neighborhood character was stressed there were perhaps lesser villages on the island. Moreover, the kingdom was not confined to the island itself. In the *Iliad*, Odysseus appears as the chieftain of the Cephallenians who not only hold Ithaca but also the surrounding islands and a strip on the coast of the mainland; and in the *Odyssey*, the suitors of Penelope are nobles from Ithaca as well as from the other islands. How this larger region was organized as a unit is no longer recognizable under the conditions of disorder which prevail in the *Odyssey*.

This typical nucleus of Achaean society was capable of considerable variations in size, wealth, and stability, as well as of creating more complex organizations through federation. The ship-catalogue of the *Iliad* enumerates a hundred ships for the Mycenae of Agamemnon (including the southern coast of the Gulf of Corinth), ninety for the Pylos of Nestor, and eighty each for the Argolid (with Tiryns and Argos) and the "Crete of the one hundred cities"; about ten other regions (among them the Lacedaemon of Menelaus) fall in the class of forty to sixty ships; the Ithaca of Odysseus (including the surrounding Cephallenian region) has no more than twelve; and the smallest region, Syme, has only three ships. About the causes of such differences in naval strength, about the economic basis of the numerous cities in the more powerful kingdoms, as well as about the sources of the wealth that built the royal palaces of Mycenae and Tiryns, the epics are uninformative. Telemachus, on one occasion, reflects that it is not a bad thing to be a king (the Greek verb would have to be rendered literally as something like "royalize"), for his house will quickly grow rich and he will earn much honor. But he does not indicate the source of revenue. One of the sources must have been war or piracy, since among the possessions of Odysseus are mentioned the slaves whom he gained as war prizes. The acceleration in royal acquisition of wealth would find a partial explanation in the greater portion of loot that was awarded to a king after a successful expedition. But the wealth of a whole civilization, the existence of large town settlements, and in particular the great wealth in the hands of individual kings, cannot be explained by war and plunder; somebody must be wealthy before robbery can have worthwhile results. The only possible explanation is royal revenue from trade. The wealth that lies on the line of Crete, Argos, Mycenae, Pylos must indicate a trade route, and the same must be true for the wealth of Troy.

A somewhat clearer picture than of the causes of regional differentiation can be gained with regard to the possibilities of an organized war
enterprise by the aggregate of kingdoms. The regional form of organization was transferable to the whole Achaean area, at least for special purposes. In the army before Troy one of the regional kings, Agamemnon,
functions as the *primus inter pares* in relation to the other kings. These
kings, or at least the six or seven more important ones among them, form
a council in the same manner in which regionally the nobles form a select
group surrounding the kings, while the army of the Achaeans at large
meets in *agore*, as a popular assembly. The leadership in war lies with the
strongest economic and military power; and, while the leaders with their
regional armies are federated for the expedition by oath, one may assume
that the pressure exerted by such superior power had something to do
with the initiation of the collective enterprise.

The constitutional organization, thus, consists of king, council and
assembly. Concerning the jurisdictions and procedures of these organs
of government the epics are comparatively rich in information because
their action hinges on legal cases. A quantitatively appreciable part of
the story is formed by expositions of points in law, by the weighing of
the relative right and wrong of the parties to a case, and by detailed
description of constitutional procedure. The constitutional preparation
of the great Achaean attack on Troy, in *Iliad* II, will offer an opportunity
to study the governmental machinery in operation.

At the opening of *Iliad* II the military situation of the Achaeans is
not the best. The siege has lasted for nine years; the temper of the leaders
is strained and the morale of the common men is low. Agamemnon is
peeved because he had to restore a beautiful girl, a part of his war loot,
to her father in order to avert the wrath of Apollo from the Achaean
army. In his anger he has compensated himself by taking the charming
Briseis, who had been awarded as war prize to the Pelide. As a consequence, the dishonored Achilles has withdrawn into his famous wrath,
swearing that he will no longer participate in the fighting however bad
it should turn for the Achaeans. At this critical juncture, with the
Achaeans deprived of their best fighting contingent, Agamemnon finds
his emotional answer to the wrathful withdrawal of Achilles (for which
he himself is largely responsible) by deciding on an all-out attack that
will conquer Troy and show Achilles that the war can be won without

him. Homer traces the procedure of preparing the attack, step by step, from the psychological formation of the royal initiative to the final assent of the army.

The fateful decision of the king is born from a turmoil of anger, frustration, envy, righteous pride, guilt, and anxiety. The masterful symbolization of the unconscious processes must be presupposed in this context. The action itself begins with the crystallization of the turmoil in a dream image. A messenger of Zeus appears to the sleeping Agamemnon, assuming the likeness of Nestor, the king's most respected counselling elder, in order to add to his persuasiveness. He reveals that he comes at the bidding of Zeus who advises the attack because the Olympians at last have become unanimous in their support of the Achaeans. The king rises from his slumber and begins to act on the divinely inspired dream. While the heralds call the army to assembly, he meets with his elders in council (*Il.* II, 1–52).

The meeting of the council opens with a speech from the king. Agamemnon lays his dream before the nobles; he then calls upon them to proceed with him to the assembly in order to move the army to battle; and, finally, he proposes an interesting procedure for moving the army toward the desired end. The procedure consists in something like a play enacted by the king and the elders. The king will first "try" (or "put to a test") the men by a speech in which he will tell them to abandon the war, to repair to the ships, and to return home; and then the elders are supposed to play their part by making counter-speeches that will hold the army back. The formulation of Homer suggests that this is not a royal whim of the moment but standard procedure for such an occasion. The "trial" is expressly designated as a legal custom or constitutional convention by the words *"he themis esti."* And since the trial is a ceremonial game, hallowed by custom, we must assume that the army is supposed to play its part in it. The assent of the army to the real will of the king should assume the form of an expressed will of the army to which the king assents (*Il.* II, 53–75).

The speech of the king to his council, in substance an order by the commander-in-chief to his generals, is answered by Nestor who addresses the other nobles. With courteous caution he remarks that they would consider such a dream, if told by anybody else, a cobweb (falsehood, *pseudos*) and turn away with contempt; but since it was seen by the man who considers himself by far the noblest (or: mightiest) of the

Achaeans the story will have to be accepted. Then he invites the others
to come with him and carry out the order. The authority of the commander prevails, though obviously the council has its misgivings; the
king is obeyed, as he indeed may be the man to whom the gods reveal
themselves truly, even if the revelation is rather at variance with common
sense understanding of the precarious situation. But Nestor's speech
has a warning undertone that the responsibility for such action, which
on the surface looks like folly, will rest with the king and his dream.
A king is not supposed to have dreams which endanger the army and
victory in war. Then the king and the elders join the assembly (*Il.* II,
76–83).

The king rises in the assembly to make his speech that will try the
army. Homer indicates the source of his authority by giving the
genealogy of his sceptre. The royal sceptre was made by Hephaestus
for Zeus, and from Zeus it was sent through the messenger Hermes to
Pelops, and from Pelops it was transmitted through Atreus and Thyestes
to Agamemnon. The authority by which the king rules over men stems
from the authority of Zeus in the Olympian dispensation of the world;
the political order partakes of the world order (*Il.* II, 100–108). In
his trial speech the king pleads an order of Zeus to lift the siege and to
return home. That, he admits, is a shameful thing to do because the
Achaeans outnumber the Trojans ten to one; but, Troy has too many
allies and the war is dragging on in the ninth year; no hope is left that
Troy will be conquered (109–41). With the end of this speech, the
procedure takes an unexpected turn. The army does not play its role
in the game. It does not wait until the other members of the council
have voiced their opposition but, overwhelmed with joy, the men rush
to the shore, begin to knock out the props and to pull the ships to the
sea, ready to start the homeward journey as fast as possible (142–54).
In that critical situation Odysseus intervenes, at the behest of Athena.
He requests from Agamemnon the Jovian sceptre and, equipped with
the symbol of divine authority, he makes his way along the ships, functioning as something like a parliamentary whip, and tries to bring the
men back into line (155–87).

The admonitions of Odysseus formulate the principle of royal order
in direct speech. The chieftains are admonished not to behave like
cowards but to sit down and make the common people do likewise;
the assembly was interrupted and they do not yet know what the in-

tention of Agamemnon really was. Common soldiers he beats with the
sceptre and chides them, telling them to sit down and listen to their
betters

For we shall not all be kings, we Achaeans;
Not good is a multitude of lords [*polykoiranie*]; one lord [*koiranos*] shall be,
One king, to whom Zeus gave
Sceptre and judgments [*themistas*] that he may take counsel for the others.

A more drastic declaration of the principle of royal rule is hardly
imaginable than this scene: Odysseus reminding the soldiers that they
are not kings but just the people for whom the king will do their
thinking, and accentuating his argument by blows with the Jovian
sceptre (188–206). This Homeric passage had a prodigious career in
Hellenistic politics, from Aristotle to Philo, as the great support for the
politico-theological analogy between the rule of one god in the cosmos
and one emperor on earth.

The assembly is at last restored to order. Before business is resumed,
however, a little symbolic byplay underlines the meaning of order. The
spirit of disorderly individualism that just manifested itself in the dangerous outburst of the army is concentrated in Thersites, an ill-favored,
cantankerous common man who now rises in speech against Agamemnon,
reviling the king and ultimately touching the sore spot of his responsibility for the wrath of Achilles. At this point Odysseus again intervenes,
administering the accustomed blow with the sceptre; he warns Thersites
not to strive singly against kings and threatens to strip him and to beat
him naked out of the assembly. That was just the incident needed to
swing the mood of the army back to order. They respond with good-
natured laughter to the punishment of their own mutiny in the shape
of the scurrilous Thersites, and express the hope that his castigation will
teach him never again to rail at kings. The atmosphere is cleansed
(211–77). The procedure can now be resumed. The elders speak in
opposition to Agamemnon, as planned; and the king lets himself be
persuaded to issue the order for battle. At the suggestion of Nestor the
contingents will fight by tribes and clans so that one can easily discern
who is brave and who is a coward (278–418).

In the *Iliad*, the constitutional order of the Achaean army still functions in the specific instance just considered. Nevertheless, the strain

under which it works, as well as the critical situation in which the fateful decision for battle is taken, are symptoms of a general malaise. And they forbode disaster.

2. *The Wrath of Achilles*

The epics are not concerned with causes and effects on the level of pragmatic history but with the phenomenon of decline itself. The Homeric society is disordered in as much as on decisive occasions the conduct of its members is guided by passion rather than by reason and the common good. The blinding through passion, the *ate,* is not the cause of disorder, it is the disorder itself. Something is badly wrong with the leading Homeric characters; and under one aspect, therefore, the *Iliad* is a study in the pathology of heroes. The retracing of Homer's analysis will appropriately begin with his deliberate parallel construction of the wrath of Achilles with the war against Troy. The great war is caused by the abduction of Helen by Paris; the Trojan prince has violated the rule that a guest should not start an affair with the wife of his host, and the violation of this basic rule of civilized societies requires counter-measures. The wrath of Achilles is caused by Agamemnon's taking of Briseis; that is an insult to the honor of a king, and it also requires some counteraction on the part of Achilles. The parallel construction offers Homer the opportunity to analyze the cases of both Achilles and Helen.

Achilles, as can be expected, makes the most of the parallel in order to keep his wrath at a fine, heroic boiling point. He will not be appeased. There the Achaeans conduct a long and costly war about Helen, in whom he is only mildly interested, and he should not indulge his wrath when he is deprived of his darling companion? Do these Argive brothers believe they are the only men who love their women? (*Il.* IX, 337–41). The argument from analogy, however, does not impress the delegation that has come from Agamemnon with an offer of reconciliation and honorable amends. He can have his Briseis back, with the guaranty of a great oath that she is untouched. And as compensation for the insult he will receive seven beautiful, skilled girls, plenty of gold and other treasure, an offer to become Agamemnon's son-in-law (with the right to take his choice from three daughters, with a huge dowry), and seven cities in Argos, all well situated near the sea on the trade routes. That offer should assuage the most magnificent wrath, as compensations for wrath go under hallowed customs. If Achilles does not accept the generous offer, something is clearly out of order. And he does not accept (IX, 260–99).

The careful elaboration of the correct solution for a quarrel of the type under debate narrows down the problem both of Achilles and Helen. As far as Achilles is concerned, the extraordinary character of his wrath can now be brought into focus. And as far as Helen is concerned, the question imposes itself: Why did the Trojans not resort to a solution similar to Agamemnon's offer to Achilles? The Trojans, too, have a constitutional government, with a council of intelligent elders. Why did not the government of Troy return Helen, with apologies and appropriate reparations, to her husband—an offer which the Achaeans would have been only too glad to accept? Why did they prefer to undergo the horrors of a long war and the serious impairment of their wealth? Homer deals with both of these questions—extensively with the wrath of Achilles at decisive junctures of the story, and in a few brief scenes with the fatality of Helen. We shall first consider the wrath of Achilles.

The wrath of Achilles is extraordinary in the literal sense. It is something outside human order. It is a gap in the order that binds men together, and through the gap is pouring an uncontrollable darkness from beyond. In order to describe this intangible, negative phenomenon Homer uses the device of confronting Achilles with the certain knowledge of his death in battle. The hero is a demi-god; and from his divine mother Thetis he has learned of the alternative fate that is in store for him: if he stays with the army at Troy he will not return home, he will perish in battle and thereby earn imperishable fame; if he boards his ship and returns home, an inglorious but long and happy life will be his lot (*Il.* I, 352, 414ff.; IX, 412f.). Homer explores the wrath of Achilles, first, by means of the divine revelation of the alternative and, second, by means of the various moods, situations, reasonings and decisions induced by the dilemma.

At this point of the analysis a source of rather common misunderstandings of the *Iliad* must be eliminated. The alternative fate of Achilles is not extraordinary by virtue of its content, but by virtue of its revelation. Homer's problem is not the fate of Achilles but the tension between a rather common fate and the uncommon reactions of the hero.

The construction of the *Iliad* depends on this tension. Hence, the common character of the fate must be ascertained with some care. The dilemma of the fate, as hinted, is not particularly exciting in the situation of a war. Even without divine information one may reasonably assume, on the one hand, that a healthy specimen like Achilles will have a long and agreeable life if he succeeds to the throne of a prosperous kingdom in a remote region and does not deliberately look for trouble; and on the other hand, that he runs the risk of getting killed sooner or later, if he engages continuously in battle with such intensity that his fame will be imperishable. Moreover, the dilemma faces most of the princes in the army. As long as the war continues they run the risk of death in battle; if they would return home and conduct themselves with some circumspection, their life expectancy would rise. And finally, it should be realized that the alternative does not imply a genuine choice. The whole army would prefer to go home; but they stay because the war is a federal political action with the purpose of punishing a violation of public order. The dilemma of Achilles, thus, is a more or less common lot. The prediction of his fate is not introduced for the purpose of creating a romantic hero who makes a free choice for early death and eternal fame. Only if the dilemma is understood as a common lot will the response of Achilles reveal its uncommon character. The tension is used by Homer with artistic circumspection for the two purposes of, first, isolating the precise nature of the Achillean wrath and, second, contrasting the wrath with the attitude of the other heroes to substantially the same fate.

The dilemma itself, thus, is not out of the ordinary. The extraordinary character of the Achillean fate begins with the fact of its divine revelation in so far as the prediction raises the probability of death to certainty. In the case of Achilles the warrior's fate of a life in the shadow of death becomes, psychologically speaking, an obsession with death that isolates him from the common life of humanity. War is for him not hardship and danger to be undergone as a public duty with the purpose of restoring order, but the fated essence of his existence. He never has experienced order as a man, for he went to war "a mere child" (*Il.* IX, 439f.). And he will not return as a man to the order for which the war is fought, since his existence will end in the death which through nine years the adolescent has dealt to others. The tension of his existence between death inflicted and death suffered is not a biographical accident but (and this is one of the points illuminated by the prediction) truly its essence.

The revelation of the fate is not an event outside the personality of Achilles; to have such a revelation is part of his character. The interpretation of the prediction as an obsession with death is not perhaps an anachronistic "psychologization" but the very meaning intended by Homer. The prediction is known not to Achilles alone but to everybody in the army. If it were considered by the Homeric characters as a piece of reliable information, from a divine source, on the impending death of Achilles before Troy, it not only would affect the Pelide but also the conduct of his friends. But his friends and comrades act as if the prediction did not exist. They seriously offer him wealth, a family alliance with Agamemnon, and an expansion of his realm, though they ought to know that such splendid prospects can hold no appeal for a man who will die and not return home. And when he reminds the embassy of the reason why their offer can hardly interest him (IX, 412f.), they continue their argument as if he had not spoken. Achilles with his revelation lives in a private world; or rather, he lives in a private world in so far as he is preoccupied with this isolating revelation. The action of the *Iliad* becomes incomprehensible unless the prediction is understood as an obsession which a hero, in so far as he is a public character, is not supposed to have. Some light will be shed on this Homeric problem by the earlier discussed dream of Agamemnon. The courteous answer of Nestor, in that instance, barely veiled the warning that kings are not supposed to have such dreams; that they come from the gods is no excuse; a man's divine revelations are his personal affairs and do not create an obligation for others; if, in Agamemnon's case, the elders obeyed orders they did not trust the dream but respected the authority of the king. The position of Achilles, however, is not that of the commander-in-chief; in his case no such respect is due. The injection of his predicted fate as an argument in the debate is a display of poor taste which the other lords are well-bred enough quietly to ignore.

The only member of the embassy who takes issue with the mental state of Achilles, at least by indirection, is his old educator Phoenix. The old man is obviously pained by the misconduct of his pupil. He, like the others, passes over the prediction with charitable silence. But he embarks on the great paraenetic, or admonitory, speech that culminates in the myth of the Wrath of Meleager; and in the course of this speech the various aspects of the hero's conduct, personal and public, are touched (IX, 434–605). As a member of the embassy, charged with an official duty, he does his best to persuade Achilles to accept the king's offer and to return to battle; and by means of the myth he points out to him the folly of his conduct on the utilitarian level. The young man cannot escape the exigencies of the situation. If he rejects the offer, he will have to fight nevertheless as soon as the Trojans have carried their attack down to the Achaean encampment and execute their plan of setting fire to the ships; and then, when he has waited until he must fight, he will be in the profitless situation of Meleager who did not receive any grateful reward for withholding his help until the last moment (IX, 600–605).

Phoenix, however, is also the educator, a second father to Achilles; he knows that the trouble is deep-seated and that the wrath will not be overcome by offers in accordance with custom or by an appeal to material interest. Hence, he prefaces the paraenetic myth of Meleager with a serious disquisition on the dialectics of guilt (*ate*) and prayers (*litai*) (IX, 496–512). The soul of Achilles must first be touched to the core, if that is possible, the obsession must be broken and a healing conversion must be initiated, before ordinary argument can be effective. He points out to his "dear child" what is wrong with him on principle. The specious prediction of fate need not even be mentioned; it is no more than one of the symptoms that Achilles has a "proud spirit [*thymos*]" and a "pitiless heart [*hetor*]." The "dear child" is violating a fundamental rule of the order of things. Even the gods who exceed him by far in worth, honor, and strength bend to prayers when men have transgressed; for prayers are the daughters of Zeus. Guilt is rash and causes men to fall, and prayers come after to heal the hurt. The daughters of Zeus must be honored. When a man rejects prayers, the insulted divinities will carry their case to Zeus himself, and then *ate* will follow the culprit and make him atone to the full.

The compact sentences of Phoenix' admonition need a little explication. The Homeric *ate* means the folly of the heart, the blindness of passion, that makes a man fall into guilt; and it also means the sinful act, the transgression of the law. And the Homeric *litai* correspondingly means the repentance of the heart, as well as the acts (prayers and sacrifices to god, prayers and offers of recompense to men) in which repentance expresses itself. *Litai* are the daughters of Zeus in so far as they express the active willingness to rise from the fall into disorder, to heal the guilt, and to return to the Jovian order. That is the reason why prayers are acceptable to the gods, and sacrifices more than a bribe. Hence, if a man repels another man's manifest willingness to repair the broken order, he himself falls into the guilt of perpetuating disorder; the disorder is now his *ate* for which he will have to make full atonement. The conduct of Achilles, thus, is more than a mere nuisance that may cause the Achaeans to lose a war; it rather is a sinister failing of the heart that places the hero outside the order of gods and men. The rhythmical movement of war and peace that goes from order through fall, transgression, punishment, repentance and healing compensation back to order is interrupted by the wrath of Achilles; the Pelide blocks the dynamics of order; with the wrath, the *cholos,* of Achilles a concrete order reaches its irreparable end.

The specific wrath that precipitates the events of the *Iliad* must be distinguished from the void, the blackness of which it is a manifestation. This void in Achilles disturbs the formation of normal social relations from his boyhood. His own father who knows the child well sends him to war with admonitions to curb his "proudhearted spirit" and to keep him out of "mischiefmaking strife"; honor will be gained rather by "gentlemindedness [*philophrosyne*]" (IX, 254–56). But the son does not take such counsel to heart. Agamemnon characterizes him as a hateful man, always bent on strife (*eris*), war (*polemos*) and fighting (*mache*), who forgets that his valor is a gift of the gods to be used in war but not a title to royal rule over all men (I, 173–87). And even his comrades in arms turn from him with embarrassment and contempt because he works up to fury his proudheartedness, does not respond with graciousness to their love and respect, is of an obdurate and ugly spirit, and disgraces his house by his haughty rejection of their request for help (IX, 624–42). The nature and source of this isolating iciness is, then, more closely circumscribed by scraps of self-analysis when Achilles reflects on the alternatives of action in face of his fate. The meaning of the divine revelation as a personal obsession can be discerned perhaps most clearly in the fact that Achilles is the only one among the princes who toys with the idea of leaving the war and returning home. Odd as it may sound, Achilles is afraid of death to the point of openly considering the possibility of desertion.

He is ardently in love with life. In one streak of his moods he does not care in the least about imperishable fame at the price of early death; he would rather live as long as possible, as an honored and wealthy king, married to a wholesome girl, without the excitements that bring fame; and he indulges in such sound but unheroic reflections that no plundering and prize winning (pleasant as it may be in other respects) will bring back the *psyche* of a man once it has passed the barrier of his teeth (IX, 393–409). But that is only one streak in his moods. It is an indulgence rather than an intention. While fear of death may have corroded his mind so deeply that he can dream of running away from his obligations, he does not seriously intend to accept the role of a royal pillar of order in his realm. The lyricism of this nostalgic passage is contradicted by the fact that for nine years he has remained before Troy, and still remains now while nursing his wrath and toying with the idea of return. For the gods have created him a warrior; he lives truly in battle, and his sulking wrath is most painful to maintain while joyous slaughter goes on without him. The alternative of fate, therefore, does not offer a true choice to Achilles any more than to the other lords—though for a different reason. The other princes are bound to their station by their oath and duty; they cannot return as long as victory has not become obviously hopeless in military terms. Achilles is bound to the war, and can never return, because he is a warrior (perhaps even killer would not be too strong a word) who would fit into the order at home even less than into the order of the army.

It will have become clear by now that in Homeric society a lordly wrath is not a private state of emotions. A *cholos*, a wrath, is a legal institution comparable to a Roman *inimicitia* or a medieval feud. If *ate* induces a man to violate another man's sphere of possessions and honor, the victim of the transgression will react with *cholos*, that is, with an upheaval of emotion, tending to inflict damage on the transgressor, with the ultimate purpose of compelling formal compensation and recognition of the rightful relation between them. Hence, in the compact Homeric *cholos* one must distinguish between the emotional, wrathful reaction against damage inflicted on a man's status and the customs that regulate the course of the emotion. The peculiar nature and problem of the *cholos* will be understood more clearly if we remember the differentiation of its components into Plato's virtues of *andreia* and *sophia*. *Andreia,* courage, is the habit of the soul to be moved emotionally to counteraction in the face of unjust action; and *sophia*, wisdom, is required for guiding and restraining courage, since emotion, however justly aroused, may overstep the measure. The Homeric *cholos* contains these components embedded in the compact medium of *themis* (right order, custom). Functioning within an established order, the *cholos*, as an emotion, will supply the force that will resist injustice and restore just order; and it will even discourage violations of order in so far as *cholos* can be expected as an expensive consequence of unjust action. The proper functioning of *cholos*, thus, is essential for the maintenance of order. If the *cholos* is not forthcoming, transgression will be encouraged; if it is unbridled, order cannot be restored. As an instrument of order *cholos* must be duly worked up and called off as required by custom.

Measured by these criteria the *cholos* of Achilles has a highly improper complexion. To be sure, it breaks out properly on occasion of the insult. But the outbreak is sensed by the others as something more than a fitting reaction to the situation; its roots seem to reach deeper into a disorderly disposition of Achilles. The proper *cholos* should be a sensitive reaction of the emotions against a threat to the customary status of a person; for if the first attack is not checked immediately, the threat may grow into a formidable danger that can no longer be met with success at a later stage. The *cholos* of Achilles, however, is not a finite reaction against a finite threat, with the purpose of repairing the momentary breach of order; it is rather an outburst of the deep-seated anxiety that has grown in him through preoccupation with his fate; it is caused by an emotional short-circuit between the diminution of his honor and the anticipation of his death. This outburst rightly causes uneasiness in the others because it is sensed as an absolute threat to the meaning of order. For the game of order, with its partial diminutions and restitutions, can be played only as long as life is accepted with a will to act it out regardless of the mystery of death. If death is not accepted as a mystery in life, as part of the mystery of life itself; if the attempt is made to transform the mystery through reflection into an experience of something, of a reality; then the reality of death will become the nothingness which destroys the reality of life. When a walking ghost like Achilles appears on the scene, the pallor of death falls over the game of order; it can no longer be taken seriously and the drama sputters out in futility and disorder. The other lords sense rightly the threat of deadly destruction in the conduct of Achilles; this particular *cholos* cannot be closed by customary compensation and reconciliation. But how, then, can it be closed at all?

The answer to this question is the content of the *Iliad*. The wrath of Achilles has an inner development, an action; and the inner drama of the wrath determines the external action of the *Iliad*. To the episode of the wrath corresponds militarily the great battle in which the Trojans throw the Achaeans back to their camp and set fire to the first ship. This terrible defeat of the Achaeans, approaching their destruction, is pragmatically caused by the abstention of Achilles from battle; but in the drama of Achilles it is a disaster that he inflicts on them by his active wish. When the hero receives the insult from Agamemnon he appeals to his divine mother: Thetis should move Zeus to bring the Achaeans to the brink of disaster so that they could see how they had profited by their great king and the king would learn what it meant to insult the best of his lords (I, 407–12). The good mother, deeply distressed that the short life of her son should be darkened by such ignoble treatment, fulfills his wish. The motivation of the wish is transparent. As Agamemnon rightly suspects, Achilles wants to triumph over the king; his overbearing conduct betrays a boundless desire to dominate. A triumph, however, would be impossible if the Achaeans were really destroyed and none were left to bear witness to the hero's exaltation; or if Achilles had returned home and could not witness the defeat. The wish, therefore, is carefully tailored to requirements: It must be a near defeat, Achilles must be on hand to witness it, and he must be able to appear as the savior at the last moment. Moreover, the wish betrays the nihilism of the Pelide's dreaming. Achilles wants a moment of triumph in which everybody recognizes his superiority; but he does not want to continue that moment into a permanent order by replacing Agamemnon as king of the Achaeans. The wish for that moment is not nurtured by political ambition; it is a subtle attempt to cheat his fate by converting the imperishable fame after death into a triumph in life. In order to achieve the fleeting moment he is quite willing to let his comrades perish in battle until his intervention is the last and uncontested means for turning defeat to victory.

Achilles carries the program out by sustaining his wrath against all reasonable attempts at reconciliation. But when the great moment approaches the chain of events slips from his hands. The Achaeans are pressed hard near the trenches of their camp and fire has touched the first ship. At last, while still not joining battle himself, he allows his friend Patroclus and the Myrmidones to intervene, so that the danger of fire will be averted. In this sortie Patroclus is killed by Hector. Achilles has cut the moment too fine and caused the death of his *alter ego*. That is the end of the murderous dream; the great moment of triumph has become a personal disaster.

The drama of the *cholos* hinges on the death of Patroclus. With the death of his friend the obsession of Achilles falls apart; and the reality of life and order is restored. The fifty verses in which Homer describes this process may justly be considered the psychological masterpiece of the *Iliad* (XVIII, 78–126). With groans the son confesses to his mother that his wishes have been granted; "but what joy [*edos*] do I have therein" now that Patroclus is dead whom he cherished like his own self (*kephale*). Patroclus is close enough to his self to let him experience death at last as the common lot; he is no longer an exception among men just because he must die. He returns to the reality of life in community; and the decisive symptom of this return is the readiness to shoulder its obligations even at the risk of death; for death has lost its horror when life again has become so supremely real that it is not worth living except at its own conditions. The first of these obligations is the revenge for his friend, even though the death of Hector, according to his predicted fate, will soon be followed by his own. He was sitting by the ships in his wrath, "a useless burden on the earth," making himself guilty by his inaction of the slaying of Patroclus and the other Achaeans, though his prowess in battle was the one gift of the gods by which he could make himself useful to others. He curses the strife (*eris*) and wrath (*cholos*) that disrupts the game of order and has burdened him with his guilt; remanding Agamemnon's insult to the past he is now ready to curb his indulgence. His fate he now accepts as do the others; and he will lie down to die like Heracles when Moira has so decided. And finally, perhaps the most subtle trait, he is now even willing to acquire imperishable renown by his deeds in the common run of his obligations as an Achaean warrior—he will no longer try to cheat fate by triumph in life.

3. The Eros of Paris and Helen

The wrath of Achilles was a disturbance of order. Still, while its generation, course, and dissolution provided the drama of the *Iliad*, it

was no more than an episode in the greater disturbance, in the war that
had been caused by the fatal attraction of Helen. We shall now turn to
the question: Why did the Trojans not prevent the war, or at least end
it, by restoring Helen to her husband with customary reparations? And
this question is inseparable from the other one: Why did they not deal
summarily with Paris-Alexander, that apparently useless individual,
who was the more immediate cause of their troubles? Homer unfolded
the various aspects of the problem in *Iliad* III, on occasion of the single
combat between Paris and Menelaus for Helen and her possessions.

The occasion itself indicates the range and complexities of the problem. The simple legal solution (restoration with compensation) is impossible because the fatality of Paris, besides Helen's, is involved in the
disturbance. The next best solution as against a long war between two
peoples would be the single combat between Menelaus and Paris, the
winner taking the prize. That is the solution on which the belligerent
parties agree with enthusiasim in *Iliad* III. Obviously the next question
will be: Why did the warring parties not resort to it somewhat earlier?
And, finally, the question must be answered as to why this attempt to
end the war proves abortive even now. The interweaving of these various
problems makes the Third Book of the *Iliad* a masterpiece of artistic
construction. Regrettably, a complete analysis is impossible in the present
context; we must presuppose the reader's knowledge of this wonderful
interpenetration of tragedy and comedy. For our purpose the various
strands will be separated, and we shall begin the work by isolating the
legal procedure which, as throughout the *Iliad*, furnishes the backbone
of the story.

The single combat is the result of a challenge issued by Paris and
accepted by Menelaus. The agreement between the protagonists must be,
and is, accepted by the commanders on both sides. A formal armistice
is concluded, stipulating that the victor in the single combat will receive
Helen and her possessions. While the combat is going on, there will be no
hostilities. And indeed, as soon as the agreement is reached, the soldiers on
both sides break their battle lines, joyously put aside their arms, and
form a ring of eager spectators around a clearance on which the combat
will take place. No matter who the victor, the combat will end the war
between Trojans and Achaeans. It looks like an ironclad agreement, and
the end of the war within an hour is in sight.

The actual course of events does not fulfill the expectations. The combat begins, but the sword of Menelaus splinters on the helmet of Paris. Then Menelaus attacks with his bare hands; he pulls Paris by the helmet and drags him, choking him with the strap; and the combat is practically over. At this moment Aphrodite intervenes, the strap breaks, Paris is whisked away by the goddess to safety in Troy, and Menelaus is left with the empty helmet, furiously looking for Paris. Understandably there is some consternation. Everybody, including the Trojans, help Menelaus in the search for the elusive Paris, but in vain. Nevertheless, there is still hope of a happy end because Menelaus obviously is the victor. Then the gods intervene again. Under divine inspiration, one of the Trojan allied leaders conceives the idea of carving a distinguished career for himself by taking a potshot at Menelaus. Not much damage is done by the superficial wound, but the truce is broken, and the battle is resumed (*Il.* IV, 85ff.). Even now all hopes for peace are not extinguished, considering that the Achaeans are still ready at any time to accept a fair settlement. In the Trojan council Antenor warns his peers that they are fighting against their oath; he admonishes them to fulfill their obligation, to return Helen and her treasure, and to close the war. But Paris refuses to surrender Helen, though he is willing to part with the treasure; and the council upholds him against Antenor (VII, 345–78). The fate of the Trojans is sealed, for the Achaeans now continue the war with the certainty that the oath-breakers will meet their due fate. Every phase of this longish procedure is gone through by Homer with care until every rational means for ending the war is exhausted. Not a shadow of a doubt is left that this war is not governed by the rationality of politics and law, but by irrational forces which spell the end of civilizational order. The analytical isolation of the disruptive force is, in the case of Helen-Paris, quite as careful as in the case of Achilles.

The irrational force governs the procedure of the combat between Paris and Menelaus from its very inception. The combat and the truce are not the result of rational action (which could have been taken at any time) but of an accident. The lines of the Trojans and Achaeans are moving to battle; in the grim moment before the clash the elegantly garbed Paris does a little parading in front and challenges the best of the Achaeans to fight him. Menelaus happens to notice the show-off and eagerly rushes toward him, with the result that Paris quickly falls back into inconspicuous safety behind the line (III, 15–37). But too late.

Hector watched the ignominious scene, and now has a few words to say to his brother. Paris is magnificent to look at, a woman-chaser and beguiler, handsome but without spirit or valor, an object of joyful contempt to the enemy, and a shame and bane to his city; the Trojans must be cowards, indeed, or they would have stoned him long ago for all the evil that he has wrought (III, 38–57). The correctness of the brotherly thumbnail sketch is borne out when, at the end of the combat, the Trojans eagerly join the Achaeans in their search for the miscreant, "for they all hated him like black death" (III, 454); and even the herald to the Achaeans, when mentioning the name of Paris, adds to his diplomatic message the private sentiment "would that he had perished long ago" (VII, 390). But Paris knows why the general contempt and hatred do not translate themselves into action against him. He candidly admits to his brother, and even admires, the justice of the portrait; but with dignity he rebukes him for holding against him the gracious gifts of Aphrodite. Such gifts must be honored, for they are bestowed without human merit, at the discretion of the immortals. Joy and fatality of divine gifts must be respected by men, by the receivers as well as by the community. Nevertheless, he is sufficiently nettled by Hector's contempt to make good his initial boast and to fight Menelaus (III, 58–75).

The accidental combat between the husbands brings Helen on the scene. She hurries toward the Scaean gate where Priam and his council are already assembled in order to watch the event. The elders see her coming and reflect that it is worthwhile to suffer the woes of a long war for a woman who looks like a goddess; but more soberly they add that after all it would be better to let her depart rather than to bring misery on themselves and their children for all the future. And Priam addresses her (like Phoenix Achilles) as his "dear child," nowise to be blamed for the war; it is all the fault of the gods (III, 146–70). The charm of the scene casts its spell today as it has always done, testifying to the greatness of the poet who ennobles disaster by making it transparent for the play of divine forces and who heightens the heroes into tragic figures by letting their human frailty carry the will of the gods. But to isolate the scene, to revel in the attraction of divine beauty and the refined humanity of Priam as a climax of the *Iliad* (as some interpreters do), would be a sentimental indulgence, a great injustice to Homer the clearheaded thinker. In the scenes with Paris and Helen we are coming near to the source of disorder on the Trojan side, and Homer uses these scenes quite deliberately for the purpose of characterizing the disordered sentiments through the ranks of the constitutional hierarchy.

Worst is the king himself; the royal gentleman exonerates the "dear child" completely and puts all the blame on the gods; and in the session of the council, when Antenor exhorts the elders to keep faith with their oath and to surrender Helen and her treasure, it is Priam who overrides the admonition to return to the sanity of order and upholds Paris. Second come the elders who, in spite of their judicious appraisal of divine beauty, are ready to admit that the woman is a bane (*pema*) and, represented by Antenor, have preserved a modicum of responsibility. And third come the people, restained from action by awe, but expressing open contempt and hatred at least for Paris, and quite willing to send the troublesome pests packing. In the *Iliad* itself the tension between ruler and people does not approach the danger of popular revolt; but in the *Odyssey*, as we shall see presently, the disorderly upper class is rather afraid of a populace whose sense for right and wrong is less deeply corroded. It would be an anachronism to read into the epics an issue of antimonarchism and revolution, but there can be no doubt that in Homer's analysis of political crisis the fish begins to putrefy from the head.

The corrosion of sentiments and actions has its center in Paris and Helen; from this center it spreads over the levels of the constitutional hierarchy. Paris and Helen are the gap in the Trojan order through which a dark force of destruction pours in, as Achilles was the gap in the order of the Achaeans. In the characterization of this force, of the *eros*, Homer uses the same technique of symbolization as in the case of Achilles. The Pelide was isolated from the community by his obsessive fear of death, symbolized by the prediction; it was a peculiar kind of open secret which the hero could freely divulge to others, while the others freely conducted themselves as if they had not heard about it; as a consequence, the conversation assumed the complexion of a dream-play, each figure talking in its own dream while acting out a common fate. In the case of Paris the erotic isolation, the disruption of real contact with the order of social relations is most drastically symbolized by the burlesque ending of the single combat. At one moment, we are still in the order of reality, with Menelaus choking his enemy to death; and at the next moment, Paris is invisible in the erotic isolation of his chamber waiting for Helen, while Menelaus, holding an empty helmet, searches for its former wearer.

The participation of Helen in the isolation of Paris is a nauseatingly profound scene. When Aphrodite has saved her darling from the battle-field, and placed him in his chamber, fresh and fragrant for sweeter combat, she goes to summon Helen who still is on the gate watching the excited search for Paris who by now ought to be dead (III, 385–94). Helen at first can hardly believe the command of the goddess; that breach of order, that outrage to decency is too much for her. She is ready to accept the agreement between the belligerents, to end the war, and to return to Menelaus, thus restoring the rightful order of society. She senses that something terrible is going to happen, and tries to hold it off. She makes a pitiful pretense at suspecting that the goddess has per-haps some lesser evil in store for her, that Aphrodite wants to throw her to some other favorite now that Paris is out of the running, continuing the miserable career of her beauty. Then the pretense falters and the horror begins to sink in. She reviles the goddess; she tells her to leave Olympus and become herself the mistress and slave of Paris if she likes him so much. She bluntly refuses to go and to commit the shameful thing (*nemesseton*) for which all women of Troy would blame her for ever after (395–412). The goddess, however, is inexorable, and her wrath (*cholos*) is now stirred. With the authoritative brutality of an Olympian brothel madame she orders Helen to bed unless she wants to meet an ugly fate that the goddess will provide for her at the hands of both Achaeans and Trojans (413–17). Under such a threat the cowed Helen repairs to the chamber. Desperately, in a last attempt, she tries to stir up some decency in Paris by telling him what sort of a coward and weakling he is, and that she would love to see him dead, but to no avail (418–36). The unimpressed Paris informs her that his mind is ob-sessed with *eros*; that never, not even on the day when he took her from Sparta, had he wanted her as much as just now; and he gently but firmly compels her submission (437–47). The construction closely parallels the case of Achilles. The Pelide wants to cheat his fate by the great, though ephemeral triumph in life; in the dream play of Paris the god-dess cheats fate by transfiguring the imminent death into the embrace of Helen.

The fish begins to putrefy from the head; and at the head—as it becomes increasingly clear—are the gods. From the chamber of Paris and Helen the scene shifts to the ultimate source of disorder, to the Olympians who are assembled and watch the events before Troy with intent interest. Zeus is pleased. In spite of the disappearance of Paris, there is still hope for a happy end that will avert destruction from his beloved Ilion, if only the Trojans will live up to the agreement and surrender Helen. The burlesque end of the combat even adds spice to the situation, and the divine ruler maliciously taunts Hera and Athena with their inactivity while Aphrodite plays a practical joke on their Achaean friends. The taunts precipitate a crisis. Zeus suggests to the council of the gods that this would be the occasion to end the war, if it should be their pleasure. But his mocking remarks have developed in Hera a fine *cholos;* with indignation she rejects the idea that all her sweat and toil for the destruction of Troy should be wasted, and grimly she assures Zeus that not all the gods will give their assent. The subsequent Jovian remonstrations only provoke pointed legal information that Zeus is not the absolute ruler of the world; the Olympian constitution is a limited monarchy, and each of the gods has inalienable rights and privileges. The crisis is overcome by compromise. Zeus cannot overrule the will of Hera to destroy his Ilion, but he can threaten her with retaliation against cities that are dear to her heart. Hera accepts the threat, and in exchange for Troy she will offer no resistance whenever Zeus wants to lay waste Argos, Sparta, and Mycenae. That appears to be a sensible compromise to the gods. They agree on the destruction of Troy as the first step in the larger program, and Athena is dispatched to inspire the previously described breach of the truce (IV, 1–72).

The problem of disorder, thus, is traced to its ultimate source in the council of the gods, and that is as far as the *Iliad* goes. The time to take stock of the results, however, has not yet come. This assembly of the gods whose principal occupation seems to be the destruction of Mycenaean civilization is odd to say the least. Before penetrating more deeply into the mysteries of Homeric theology we shall do well to broaden the basis of the study by the ideas which the *Odyssey* has to contribute to the subject of order and disorder.

4. The Odyssey on Disorder

The *Odyssey* opens with an assembly of the gods in a somewhat different mood. The great war now lies ten years in the past; Zeus indulges in remembrance and reflection. Evil there is in the world, like the fate of Aegisthus who slew Agamemnon and in his turn was slain by Orestes. But the mortals are wrong when they say that evil comes from the gods; through their own perversity they create sorrow for themselves beyond their share, as is proven by the case of Aegisthus who was forewarned of his fate if he committed his crimes. Such pious reflections allow Athena to draw the attention of her divine father to the case of Odysseus. He is in the miserable captivity of Calypso on Ogygia, while far away his home is rapidly ruined by the insolent suitors of Penelope. Here is evil without any apparent misdeeds of Odysseus; and one may even say that the gods are its cause. For the goddess Calypso retains him because she wants him as a lover, and Poseidon chases him over the seas relentlessly because he got the better of Polyphemus in quite reasonable self-defense. Zeus admits that the case needs cleaning up if his reflections are to be vindicated. Fortunately Poseidon is absent in a distant country so that the first measures can be taken behind his back; and later he will have to lay by his *cholos* when he sees the other gods united against him. Hermes, thus, is dispatched to Ogygia to inform Calypso that she will have to frustrate her passion and let Odysseus go; while Athena repairs to Ithaca in order to groom Telemachus for resistance to the suitors of his mother (*Od.* I, 31–95).

As far as the gods are concerned the evil that still can be attributed to their little indulgences in *eros* and *cholos* will be liquidated under the new regime of mellow morality. As far as the mortals are concerned, the Jovian reflections are the prologue to the disorders of Ithaca and their punishment by the returning Odysseus. We must dispense with the intricacies of Achaean marriage law (meticulously described by Homer in order to isolate the precise crime of the unwanted suitors), with the subtle degrees of rottenness in the princely suitors, as well as with the colorful story of the return and punishment. We rather must concentrate on the fundamental traits which characterize the disintegration of public order. In describing the symptoms of disintegration Homer uses the same method as in the corresponding description of disorder in Troy, in so far as he traces the symptoms through the ranks of the constitutional hierarchy.

The evil at the royal top of the pyramid is obvious. The king is absent for almost twenty years, while his old father is powerless in retirement. The son, Telemachus, is an unimpressive youth of twenty. His decency, it is true, is not impaired by the embarrassing situation in the house, and he even gives some promise of development under the guidance of Athena, but he will at best grow into a friendly average. Even the goddess shows impatience with his dispiriting insignificance and reflects gloomily: "Few sons grow like their fathers; most are worse, and only few are better" (*Od.* II, 276f.). With this generalization from the disheartening appearance of Telemachus, Athena continues the reflections of Nestor in the *Iliad* that the generation of Troy is no match to the companions of his youth; the generation of Telemachus is a further decline.

Next in the hierarchy come the nobles of the Cephallenian region. The most distinguished among them should form the constitutional council and see to it that a regency is established in the absence of Odysseus, or that the succession to the kingship be regulated. The older members of the nobility, as far as they have not joined the expedition against Troy, are on the whole decent-minded but few in number and powerless against the trend of the younger generation. And the younger lords are the wastrels who, a hundred strong, have occupied the manor of Odysseus and devour its substance while beleaguering Penelope. They presume Odysseus to be dead but neither do they recognize his son as the king, nor does any one among them have sufficient stature to reach for the kingship himself. The kingdom is in leaderless anarchy. The contrast between the old and the young, for the rest, plays an important role throughout the *Odyssey*. Its meaning appears perhaps most clearly in the figures of the swineherd Eumaeus and the Odysseus in beggar's disguise: The old men of quality are in disguise and low station, while rank and public status belong to the young vulgarity.

The role of the people, finally, as well as its relation to the nobility, is characterized on occasion of the assembly which Telemachus convokes at the behest of Athena. No session of the assembly has been held since Odysseus left for Troy. An old lord (one of whose sons is among the suitors), a friend of Odysseus, presides over the meeting. Telemachus appears, not as king or successor to the kingship, but as a private plaintiff, seeking help from the people against the nobles who destroy his property. The constitutional order as a whole thus comes into play. The noble suitors are incensed by this appeal to the assembly; but they are also afraid, and by heated argument they try to avert the people's attention from the issue. The assembly, however, has not much stomach anyway for armed action, amounting to civil war, that is, for the only action that could dislodge the brazen suitors. The sullen hesitation of the people becomes so nauseating that Mentor puts a curse on them: May no king in the future be kind and righteous, let him be stern and unrighteous, since Odysseus is not remembered by the people over whom he ruled like a father! (*Od.* II, 229–41). The corruption reaches down to the people; if the future should bring a decline from kingship to tyranny they would not deserve any better.

5. *The Aetiology of Disorder*

It will be possible now to appraise the theory of order that emerges from the Homeric epics—if, for lack of a more appropriate one, the term theory will be allowed to signify a technique of symbolization which is distinctly pre-theoretical. The appraisal will best commence from a problem that lies at the heart of the Homeric symbolism, that is, from the function of the gods. It has been frequently observed that the reflections of Zeus at the opening of the *Odyssey* are something like a theodicy. The gods are absolved from causing evil in the world. That seems to be a purer, or at least more carefully reflected, conception of the gods than can be found in the *Iliad;* and the apparent advance of religious sentiment and theology is used as an argument for dating the *Odyssey* later than the *Iliad*.

We do not question the later date of the *Odyssey,* but we are inclined to question the premises on which the argument is based. For the argument from increasing purity presupposes that "gods" are something of which one can have purer or less pure conceptions independent of a larger context; that there is a "theological" development in isolation from a general view concerning the order of human existence in society. Such presuppositions, however, will appear dubious as soon as they are examined more closely. Let us assume, as an hypothesis, that there are no more than two sources of evil, *i.e.,* gods and men. In that case a shifting of responsibility from one source to the other can only purify gods at the expense of men, or men at the expense of gods; the purer the one side becomes, the impurer will be the other side. Neither the reality nor the amount of evil are touched by such shiftings; and what precisely is to be gained by locating evil in man rather than in the gods will remain obscure as long as such operations are interpreted under the aspect of their "purifying" results.

The opening of the *Odyssey* will acquire a new significance if we recognize that Homer is concerned, not with purification of the gods, but with the aetiology of disorder. Evil is experienced as real; and the evil forces which disrupt order certainly are disturbing enough to invite exploration of their nature and source. The location, or transfer, of responsibility will become of lively interest if it is understood as a search for *truth* about the source of evil. Truth is Homer's concern rather than purification. And since the "gods" are not self-contained entities but power complexes in the order of being that also embraces man, an increase of truth about the gods will also be an increase of truth about man. What really is at stake, therefore, is not a progress of morality or theology but the genuinely theoretical issue of the nature of being as far as order and disorder of human existence in society are concerned.

If the issue, thus, is restated in ontological terms, the relation between gods and men will appear in a new light. Gods and men are not fixed entities but more or less clearly discerned forces in an order which embraces them both. The primary experience is that of an order of being which permeates man and transcends him. Both relations are of equal importance; there is no clearly circumscribed order of man, over-arched by a transcendent order of the gods; the forces that operate and interact in the comprehensive order of being rather reach into man himself in such a manner that the borderline between human and transhuman is blurred. If in the interplay of forces man is distinguishable as a unit at all, it is by virtue of his bodily existence in space that will be terminated by death. And even this formulation attributes to the complex called man more of a demarcation than it actually has in the epics. For in the language of Homer there are no words for body and soul.

The word *soma* which in later Greek means "body" occurs indeed but it has the meaning of "dead body," "corpse." The living human shape can only be designated by *chros,* skin; and *chros* does not mean skin in the anatomical sense (the skin or pelt that can be skinned off an animal, *derma*), but skin in the sense of a surface that is the bearer of color and visibility. This Homeric visibility of surface (as distinguished from our notion of bodily existence) is an immaterial, intangible quality to which unexpected things may happen. The visible shape may become invisible at the right tactical moment and reappear elsewhere, as in the case of the vanishing Paris. And then again it may expand demonically as in the appearance of Achilles when he frightens the Trojans from the body of Patroclus, with a thick golden cloud around his head and shining flames rising from the cloud, shouting with the sound of a trumpet. Such diminutions and exaltations of visible shape, however, are understood as more than human; they only occur with the help of the gods, an intermediate phenomenon as it were between normal human appearance and the occasional donning of visible shape by the immortals. The conception of a "living body" as it is familiar to us does not exist in the epics; it would presuppose the notion of an animating principle that endows the body with form, the notion of a "soul"—and there is no word for "soul" in the epics.

Again, to be sure, the word *psyche* which in later Greek means "soul" is present as is the word *soma* but it signifies an organ of man rather than the organizing form of a body. Not much information can be extracted about this *psyche* from the epics, except that it means a life-force which leaves man in death and then leads a miserable, independent existence as the shadow, the *eidolon*. And since there is no conception of the soul, such phenomena as "emotions," "stirring of emotions," "thinking," cannot be conceived as functions of the psyche but must be understood (by the terms *thymos* and *noos*) as additional organs of man. The problems of man and his soul are not absent from the Homeric work, as we shall see presently; nevertheless, this peculiar articulation of man into a bundle of organs and forces compels the poet to treat such questions by means of a symbolism which barely recognizes man as a well-circumscribed, world-immanent center of action.[9]

The Homeric problems of order originate in the uncertainties concerning the nature of man. Only one thing is really certain even about Homeric man: he must die. Hence, "mortal" is the preferred synonym for man, distinguishing his nature without a doubt from that of the immortal gods. For the rest, the transhuman elements of the order of being penetrate so deeply into man or, from the other side, man is yet so imperfectly closed as a self-conscious, reflecting agent, that the status of various phenomena as human or divine must remain in doubt and, in particular, that quite frequently it will not be certain to what extent the actions of man are his actions at all. Homer's difficulties in dealing with these problems, as well as the importance of his partial solutions, can be understood only if we place ourselves in his position. If, on the contrary, we interpret the epics under the assumption that he knew already what gods and men were, his specific achievement in clarifying the nature of man and the meaning of order will be obscured.

[9] For Homer's anthropology cf. Bruno Snell, *Die Entdeckung des Geistes. Studien zur Entstehung des europaeischen Denkens bei den Griechen* (Hamburg, 1946), the chapter "Die Auffassung des Menschen bei Homer."

Hence, we shall approach the problem casuistically by analyzing the two main classes of action as they appear in the epics, that is, first the actions which maintain and restore order, and second the actions which disturb order.

All through the epics run divine interventions which result in human decisions of public importance. A typical case is the energetic action of Odysseus, in *Iliad* II, when he holds back the army that is on the point of boarding ship for home; it is an action at the behest of Athena. The cases of this type are rather frequent. Any human decision, hesitation, or resolution somewhat out of the ordinary is apt to appear as inspired by divine counsel. They are so frequent indeed that sometimes the interventions themselves become a routine; Athena is a ubiquitous lady, especially in the *Odyssey,* arranging the voyage of Telemachus step by step, from pushing the young man into action, to outfitting the ship and getting him on his way. On the whole, however, the interventions effectively serve the purpose of raising the otherwise irrelevant doings of man to the rank of actions which are transparent toward the order of being. Ordinary men, going about their ordinary business, are not favored in this manner; the divine appearances are bestowed on the heroes when the consequences of their action affect public order. Hence, action in this limited sense acquires the more-than-human meaning of a manifestation of divine order; and the hero in the Homeric sense can be defined as the man in whose actions a more-than-human order of being becomes manifest. The Homeric clarification of the meaning of action was continued by Aeschylus. In his *Suppliants* especially, Aeschylus characterized heroic action (that is the only action deserving the name, as distinguished from ordinary doings) as the decision for Dike against demonic disorder; the order of the polis, in so far as it was established and maintained by such action, represented the order of Zeus. Action at the heroic height, thus, is as much human as it is the manifestation of a divine force. And the public order of a society, in so far as at critical junctures it depends on the forthcoming of such action, is precariously maintained in being at the borderline of this meeting of human with divine forces.

The aetiology of order and disorder obviously cannot be reduced to a simple formula. Are the gods who inspire, or the men who obey, responsible for heroic action? And who is responsible for a debacle when a hero did not receive a divine inspiration at the right moment—the god who played truant or the man who embarked on an unfortunate course of action by his own light? And such questions become even more pungent when actions are disruptive. What is the status of *ate* in Homeric ethics? On the one hand, she is blinding passion that motivates actions in violation of just order; on the other hand, she is a goddess, the oldest daughter of Zeus who, on occasion, plays a trick even on her own father. Who is responsible for misdeeds caused by *ate*? A detailed answer to such questions would require a monograph. We can do no more than state the principle of Homer's position, supported by a few cases.

Throughout the *Iliad* the poet seems to be engaged in a subtle polemic against the morality of several of his figures—and the polemic quite probably is also aimed at his social environment which sympathized with the figures. Take the case of Achilles. From Homer's descriptions he emerges as a splendid warrior, useful to have on your side in an emergency, but as a not very appealing figure, almost a pathological case. And the poet leaves no doubt that the trouble stems from toying and tampering with fate, from misusing the divine Thetis for satisfying the hero's childish desires, and from a reluctance to shoulder the burden of humanity. The difficulties fall apart when the burden of fate and responsibility is accepted with humility.

A second important instance is furnished by Agamemnon's apology to Achilles (*Il.* XIX, 78–144). The king casts the responsibility for his unjust action on a whole assembly of gods (Zeus, Moira, Erinys, Ate) who blinded him. But when the blindness falls from him, and he becomes seeing again, he assumes responsibility for his action and offers amends. With Homer a man's actions are his own only when he sees what he is doing; as long as he is blinded they are not his own and he is not responsible for them; but when in retrospect he sees again, then what he committed in blindness becomes his own through seeing and he compensates for his misdeeds. The analysis by means of the symbolism of "blindness" and "seeing" is of considerable interest for the later development of a theory of action. For Homer is on the way toward discovering what the philosophers will call the "true self," that is, the area in a man's soul in which he is oriented toward noetic order. When the true self dominates, then the man "sees"; and through the retroactive recognition of "blindness," the misdeed is integrated (as it were by a "conscience") into the acting self. Still, in the case of Agamemnon, the blindness re-

mains the work of the gods; the absorption of the misdeed into the self
does not yet go to the point of accepting the guilt for temporary
"blindness." And in general there is no tendency toward an understanding of guilt in the Christian sense—either in Homer, or in the philosophers of the classic period who, though they develop the problem further, retain the Homeric position on principle. The continuity with
regard to this problem, from Homer to the fourth century, will go far
to explain the odd idea of Socrates-Plato of solving the problem of true
order in the soul and society through "seeing," that is, through knowledge.

Nevertheless, the self-interpretation of Agamemnon in his apology
to Achilles is perhaps not the last word of Homer in this matter. A wary
psychologist will ask himself the question how "true" Agamemnon's
story about his temporary blindness really is. Does a man, even in anger,
not know in some corner of his mind that just now he is doing something
which he ought not to do? Is there really a time interval between blindness and seeing? Is man really at one time a passionate self, blinded, and
at a later time a true self horrified at the deeds of his passionate self?
Homer certainly asked himself such questions. The proof is the scene
of Paris in his chamber. There is the case of the elegant rotter who, in
excellent self-analysis, informs Helen that his mind is obsessed by Eros,
and then pleasantly proceeds to act not on the "seeing" of his analysis,
but on the "blindness" of his passion. The case of Paris shows the simul-
taneity of blindness and seeing. And what happens in this case is most
illuminating for Homeric as well as for Greek theory of action in general.
We do not fall into the abysmally desperate situation described by St.
Paul in Romans 7, but into a refined rascality, not lacking in profoundness.

The case of Paris shows that Homer knew about the mysteries of
blindness and seeing. Nevertheless, it should not be taken as an expression
of his own opinion in the matter. The apology of Agamemnon certainly
does not mean to characterize the king as a hypocrite who tries to cover
up the fact that he knew quite well what he was doing at the time and
preferred to indulge in the voluptuousness of his anger.[10] The case of
Agamemnon must be taken at its face value as one of the various types
in a psychology of action. Homer's own position should rather be in-

[10] "*Cholos* . . . sweeter far than honey" (*Il.* XVIII, 108–109).

ferred from the manner in which he constructs the story of the epics on principle. In both epics the story rests, as we have seen, on the careful analysis of the legal issues involved in the various actions. The public knowledge of order, of *themis,* of what is right, is the foundation for the actions of the heroes. *Everybody* knows, as a matter of public knowledge, exactly what he *ought* to do—and then he does something else. As an extreme case, to support this point, let us remember the old Priam who knows quite well what is wrong but cannot wrest from himself the effort to maintain public order; he throws the responsibility on the gods and lets Troy go to destruction. The various figures of the epics, thus, are set by Homer against a background of public knowledge about what is right. They all "see" while they are "blinded"; but there are various degrees of blindness and sight, as well as a variety of relations between them.

On the basis of the preceding analysis we can venture to formulate the relation between the two epics. The *Iliad,* so it seems, is much richer in its exploration of the mysteries of action than the second epic. It is hardly permissible to consider the *Odyssey* an advance beyond the *Iliad* with regard to theology or religious sentiments. At most one can say that in the prologue in heaven Homer states in explicit terms the problem that occupied him all through the *Iliad, i.e.,* the aetiology of evil. The term "aetiology," hitherto used undefined, does require, and can now receive, some precision. We are using the term because it is Homer's word in dealing with his problem. The question is whether the gods are *aitioi* or not *aitioi* with regard to the evil that befalls man. The meaning of *aitios* (*Il.* III, 164) ranges, in the Homeric contexts, from "guilty" or "blame-worthy" to "responsible for" or "being the cause of." When Homer speaks of men who ascribe evil to the gods, he uses the word *aitioontai,* (*Od.* I, 32), with a corresponding range of meaning from "they accuse" or "blame" the gods to "they make them responsible," or see in them the "source" or "cause" of evil. The primary concern of Homer is not a vindication of the gods but the interpretation which men put on their own misconduct. The tendency of his aetiological interest can, therefore, be circumscribed by the following theses:

(1) Man is in the habit of making the gods responsible for his misdeeds, as well as for the evil consequences engendered by his misconduct.

(2) Theoretically, this habit implies the assertion that the gods are
the cause of the evil which men do and suffer. This assertion is
wrong. It is man, not the gods, who are responsible for evil.

(3) Practically, this habit is dangerous to social order. Misdeeds will
be committed more easily if responsibility can be shifted to the
gods.

(4) Historically, a civilizational order is in decline and will perish,
if this habit finds general social acceptance.

This circumscription of Homer's aetiological concern can be based on the
Iliad alone. The reflections of Zeus, in the *Odyssey*, do no more than state
a part of the problem in direct language, preparatory to the evil which
the suitors bring on themselves by their deeds.

The most impressive phenomenon, as always in the decline of an
order, must have been the acts of wanton indulgence, due to *eros* and
cholos, as well as of ambition "beyond the share" (*hyper moron*)
(*Od.* I,35), which break the right order (*themis*) so frequently and so
deeply that a society is no longer capable of self-defense. This is the
phenomenon which Toynbee has called the suicide of a civilization.
Since this is the same phenomenon which Plato tried to analyze in the
Hellenic case, it should not surprise us that the Homeric aetiological
concern (as set forth in the four theses) bears a remarkable resemblance
to Platonic problems.

In the present context, however, the resemblance is less important
than the great difference which is due to the fact that Homer wrote before, while Plato wrote after the discovery of the psyche. The Homeric
achievement is remarkable as a struggle for the understanding of the
psyche with the rather crude symbols that we have studied. Homer
astutely observed that the disorder of a society was a disorder in the soul
of its component members, and especially in the soul of the ruling class.
The symptoms of the disease were magnificently described by the great
poet; but the true genius of the great thinker revealed itself in the creation of a tentative psychology without the aid of an adequate conceptual apparatus. Without having a term for it, he envisaged man as having
a psyche with an internal organization through a center of passions and
a second center of ordering and judging knowledge. He understood the
tension between the two centers, as well as the tricks which passion plays
on better knowledge. And he strove valiantly for the insight that ordering action is action in conformance with transcendent, divine order,

while disruptive action is a fall from the divine order into the specifically human disorder. We can discern the dim outlines of the Platonic anthropology, and even of the Platonic postulate that God rather than the disorderly velleities of man should be the measure of human action.

This strand of Homer's thought, however, had to dangle as a loose end because the theoretical means for weaving it into a consistent conception of order were not available. If we read the famous opening of the *Odyssey* with care, we find Zeus reflecting that men, through their own folly, create sorrow for themselves "beyond their share" (*Od.* I,34). The gods are not responsible for the evil that men bring on themselves—but who is responsible for the evil that is not caused by man, and apparently not by the gods either? The clean division into divine order and human disorder leaves a considerable residue of evil, symbolized in the epics by various means. First of all, the divine order of the Olympians extends only to the inhabited earth with its human societies; it does not extend to the elemental realm of Poseidon, or the underworld of Hades; Zeus is the highest of the gods and has sovereign prerogatives, but his jurisdiction has definite barriers. In the second place, the Olympian gods themselves are a dubious source of undisturbed order, beset as they are by jurisdictional quarrels of their own and by domestic strife. And, thirdly, there is Moira, Fate, with its decisions beyond the influence of the other gods. Homer did not attempt a theoretical penetration of this wilderness beyond the island of precarious Jovian order. Such symbols as the Platonic creation of the divine puppet player, who pulls the various cords and leaves it to man to follow the right one, were not yet at his disposition.

Nevertheless, as far as the central problem, the breakdown of Mycenaean civilization, was concerned, it was clear that something more was needed by way of an explanation than the misconduct of a few members of the ruling class. Individuals, as for instance Aegisthus or the suitors, could be forewarned that their personal crimes would find terrible retribution. But the historical process in which a society declines, as well as the infinitude of acts which in the aggregate of centuries spell destruction, had a pattern of their own that could not be described in terms of individual misdeeds. Homer had to face the problem that the day-to-day causality of human action will explain the detail of the historical process but not its configuration. His answer to this mystery of the rise and fall of civilizations was the extraordinary Olympian assembly at which Zeus and Hera agreed on their program for the destruction of Mycenaean civilization, including both Trojans and Achaeans. The answer may seem crude today; but again, Homer could not yet invent a highly theorized symbol like the myth of the alternative motions of the universe in Plato's *Statesman*. And if we remember that even a modern thinker, with the experience of two thousand years of metaphysics at his disposition, could do no better than invent the *List der Vernunft* in order to explain the pattern of history, the achievement of Homer in recognizing the problem will command our respect.

PART TWO

From Myth to Philosophy

CHAPTER 4

The Hellenic Polis

When the darkness after the Mycenaean breakdown gave way to a new light, the form of political existence in the Greek civilizational area was the polis. About the origins of the polis we know next to nothing from firsthand sources. For the critical period of the so-called synoecism we must rely on reconstructions. At the time of the earliest literary sources around 700 B.C., the new form of political existence was firmly established and had a prehistory of indeterminate length. A phase of early kingship belonged already to the past. And even the next phase, the rule of a landed aristocracy, was in a stage of unsettlement through the pressure of increasing population, as well as through the rise of a mercantile economy. Both unsettlement and vigor in coping with it were manifest in the great movement of colonization from 800–600 B.C. The phase of aristocratic rule had indeed so far advanced toward a crisis that the work of Hesiod, the first literary occupation with the order of the polis, was a work of discontent and critique.

Before we enter into the study of the Hellenic occupation with the order of the polis, we shall, in the present chapter, deal with the institution of the polis and its history, with the diversification of the institution, and with the attempts to overcome the parochialism of the form by larger regional organization.[1]

1. Synoecism and Gentilitian Structure

The polis did not spring up as a uniform type of organization throughout the area of Hellenic civilization. The various poleis were organized neither at the same time, nor under the same circumstances.

[1] For the institutional history of the polis cf. Georg Busolt, *Griechische Staatskunde*, I, 248ff., 264; II, 957ff. (3d ed., Munich, 1920). Also used were U. von Wilamowitz-Moellendorf, *Aristoteles und Athen*, II (Berlin, 1893); Max Weber, *Wirtschaft und Gesellschaft* (Tuebingen, 1922), Part II, Chapter 8 on "Die Stadt"; the articles in the *Cambridge Ancient History* by F. E. Adcock, "The Growth of the Greek City State" (III, 26), "The Reform of the Athenian State" (IV, 2), "Athens under the Tyrannis" (IV, 3), and by E. M. Walker, "Athens: The Reform of Cleisthenes" (IV, 6). Very helpful were Arnold J. Toynbee, *A Study of History*, II, 37ff.,

And the variations of the founding process decisively determined the structure of the single poleis in historically recorded time.

Town settlements in the Aegean area at large went as far back as the third millennium B.C. The principal centers of Mycenaean civilization assumed the form of a fortified citadel, the residence of the prince, surrounded by an open settlement, the asty. This aggregate, the pre-Doric city, in most cases did not survive the Doric invasion—though in the most important instance, that of Athens, the continuity between the Aegean settlement and the later polis seems to have remained unbroken. The Hellenic type of the polis was probably created by refugees from the Greek mainland who had either conquered old settlements or founded new ones in a foreign environment on the eastern coast of the Aegean. From the Anatolian coast the newly created form then spread, through mimesis, to the Greek mainland. Concerning the motivations of the form nothing but surmises are possible. Usually the topography of the area, with its relatively closed landscapes, is emphasized as the cause of political organization in small towns with an agricultural hinterland. Still, the succession of Phrygian, Lydian, and Persian conquests of the poleis in Anatolia proved that the area could be quite well integrated into larger realms, if the power and the will to do so were given. While the topographic factor must not be rejected, the numerical smallness of the refugee groups who settled in Ionia also affected the form in which they had to organize themselves. That the circumstances of the first foundations were somewhat extraordinary is suggested by the terminology. The "tribes" which constitute the polis are called *phylai,* while the language has another term to signify a tribe settled on a territory, *ethnos.* Hence, the conjecture is plausible that the *phylai* of the poleis were originally military units, perhaps ship companies, as they may have been formed on occasion of a transmarine migration to Anatolia. The probability is corroborated by the origin of the Spartan *phylai*—the Hylleis, Dymanes, and Pamphyloi—in the military units of the Doric migration. A break of continuity with the social organizations of the pre-polis time, a growth of new social units in the course of the migrations, can be sensed as the background of the polis.

The process in which the poleis were founded, the so-called synoecism,

97ff., and III, 336ff., 477ff. (Oxford, 1934). For the phases of intellectual history cf. Jaeger, *Paideia* I, (1945). The best recent study is Fritz Schachermeyr, "Geschichte der Hellenen bis 356," *loc. cit.,* 116–215.

extended over centuries and in some cases it was concluded only in the classical period. For Athens the synoecism was completed approximately by the end of the eighth century. The resulting constitutions of the poleis marked a distinct break with the earlier tribal constitutions, as well as with the symbioses of tribes after the Doric conquest. Nevertheless, the tribal age left an imprint on the structure of the polis, deep enough to become a decisive factor in shaping both its internal and external history to the end in the Macedonian conquest, in so far as the polis preserved the order of blood-relationship for its subdivisions, however fictitious the relationship had become in course of time. As a city, therefore, the polis never developed into a community of individual citizens held together by the bond of a *conjuratio* like the Western medieval towns; and as a territorial state, the polis was never able to expand into a nation consisting of individual citizens like the Western national states. The individual never gained the personal status in his political unit which, under the influence of the Christian idea of man, characterized the political formations of Western civilization; it always remained in a status of mediation through the fictitious tribal and narrower blood-relationships within the polis.

The example of Athens will illustrate the problem. Beyond the household community, consisting of parents and children, the smallest organized blood-relationship was the *anchisteia* which included three generations, counting from the head of the family to his own grandchildren, the children of his nephews and nieces, and the grandchildren of uncles. This body of relatives formed a unit in family and sacred law with claims to inheritance, with burial obligations and death rites. Beyond the *anchisteia* we find the *genos*, the aristocratic family unit which could form if external circumstances (such as inherited wealth, social standing, and so forth) were favorable. The unifying bond of a *genos* was the descent from a common ancestor, whether real or fictitious, and the cult of the ancestor. The Athenian *gene* were formed in the Hellenic late middle-age, in the time of political and military predominance of the landed aristocracy. Every *genos* had its cult-places, a priesthood, an assembly-house, a common treasury, and an executive, the *archon*, probably determined annually by lot. The *phratria* was a still larger community comprising the narrower blood-units, again held together as a brotherhood by descent from a common ancestor. And again the *phratria* had its temples, cults, festivals and its legal functions with regard to family relationships. Beyond the phratries, finally, we find the *phylai* with their cult functions. Down to the reform of Cleisthenes in 508 B.C., membership in a *phratria* was the prerequisite for Athenian citizenship.

The strength of the gentilitian experience of order was fully revealed on occasion of the reform of Cleisthenes, in 508 B.C. The reform intended to break the domination of genes and phratries by the aristocratic families. In order to achieve his purpose Cleisthenes divided the Attic territory into ten regions and constituted their inhabitants as ten new *phylai*. Each of the ten *phylai* was subdivided into ten districts, the demes. Citizenship was now made dependent on membership in one of the demes. Since at the same time a considerable number of persons received the franchise as citizens and the old tribes were confined to their religious functions, the net effect was a successful democratization of the constitution, breaking the power of the old gentilitian structure. Nevertheless, only the power of the aristocratic *gene* was broken, not the gentilitian spirit of the institutions. The *demos*, in spite of its territorial basis, was a corporation of persons just like the older blood-relationships. The Athenian still had his citizenship, not through a legal act making his person a member of the polis, but by virtue of his membership in a *demos*. In addition to his personal name he, therefore, bore the *demotikon*, the name signifying the *demos* of his origin; and the *demotikon* followed him and his descendants regardless of change of residence from the original district, of 508, to another district. The *demos* substituted for the former *genos* and *phratria*. It has rightly been said that Cleisthenes extended aristocratic, gentilitian status to every Athenian citizen. By the side of the former aristocratic, now developed a demotic genealogy leading back to the ancestor who had his residence in the *demos* at the time of its organization. The members of the *demos* had their local cult-heroes just as the nobility had its ancestor cults, and they formed communities in sacred law like the genes and phratries. This form which the democratic reform of Cleisthenes assumed perhaps shows best the strength of the gentilitian sentiment, as well as the resistance to any idea that would give the individual a personal status within the larger political community.

2. The Polis

An understanding of the Hellenic polis must start with the gentilitian structure but it cannot end with it.

It must start with it because the style of existence created by the aristocratic genes, as we know it from the Homeric poems, has remained the dominant style of Hellenic political culture through all transformations and democratizations down to the Macedonian conquest in the fourth century B.C. The political power of the aristocracy might be broken but its culture permeated the people; democratization in Hellas meant an extension of aristocratic culture to the people—even though in the process of diffusion the quality was diluted. We must never forget that the people who committed the atrocities described by Thucydides were the people of the Periclean Golden Age, that the corrupt slaughterers and conspirators were the men who performed and appreciated the drama of Sophocles and Euripides, and that the enlightened urbanized rabble, hated by Plato and Aristotle, were the people in whose midst the Academy and Lyceum could flourish. In the history of the Hellenic polis we do not find the dramatic cultural upheavals which accompany the social rise of the urban classes in Western civilization. With the changes in social and economic structure, and with the development of personality, the epic gave way to lyric, lyric to tragedy, and tragedy to philosophy—but the music and gymnastic culture of Homeric society remained the paradigm of culture from Homer to Plato and Aristotle.

The gentilitian structure, while securing the unity of Hellenic culture through the centuries, did not provide the institutional order in which it developed. Above the manifold of tribes, phratries, and genes rose the polis which embraced them all. The polis was the autonomous, nontribal unit of political order.

With regard to the early period of this autonomous factor, as we said, we know next to nothing. And when the literary sources begin to flow more richly, we still can only form reasonable conclusions with regard to the social changes which must underlie the changes of literary form and of the experiences expressed. Moreover, the several regions of Hellenic civilization—Anatolia and the islands, the mainland, Sicily and *Magna Graecia*—differed in the nature of their political problems and in the rhythm of their development. The history of the poleis was not uniform and, as a consequence, institutions and ideas differed from region to region, and even within a region from polis to polis. Only in the fifth and fourth centuries, after the Persian Wars, when Athens became the center of power and culture, do we find the continuous occupation with the problem of order that culminated in the work of Plato and Aristotle.

The earliest literary documents convey the impression of a decline of the old aristocratic order rather than of a strong consciousness of the polis. On the mainland, the work of Hesiod (c.700 B.C.) is the magnificent beginning of articulate concern about right order, but with regard to the polis, however important in other respects, it is rather negative. For Hesiod was in the position of a victimized subject. He complained about the princes whose corruption endangered his property; he expressed the ethos of work; but he had nothing to say about rulership and constitutional order. The pathos of the polis was not alive in him. In Ionia, the century of lyric from Archilochus (c.700) to Sappho (c.600) marks the beginning of the life of the soul. But again, it attests the decline of an aristocratic order of life, setting the individual soul free, rather than betraying a new political will. Nor does the Milesian speculation of Thales, Anaximander, and Anaximenes (c.650–550) suggest anything but a new intellectual freedom as it will unfold when style and tension of a political culture dissolve.

Literary evidence for the process in which the consciousness of the polis was formed becomes tangible for the first time on the mainland, in Sparta and Athens. The political circumstances of the two occasions differed greatly. In Sparta it was the emergency of the Messenian revolt which occasioned the poems of Tyrtaeus in praise of the specific virtue, different from aristocratic heroism, that will defend and maintain the polis. And in the wake of the revolt, the Eunomia (c.610) was resolved upon which transformed Sparta into a formidable military organization, ready and able at all times to cow rebelliously inclined subjects. In Athens it was the social and economic paralysis, due to debt-slavery, which induced the Seisachtheia and the constitutional reform of 594. The poems of Solon described the difficulties of the polis and, for the first time, they expressed its pathos through the principle of *eunomia*, of the right order that will integrate all sections of the people into the one unit of the polis.

The aftermath of the reform, the tyranny of Peisistratus (561–527), reminds us that the Solonian effort was probably no more than a partial solution of the type of crisis which engulfed the whole polis world from Ionia to Sicily and manifested itself in the rise of tyrants, in the period from 650–500 B.C. In the Athenian case we are informed, through Aristotle, about the nature of the social problems which required tyrants for their solution. At the time of Peisistratus there were three parties in Athens: The *paralioi,* the men of the coast, a trading middle class which aimed at a "middle form of constitution"; the *pediakoi,* the men of the plain, the landed aristocracy that wanted an oligarchic constitution; and the *diakrioi,* the men of the highlands, consisting of small artisans, shepherds, poor farmers who through the Solonian reform had gained freedom but no means, impoverished malcontents who through the Seisachtheia had lost their capital, and men who feared loss of their citizenship because they were not of pure descent. The third group, the *diakrioi,* was formed into a party and led by Peisistratus.[2]

The administration of Peisistratus not only was humane (*philanthropos*) and moderate, but also pursued a definite policy. The tyrant advanced money to poor peasants who were free without means, so that they could build up their small farm economies. By this measure he removed them from Athens and scattered them over the countryside; he thus kept the poor people busy with their homesteads and prevented them from loitering in the city as well as from attending to public affairs. At the same time the thorough cultivation of the country increased private income as well as public revenue. For the same purposes he held assizes in the country so that the peasants would not lose time with trips to the town. His respect for constitutional government, his appearance in court when accused, and his good personal relations with the upper class helped to maintain a general state of peace and satisfaction in the polis.[3] The "tyrant" was the statesman who by his skilful policy and personal tact eased the social conflicts and forged the state in which even the poor could feel they had a stake. After the polis had passed through "tyranny" it could embark on its stormy career of conflicts between the rich and the poor without breaking asunder.

The function of the tyrant as the moderator of the polis is confirmed by Aristotle in his interpretation of constitutional history as a succession of the "heads of the people" (*prostates tou demou*). "Solon was the original and first head of the people, the second was Peisistratus, a man of nobility and note."[4] Peisistratus was followed by Cleisthenes and a

---

[2] Aristotle, *Athenian Constitution,* XIII (Loeb Classical Library).

[3] *Ibid.,* XVI.

[4] *Ibid.,* XXVIII, 2. The designation of Solon as the "first head of the people" occurs also in II, 2. Solon apparently created the type of nobleman who became "head of the people" and served as the mediator between nobility and people.

line of successors down to Pericles. After Pericles began the decline of the
institution because the people now adopted a head, Cleon, who was not
in good repute with the upper classes. And after Cleophon "the leadership of the people [*demagogia*] was handed on in unbroken succession by
the men who talked biggest and gratified the many, looking only to the
interest of the moment." [5] The "head of the people" was the accepted
designation for the leader of the democratic party; no comparable title
had evolved for the leader of the aristocratic party. To the critical observation of Aristotle, the line of the great "heads" defined the significant
sector of the constitutional history of Athens. It began with Solon and
the tyrant Peisistratus, and it came to a close with Cleophon, toward the
end of the Peloponnesian War. The history of the polis in the narrower
sense became identical with the period from the first stirring of its pathos
to its conquest by urbanized democracy. The effective polis, from its
integration through Solon and tyranny to its dissolution by the dema-
gogues, lasted barely two centuries.

The pattern of Athenian constitutional history can be no more than
a means of orientation in the maze of Hellenic political history. It is not
transferable to other regions and not even to other poleis of the mainland. In Anatolia for instance, the course of constitutional history was
decisively interrupted by the external event of the Persian conquest in
546 B.C. In Sicily, on the other hand, the "tyranny" was much more than
a passing phase in the process of democratization because the dangerous
situation of a frontier against Carthaginians and Etruscans, as well as
against the non-Hellenic native population, required a more effective,
permanent military organization of greater striking power than could
be afforded by the small-scale single poleis. And Sparta, finally, had
neither a tyranny nor a democratic development because, after the Messenian revolt, the situation of conquest was permanently fossilized as
the "aristocratic" constitution.

With due allowance for all necessary qualifications, we may venture
the generalization: The pathos of the polis was the pathos of a dynamic
participation of the people in a culture that originated in the aristocratic
society. The dynamics was on the side of the "people." That may be the
reason why we hear so little about the aristocracy which after all had
created the paradigm of Hellenic culture. In fact, no early post-Homeric
expression of aristocratic pathos is preserved at all. The aristocracy be-

[5] *Ibid.,* XXVIII, 1 and 4.

came vociferous only when under the impact of democracy its position
was seriously endangered; only when it had become a "party" in the
losing constitutional battle within the polis did its pathos find a brief but
grandiose expression in the poems of Theognis of Megara (*floruit c.*545)
and Pindar of Thebes (518–442).

3. *Sympoliteia*

The strength of the gentilitian sentiment, and its expansion from the
aristocracy to the people, were the great obstacles to an evolution of the
polis toward a territorial, national state. Once the gentilitian structure
of the polis was fixed the possibilities for the formation of larger units
were limited. The problem that faced the city-state, we may say, was the
opposite of the problem which the Germanic tribes of the Migration had
to solve after their conquest of large Roman provinces. The conquering
Germanic tribes started with the possession of a large territory; and they
had to organize, administer, and unify its population politically and
culturally through centuries until the sentiment of nationhood and
the forms of self-government through election and representation had
evolved. The polis started with intensive self-consciousness and self-
government; and it had to invent the forms that would transcend local
institutions and integrate a plurality of poleis into a larger territorial
unit. The basic legal form which the polis had at its disposition for this
purpose was the sympoliteia, that is, the extension of citizenship to the
population of the surrounding countryside or of other poleis.

The form of sympoliteia had been used sucessfully on a small scale
in the so-called Athenian synoecism. The Athenian settlement reached
back into the pre-Doric time. Hence, what is called the Athenian synoecism was not a voluntary or compulsory settlement of a hitherto scattered
agricultural population in a newly founded city, but rather an extension
of Athenian citizenship to the villages of Attica; it was a process of
peaceful integration through agreement, extending over a long period
of time. On a larger scale, under more difficult circumstances, the sympoliteia was employed again, in the fifth century, in the creation of a
Greater Olynthus (*c.*432 B.C.). The Chalcidian communities which
combined in this form retained their status as poleis, each with its own
citizenship, while their populations received the citizenship of Olynthus.
It is the same device of dual citizenship that was later used in the extension of Roman citizenship to the Italian municipalities. The Olyn-

thian experiment came to an untimely end through the Lacedaemonian intervention of 382–379, which nipped the rising Hellenic great-power in the bud. The breaking of Greater Olynthus decided historically that the unification of Hellas fell to the Macedonian monarchy. When in 349 the poleis of Chalcidice applied for Athenian help against Philip II, the internal disintegration of Athens had proceeded so far that decisive action, comparable to the Lacedaemonian of 382, had become impossible. It is rather doubtful, however, whether unification through dual citizenship could have been achieved for an appreciable section of Hellas even if the Olynthian enterprise had not been broken by the Lacedaemonian intervention. In the Roman case, at any rate, the extension of citizenship was of minor importance compared with the transformation of the population of the Empire into the personal clientele of the princeps. The institution of the clientele and the evolution of Paganism as the state religion created such coherence as the Empire had, rather than any legal construction that drew on the forms of the polis.

4. The Failure of the Leagues

The only device that could overcome the radical autonomy of the poleis, and provide at least a degree of unification for larger areas, was federation. All through Greek history can be traced the attempts at forming leagues among the poleis. At the time of the Persian War the movement acquired momentum, resulting in temporary military alliances and in the formation of large confederacies. The attempts, however, remained sterile. The leagues either dissolved when the danger decreased, or they degenerated into unions held together by sheer force, ready to break up as soon as the hegemonic power showed any signs of weakness. These federative attempts require brief consideration, especially since federation ultimately became the technique for submitting Hellas to the Macedonian power.

The process of synoecism had not completely destroyed the earlier clan and tribal affiliations. Over large areas, such as the Doric or Ionic, we see the same tribes as religious units constituting the poleis. Such clan affiliations seem to have played a role in the construction of the oldest leagues among the newly created poleis, in the Northern Peloponnese as well as in central and northern Greece. The actual clan relationships within a group of poleis induced them, frequently under the leadership of the strongest polis, to enter into more or less voluntary defensive

alliances, the symmachies against other federations, as well as into agree-
ments for a certain restraint in warfare among themselves.

A second type of federation is characterized by the possession of a
common religious center. Federations of this type were called amphictyonic leagues. The most famous of them was the Delphian Amphictyony. The members of the Delphian federation took an oath neither to
destroy to the ground the city of a member polis when they fought
among themselves, nor to cut off the water supply in war or peace; and
they agreed, furthermore, to protect the Delphian temple with all their
strength. Such stipulations (as well as others concerning arbitration of
boundary disputes, and so forth), however, should not be optimistically
understood as the important beginnings of international organization.
It is obviously out of keeping with elementary facts of Greek history
if we interpret an agreement between small neighboring cities of the
same stock and civilization not to exterminate each other in a dispute
over an acre of land as a great achievement in international law. There
is no cause for enthusiasm when closely related cities agree to leave a few
houses standing and to stop slaughtering when half the population is
killed. It is, on the contrary, a cause for astonishment that such rules were
about the best that could be achieved in the direction of national unification. The federations must be seen against the background of the death-
struggle that was permanently going on among the poleis. They achieved,
it is true, an approximate pacification of certain areas; but the strength
which they preserved by those means was used for the purpose of con-
ducting a war of all against all on the level of the federations. All that
was gained was a certain chance of survival for the member poleis. In
order to reach this aim some federations went even so far as to make
arbitration of disputes between their members compulsory. The judgments rendered, however, were not always accepted; the losing party
often resorted to warfare; and that happened even in the hour of
national emergency. The Second Holy War started because the Phocians
did not submit to a fine inflicted on them by the Amphictyonic Council;
they countered the sentence by plundering the temple treasure of Delphi
and using it for military equipment. The ensuing war lasted ten years
and led to the intervention of Philip of Macedonia, the first step in the
subjugation of Greece.

Leagues of the amphictyonic type were formed and reformed,
entered into alliances, and broke down temporarily or permanently.

With the exception of the Boeotian League they had, on the whole, little influence on the political affairs of Greece. The great power centers which shaped the history of Greece in world politics were the Spartan League and the Athenian Empire. The Spartan League was the first to be formed. Clan and religious factors were at best of minor importance in its organization. Its formation was due to the military superiority of the Spartan state and its unwillingness to tolerate independent leagues in the neighborhood. After the battle of Thyrene, in 549 B.C., which resulted in the dissolution of the Argive League, the unification of the Peloponnesian communities in a military league under the hegemony of Sparta was practically complete. Its great efficiency as a military machine made it the hegemonic power of all Hellas at the beginning of the Persian Wars, when the Greek poleis united in an effort of national defense and gave the military command of the campaign to the Spartans. After the battles of Plataea and Mycale in 479, however, when the immediate danger to the Greek mainland had been averted, the Spartan League proved to be incapable of leadership. The Greek internal strife revived in the form of the increasingly vicious attacks of Sparta against Athens as well as in the form of internal conflicts in the Peloponnesian League itself.

In 478 the hegemony in the Persian War was transferred to Athens because she had the greatest interest in averting the Persian danger to the island world and to the Anatolian Greeks. An Hellenic Confederacy was formed which consisted of the Aegean insular and coastal cities, with Athens as the hegemonic power and Delos as the religious and financial center. This new confederacy was a more hopeful enterprise than the Spartan League, because it was not based on a victory of the hegemonic power over the members of the federation but on a community of interests in face of a foreign danger. It was a symmachy, a voluntary military alliance among the interested governments for the conduct of the war. Though the facts of the situation and the construction of the League favored the domination of Athens over all the other members, the circumstances of its formation held the promise of a more stable union which might expand into a pan-Hellenic organization. The actual warfare against Persia, however, was not too successful. Moreover, it was gravely hampered by the Spartan-Boeotian resistance against an expansion of the Athenian maritime league. By 454 the momentum of the symmachy had been weakened to such a degree that Athens had to give up all attempts at imperial expansion and even found herself compelled to consolidate the existing status by transforming the symmachy into the Athenian Empire. The treasury was transferred from Delos to Athens, the federal contributions became tributes, the courts of Athens became superior courts for trials in the member poleis, the voluntary element disappeared and a continuous series of revolts ensued which had to be quelled with severity. The Empire became a hegemonic confederation similar in its general structure to the Spartan hegemony over the Peloponnese. By the Thirty Years' Peace between Athens and Sparta in 445, the existence of the two confederacies was mutually recognized. The pan-Hellenic dream was dead.

The following century, the century of the sophists, of Thucydides, of Socrates, Plato and Aristotle, saw the death struggle of the Greek federations. The Peloponnesian War (431–404) ended with the defeat of Athens and her incorporation into the Second Spartan Hegemony (404–371). The war between Sparta and Persia ended with the Peace of Antalcidas (387–386); the poleis of Asia Minor were surrendered to Persia, while the other islands and poleis were to be independent under a Spartan-Persian guaranty. This was the first time that the status of Greek cities was guaranteed by a non-Hellenic power. The internecine warfare went on nevertheless, and after the short-lived Theban Hegemony of 371–362, the Second Holy War against the Phocians brought on the previously mentioned Macedonian intervention with the result that Phocis was replaced in the Delphian Amphictyony by Philip of Macedonia. A monarch had become a member of an Hellenic confederacy. The new position was used by Philip for further interventions in Greek affairs, ending in 338 in the defeat of the Hellenic national opposition led by Demosthenes, and in the foundation of the League of Corinth under Macedonian hegemony. The Spartans, who for a time could resist their incorporation into the League, had to submit in 331. All the Greek states were now united in one confederation for the purpose of the final war against Persia and for the liberation of the Asiatic Greeks. By now, however, the initiative of historical action had passed from the Hellenic polis to a foreign monarchy.

CHAPTER 5

Hesiod

The creation of philosophy as a symbolic form is the achievement of Hellas. The new form begins to disengage itself from the myth, toward the end of the eighth century, in the work of Hesiod inasmuch as in his *Theogony* the myth is submitted to a conscious intellectual operation, with the purpose of reshaping its symbols in such a manner that a "truth" about order with universal validity will emerge. Metaphysical concepts are incipiently formed, and their formation raises problems which in their turn press toward further consistent elaboration. In brief: The speculative reason of the thinker asserts its autonomy against the mythopoetic mode of expression. The pathos of being and existence, which hitherto had expressed itself compactly in the form of the myth, now tends toward a more differentiated expression through the instrument of speculation.

1. From Myth to Metaphysics

The transition from myth to metaphysics is fraught with problems which science has not yet resolved by far. Still, one can formulate the central issue: that rational speculation, while it can be used within the symbolic forms of both myth and philosophy, is neither the one nor the other.[1] Myth and philosophy, just as myth and revelation, are separated by the leap in being, that is, by the break with the compact experience of cosmic-divine order through the discovery of the transcendent-divine source of order. The leap in being, however, notwithstanding the radicalism of the event when it occurs, is historically prepared by a variety of modes in which the myth is loosened up and made transparent toward transcendent order. In the Egyptian form of order,

[1] Throughout the present chapter on Hesiod the analysis of the Egyptian "Dynamics of Experience" in *Order and History* I, Ch. 3, § 3, is presupposed.

the theogonic speculation of the Memphite Theology, the summodeistic speculations of the empire theologians, culminating in the symbolism of Akhenaton, as well as the personal piety of the Amon Hymns, made the cosmological myth so transparent for transcendent being that the resulting formulations could be misunderstood by historians as "monotheistic." The carrier of this advance is man inasmuch as his existence under God is real even though it is not yet illuminated by the leap in being. The desire to know the truth of order, which Aristotle recognized as natural to man, is present even where it has to struggle with the compactness of experience and its cosmological expression. In Hellas these preparatory steps toward the leap in being were taken by the "singers." Homer created the present of man, if not under God, at least under the monarchically organized Olympians, and with it the past of memorable deeds and the future of survival in song. Hesiod, to whom the symbolism of existence under the Olympian gods was already given, applied rational speculation to it in his pursuit of truth. The Hesiodian speculation, however, does not belong to the same type as the Egyptian, for the Olympian myth of Homer, to which it applied, was no longer cosmological. The decisive step toward the creation of historical form had been taken by Homer when he transfigured the Achaean fall into the past of Hellenic society. Unlike the Egyptian speculation, which remained an event within the medium of the cosmological form, the Hesiodian work has its sequel in philosophy because it moves within the mnemosynic form of the singer; the poems of Hesiod are a symbolism *sui generis* in as much as they establish a genuinely transitional form between myth and metaphysics. To be sure, since the compact symbols of the myth comprehend shades of experience that escape the differentiated concepts of metaphysics, while the language of metaphysics lends precision to meanings which remain inarticulate in the myth, the units of meaning cannot be simply paired off against each other. Nevertheless, the transition is an intelligible process, because the experiential substratum provided by Homer remains recognizable in its sameness through the change of symbolic forms; and this sameness is most clearly recognizable in the Hesiodian beginnings of the process when, in faltering and stumbling speculation, the symbols of the myth point searchingly towards meanings for which later generations of philosophers will develop a technical vocabulary. The *Theogony* represents such an incipient penetration of the Olympian myth with a speculative intention; and an intelligible line of speculative evolution runs from these beginnings through the Ionian and Italian philosophers to Plato and Aristotle.

The continuity of this evolution was recognized in antiquity. The term "theology," coined by Plato, was used by Aristotle for designating his *prima philosophia* (the later "metaphysics") : "There are three theoretical philosophies: The mathematical, the physical, and the theological." [2] With a fine sense for historical derivation Aristotle understood the Hesiodian *Theogony* as the first clear step toward philosophical speculation. He was inclined, however, to distinguish Hesiod and his followers as the "early theologizing" from the Ionians as the "early philosophizing" thinkers; [3] and he found the specific trait of the "theologians" in their habit of speculating "mythologically" (*mythikos*).[4] In one of its meanings the new term "theology" was used by Aristotle for designating the form of symbolization, intermediate between myth and philosophy, that we find in Hesiod.[5]

The preliminary characterization of Hesiodian form leads to the question why the myth should have been found wanting as a medium of expression, and what changes in the substratum of experience made speculation appear necessary as a supplementary medium. Fortunately Hesiod himself supplies the answers. His incipient speculation is a response to the experience of social unsettlement.

Hesiod's father came to Boeotia over the sea from the Aeolian Cyme in Asia Minor. The father took to seafaring in order to improve his insufficient livelihood. One of these trips was final. He "left Aeolian Cyme and fled, not from riches and substance, but from wretched poverty which Zeus inflicts upon men," and he settled in Boeotia in

[2] Aristotle, *Metaphysics* VI, 1026a18f. For the same classification of "theoretical sciences" cf. *Metaphysics* XI, 1064b1ff.

[3] *Protoi theologesantes, protoi philosophesantes, Metaphysics* I, 983b29 and 982b11ff.

[4] *Metaphysics* III, 1000a9, with special reference to Hesiod as a theologian, and 1000a18. Cf. Werner Jaeger, *The Theology of the Early Greek Philosophers* (Oxford, 1947), 9–17.

[5] A very important attempt to deal with the intermediate symbolic form of Hesiod was made by Olof Gigon, *Der Ursprung der Griechischen Philosophie. Von Hesiod bis Parmenides* (Basel, 1945), especially 36–40. I find myself in agreement with Gigon's analysis as far as it goes, but I doubt that his distinction of symbolic means ("*Alles wird Person*"—"*Alles wird zum Gegenstand*") is sufficient to cover the problems which in Greek philosophy arise, not from the side of the symbols, but from the side of the experiences expressed by their means. The symbolization of transcendent reality as *eidos*, form, in Plato's philosophy, for instance, illustrates the predominance of "*Sachanalogie*." Nevertheless, the Platonic experience of transcendent being is of importance in itself—and it is closer to the Hesiodian range of experience, with its expression through the personal symbols of the myth, than to the world experience of the Ionian philosophers.

the miserable village of Ascra which is "bad in winter, sultry in summer, and good at no time." [6] He found subsistence but no riches. On his death the inheritance was divided between Hesiod and his brother Perses. A not too rosy situation was aggravated by the corruption of the village notables in so far as Perses was able to obtain the larger part through bribing the magistrates.[7] Experience with women also seems to have not been the best, for references to the deadly race of women who are "no help in poverty," who stay at home and let the man work, have an autobiographical ring.[8] By economic status he was a "shepherd of the wilderness," an "ugly shame," a "mere belly." [9] And to make the measure full, the tricky Perses was just involving him in another lawsuit to rob him still further with the help of conniving judges, the princes (*basileis*) of *Works and Days*.[10]

Such hardships will cause a man to reflect on his position in the world and society, as well as on the meaning of an order which on the surface has become doubtful, if reflection be his talent and if the state of civilization furnish him with the means for articulating his thought. Both conditions were fulfilled in the case of Hesiod. The literary form in general, which will be discussed further, was provided by the Homeric poems, and the means of articulation in detail by a wealth of highly developed myths and fables. Moreover, the personal factor, *i.e.* the will and talent of using these instruments for a reflective penetration of the meaning of order, was certainly present as evidenced by the Hesiodian work; and it was present not only in fact, but also reflectively to the poet's consciousness as a new adventure of man in dealing with problems of order. For the *Theogony* opens with the story of the Heliconian Muses, who appeared to the shepherd Hesiod, endowed him with the staff of the rhapsode, and breathed into him the voice of the singer who celebrates things past and to come. This story in itself was an innovation in so far as the poet stepped out of the anonymity of the older epic and appeared

---

[6] *Works and Days*, text and translation by Hugh G. Evelyn-White (Loeb Classical Library), 631–40. Throughout this chapter I am using the translation by Evelyn-White but take the liberty of making small changes whenever they seem desirable for sharpening the meaning. Also used were the text of *Hesiodi Carmina*, Recensuit Aloisius Rzach (3d ed., Leipzig, 1913), as well as the following works of interpretation: Ulrich von Wilamowitz-Moellendorf, *Hesiods Erga* (Berlin, 1928); Jaeger, *Paideia* I (1945); Jaeger, *The Theology of the Early Greek Philosophers* (1947); Friedrich Solmsen, *Hesiod and Aeschylus* (Ithaca, N.Y., 1949); and Frederick J. Teggart, "The Argument of Hesiod's *Works and Days*," *Journal of the History of Ideas*, VIII (1947).

[7] *Work and Days*, 37ff.   [8] *Theogony*, 590ff.

[9] *Ibid.*, 26ff.   [10] *Works and Days*, 33ff.

in person, naming himself as the vessel of inspiration. Moreover, the personal appearance was motivated by Hesiod's consciousness of the difference between the inspiration of the older poetry and his own, and even of an opposition to that of Homer. For the Muses, when breathing the voice into Hesiod, informed him that they were quite capable of telling falsehoods (*pseudea*) which sounded like the real thing—apparently a slap at Homer—but that they also knew how to tell the truth (*alethea*) when they chose, and that is what they intended to do in the case of Hesiod.[11] Apparently it was the personal distress of Hesiod, his suffering from injustice, which motivated him to break the older anonymity, to appear as the individual man in opposition to the accepted order, and to pit his knowledge of truth against the untruth of society.

With the speculative penetration of the myth we see the problem of truth developing a gamut of shades. What is the truth of the old myth? What is the source of truth in the philosopher's speculation? What change of meaning does an old myth undergo when it is told as a paradigmatic fable in a context of speculative truth by Hesiod? What kind of truth has a god when he is shaped by Hesiod, as far as we can see, to fit a speculative requirement? What kind of truth have the genealogies of gods invented by Hesiod? These questions run from now on through the history of Greek thought until they come to their head in Plato's struggle with the truth of the old myth to which he opposes the truth of his new myth of the soul, and especially in Plato's much misunderstood invention of a false myth, a "lie" (*pseudos*), by the side of his true myths in the *Republic*.[12] A new kind of truth is the fundamental concern of Hesiod, and the assurance that he is telling "true things" (*etetyma*) recurs in the *Works and Days*.[13]

It is in the light of this concern that we must read the curious passage, in the *Theogony*, on the cathartic effect of articulating the inspired truth. The Muses, and in particular Calliope, attend to the princes and to the singers. When the Muses honor a prince, gracious words will flow from his lips, and his wisdom and judgment will settle great quarrels. When the people are misguided in assembly, he will set matters straight with the ease of his persuasion. And when such a true

[11] *Theogony*, 26ff.
[12] On the problem of truth and lie in Greek thought cf. Wilhelm Luther, *Wahrheit und Luege im aeltesten Griechentum* (Borna-Leipzig, 1935).
[13] *Works and Days*, 10.

prince passes through the place of assembly, people will greet him reverently like a god. The cathartic, ordering effect of the prince on the turbulence of the people is paralleled by the rhapsode's effect on the turmoil of the individual soul. When the soul of a man is in sorrow through recent grief, and distress fills his heart with anxiety, he will forget his disturbance when the servant of the Muses sings the glorious deeds of the men of old and of the blessed gods.[14]

The Muses are the daughters of Zeus, of the ordering force of the universe. They transmit the Jovian order to the prince and the singer, for further transmission to the people, as well as to man in his solitude. The Music truth of the prince and the singer that has such cathartic effect is not a piece of true information. It rather is the substance of order asserting itself against the disorder of passion in society and man. Hesiod, thus, distinguishes the three levels of truth and order in God, society, and man that we still can recognize, in their philosophical transformation, in Aristotle's three levels of autarky in God, polis, and man.

Moreover, the Muses are the daughters of Zeus from Mnemosyne, from Memory. Zeus fathered them with Mnemosyne when he sought forgetfulness (*lesmosyne*) from ugliness and a rest from his own unruly immortals.[15] Zeus himself, thus, needs an assuaging of his heart, and he finds it in cosmic Memory as the mortals in the memory of their myth. And again we can hear the late echo of the Hesiodian catharsis through Mnemosyne in Plato's anamnesis, especially in the late symbolic form of the *Timaeus* where memory hearkens back to the cosmos for the hints of true order that will overcome the disorder of the age.

2. *The* Theogony. *The Origin of Order*

An interpretation of the Hesiodian poems presents certain difficulties. At a first reading they seem to be neither well-constructed stories nor closely knit pieces of reasoning but rather loosely jointed sequences of myths, fables, philosophical excursions, apocalyptic visions, exhortatory speeches, economic advices, and wisdom of the kind that can be found in a farmer's almanac. Since the thread on which these variegated materials are strung is barely visible, the temptation is great to isolate the pieces and to interpret them out of context. And since we cannot analyze the works as a whole but must concentrate on the problems

[14] *Theogony*, 75–103. [15] *Ibid.*, 53ff.

pertinent to our study, it is all the more necessary to be aware of the embracing literary form which in fact determines the meaning of the component parts. As to their literary form, now, the poems derive from Homer. The *Theogony* is an Aristeia, *i.e.* a ballad or story of an heroic adventure; and the *Works and Days* is a Paraenesis or Protrepticus, *i.e.* an admonitory speech.

We shall, in the present section, deal with some problems of the *Theogony* that will illustrate the state of theoretization reached by Hesiod. The subsequent section will deal more extensively with Hesiod's speculation on political order in the *Works and Days*.

The *Theogony*, as we said, is an Aristeia. Its subject matter is the victory of Zeus over the older divinities; and the story culminates in the Titanomachia, the description of the battle between Zeus and the Cronian generation of gods. Since Zeus is the father of Eunomia (Order), Dike (Justice), and Eirene (Peace), the Titanomachia brings the victory of the forces of true order over the savagery of cosmic and telluric forces. This is the level of meaning determined by the literary form.

The story of the *Theogony* is a cardinal problem in a philosophy of history and order. In nonmythical language, it is the tension between a hard-won civilizational order, precariously in balance, and a rumbling underworld of demonic forces which at any time may break loose and destroy it. The danger of such a break, experienced by Hesiod, lies back of his urge toward clarification and persuasive articulation of the principles of order represented by Zeus. In the execution of this program (if we may use this rational term in connection with a theogonic poem), however, Hesiod is bound by the rules of mythical language. The tension itself becomes the epic struggle of Zeus with the forces of disorder; and the meaning of order must be found in the development of the god's personality. Hence, when from the general problem, we turn to the specifically Hesiodian achievement in its formulation, we should above all note the evolution of Zeus as an ethical personality.

This evolution does not begin with Hesiod—it is noticeable even in the *Odyssey*—,[16] but now it progresses beyond the Homeric range inasmuch as the predominance of ethical forces becomes the *raison d'être* of the reign of Zeus. The other gods are "earlier" gods because

---

[16] On the opening of the *Odyssey* cf. Ch. 3, § 2, 4 and 5.

of their savage lusts, their tyrannical cruelties, and, especially because of the uncivilized habit of swallowing their children in order to avoid an aristocratic sharing of rule among the immortals. Atrocities beget atrocious revenge, and the revenge begets new atrocities. Only Zeus puts an end to this dreary sequence; for, while his victory is won by force, it is held by the just distribution of his honorable share (*time*) to each of the immortals.[17] This is substantially the conception of Zeus that was further developed by the Aeschylean *Orestia* into the figure of the God who gains wisdom through suffering, and by Plato's *Phaedrus* into the Zeus whose followers are the philosophers, in particular the Son of Zeus, Plato himself.

The Zeus of the *Theogony* stands at the beginning of an evolution that ends in the Platonic divinity of the philosophers. In the work of Hesiod, however, he is still one of the many gods of the myth, not yet a symbol whose meaning is fixed, without regard for the traditions of the myth, by the philosopher's experience. Hence his existence and specific function had to be clarified in terms of his relations with the other gods. Hesiod, though in an entirely different experiential situation, had to cope with the problem that motivated the summodeistic constructions of the Mesopotamian and Egyptian empire theologians; and as his Near Eastern predecessors, he resolved it through a theogony. He assumed three generations of gods descending one from the other: Ouranos (Heaven) and Gaea (Earth), Cronos and Rhea, Zeus and Hera. Hesiod, however, was not burdened, as the imperial theologians of the Near East, with the task of rationalizing the position of a highest god as the source of imperial order; he was free to penetrate to the problem of order and its origin on principle. In Hesiod, there is already alive the Hellenic universalism that has no parallel in the constructions of the Memphite Theology or the *Enuma Elish*. The theogonic speculation, free as it was from imperial concerns, could issue into the philosophical speculation contained in it in compact form. Each god of the myth, it is true, had yet to be assigned a place on the family-tree but in this ordered derivation of the gods from their ancestors, there was prefigured, in the medium of the myth, the later aetiological speculation, the search for the ultimate cause (*aition*) of the phenomenon that is presently experienced. Hesiod's explanation of the Jovian order through ascent to the first generation of gods becomes, with the Ionian philoso-

---

[17] *Theogony*, 71–74.

phers, the ascent from the experienced world to a generative principle (*arche*), be it water, fire or air.

The genealogical construction seems to be marred by a rather obvious flaw. If the existence of Zeus and his generation of immortals requires an explanation, the existence of the first generation of gods (Chaos Gaea) requires one, too. The gods are immortal, but they come into being; and how did the first gods come into being? The manner in which Hesiod meets this pertinent question reveals the unusual quality of his speculative genius. For the generations of the gods who descend one from the other through what—with poetical license—may be called marital relations, are preceded by gods who come into being from no-where. These primordial entities are Chaos, Gaea, and Eros. With Eros in existence, Chaos and Gaea become productive. Chaos produces Night and Erebus, Gaea produces Ouranos. Only after these cosmic preludes is there a sufficient personnel of gods to start the generations.[18] Hesiod, thus, distinguishes between the procreative generations of the gods and the gods who come into existence without the benefit of procreative symbolism. Within the realm of the myth itself the trinity of Chaos-Gaea-Eros is set off as the *arche* of the gods in the same manner as one of the elements is posited as the *arche* of things in the Ionian specula-tion. Hence we cannot agree with the older interpretations (which still find acceptance) that the Hesiodian theogonic system has left the question of the "origin" unanswered and that only the Ionians pene-trated the problem speculatively. The error is caused by the symbolic language which Hesiod inevitably must use even when expressing a strictly speculative problem. The three primordial divinities do not exist, in his language, from eternity but "come into being" like the other gods. This language of "coming into being," which belongs to the rules of the Hellenic myth, if taken (or rather mistaken) as *oratio directa* will leave the question of the "origin" unanswered. If we how-ever distinguish—as we must in an analysis of myths—between the language of the myth and the meaning which it is meant to convey, we shall recognize that Hesiod took great pains to distinguish the pre-erotic "came to be" (*geneto*) from the erotic generation. Hence, the *Theogony* is, on the level of the myth, as accomplished and complete a speculation on the origin of things as the Ionian physicism.

Once this point is secured we can deal with the intricacies of the

[18] *Ibid.,* 116ff.

primordial trinity itself. The moderns have had a less lucky hand at this problem than the ancients. The most perceptive observations on the subject are Aristotle's. In *Metaphysics* I, when he explores the ancestry of the four causes which he had distinguished in *Physics*, he finds that the Ionians with their assumption of an elemental *arche* had touched at least the problem of the *causa materialis*. This type of speculation, however, he considers metaphysically insufficient: "However true it may be that all generation and destruction proceed from some one or (for that matter) from more elements, why does this happen and what is the cause?" [19] The material substratum does not itself produce its own change; we need a second principle in order to understand change. With regard to this second principle (the *causa efficiens*) "one might suspect that Hesiod was the first to look for such a thing." And then Aristotle quotes the passage on the primordial divinities "which implies that among existing things there must be from the first a cause which will move things and bring them together." [20] For the rest he deplores that the pre-Socratic philosophers never advanced beyond these two causes and did not grasp the problems of form and end.[21]

While Aristotle's observations are open to criticism in more than one respect, they discern the essential point that the Hesiodian trinity has something to do with the problem of the world-process. The quest for the origin must take into account that the world of our experience is not a static structure but a process; and the speculation on the origin must project (in one symbolism or another) this experience into a process in the origin itself. The Hesiodian speculation, far from being "primitive" in this respect, is indeed of the greatest interest in the history of symbols because here we find, within the medium of the Hellenic myth, an internal organization of the origin which corresponds to the gnostic speculation of later periods. There is a beginning from nowhere, resulting in the empty extension of Chaos, an articulation within nothing producing an articulated nothing (very similar to the Cabbalistic articulation of the *En Sof* into the first *Sefirah*), followed by the articulation into a matrix of creation and a desire for definite forming. As far as such complicated problems can be rendered in the roughhewn symbolism of separate, personalized divinities, we have in the Hesiodian

---

[19] *Metaphysics* I, 984a19ff.   [20] *Ibid.*, 984b23f.
[21] The Aristotelian complaint is of older standing. Cf. the characterization of the philosophic situation in his youth by Socrates in the *Phaedo*.

trinity a piece of speculation resembling by its intention the gnosis of *Sefiroth* or potencies.[22] The appearance of this type of speculation in the Hesiodian myth is neither anachronistic nor surprising. In view of the scarcity of preserved sources we must always reckon, in the Hellenic eighth century B.C., with a vast mass of floating ideas of which only fragments have come to us through the literary remains. That the speculation on the origin was part of this mass is sufficiently attested through the pervasive trinitarian symbol of the fleur-de-lis in Cretan civilization. The reader should refer back to what we had to say about this problem in Chapter 2.1, on the Cretan Society, as well as to the remarks on that occasion about the probable meaning of the Pythagorean *tetraktys*.

It must be, finally, noted that the Hesiodian speculation presupposes a considerable flexibility of the myth, a wide range of freedom granted to invention and transformation. For the single myths which have entered the *Theogony* are by far not the people's myths which are bound to specific localities and rites. On the contrary, Hesiod makes a deliberate effort to overcome, if not to abolish, the manifold of the local myths and to replace it with a system of typical gods—sometimes the local variants can still be discerned in the new type, as for instance in the story of the birth of Aphrodite with its explanation of her various names as Cytherea and Cyprogenea.[23] Hesiod, as Homer, was a creator of gods for the whole area of Hellenic civilization and thereby one of the great formers of its unity. The mythopoetic work of the two poets was a spiritual and intellectual revolution; for inasmuch as it established the types of cosmic and ethical forces, as well as the types of their

[22] Gershom G. Sholem, *Major Trends in Jewish Mysticism* (Jerusalem, 1941), 213: "The crisis can be pictured as the break-through of the primordial will, but theosophic Kabbalism frequently employs the bolder metaphor of Nothing. The primary start or wrench in which the introspective God is externalized and the light that shines inwardly made visible, this revolution of perspective, transforms En-Sof, the inexpressible fullness, into nothingness. It is this mystical "nothingness" from which all other stages of God's gradual unfolding in the Sefiroth emanate." Cf. also G. Sholem, *Die Geheimnisse der Schoepfung. Ein Kapitel aus dem Sohar* (Berlin, 1935). The Cabbala type of gnosis differs from the Hesiodian speculation in so far as the En-Sof is the point of origin of creation as well as the medium in which the process runs its course; such a medium does not appear as a separate person in Hesiod. The idea of the En-Sof (or Boehme's *Ungrund*) can develop only within the symbolism of a monotheistic religion. While this is not the place to develop the problem further, the suggestion may be thrown out that gnostic speculation, when it appears as a theosophic movement within a monotheistic culture, is a reversion to the myth. The demythization of the world is not an unbroken process; there may break through again, in the monotheistic phase of religiousness, a desire for remythization on the highest level of intellectual speculation. This certainly was the case of Schelling's *Weltalter*.

[23] *Theogony*, 188–200.

relations and tensions, it created, in the form of the myth, a highly
theorized body of knowledge concerning the position of man in his
world that could be used by the philosophers as the starting point for
metaphysical analysis and differentiation.[24] The freedom of such creation, while it assumes revolutionary proportions in Homer and Hesiod,
is a general characteristic of the mythopoetic process in Hellas.[25] It remains the presupposition for the further evolution of the gods from
Hesiod, through the tragedy of the fifth century, down to Plato who,
after the disintegration of the myth in the age of enlightenment, regains
its true function as the instrument of symbolization for transcendental
border-problems beyond the reach of world-immanent metaphysical
construction.

3. *The* Works and Days. *Invocation and Exhortation*

The *Works and Days* is a Paraenesis, an exhortatory speech addressed
by Hesiod to his brother Perses. As in the case of the *Theogony*, the
meaning determined by the literary form must be established before we
can proceed to an analysis of various subdivisions of the poem. This is
especially necessary, because the argument of the poem is supported
by the famous paradigmatic fables of Pandora and of the Ages of the
World (or, more precisely, of the races of men), which have tempted
more than one interpreter to treat them without regard for the meaning which they have in the larger context.

The theme of the exhortation is formulated in the opening invocation of the Muses. They are called upon by the poet to chant the praise
of Zeus, since the fate of man is in the hands of the God; men will be
famed or unfamed, sung or unsung as the God wills. Easily he raises
a man, and easily he breaks him; easily he humbles those who walk in
the light, and easily he advances the obscure; easily he straightens what
is bent, and easily he brings down the overbearing. And then the poet

[24] In the construction of the *Symposion*, for instance, Plato lets the first speaker, Phaedrus,
render a survey of what has hitherto been said about Eros. And this survey begins with the
respective passages from Hesiod and Parmenides (178). The same procedure, though leading
to an entirely different metaphysical result, is followed by Aristotle: In *Metaphysics* I, 4 he
opens the discussion again with the same passages from Hesiod and Parmenides.

[25] For the impressive production of gods in a continuity which links the Cretan with the
Hellenic society, cf. the fine survey in Axel W. Persson, *The Religion of Greece in Prehistoric
Times* (Berkeley-Los Angeles, 1942), Chapter V: "Minoan-Mycenaean Survivals in the Greek
Religion of Classic Times."

turns to his brother: Attend with eye and ear, and make lordly judgments straight with righteousness (*dike*), for what I tell you, Perses,
of a certainty is true (*etetyma*).[26]

The lines are self-explanatory. Nevertheless, it will do no harm
to stress the prophetic tone and the affinities with the Hebrew turning
of the tables. Not that we have to look for "influences"—all parallels
with Babylonian and Hebrew literary expressions can be sufficiently ac-
counted for by the assumption of a floating stock of tales, fables, typical images and metaphors, which pervades the whole eastern Mediterranean area (and perhaps India and China) and determines closely
similar expressions when, in the eighth century B.C., the lower classes
gain a literary voice.[27] We are, rather, interested in the influence which
Hesiod has exerted on the Greek philosophy of order through his creation of types which recur as the constants of later speculation.

In this respect the introductory lines of *Works and Days* are of
considerable importance because not only do they establish Zeus as the
god of the just, political order, but because their exemplification of
divine justice implies that the men in power are unjust and that the
restoration of just order entails a breaking of the great and a raising
of the humble. We find this conception of justice still as a typical
content in Plato's notion that the men who have held power in this
life will be most likely condemned by the Sons of Zeus in afterlife,
while those who have not engaged in political affairs will receive their
reward before the eternal tribunal. Moreover, the type continues into
the literary production of the Socratics where the socially and spiritually
humble Socrates is victoriously opposed to the aristocrat Alcibiades and
to the intellectually proud sophists, while the respective attitudes are
sublimated to the opposition of Alcibiadic *alazoneia* (overbearing, pride)
to Socratic *eironeia* (irony). The remembrance of the Hesiodian origin

[26] *Works and Days*, 1-10.
[27] Cf. Persson, *The Religion of Greece in Prehistoric Times*, 1: "To suppose that the great
cultures in the eastern Mediterranean area and in the Near East were separated from each other,
in the beginning, by the broadest of gulfs is an interpretation wholly at variance with the facts.
On the contrary, it has been clearly enough established that we have to deal, in this region, with
an original or basic if not completely uniform culture so widely diffused that we may call it the
Afrasian. It extended westward as far as Thessaly and southern Italy, perhaps as far as China in
the east, and certainly covered a large part of the African continent." Cf. further Sir John
Marshall, and others, *Mohenjo-Daro and the Indus Civilization*, I (London, 1931), 93ff.; the
suggestions in Ernest Mackay, *Early Indus Civilizations* (2d ed., London, 1948), Chapter VIII;
Leo Frobenius, *Kulturgeschichte Afrikas* (Zurich, 1933), *passim*; and, most recently, Cyrus H.
Gordon, *Homer and Bible*.

of the type will sharpen our ear for the eschatological overtones in Plato.

The structure of the *Works and Days* is still so much a matter of debate that we feel justified in advancing our own opinion without further ceremony. We find two main parts in the poem, each introduced by an exhortation to Perses. The first exhortation (11–41) is followed by the great fables and the apocalyptic sections dependent from them; the second exhortation, (274–97) is followed by the detailed advice for the industrious farmer's life, seafaring, marriage, general wisdom and superstition, as well as by the calendar of good days. We shall first consider the exhortations because they supplement, not only one another, but also the invocation of the Muses.

The first exhortation opens with the reflection: "So, after all, there was not one kind of Eris (Strife), but two of them are roaming the earth" (11f.). That casual remark refers to *Theogony* (225) where Eris (Strife) is enumerated as one of the daughters of Night. With magnificent mythopoetic freedom a new goddess is now added to the system. The evil Eris of *Theogony* receives a sister, the good Eris. The evil one stirs up war, battle, injustice, cruelty and all kind of mischief among gods and men. The good one, set "in the roots of the earth," stirs up the shiftless to toil, engenders a wholesome sense of competition among neighbors, and stimulates craftsmen to surpass each other in the quality of their work. Perses is admonished to follow good Eris. He ought to find his prosperity through industry, and not persecute his brother with legal chicaneries inspired by evil Eris.

The second exhortation (274–97) relates the two Erides with the Dike of Zeus. Perses should listen to Dike and wholly forget violence (*bia*); for this is the way of life ordained by Zeus for men.[28] Fishes, wild beasts and winged birds devour one another, for the animal kingdom is not the dwelling-place of Dike, but men have received Dike and should live by it. Those who observe Dike will prosper with their offspring while the others will sink into obscurity. The road to Misery (*kakotes*) is easy and smooth; "but the immortal gods have placed sweat before Success [*arete*]; long and steep is the path to it, and rough at first; but when the top is reached, then it is gained easy despite its hardness." [29]

[28] The Greek term rendered by "way of life" is *nomos*. The term does not yet have the meaning of "law." Cf. on this question Jaeger, *Theology*, 68, note 4.

[29] With the translation "Misery" and "Success" I am following Jaeger. Cf. *ibid.*, 70 and note 51 for the reasons.

By the Dike of Zeus it is ordained that we can achieve *arete* only through hard work under the impulsion of the good Eris. This Hesiodian *arete* of the peasant (as contrasted with the Homeric *arete* of the aristocratic warrior) is, then, detailed in the second part of the poem in a wealth of rules. The way of life of the peaceable, hard-working peasant is the order in conformity with Dike, and Hesiod undergoes the labor of its exposition because he hopes that after all the "foolish Perses" may be induced to follow the advice. Without this fundamentally hopeful tone the whole poem, as an exhortation, would not make sense; and we must keep this governing sense in mind when we deal with the fables of the first part which, if taken in isolation, might convey the impression that Hesiod is a philosopher of cultural pessimism.

Before we turn to the fables, however, we must consider the closing lines of the second exhortation (293–97). An admonition presupposes that the admonished is not in a position to know the truth himself and to act on it; and it must further assume the alternative possibilities that the admonished will take the advice or will fail to do so. This situation Hesiod has concentrated in the apophthegm: "The very best is the man who understands all things himself; good is a man who listens to a good adviser; but who neither can think for himself, nor keep in mind what another tells him, is a worthless [*achreios*] man." In the context these lines mark the transition to the second part of the poem with its detailed advice, but they have unfolded into one of the major problems in the Greek science of politics. For Aristotle quotes them in *Nicomachean Ethics* (1095b10–13) in confirmation of his thesis that the truth of a prudential science is accessible only to those who by inclination and training are predisposed toward it, while it will be rejected by the "worthless men." The Hesiodian situation of the admonition develops into the epistemological principle that the science of ethics can be cultivated only by men whose character is sufficiently mature to serve as an instrument of cognition.

4. The Fables. Paradise

The first part of *Works and Days* contains the three fables and the apocalypses depending on them.

The use of the fable is part of the exhortatory style stemming from Homer. The persuasive force of the admonition is increased by suitable illustrations taken from the common stock of the myth; and the argument itself is supported by the authority of the paradigmatic wisdom embodied in the mythical lore of the community. The classic example of this type of Paraenesis is the exhortatory speech of Phoenix addressed to Achilles in *Iliad* IX, 434–605, with its climax in the paradigmatic myth of the Wrath of Meleager.[30] Hesiod brings out the meaning of his exhortatory instrument by specifically calling the Fable of the Hawk and the Nightingale (the third one in the series) an *ainos*. While the term *ainos* applies more narrowly to the animal fable, it still designates in the older language (Homer, Pindar) the paradigmatic tale at large; the *ainos* as an illustration with a moral carries the meaning of advice. "So the ainos is not merely the animal-fable of the hawk and the nightingale. That is only the example which Hesiod gives to the judges. Both the tale of Prometheus and the myth of the five ages are true ainoi also." [31] Through the paradigmatic exposition of truth Hesiod, together with the other early poets, has created a type that unfolds in continuity into the philosophical speculation of the fourth century. Plato's pattern of the polis, the paradigm that is laid up in heaven, is the ultimate speculative transformation of the mythical paradigms of the early poets.[32] Moreover, the poets' technique of authoritative illustration has unfolded into the rhetoric of the polis, and Aristotle has devoted one part of his logical work, the *Topica*, to the correct use of authoritative *topoi*.

In the light of these reflections an analysis of the fables must distinguish between the story itself and its paradigmatic purpose. For the story may be a tale of woe, while its narration is animated by the hope that the hearer will take the lesson to heart and avoid the woe by more intelligent conduct. Such a conflict of meanings occurs in the case of the Hesiodian fables. If we place them side by side and try to harmonize their contents into a consistent picture of Hesiod's political views, as some interpreters have done, we run into insurmountable difficulties. If we take them as paradigms in the context of the exhortation, we shall find them identical in purpose inasmuch as all three of the fables convey the moral that the order of Zeus must be accepted and that anybody who violates Dike will come to grief. By the authority of the myth they try to impress Perses with the consequences of his unrighteous conduct; and all three of them, while groaning under the

[30] Cf. Jaeger, *Paideia* I, 1945, 26ff.   [31] *Ibid.*, 68.   [32] *Ibid.*, 32–34.

misery that is a consequence of the revolt against Zeus, are animated by the conviction that the order of Dike will ultimately prevail.

While all the fables, thus, point the same lesson, their contents have a life of their own. From the reservoir of mythical tales they draw the images that will symbolize the burden of existence, the sources of anxiety, the melancholy of a paradise lost, the hope of a better time to come, and the hardheaded will to survive. For the experiences of this class, the genius of Hesiod has found the symbols which have become types, not only for Hellenic speculation, but for the Romans and Western civilization as well.

The first is the Fable of Pandora, telling the story of the deceits of Prometheus and of the punishment visited by Zeus on mankind (42–105). In his anger over a deceit of Prometheus, Zeus hid from men their livelihood (*bion*), so that they had to keep themselves alive by hard work. Then Prometheus stole back fire for man; and as punishment for this second trick Zeus ordered the fashioning of Pandora, a human being in maiden shape, imitating the immortal goddesses, endowed with all graces and skills, and in addition equipped with a jar full of plagues for man. The slow-witted Epimetheus accepted the gift of the gods—and that is how evil (*kakon*) started. "Ere this the tribes of men lived on earth free from evil and grievous toil and sore diseases which bring the black Fates upon men—for in misery [*kakotes*] the mortals grow old speedily. But the woman took off the great lid of the jar with her hands and made a scattering of all these and devised woeful sorrows for man" (90–95). Only Hope, by the decree of Zeus, was kept under the rim. "Thus, there is no way to escape the will [*noon*] of Zeus" (105).

The Fable of Pandora is related with the story of the Fall and the expulsion from paradise in Genesis. A common reservoir of preliterary myths may be assumed on which both symbolisms could draw. The Hesiodian, however, is distinguished from the Biblical form by its distribution of accents. The motif of rivalry between man and God is subdued, while the complaint about the human condition is moved into the foreground. To be sure, the rebellion against the order of Zeus is the cause of man's misery—that is the point of the Fable; twice has Prometheus deceived Zeus. But the first deceit is not specified, and the second deceit is the rape of the fire; the symbolism does not have the

Biblical clarity of man's striving for the knowledge and life of the *elohim*. This reduction of the scale of ambition, while it veils the spiritual enormity of the Fall, has the consequence, one might even say the advantage, of bringing into focus a more humble area of experience; for the Hesiodian dream of paradise is the counterimage to the burden of existence as experienced by the common man. The Pandora fable, especially if supported by parallel dream expressions from other passages, has the merit of listing with rare precision and completeness the elements which go into the making of everyman's paradise and, therefore, recur constantly as a type in the process of politics. This average dream is less interested in possessing the knowledge of the gods than in having the work load reduced and in not suffering from hunger and sickness; it is less interested in immortality than in living indefinitely longer, in something like Hesiod's "practical immortality" of his mortals before the advent of Pandora. And, in the personal case of the poet, he would not be happy unless he is freed of the Pandora type of woman —with the grace of golden Aphrodite on her head, a shameless (literally: bitchy) mind, and a tricky character (65–67).

The Hesiodian dream of no work, no hunger, no sickness, no old age and death, no women, lists the negatives of the experiences which are the principal sources of anxiety in human life. The paradise in this sense, as the dream of freedom from the burden and anxiety of existence, is a constant dimension of the soul that will express itself not only in the imagery of immortal existence in the beyond but generally pervades the imaginative occupation with a desirable state of mundane existence. One does not have to insist on coarse expressions that will first come to the mind, such as the "freedom from want and fear" of the Atlantic Charter. More subtly, the dream is the dynamic component in the attempts at creating an earthly paradise by reducing the hours of labor (no work), by getting a living wage (no hunger) and medical care (no sickness) for everybody, and by increasing the length of human life (no death). And even the problem that man is created both man and woman, while it cannot be resolved, can be psychologically diminished to the famous "satisfaction of biological urges." Moreover, the dream of paradise generally animates the imagery of a changeless order expressing itself in the desire for stabilization, conservation, preservation of the *status quo,* as well as in the monopolistic appropriation of gainful chances and the resistance to the rise of rivals and competitors. An explanation of such phenomena in terms of a psychology of material interests touches only the surface of the problem. The strength of the Pandora fable rests in its penetration to a constant dimension of dreams which correspond to the experienced burden of existence. The paradise is indeed lost—that is the mystery of existence—and it cannot be regained within the life of man in society; but through the attempt at regaining it, the endeavor of man becomes the "material interest" that violates the order of Zeus and Dike. Submission to the order of life as decreed by God for man means shouldering the burden of existence in competition and co-operation with fellow men: "Fools, who know not how much more the half is than the whole!" (40).

5. *The Ages of the World*

The analysis of the second fable is entitled "The Ages of the World," because the term is in general use for designating the class of speculation of which the Hesiodian fable is a specimen.[33] The title, however, must not prejudice the analysis—what the subject matter of the fable really is will have to be decided by recourse to its text (106–79). Since the following analysis will deviate from established interpretations on several points, I shall first give a summary of the fable's content.

The fable is introduced by a brief remark addressed to Perses that now he will hear another story (*logos*) which he should keep in mind, the story of how gods and mortal men had the same origin (*homothen gegaasi*). This is the story:

> The immortal Olympians first created a golden race [*genos*] of men. When Cronos reigned in heaven, they lived like gods without sorrow, toil, suffering and the misery of aging. Their happiness was full; earth brought forth food and flocks in abundance; in peace, comfort and feasting ran their lives. They were loved by the gods; and they died as if they were overcome by sleep. Being mortals they had to die away and the earth covered them; but in afterlife they became good spirits [*daimones hagnoi*], roaming the earth as guardians of men, watching over right and wrong, and enjoying bliss.

> Then the Olympians created a silver race, much inferior in quality, not resembling the golden race in appearance or mind. The

[33] See the article "Ages of the World," as well as the related article "Cosmogony," in the *Encyclopedia of Religion and Ethics.*

children grew up under their mothers' protection for a hundred years, simpletons. And when they had reached their prime they lived only a short while and only with sorrow for they could not keep from *hybris*, wronging each other and neglecting to honor the gods. Then Zeus was angry and put them away under the earth. Still, in afterlife they became the blessed spirits of the underworld [*hypoch-thonioi makares*], second in rank to the good demons but nevertheless to be honored.

Then Zeus created the bronze race, from hard wood, strong and powerful, not similar to the silver. They loved the work of war [*Ares*] and acts of violence [*hybris*]. Their armor, houses and implements were of bronze; there was not yet black iron. They destroyed each other and passed to Hades, leaving no name.

Then Zeus made a fourth race of men, nobler and more righteous, the race of the hero-men, who are called demigods, the race preceding our own. Many of them were destroyed in the grim wars at Thebes and Troy; but the others Zeus removed to the ends of the earth where they live on the Islands of the Blessed, along the shore of Oceanos; there the earth brings fruit thrice a year, and there live the happy heroes under the rule of Cronos whom Zeus released from his bonds for this purpose.

And then Zeus made the fifth race, the iron, never resting from labor and sorrow by day, and the fear of perishing by night. But nevertheless even they have some good mixed with their evil.

Even the most superficial reading of the story will reveal that the sequence of golden, silver, bronze, heroic, and iron ages is disorderly in so far as the series of the metals is interrupted by the heroes. The conjecture is suggestive that Hesiod drew on some myth of the four metal ages, perhaps a Babylonian one, and adapted it for his purposes by inserting the world of the Homeric epic between the bronze and the iron ages. Stories of the four ages, indeed, exist in the Near East and India which may go back to sources similar to the Hesiodian. Reitzenstein, for instance, has suggested an interesting parallel in the ages of Krishna as preserved in the Jainist tradition. According to this myth there are four ages characterized by the colors light, red, yellow, and black. Through the four ages the state of the world deteriorates. In the light age there are no diseases, no misery of old age, no passions and no war. In the red age justice and piety are reduced by one-fourth; religion becomes externalized, new customs appear, and the consciousness of duty awakens. In the yellow age justice and piety are reduced to one-half; the formation of sects begins; passions and diseases appear; and the fate of men becomes heavy. In the black age only one-fourth of justice and piety is preserved; men are governed by their wrath; it is the age of hunger, fear and plagues.[34] The myth is instructive in so far as it shows the type of symbolism that may have been available to Hesiod for expressing the deterioration of the world in successive phases; but it also makes it clear that the Hesiodian logos, unlike its Oriental counterpart, is not inspired by the clear conception of a cycle of the cosmos in which the sacred order deteriorates until the cosmos perishes with its law.[35] It is not even certain that Hesiod entertained an idea of a cycle at all. To be sure, there is the expression of his wish not to be among the men of the fifth race, and to have "either died before or been born afterwards," [36] which seems to imply a better future after the iron age. But whether this wish justifies the conjecture that Hesiod envisaged an *ekpyrosis,* a general conflagration, to be followed by a new cycle of the world, must be doubted, considering that the idea would be in conflict with the exhortatory purpose of the poem.

The exploration of the field of possible Hesiodian sources and parallels that we owe to distinguished Orientalists should not be deprecated at all—especially since we intend to indulge in such exploration presently ourselves. Nevertheless, the search for such parallels has seriously hampered an understanding of the logos because it has distracted attention from its content. The following analysis concentrates on the text itself and tries to interpret it in terms of the Hesiodian mythico-speculative categories with which we are already acquainted.

Above all, the logos is not primarily concerned with "ages of the world" but with "races of men." And when we take a closer look at these "men" we shall see that the first three races can hardly be called "men" at all. They are amiable creatures of a topsy-turvy world who live out their allotted time; or deplorable simpletons who get themselves into trouble until they are put away; or fabulous monsters, apparently

---

[34] R. Reitzenstein, *Altgriechische Theologie und ihre Quellen* (*Vortraege der Bibliothek Warburg 1924–1925*), (Leipzig-Berlin, 1927). For further Mandaean, Iranian, and Indian sources see R. Reitzenstein and H. H. Schaeder, *Studien zum antiken Synkretismus aus Iran und Griechenland* (*Studien der Bibliothek Warburg,* VII), (Leipzig-Berlin, 1926). For a critical evaluation of the work of Reitzenstein and Schaeder cf. A. D. Nock in his review in *Journal of Hellenic Studies,* Vol. 49 (1929), 111–16.

[35] Reitzenstein, *Altgriechische Theologie,* 4.   [36] *Works and Days,* 175.

made of hard wood, who destroy each other and are never heard of again. Only the fourth race has the comprehensible, though heightened, humanity of the Homeric heroes; while with the fifth race we are quite at home in the sphere of the all-too-human. If we follow the suggestion of the text, an incision must be made between the fabulous creatures of the first three races and the intelligible humanity of the fourth and fifth. If that incision be made, we need no longer be fascinated by the series of the four metals in the abstract; we can forget our erudition with regard to Oriental parallel myths of the four ages; we are not compelled to construe the "heroes" as an interruption of an original sequence; and we get rid, at the same time, of the notion that the myth must necessarily deal with the deterioration of the world through successive phases. We are then free to look at the poem itself and to see that the first three races, indeed, form a series of deteriorations, that with the heroes a better race appears on the scene, but that the transition from the fourth to the fifth race again brings deterioration. The first three and the last two races, thus, are distinct groups deteriorating within themselves.

With the clear incision between the two groups in mind, we can now consider the introductory verses addressed by Hesiod to Perses which, in our opinion, contain the key to the structure of the logos. Hesiod informs his brother that he is going to tell him the story of how the gods and mortal men came into being from the same point of origin (*homothen*). Since Hesiod does not say anything about the origin of the gods in the course of the fable, it has been conjectured that the line in question (108) is the remnant of a plan that was not executed. The line, however, makes sense if we assume that Hesiod refers back to his *Theogony* and now intends to show that men have the same type of origin as the gods. If we read the logos in this sense we find that the first group of three races corresponds to the three generations of gods in the earlier work. It looks as if Hesiod had paralleled his theogony by an anthropogony.

If the creation of an anthropogony was the intention, it would explain the peculiar vagueness in the characterization of the three races that has always been observed by historians. Beyond the abstract assurance of deterioration, there is no concrete description of a decline in religion, justice, mores, fertility of the soil, or climatic conditions, as we find it in Eastern tales of the ages, or later in the West in the ages of Ovidius.[37] Hesiod was less interested in the content of the supposed source, if it was articulate enough, than in securing three fabulous, humanly not too intelligible races that could serve as a parallel to the theogony. Moreover, the genesis of the races seems to have been left deliberately vague in order to serve this purpose. The first race was created by the "Olympians" and lived "under Cronos"; but was it created by Cronos, or, rather, under the first generation of the *Theogony?* The second race, again created by the "Olympians," gets into trouble "under Zeus"; but was it created by Zeus, or perhaps under the second generation of the *Theogony?* Only the third race was certainly created by Zeus. That causes a difficulty for Hesiod because he runs out of generations of gods and must let the heroic race also be created by Zeus; and that makes us wonder why Zeus should have created the rather hopeless-looking hard wood creatures in the first place.

All these curiosities become meaningful as soon as we cease to insist that an unbroken line of evolution or dissolution must run through the five ages, as soon as we recognize the incision between the two groups as determined by a principle of mythico-speculative construction. Then the first three races become an anthropogony paralleling the theogony, while with the fourth and fifth races we enter the realm of man proper under the rule of Zeus. We shall, therefore, distinguish the two groups terminologically and speak of the first part of the logos as the "anthropogonic myth," and of the second part as the "epic myth."

We designate the second part of the logos an "epic myth" because Hesiod's view of the problem of man under the dispensation of Zeus obviously develops within the horizon of the epics of Homer and the Homerids. The noble society whose historical existence is well attested by the *Iliad* and *Odyssey* belongs to the past; as far as the experience of Hesiod is concerned, no trace of it is left. Mankind has two ages, the heroic past and the iron present. This raises the question whether the meaning of the "iron" age cannot be determined within the epic myth, independent of the metals of the anthropogonic myth. The logos itself offers a clue to the answer. The metals of the anthropogonic myth seem to have no other function than to symbolize the decrease in value of the successive races—unless we want to assume (what also has been done on occasion) that the three races were really meant to consist of gold, silver, and bronze respectively. In the description of the third race,

[37] Ovidius, *Metamorphoses*, I, 89–150.

however, Hesiod insists in a peculiar manner that the houses, arms, and implements of the race consisted of bronze, and that "there was no black iron." [38] In this instance, the "bronze" apparently is not only a mythical symbol but also characterizes the bronze age in the sense of cultural history. It seems possible, therefore, that Hesiod meant his iron race primarily to be the race that lived in the cultural iron age, that is, in the age that was historically ushered in by the Doric invasion which put an end to the Mycenaean glory of the bronze age. The suggestion will make sense of the two races of the epic myth as the representatives of the two great periods of Greek history.

If we adopt this view we also can dispose of the bothersome problem of a myth of the four metal ages that was found by Hesiod and garbled by him through the insertion of the heroic age. While such a myth may have existed, we certainly have no evidence of it. Its existence is assumed for the exclusive purpose of explaining the structure of the Hesiodian logos. A. D. Nock has excellently formulated the motive of the assumption: "Certainly the insertion of the Heroic Age in the sequence of metals suggests that the poet has borrowed a scheme, but modified it because the popular memory of the Heroic Age excluded belief in continuous degeneration." [39] And another authority states: "No reference to this version is found in the Homeric poems, but, even at that early period, some form of it was probably current among the Greeks." [40] If the structure of the logos is meaningful on its own terms, the assumption will be unnecessary. While Hesiod most probably could draw on a store of myths of ages of the world, of myths of a golden age, and on ascriptions of other metals to other ages, there will be no reason to assume that the various elements appeared in the combination of a myth of four metal ages before his time. Instead of an Hesiod who garbles a good myth, we gain the more appealing, and much more probable figure of an Hesiod who constructs a new myth from less highly organized materials. The construction of a consistent myth of four metal ages as a series of descending periods—as we find it in Ovidius, probably mediated through Orphic sources—would then be a further mythopoetic step based on the work of Hesiod.

The assumption of a pre-existing myth of the four metal ages is, in

[38] *Works and Days*, 151.

[39] A. D. Nock in the previously quoted review of Reitzenstein—Schaeder, *loc. cit.*, 114f.

[40] Kirby F. Smith, "Ages of the World (Greeks and Romans)," *Encyclopedia of Religion and Ethics*, I, 193.

our opinion, unnecessary. We are free, therefore, to consider what we really know about the elements that went into the Hesiodian construction. The ages of the world in general, and the metal ages in particular, point to Babylon as their origin. The theory of the ages as such was a common possession of the ancient Orient, and it was carefully elaborated in the Babylonian cosmological system. The world year, the later *magnus annus* of the Romans, is determined by the precession of the vernal equinox. Every 2,200 years the vernal equinox traverses one figure, that is, one-twelfth of the Zodiac; and each one of the world years is considered to be ruled by the respective figure of the dodekaoros. In the historical time that comes under our observation, the Babylonian calendar counts the Age of the Bull. The bull becomes the symbol of the god; and we find the full symbolism contemporaneously predominant throughout the Near East, in Egypt as well as in Crete. The Age of the Bull begins *c.*2800 B.C. In the eighth century B.C. the calendar was changed, and the Age of the Ram followed the Age of the Bull. Though the change of calendar coincided with the breakdown of Babylonian power, it spread through the Near East and it seems to have found its chief support in Egypt. The symbolism of the political gods changed with the calendar, and the bull-god was superseded by the ram-headed Jupiter-Amon, to whose oasis Alexander repaired (when he conquered Egypt) in order to receive the supreme sanction of his power.

The conception of ages based on zodiacal calculations alone lets the ages follow each other without qualitative differences between them. The notion that the successive ages are becoming worse has its independent source in the experience of decline in the course of history. Wherever the experience combines with the rhythm of time that we call an "age," it results in the symbol of an evil present state of the world, preceded by a better state; the world was good when it sprang fresh from the hands of the gods and it became worse in course of time for one reason or another. Two ages are the minimum needed for such symbolization; and hence the myth of a golden age preceding the historical misery can always unfold independently of any further speculation on ages. Whether the speculation will expand into triadic, tetradic, pentadic, or even more elaborate myths of a sequence of deteriorating ages, will depend on its combination with elements that develop independently in other areas of cosmological speculation. And whether such a series of ages will be combined with a series of metals, or of other organic or inorganic objects or substances, will again be a question of the independent development of such series in further areas of speculation on natural phenomena. In the Babylonian civilization there were indeed present the various independent elements that could have coalesced into a myth of the metal ages, though of the triadic rather than the tetradic variety. For the leading planets of the Babylonian cosmological system—Sun, Moon, and Istar (Venus)—formed a divine trinity similar to other Near Eastern groups of this type, while the four other planets—Jupiter, Mercury, Mars, Saturn—formed a tetrad symbolizing the four corners of the world. And the members of the leading trinity were associated with the metals gold, silver, and copper.[41]

The elements thus were present for the formation of a myth of the metal ages. But was it actually formed? All we know is that the value relations between the metals have exerted an enormous fascination because of their divine association. At times the commercial ratio of gold to silver was $1:13\frac{1}{3}$, because that was the relation between the lengths of the lunar and solar courses (27:360). But if such a myth which expressed the relative values of the ages by the divine metals was formed at all, it would have been a triadic myth—and that is the type of myth that we find in the anthropogonic section of Hesiod's logos. Hence, it must remain doubtful whether a tetradic myth of metal ages existed before it could be extracted from the Hesiodian assemblage of elements. In this connection it is also worth noting that the earliest documented case of a Near Eastern myth of the four metal ages occurs in a Persian speculation of the ninth century A.D. While the literary form does not date the myth itself, it is curious that no earlier literary fixations should be known, if myths of this type were current in the Near East for more than a millennium and a half before this date.[42]

The two parts of the Hesiodian logos are intelligible constructions separately. We can now turn to the problem of their integration into a meaningful whole. In understanding the meaning of the whole we shall be greatly aided by the existence of a Chinese myth of five ages

[41] The materials in this account of the Babylonian elements of the myth are drawn from Alfred Jeremias, "Ages of the World (Babylon)," ERE.

[42] Nathan Soederblom, "Ages of the World (Zoroastrian)," ERE. The myth is contained in the Dinkart IX, 8, SBE XXXVII, 181, a compilation of the ninth century. Concerning the date of the origin of the myth, Soederblom (loc. cit., 209) suggests: "The four Ages of Gold, Silver, Steel and Iron were adopted, at first probably by an orthodox compiler, during the early controversies with Manichaeism and other heresies." That would allow the third century A.D. as the earliest date of origin.

which has certain formal characteristics in common with the Hesiodian logos. It originated in the Tsou Yen school of the Five Elements, shortly before the final victory of Ch'in Shih Huang Ti in 221 B.C. There is no suspicion of "influences" from the West; it is a case of parallel motivation resulting in parallel speculation. The content of the myth is the following:

> Whenever any Emperor or King is about to arise, Heaven must first make manifest some favorable omen among the lower people.
>
> In the time of the Yellow Emperor, Heaven first made a large [number of] earthworms and mole crickets appear. The Yellow Emperor said: "The force of the element earth is in the ascendancy." Therefore he assumed yellow as his color, and took earth as a pattern for his affairs.
>
> In the time of Yu (founder of the Hsia dynasty), Heaven first made grass and trees appear which did not die in the autumn and winter. Yu said: "The force of the element wood is in the ascendancy." Therefore he assumed green as his color, and took wood as a pattern for his affairs.
>
> In the time of T'ang (founder of the Shang dynasty), Heaven first made some knife blades appear in the water. T'ang said: "The force of the element metal is in the ascendancy." Therefore he assumed white as his color, and took metal as a pattern for his affairs.
>
> In the time of King Wen (founder of the Chou dynasty), Heaven first made a flame appear, while a red bird, holding a red book in his mouth, alighted on the altar of the House of Chou. King Wen said: "The force of the element fire is in the ascendancy." Therefore he assumed red as his color, and took fire as a pattern for his affairs.
>
> Water will inevitably be the next thing which will replace fire. And Heaven will first of all make the ascendancy of water manifest. The force of water being in the ascendancy, black will be assumed as its color, and water will be taken as a pattern for affairs.
>
> If the power of water arrives without being recognized, the operation, when the cycle is completed, will revert once more to earth.[43]

The formation of the myth takes place in the full light of history. While the symbolism of the Five Elements is of much earlier date, it becomes a principle of speculation in a school only in the third century;

---

[43] Fung Yu-Lan, *A History of Chinese Philosophy*, I, trans. by Derk Bodde (Princeton, 1952), 161f.

and the application of the principle to the course of history can be
dated fairly closely through the fact that the author hedges on the
question of the symbol for the fifth period. The Chou period was drawing to its close and the victory of Ch'in was impending; but it was
yet undecided whether the conqueror would use water as the symbol of
his reign (as he actually did in 221) or the earth of the mythical Yellow Emperor.[44] Moreover, we are amply informed about the intentions
of the author through the account given by Ssu-ma Ch'ien in his *Shih
Chi*. Ssu-ma Ch'ien reports on Tsou Yen:

> In Ch'i State . . . there was Tsou Yen who came after Mencius.
> Having observed that those who were possessed of countries were
> becoming increasingly licentious and incapable of appreciating moral
> power . . . and of influencing the common people, he proceeded
> to make a profound survey of the ebb and flow of the Yin and Yang,
> and to write essays running to more than a hundred thousand words
> on their permutations and the cycles of the great ages. . . . He was
> first to put the present in exact relation to a past going as far back
> as the Yellow Emperor. He took what the learned had all narrated
> and made a great correlation of the ages in their rise and fall, work-
> ing out their omens, both bad and good, and their institutions, and
> making far-reaching inferences from them. This brought him to the
> time before heaven and earth existed, to what is so hidden that its
> origin cannot be investigated.[45]

The parallel between Tsou Yen and Hesiod is striking with regard
to both their situation and their response. The decline of political
morality provides the motivating experience; the speculation on the
rhythmical ebb and flow of political power and order is the response.
Both mythologists utilize symbols of periods and cycles which they
find in the tradition; and both apply them to the historical materials
within their range of knowledge. And above all, both think in the
categories of the cosmological myth and feel, therefore, obliged to
build the problem of present order into a chain of periods ascending
to pre-historic ages. Tsou Yen ascends beyond the historical periods
to the mythical Yellow Emperor, Hesiod beyond the Homeric-Achaean
period to the races of his anthropogonic myth. Moreover, the account of
Ssu-ma Ch'ien informs us that Tsou Yen went beyond the periods

[44] Concerning the situation in which the myth was created cf. Derk Bodde, *China's First
Unifier. A Study of the Ch'in Dynasty as Seen in the Life of Li Ssu* (*Sinica Leidensia*, III),
(Leiden, 1938), 112ff.
[45] E. R. Hughes, *Chinese Philosophy in Classical Times* (Everyman's Library, London, 1942),
213.

characterized by the five elements and ascended to the cosmic origins in Heaven and Earth, and even further to the hidden origin of these first cosmic principles. The myth of the five ages, thus, was supplemented by a speculation on the cosmic origin in the same manner as Hesiod's logos of the *Works and Days* was supplemented by the speculations of the *Theogony* on the question of the origin of both gods and men. In both cases the political order had become problematic; in both cases the mythologists, in their restorative efforts, appealed from the disorder of the time to the divine order of the cosmos.

6. The Apocalypse

Under the title of apocalypse we shall deal with the lines 180–285 of *Works and Days*. The delimitation of the passage involves a measure of arbitrariness in so far as the sections into which we divide the poem for the purpose of our analysis were not made by Hesiod. An intricate pattern of motifs runs through the whole poem so that a particular passage, loaded with the meanings of several themes, might be included justly in more than one subdivision. The lines 180–201, for instance, immediately follow the logos of the races of man; and they might quite properly be treated as an integral part of the logos itself since they contain a vision of the dire future of the iron race. Nevertheless, one might also consider that the logos has fulfilled its function and that in 180–201 Hesiod is dealing with present mankind, regardless of its interpretation as the last of the five races. Moreover, the passage is set off from the logos itself stylistically through the use of the future tense. At the end of the whole section (180–285) we have, then, included the lines 274–85 which earlier in the present chapter we treated as part of the second main exhortation addressed to Perses, for these lines can indeed be understood either as the conclusion of the apocalypse or as the opening of the second exhortation.

The unit of 180–285 is formed by the theme that runs through the lines. It can be described as the future of mankind under the alternative aspects of its obedience to, or revolt against, the just order of Zeus. The theme, then, is interwoven with the special Hesiodian grievances against Perses and the corrupt magistrates. Alternately the magistrates and Perses are admonished to desist from their iniquity and, thus, to secure for themselves and their polis the happy fate of the just. By weaving the alternatives of human future, as well as the alternating admonitions, into the general background of dark foreboding, Hesiod achieves the following structure for the whole passage:

(I) 180–201—General apocalypse of the dark future for the iron race. "Zeus will destroy this race of mortal men" (180). Nevertheless, there is "some good mingled with the evils" of this race (179). Without this concession the following exhortations and alternatives would not make sense.

(II) 202–24—The admonitions to the princes and to Perses.
    (1) 202–12—The Fable of the Hawk and the Nightingale, the "fable for princes."
    (2) 213–24—The admonition to Perses.

(III) 225–47—The apocalypses of the just and the unjust cities.
    (1) 225–37—The apocalypse of the just city.
    (2) 238–47—The apocalypse of the unjust city.

(IV) 248–85—Concluding admonitions and reflections.
    (1) 248–66—Warning to the princes that the messengers of Zeus watch their injustice, and that they must expect punishment.
    (2) 267–73—Expression of Hesiod's own suspense between hope and apprehension of the worst.
    (3) 274–85—Warning to Perses that prosperity or evil will come from Zeus in accordance with his obedience to the order of Dike.

The *Works and Days* is a poem, not the discursive exposition of a thesis. One must read and study the work itself in order to gain an understanding of the richness of its contents. We can do no more than aid such understanding by circumscribing the areas of experience in which the apocalypse is rooted.

The area itself, as well its symbolization, will be circumscribed best, as in the case of the Pandora fable, by relating it to the parallel Israelite phenomena. The Hesiodian apocalypses of the just and unjust cities, corresponding to the alternatives of obedience to, or revolt against, the order of Zeus, obviously have their parallel in the prophetic types of existence in faith or defection, with the corresponding dual symbolism of salvation or punishment for Israel.[46] The paraenesis of the poet is an

---

[46] On the dual symbolism of the prophets cf. *Order and History* I, 461ff.

existential appeal of the same type as the prophet's call to return to the order of Yahweh. To be sure, the order of Zeus and Dike is not the order revealed from Sinai. Hesiod's apocalypse, moving from the myth toward the leap in being, does not have the spiritual tension of the prophets' appeal after the leap in being; his visions of good and evil remain within the bounds of earthly prosperity and disaster; but this lesser tension also preserves him from the metastatic derailment of an Isaiah.[47] Still, Hesiod has experienced the anxiety of existential disorder, and has discovered its connection with the order of society, as have the prophets; and for the expression of his experience he has developed closely parallel symbols. If Hellenism and Christianity could blend into a common Mediterranean civilization, it was due to the parallel rhythm of spiritual development of Hellas and Israel; and in the beat of this rhythm Hesiod keeps time with the prophets.

The Hesiodian experience which motivates the apocalypse must furthermore be set off against the variety of experiences which motivate similar symbols in his work. The visionary revelations are not stories about gods and men; they are symbolic forms, moving distinctly in the direction beyond the myth, which express the anxiety of the soul when it senses the possibility of its spiritual and moral destruction. The significant symptom of the new anxiety is Hesiod's anticipation that he and his son must cease to be righteous men, "for it is a bad thing to be a righteous man when unrighteousness has the greater right"; he can only voice his hope that all-planning Zeus will not let that happen (270–73).[48] If this anxiety and hope be considered the experiential core motivating the apocalypse, one can distinguish, by recourse to the motivating experiences, the following types of symbols which resemble each other closely:

(1) The visions of the just and unjust cities (255ff.) originate in the anxieties and hopes just indicated.

(2) The blessed existence that man has lost through the deceits of Prometheus and the gifts of Pandora originates in the experience of "paradise lost" discussed in an earlier section of this chapter.

(3) The symbolism of better, preceding ages, and in particular the happy innocence of the Golden Age, originates in the experience of historical deterioration of society.

[47] On metastatic experiences and their symbolization cf. *ibid.* 447ff.

[48] On the Egyptian response to disorder cf. the respective section in *Order and History* I, Ch. 3, § 3, 3. On Plato's resumption of the Hesiodian problem, in the *Republic*, cf. *Order and History* III, Ch. 3, § 3.

(4) And the closely related symbols of the existence of blessed demons, as well as of demigods living eternally on the Islands of the Blessed, originate in the experienced potentiality of more perfect being, halfway between man and God, which in the third century develops into the demonology of the schools and later can blend with Eastern angelology. All of these experiences, as well as their symbolic expressions, can be clearly distinguished in the work of Hesiod while in later history, when the symbols are severed from their experiences and have become topical units in poetry and speculation, their meanings will blend. It will then become difficult to distinguish a paradise from a golden age, or a golden age of the past from a golden age of the future, or a paradise lost from a terrestrial paradise to be realized by organizational efforts, or an Island of the Blessed from a Utopia.

We have delimited the area of experience in which Hesiod's apocalypses originate; and we can now consider the concrete structure of the experience. The anxiety of annihilation assumes the specific form of the fear that Hesiod himself, and his son, will have to become unrighteous in order to survive. This fear cannot yet be met by the resistance of a soul that has become conscious of its own life. The soul still is inextricably interwoven with the fabric of social and cosmic order; when the order becomes unrighteous, the soul must become unrighteous too, because life has no meaning beyond life within the order. Strictly speaking, the soul does not yet exist. The self-conscious resistance of a Xenophanes or Heraclitus was out of the question; and it took several centuries before the soul was sufficiently formed to become a source of order in opposition to society, as it did in the life and work of Plato. While the soul begins to "come into being"—if we may use the poet's own term— the primary being is still the order of social and cosmic reality of which man is no more than a subordinate part.

As a consequence, the Hesiodian experience is a curious complex of conflicting elements. In some respects the individualization of the soul has advanced farther than in others. The exhortation, for instance, presupposes areas of sensitiveness in the soul that will respond to the appeal. In the great vision of the end of the iron race Hesiod names them Aidos and Nemesis, the two goddesses who will return to their Olympian company when the corruption of the iron race has become irreparable. Aidos is the sense of shame; when it is alive in a man he is able to respond to an appeal that brings the shamefulness of his conduct to his attention. In Aristotle's *Nicomachean Ethics* Aidos becomes the condition of a

good society; where shame does not respond, fear must be used to preserve the order of society. Nemesis is a sense of indignation aroused by
the spectacle of successful unrighteousness. With Homer it has the colora-
tion of a personal insult suffered through the recognition and preferment
of the lesser man; with Plato its meaning and function are absorbed by
the *andreia,* the courageous reaction against injustice. When Aidos and
Nemesis disappear, the last barriers against evil have broken down (197–
201).

Without shame and indignation in the soul of the addressee, the exhortation would have no aim. As soon, however, as Hesiod goes beyond
the personal appeal, he goes beyond the life of the soul and reaches out
into the surrounding fabric of order. Perses is assured that the reward
of good behavior will be prosperity for himself and his offspring
(280–85). The princes are warned that Dike and the myriads of immortal watchers will report the wicked acts to Zeus, and that the god will
punish them, not with personal affliction of their souls, but with the
misery of their people so that the pleasures of rulership will be seriously
impaired (248–64). The consequences of misconduct, thus, will appear
in the external fabric of individual and social life, and the evils are fitted
to the social status.[49] Hesiod even goes so far as to make a certain
allowance for hybris in princes. This at least seems to be the implication
of the Hawk and the Nightingale, the "fable for princes":

> The hawk carried the nightingale high up among the clouds, gripped
> fast in his talons. The nightingale, pierced by the talons, cried piti-
> fully. Contemptuously the hawk said: "Wretch, why do you cry
> out? A stronger one holds you fast; you must go where I take you,
> whatever of a singer you are. I shall make a meal of you or let you
> go, as I please. Witless is he who tries to withstand the stronger; for
> he cannot gain victory and will suffer pain in addition to his shame."
> Thus spoke the swift-flying hawk, the long-winged bird.

It is a "fable for princes who understand by themselves" (202)—Hesiod
himself does not point the lesson. There is a tone of acceptance in the
verse. Although the princes know better, they will on occasion indulge
their hybris; such princely behavior is part of the order of things; and
the subjects had better be aware of their weakness. In its context the
fable for princes, thus, becomes rather a fable for Perses who is warned

---

[49] The reader should refer to the chapter on Plato's *Gorgias* in *Order and History* III,
especially to the analysis of the "Judgment of the Dead," in order to gauge the advance in the
understanding of the soul from Hesiod to Plato.

that such hybris is bad for a poor man, since even the prosperous will be weighed down by its consequences—for "Dike beats Hybris when it comes to the end of the race" (213–19).[50] While the great and the humble, thus, seem to have different ranges for the indulgence of their hybris, the result will be the same in the end. The community as a whole will suffer under the punishment of Zeus. "Often a whole polis suffers for a bad man . . . when Zeus lays great trouble on the people, famine and plague, so that the men perish and the women bear no children and their houses become few . . . or, when he destroys their vast army, or their walls, or makes an end of their ships on the sea" (238–47).

It is well to be clear about the structure of the Hesiodian experience if one wishes to preserve a balanced view with regard to the parallels between Hesiod's vision of bliss and doom and the corresponding visions of the Israelite prophets of the eighth century B.C. While the search for Oriental parallels should be deprecated no more than in the cases of the Pandora fable, or of the logos of the Ages of the World, one must realize that no question of literary influences can arise. We are dealing with the history of experiences and their symbolization; and the experiences of Hesiod as well as their expressions are intelligible within Hellenic history, without recourse to "influences." Every line of the Hesiodian apocalypse could be written without a knowledge of the Hebrew parallels. With this warning in mind let us now juxtapose some passages of Hesiod and a few verses from the prophets.[51]

In the great vision of the future of the iron race Hesiod writes (182ff.):

> Neither will the father be of one mind [*homoiios*] with his children, nor the children with their father; neither guest with host, nor friend with friend; neither will brother be dear to brother as aforetime. Men will dishonor their quickly aging parents, finding fault with them and abusing them with bitter words, monstrously over-

[50] The plain translation does not do justice to the original. The "poor man" renders the Greek *deilos brotos,* and the meaning of that phrase is conditioned by the following *esthlos* (prosperous). *Deilos* and *esthlos* signify the poor and the rich or noble in the social sense. Cf. on this point the note in T. A. Sinclair, *Hesiod. Works and Days* (London, 1932), 26. *Deilos brotos,* however, can also mean the "miserable mortal" contrasted with the gods. From this meaning the *esthlos* receives by reflection the aura of a being who by his social status is elevated beyond the rank of the "miserable mortals."

[51] For a richer selection of Hesiodian and prophetic parallels cf. Teggart, "The Argument of Hesiod's *Works and Days,*" loc. cit.

bearing, not knowing the vengeance of the gods; nor will they make return to their aged parents of the cost of their upbringing. . . . Neither will be in favor the man who keeps his oath, or the law-abiding, or the man of excellence; men will rather praise the evil-doer and the works of hybris. Right will lie with brute strength, and shame will be no more; the worse will damage the better man, speaking crooked words against him and swearing an oath upon them. Envy, discord-talking, rejoicing in mischief, will be the companion of all men to their sorrow.

To this vision we find such parallels in the prophets as Isaiah 3:4ff. :

> And I will give children to be their princes,
> and babes shall rule over them.
> And the people shall be oppressed, every one by another,
> and every one by his neighbor.
> The child shall behave proudly against the ancient,
> and the base against the honourable.

Or, Hosea 4:1ff.:

> No truth, nor mercy, nor knowledge of God in the land.
> By swearing, and lying, and killing,
> and stealing, and committing adultery,
> they break out, and blood toucheth blood.
> Therefore shall the land mourn,
> and everyone that dwelleth therein shall languish,
> with the beasts of the field, and with the fowls of heaven;
> yea, the fishes of the sea also shall be taken away.

Or, Micah 7:2ff.:

> The good man is perished out of the earth:
> and there is none upright among men:
> they all lie in wait for blood;
> they hunt every man his brother with a net.
> That they may do evil with both hands earnestly,
> the prince asketh, and the judge asketh for a reward;
> and the great man, he uttereth his mischievous desire:
> so they wrap it up.
>
> .　　.　　.　　.
>
> Trust ye not in a friend,
> put ye not confidence in a guide;
> keep the doors of thy mouth

from her that lieth in thy bosom.
For the son dishonoreth the father,
the daughter riseth up against her mother,
the daughter in law against her mother in law;
a man's enemies are the men of his own house.

Against this vision of doom Hesiod holds his hope for the just city (225ff.):

> But when they give straight judgment to strangers and to the men of the land, and go not aside from what is just, their city flourishes and the people prosper in it. Peace, the nurse of children, is abroad in their land, and all-seeing Zeus never decrees cruel war against them. Neither famine nor disaster ever haunt men who do true justice; but light-heartedly they tend the fields which are all their care. The earth bears them victual in plenty, and on the mountains the oak bears acorns upon the top and bees in the midst. Their woolly sheep are laden with fleeces; their women bear children like their parents. They flourish continually with good things, and do not travel on ships, for the grain-giving earth bears them fruit.

With this vision one might compare Micah 4:3f.:

> And he shall judge among many people,
> and rebuke strong nations afar off;
> and they shall beat their swords into plowshares,
> and their spears into pruninghooks:
> nation shall not lift up a sword against nation,
> neither shall they learn war any more.
> But they shall sit every man under his vine
> and under his fig tree;
> and none shall make them afraid:
> for the mouth of the Lord of hosts hath spoken it.

Or, Isaiah 30:23:

> Then shall he give the rain of thy seed,
> that thou shalt sow the ground withal;
> and bread of the increase of the earth,
> and it shall be fat and plenteous:
> in that day shall thy cattle feed
> in large pastures.
> The oxen likewise and the young asses that ear the ground
> shall eat clean provender,
> which hath been winnowed with the shovel and with the fan.

But let us not overlook the fact that closer to Hesiod's vision than any utterances of the Prophets are a few verses from the Odyssey (XIX, 109ff.) where Odysseus unrecognized praises Penelope:

> For thy fame goes up to the broad heaven, as does the fame of some blameless king, who with the fear of the gods in his heart, is lord over many mighty men, upholding justice; and the black earth bears wheat and barley, and the trees are laden with fruit, the flocks bring forth young unceasingly, and the sea yields fish, all from his good leading; and the people prosper under him.

Parallels, thus, exist—but precisely in the case of the apocalypses, and in particular in the case of the apocalypse of doom, their existence does not point to common sources. For the apocalypse of doom has for its core an intensification of evils which are experienced by the prophet. The apocalyptic vision is something like the heightening of an empirical description of an unsatisfactory state of things into an ideal type of evil. The prophet of doom does not have to search foreign civilizations for symbols that will adequately express his anxiety of annihilation— all he has to do is to grasp the essence of the evil that surrounds him and to paint its phenomena without the extenuating admixture of good. The parallel symbols are due to the parallel genius in apperceiving the empirical phenoma of evil. Even more so this is true for prophecies of bliss. The hope for peace, fertility, and prosperity, in the setting of a rural economy, is bound to produce parallel symbols.

This relation between experience and apocalyptic symbol is of considerable importance for the philosopher of history because apocalypses of doom, when the prophet is perspicacious, may come true. The annihilation which anxiety apprehends as a danger may become historical reality; and when it has become empirically real, the description of its reality may strangely coincide with the apocalypse. Such a confirmation of the apocalypse by history has happened to Hesiod through Thucydides. With the Fable of the Hawk and the Nightingale in mind, let us read a few passages from the famous Melian Dialogue. Thucydides lets the Athenian delegates admonish the Melians to dispense with futile expressions of sentiment concerning right and wrong "since you know as well as we do that right, as the world goes, is only in question between equals in power, while the strong do what they can and the weak suffer what they must." [52] When the Melians express their trust in the gods who will support the just man in his fight against the unjust, the Athenians answer:

> When you speak of the favour of the gods, we may as fairly hope for that as yourselves; neither our pretensions nor our conduct being in any way contrary to what men believe of the gods, or practise among themselves. Of the gods we believe, and of men we know, that by a necessary law of their nature they rule wherever they can. And it is not as if we were the first to make this law, or to act upon it when made; we found it existing before us, and shall leave it to exist for ever after us; all we do is to make use of it, knowing that you and everybody else, having the same power as we have, would do the same as we do.[53]

We remember Hesiod's warning to his brother (attached to the fable) that hybris is bad for a "poor man," with the implication that the "princes" are granted a somewhat larger range in this respect than "miserable mortals." This subordinate strain in the Hesiodian experience has now gained a monstrous life of its own by making the order of the gods identical with the order of hybris, and by identifying the order of hybris with the order of politics. The appeal to the gods is cut off when the order of power unrelieved by Dike is experienced as the order of the gods. The apocalypse becomes historical reality when the apocalyptic tension of the soul is crushed and the bleakness of annihilation creeps over a society. When this comes to pass it is doubtful whether one can still speak of order at all. We remember Hesiod's vision of the future of the iron age (182ff.) with its destruction and perversion of social relations. We may compare with it the Thucydidean description of society in revolution:

> Words had to change their ordinary meaning and take that which was now given them. Reckless audacity came to be considered the courage of a loyal ally; prudent hesitation, specious cowardice; moderation was held to be a cloak for unmanliness; ability to see all sides of a question inaptness to act on any. . . . The advocate of extreme measures was always trustworthy; his opponent a man to

[52] Thucydides, *Historiae,* ed. by H. S. Jones and J. E. Powell (Oxford, 1942), V, 89. The translation is Crawley's in Everyman's Library.
[53] Thucydides, V, 105, 1–2.

be suspected. . . . Oaths of reconciliation, proffered only on either side to meet an immediate difficulty, only held good so long as no other weapon was at hand. . . . Thus religion was in honour with neither party; but the use of fair phrases to arrive at guilty ends was in high reputation. Meanwhile the moderate part of the citizens perished between the two, either for not joining in the quarrel, or because envy would not suffer them to escape.[54]

The parallels between Hesiod and Thucydides suggest serious problems for an epistemology of political science. If the visions engendered by the anxiety of annihilation can become the structure of society— what is reality? Is it Hesiod's anxiety, or the nihilism of the Athenians? What status of reality has a society that could be created by an apocalyptic vision? And what is the "realism" of a Thucydides when his types are fables and visions? These are the questions from which the science of politics has sprung with Plato and Aristotle. There is an interesting sentence in the passage of the Melian Dialogue that we quoted: "all we do is to make use of [the law of rule by power], knowing that you and everybody else, having the same power as we have, would do the same as we do." This assumption of the nihilist that his personal nothingness is the measure of man is the great error of "realism." The assumption recurs in the mouth of Polus, the sophistic representative of nihilism, when (in Plato's *Gorgias*) he charges the disagreeing Socrates with ill-will:

> *Socrates:* I cannot admit a word which you have been saying.
> *Polus:* That is because you will not; for surely you must think as I do.[55]

If we understand the "reality" described by Thucydides as an apocalyptic nightmare, we gain a first approach to Plato's much-misunderstood "idealism" as the attempt to overcome a nightmare through the restoration of reality.

[54] Thucydides, III, 82, *passim.*   [55] Plato, *Gorgias,* 471 d–e.

CHAPTER 6

The Break with the Myth

§ 1. The Emergence of Philosophy

Our picture of Greek intellectual history is still substantially influenced by historiographic conventions of the Hellenistic period. The development of philosophical schools in the fourth century B.C. induced the later historians, who themselves were members of schools, to project the institution into the earliest times and to construct the famous "Successions." The result was a linear development of Greek thought from the Milesian "school" to Socrates, and a bi- or tri-furcation of schools in his succession.

The picture that results from a critical study of history shows entirely different traits. Hellenic civilization was far-flung from Sicily to Anatolia, and from the Macedonian to the North African outposts. The political and intellectual development in that wide area was neither uniform nor continuous; and it was carried not only by the philosophers but first in order by the poets. Of the carriers we have studied Homer and Hesiod, the poets of the eighth century; and we have touched incidentally on the Ionian lyric of the seventh, as well as on the Milesian speculation of the sixth centuries. The Milesian speculation, now, did not find immediate successors. The conquest by the Persians in 546 B.C. apparently had disturbed the internal development of the Anatolian poleis deeply. Xenophanes of Colophon (c.565–470) emigrated to Italy; and in 494 Miletus was destroyed. In the sixth century, then, the Orphic movement with its mystery of the purification of the soul spread through Greece, while in Italy arose the related Pythagorean movement; and both of these movements enriched with their experience of the soul the work of the philosophers at the turn from the sixth to the fifth century B.C. The Orphic knowledge of the soul was pervasively present in the work of Xenophanes and Heraclitus (c.535–475). Both of the great philosophers spoke with the authority of the mystic and represented the order of the soul in opposition to the order of the polis. By the middle of the fifth century, finally, the philosophical scene shifted from the Italy of Parmenides and Zeno to the Athens of Anaxagoras and Democritus.

Most important, however, is the point that there were no "schools" in any conceivable sense of the word. The style of Hellenic civilization is indelibly characterized by the absence of temporal and ecclesiastic bureaucracies. Through a miracle of history the geographic area of Hellenic civilization remained undisturbed by foreign invasions from the Doric migration to the Persian Wars, that is, roughly from 1100–500 B.C. During six hundred years, while in the Near and Far East the imperial civilizations with their inevitable bureaucracies were founded, overthrown, and re-established, the geopolitical paradise around the Aegean could develop the "free" civilizations, first, of local clans and aristocracies, and later, of poleis that were so small that no bureaucratic administration of formidable size was needed. Under these historically unique circumstances the transition from archaic to classic Hellas could assume the form of intellectual adventures by individuals, unhampered by the pressure of hierarchies which tend to preserve traditions.

The earliest recorded adventure of this type, the Homeric epic, revealed the free manipulation of a stock of myths. The mythical form was transformed into the image of an aristocratic, courtly society of gods and men, into a world of masterly drawn, intelligible personalities of the "Olympian" clearness that is due to the radical elimination of chthonic horrors. Here was born and moulded the Ionian component of Greek religiousness, that peculiar freedom from horror as well as from the *tremendum* of a "dread God." Man faced the immortals, not with a shudder at his own nothingness, but with a sense of wretchedness, as "the creature of the day," before the splendor of such heightened life, or with the Homeric astonishment, shading off into admiration, when Achilles turns around and sees Athena standing behind him, counselling restraint with a courteous "if you will obey me." From the respectful intimacy of such astonishment (*thambos*) stems the wondering admiration, the Ionian *thaumazein,* before the spectacle of the cosmos which Aristotle still recognized as the origin of philosophical inquiry.

The next adventure, the Hesiodian, brought the inrush of primordial, chthonic divinities into the material of speculation. That inrush was characteristic of the Greek mainland where the continuity of the myth was less broken than in the Ionian cities of the refugees who had been separated from the divinities of their rivers and hills and of the earth under their feet. While the basis of the myth, thus, was broader for Hesiod than for Homer, his work was nevertheless the first great document of both the awakening and the effects of speculation. The materials of the people's myth were submitted, with an almost incredible freedom and insouciance, to the exigencies of the speculative quest for the origins of being and order. Moreover, at the dynamic center of the mythopoetic and speculative effort the personality of a great poet and thinker did not have to be surmised, as in the case of Homer; the creator of the work presented himself in person, fully conscious of what he was doing when he opposed the principle of his new Aletheia to the untruth of older pseudo-inspirations. With the victorious emergence of Jovian Dike over the cosmic and telluric gods, there emerged the self-consciousness of the thinker as the carrier of a new truth in history. The personality of the man who can distinguish verities of order and create the symbols to express them became with Hesiod a new element in the structure of reality.

The same style of intellectual adventure characterized the philosophizing of the great Milesians, of Thales, Anaximander, and Anaximenes, when they replaced the divine figures of the myth, in their search of origins, with symbols drawn from objects and substances of the world of sense perception. Unfortunately we know entirely too little about their work because the Persian conquest, as we have indicated, apparently interrupted the formation of a tradition. The memory of Thales was preserved through anecdotes; his works were so thoroughly lost, that one cannot be quite sure he ever wrote a treatise. Anaximander and Anaximenes were completely forgotten. Their names came to light again when Aristotle and his school undertook a search for predecessors; practically all that we know about their work stems from the excerpts which Aristotle and Theophrastus made from a manuscript they must have obtained. That is not to say that the work of the Milesians remained without effect. For the elimination of the mythical personnel from speculation proper was established. Neither the attack of Xenophanes on the myth, nor the Heraclitean analysis of the soul, nor even the speculation of Parmenides in spite of the fact that it is embedded in a *mythos,* can well be imagined without the Milesian background.

A "school," in the sense of successive generations of thinkers who draw on a common substance provided by the "founder," is possible only when the substance is spiritually and intellectually rich enough to become an effective center for the organization of human souls in rivalry with the common stock of traditions, or when it is a specific, intense variant within the tradition. Before the foundation of the Academy under the impact of Socrates on Plato, only two men can be considered, with appropriate qualifications, as founders of "schools," that is, Pythagoras and Parmenides.

The Pythagorean association was a religious community, with a distinct "way of life," resting on doctrines concerning the fate of the soul, and with a discipline required for securing its purification and immortalization. The instance of Pythagoreanism as a school, however, must be qualified by the political character of the association. As far as the insufficient sources allow a judgment, the Pythagoreans were a political organization or club, similar in type to the *hetaireia,* which evolved, from the free formation of bands of nobles for various purposes of war, plunder, and peaceful banqueting in the pre-polis time, to the small aristocratic clubs in the democratic polis of the fifth century. The Pythagoreans were distinguished from the ordinary *hetaireia* through the considerable size of the association, as well as by the internal, hierarchical organization into initiates and novices. The opinion that Pythagoreanism was sociologically an aristocratic (or oligarchic) branch of the movement of mystery religions, which on the populist side expressed itself in Orphic cult communities, has much to recommend itself.[1]

In the case of Parmenides, on the other hand, there were no traces of formal organization at all. The effect of a "school" resulted from the nature of his didactic poem which, for the first time in the history of philosophy, provided a coherent, argumentative piece of ontological speculation. Here was a mine of metaphysical, epistemological, and logical problems, fit for elaboration by successors who, even without social formalities, would be a "school" through the theoretical intentions derived from their common source.

Hellas did not rise above the level of the city-state, as did the Mesopotamian civilizations, through imperial unification and the development of a political summodeism of the same symbolic type as the myth of the single city-states, but through the efforts of individuals who discovered

---

[1] On the political aspects of Pythagoreanism cf. Kurt von Fritz, *Pythagorean Politics in Southern Italy* (New York, 1940) and Edwin L. Minar, Jr., *Early Pythagorean Politics* (Baltimore, 1942).

the order of the human psyche beyond the order of the polis and articulated their discovery in the symbolic form which they called philosophy. Hence, philosophy was more than an intellectual endeavor in which certain Greek individuals excelled; it was a symbolic form which expressed definite experiences of order in opposition to the polis. The tension between the Hellas of the poets and philosophers, and the polis to which they were in opposition, was the very form of Hellenic civilization. Nevertheless, this form had something elusive in comparison with the Near Eastern empires, because the personal order of a soul through orientation toward transcendent reality could not be institutionalized, but had to rely on its autonomous formation by individual human beings. And since this elusiveness of the form is the cause of the error that philosophy is an "intellectual" or "cultural" activity conducted in a vacuum, without relation to the problems of human existence in society, it becomes all the more important to stress the roots of philosophy in the order of the polis. This problem can be clarified best by a comparison between the Hellenic and the Israelite mortgage of society on the symbolic form.

The leap in being had different results in Israel and Hellas. In Israel it assumed the form of historical existence of a people under God; in Hellas it assumed the form of personal existence of individual human beings under God. If the issue be formulated in this manner, it will be apparent that the "perpetual mortgage of the world-immanent, concrete event on the transcendent truth that on its occasion was revealed," of which we had to speak in the case of Israel,[2] would be less of a burden on Hellenic philosophy than on Israelite revelation. The universal validity of transcendent truth, the universality of the one God over the one mankind, could be more easily disengaged from an individual's discovery of the existence of his psyche under the gods than from the Sinaitic revelation of a people's existence under God. Nevertheless, as Israel had to carry the burden of Canaan, so philosophy had to carry the burden of the polis. For the discoveries, though made by individuals, were made by citizens of a polis; and the new order of the soul, when communicated by its discoverers and creators, inevitably was in opposition to the public order, with the implied or explicit appeal to the fellow citizens to reform their personal conduct, the mores of society, and ultimately the institutions in conformity with the new order. Hellenic philosophy became, therefore, to a considerable extent the articulation of true order of ex-

[2] *Order and History* I, 164, 180.

istence within the institutional framework of an Hellenic polis. That is not necessarily the great defect which moderns frequently believe it to be. For, after all, philosophy grew within the polis; and true philosophical existence is perhaps possible only in an environment resembling the culture and institutions of the polis. That, however, is a complicated question; it will occupy us at length in later volumes of this study, when we have to deal with the problems of a specifically "Christian" and "modern" philosophy; for the moment it will be sufficient to say that the question is far from settled. At any rate, the institutions of the polis were distinctly a limiting factor in the Hellenic exploration of order, down to the great constructions of paradigmatic poleis by Plato and Aristotle.

The preceding reflections, in spite of their brevity and simplifications, will be sufficient as a preliminary orientation. For philosophy as a symbolic form is distinguished from myth and history by its reflective self-consciousness. What philosophy is, need not be ascertained by talking *about* philosophy discursively; it can, and must, be determined by entering *into* the speculative process in which the thinker explicates his experience of order. The philosophers' conscious break with the form of the myth occurred about 500 B.C. The individual steps taken toward a differentiated experience of the psyche, during the two centuries after Hesiod, had the cumulative result of letting the self-conscious soul emerge as the tentative source of order in competition with the myth, as well as with the aristocratic culture of the archaic polis. Ionian lyric and Milesian speculation, the revision of political *aretai* through Tyrtaeus and Solon, tyranny and democratization, the Orphic movement, the Pythagoreans, and the public recognition of Dionysian cults—they all had contributed to the experience of the soul and its order that now became the motivating force in the work of Xenophanes (*c.*565–470), Parmenides (*fl.c.*475), and Heraclitus (*c.*535–475).

With the exception of a few longer passages from the didactic poem of Parmenides, the work of the three mystic-philosophers is preserved only in small fragments. A reconstruction so that the single sentences could be understood in their context is impossible. We shall proceed, therefore, by selecting groups of fragments which bear upon the basic issues in the revolt against the myth and consequently illuminate the meaning of the new order. The first such group will consist of a number of fragments from Xenophanes. He was the first thinker to challenge the authority of Homer and Hesiod on principle on the ground that they accepted the myth, as well as the anthropomorphic conception of the gods, in their work.[3]

§ 2. Xenophanes' Attack on the Myth

1. *The Seemliness of Symbols*

The myth had received its panhellenic form through the poets: "From the beginning [*ex arches*] all have learned from Homer. . . ."[4] Hence the assertion of a truth in opposition to the myth had of necessity to assume the form of an attack on its creators. Xenophanes was the first to dare it. And his attack became the paradigmatic expression of the tension between the mystic-philosopher and the poet which still, in the fourth century, motivated Plato's attack on Homer in the *Republic*.

The tension did not originate in a banausic aversion to poetry— though even today critics of Plato indulge in that wild assumption— but was caused by the authority which the poet had acquired in Hellas. Homer and Hesiod had transformed the primitive and local myths into the intermediate form of a speculative myth with panhellenic validity. For the area of Hellenic civilization they had acquired a public authority with regard to the right understanding of the order of human existence that corresponded to the royal and sacerdotal authorities of the Near Eastern empires. The attack of Xenophanes was directed, not against poetry (which in that bourgeois abstraction did not exist in Hellas), but against the form of the myth as an obstacle to the adequate understanding of the order of the soul. The poetic form itself he did not question at all, but accepted it as the adequate instrument for expressing his own truth. Xenophanes primarily used the form of the *silloi*, of short satirical poems. Even a truth opposed to the myth still had to be couched

---

[3] In the following chapters all quotations from pre-Socratic thinkers, unless other sources are mentioned, refer to Diels-Kranz, *Fragmente der Vorsokratiker* (7th ed., Berlin, 1954). A complete English translation of the B-Fragments is available in Kathleen Freeman, *Ancilla to the Pre-Socratic Philosophers* (Oxford, 1948). Valuable as an aid is the same author's *The Pre-Socratic Philosophers* (Oxford, 1946). Most of the fragments are accessible in English translation in John Burnet, *Early Greek Philosophy* (4th ed., London, 1948). The fragments of Xenophanes are also available in the English translation of J. M. Edmonds in *Elegy and Iambus* I (Loeb Classical Library). The works of interpretation most frequently used are Werner Jaeger, *Paideia* I (2d ed., New York, 1945); Olof Gigon, *Der Ursprung der griechischen Philosophie* (Basel, 1945); Werner Jaeger, *The Theology of the Early Greek Philosophers* (Oxford, 1947); and Bruno Snell, *Die Entdeckung des Geistes,* (2d ed., Hamburg, 1948). Basic is still Eduard Zeller, *Die Philosophie der Griechen,* I/1–2 (6th and 7th eds., Leipzig, 1920–23).

[4] Diels-Kranz, *Fragmente der Vorsokratiker* (1954), Xenophanes B 10.

in verse in order to appear in authoritative garb before the public; prose was not yet a vehicle of authoritative communication.

We arrange the pertinent fragments in three groups:

(1) The attack itself was directed against the improper presentation of the gods. "Homer and Hesiod have ascribed to the gods all things that are a shame and disgrace among men, such as stealing, adultery and cheating each other" (B 11). The reason for such misrepresentation Xenophanes apparently sought and found in the naiveté of the early poets. "Mortals suppose that gods are born, and have clothes, voices and bodily forms like theirs" (B 14). Men create gods in their image, down to racial differences: "Ethiopians make their gods flat-nosed and black, the Thracians let theirs have blue eyes and red hair" (B 16). And if horses and oxen and lions could make works of art like men "they would form their gods horse-like and oxen-like, each after its own kind" (B 15).

(2) To such fancies Xenophanes opposed his own conception of God: "One God is greatest among gods and men, not like mortals in body or thought [noema]" (B 23). The divine is a living being (zoon) though not of articulated form, for "all through it sees, all through it thinks, all through it hears" (B 24). Without effort it sways all things through its thought (B 25). "It ever abides in the self-same place and never moves; nor is it seemly [epiprepei] for it to go now hither now thither" (B 26).

(3) Concerning source and certainty of his knowledge Xenophanes raised no specific claims: "The gods did not grant knowledge of all things to mortals from the beginning, but by seeking they find in time what is better" (B 18); and "there never was nor will be a man who knows about the gods and all the things I speak of. Even if by chance he should say the full truth, yet he would not know that he does so; there is fancy in all things" (B 34).

We know nothing about the larger context of these fragments; each of them must stand for itself. The arrangement in three groups does not reflect an intention of their author.

The key to the understanding of the fragments lies in the word *epiprepei* which means "it is seemly." What Homer and Hesiod have to say about the gods is unseemly; what Xenophanes has to say in his turn presumably is seemly. No criteria of seemliness, however, are given, and Fragments 18 and 34 indicate that they are in historical evolution. There is an element of fancy (*dokos*) in assertions concerning gods and other things whereof Xenophanes speaks; and since there are no objective criteria the full truth will not be recognized as such even if attained. Xenophanes himself might even be exposed to charges similar to the ones which he levels against Homer and Hesiod if the notions about seemliness should change.

That is exactly what happened to Xenophanes in the next generation at the hands of Heraclitus. For the Ephesian said: "Much learning [*polymathie*] does not teach understanding [*noon*]; else it would have taught Hesiod, Pythagoras, Xenophanes, and Hecataeus" (B 40). On this occasion, however, it became clear that the criteria of seemliness, though changing, were not arbitrary. For Heraclitus gave, if not a definition of criteria, at least an indication of the region of experience which authorized the notion of seemliness; in one of the fragments (B 45) he said: "You will not find the boundaries of the soul though travelling every path; so deep is its logos." Heraclitus had discovered the soul and its dimension in depth; he could oppose "deep-knowing" (*bathys*) to "much-knowing" (*polys*). The depth of the soul revealed itself as the new source of knowledge. We shall return to this problem in the chapter on Heraclitus.

While the notion of *epiprepei* required considerable further elaboration it was, nevertheless, Xenophanes who conceived it for the first time. With his opposition to the myth of Homer and Hesiod began the conscious distinction between various types of symbolic forms that unfolded in the following centuries until it culminated in the Varronic classification of the *genera theologiae* as mythical, civil, and physical theology. From Varro's *De rebus divinis* and Cicero's *De natura Deorum* it entered the Christian literature and developed into the Augustinian distinction between a *theologia naturalis* (the former physical or philosophical) and a *theologia civilis* (to which St. Augustine was inclined to subordinate also the poetic or mythical theology); to both of these latter categories was then opposed the Christian *theologia supranaturalis*.[5] The classification of symbolic forms, thus, has a long history, beginning with Xenophanes.

An epoch in that history was marked by Plato's treatment of the problem in *Republic* II, since it involved the creation of the term *theology*. In discussing the education of children who will grow into the

---

[5] Jaeger, *Theology*, 1ff. and 49ff.

guardians of his Politeia, Plato raised the question which kind of stories should be told to the young in order to inculcate in their souls the proper traits of character. Again the fables of Homer and Hesiod were attacked as unsuitable, and now the unsuitability was specifically characterized by the term "lie" (*pseudos*) (377 d–e). The term *pseudos* continued the Hesiodian procedure (*Theogony* 27) of designating the older myths as falsehood (*pseudea*). As examples of lies Plato gave instances of immoral conduct, violation of filial piety, wars between the gods, Gigantomachia and Titanomachia. Such lies should be replaced, in the education of the young, by stories following a more fitting pattern. And on that occasion Plato introduced the term "types of theology" (*typoi peri theologias*) (379 a) as a technical term for such patterns. The rest of Book II then was concerned with an exposition of the true "types."

Plato's exposition culminated in the notion of the "true lie" (*alethos pseudos*), the lie in the heart of the soul where we know about the true nature of the gods. Misconception about the gods is not an ordinary lie for which may be found extenuating circumstances. It is the supreme lie which consists in an "ignorance within the soul" (*en te psyche agnoia*) (382 a–b). The ignorance of the soul is the source of mythopoetic figments. To the *phantasmata* or *plasmata* of the myth Plato opposed the truth of the Idea. In so far as his own "types of theology" were concerned with goodness, changelessness and truthfulness, Plato offered in this section of the *Republic* the most explicit self-interpretation of philosophy as the new theology in opposition to the types of the older myth.

2. *Anthropomorphism*

The conscious differentiation of the new theology from the myth begins with the Xenophantic *epiprepei*. Before we can examine the seemly and unseemly features themselves, however, we must remove a further problem which from Xenophanes onward has agitated the philosophy of symbolic forms.

Xenophanes does not simply berate the poets because they attribute disgraceful actions to the gods, but also develops a theory concerning the motives of such unseemly attributions, as well as a theory concerning the fallacy involved in them. The gods, he opines, are endowed with improper attributes because man creates gods in his image. This is the fallacy which modern sociologists call "anthropomorphism." According to Comte the history of human thought moves from anthropomorphic theology, through metaphysics, to positive science. Xenophanes must be credited with the formulation of the theory that the myth is an anthropomorphic representation of divinity, to be superseded with the advance of insight by more appropriate symbols. Since the theory has had far-reaching consequences, we must briefly examine the nature of the problem.

The characterization of mythical symbolization as anthropomorphic is a theoretical mistake. In the first place, the theory would require certain elementary emendations in order to be debatable at all. Obviously, in the Greek myth the gods never were really represented as human beings. The gods were distinguished from men through their immortality; they were physiologically distinguished through their living on a special diet; and they were endowed with a variety of nonhuman qualities such as superior knowledge and strength, the ability to be invisible and to change their form; and so forth. To speak of anthropomorphic representation of gods without such qualifications is as inapposite as to find angels in a Renaissance painting represented "realistically," overlooking the minor point that the representation of human-shaped creatures floating on clouds is in itself unrealistic. As soon, however, as such emendations are made, and the meaning of anthropomorphism is properly restricted to the representation of gods as beings who on occasion assume human shape, and talk and act like men, we become aware of the fundamental theoretical problem that such partial transfer of human qualities (which does not affect the essential divinity of the gods) may have something to do with the idea which man has of himself. Is it not probable, we may ask, that human qualities are transferred to gods only as long as the spheres of the divine and human are not quite clearly set off against each other? That "anthropomorphism" is possible only as long as the idea of man is not too clearly differentiated? That "anthropomorphism" occurs only when it cannot occur at all because an idea of man that could be transferred to the gods has not yet developed? And that it tends to disappear precisely when a transferable idea of man has been formed at last?

As a matter of historical fact the problem of anthropomorphism becomes visible, as in the case of Xenophanes, when the psyche and its self-consciousness begins to emerge. That is the occasion on which thinkers discover that something is wrong with the representation of gods, even if they do not know precisely what is "unseemly." To be sure, part of the unseemliness is found in the attribution of human shape, voice, and dress to the gods; but to a much more important part, it is found in the attribution of conduct that is considered a "disgrace and reproach" among men. A new, differentiated sensitiveness of man recognizes as improper among gods what is improper among men. With the discovery of the psyche and its order as the specifically human characteristic, the gods must live up to the new standards of man. This is the problem even of Hesiod, though in his work it does not yet break through to the level of critical discussion. The story of the *Theogony* is, after all, the story of the elimination of the "unseemly" gods through the Titanomachia, and of the advent of the more seemly order of Zeus and his Dike. Xenophanes, through his very attack on Hesiod, continues the purifying operation on the myth that was begun by the earlier poet. Hence we may say that anthropomorphic representation of gods is experienced as embarrassing when the gods do *not* act as a more differentiated, sensitive man would act. Anthropomorphism appears in retrospect as a symbolization of gods that corresponds to a past phase in the self-understanding of man. The problem does not arise within any given phase of self-understanding, because in every present the symbolization of gods is in harmony with the degree of differentiation which man has reached. Xenophanes for instance, while criticizing Hesiod for his anthropomorphism, is not at all troubled by his own symbolization of god as a being which hears, sees, and thinks, and always abides in the same place. Behind the term anthropomorphism, which has become a scientistic cliché, hides the process in which the idea of man differentiates and correlatively with it the symbolization of transcendence.

Obviously, this process has a limit. It reaches its climax when the differentiation of man has advanced to the point where the nucleus of the spiritual soul, the *anima animi* in the Augustinian sense, is discovered. At this ineffable point of openness towards transcendent reality, at this heart of the soul where the infusion of grace is experienced, the divinity becomes ineffable, too. The god of the mystic is nameless, beyond dogmatic symbolization. At this climax of the process the problem of anthropomorphism dissolves into the new problem of the *nomina Dei* as analogical predicates of the ineffable *ens perfectissimum*. In so far as this problem has through St. Thomas received the technical name of *analogia entis,* the Xenophantic criticism of the myth, as well as the postulate of seemliness, is the first conscious, though still primitive, attempt at dealing with the analogy of being.[6]

The fallacy of interpreting an earlier complex of symbols as a rational construction that would presuppose a later degree of differentiation, as we find it for the first time in Xenophanes, has remained a pattern of historical misinterpretation to this day. We must briefly consider a modern variant of the fallacy, the Animism of Tylor, because it has become a source of misunderstandings of the Hellenic history of order through the mediation of Rohde's *Psyche.*[7]

Tylor has developed the Xenophantic fallacy into a principle of historiography. "As to the religious doctrines and practices examined, these are treated as belonging to theological systems devised by human reason, without supernatural aid or revelation; in other words, as being developments of Natural Religion."[8] The laudable resolve to treat symbols as historical phenomena, without regard to a transcendental source of inspiration, derailed (through a complicated chain of misunderstandings that we cannot unravel on this occasion) into the assumption that the symbolization of transcendence is a "system devised by human reason." Consistently Tylor created the figure of the "ancient savage philosopher"[9] who performed the most astonishing feats of ratiocination, culminating in the doctrine of "spiritual beings." "I purpose here, under the name of Animism, to investigate the deep-lying doctrine of Spiritual Beings, which embodies the very essence of Spiritualistic as opposed to Materialistic philosophy."[10]

It is hardly necessary today to elaborate on the anachronism of projecting such concepts into primitive cultures. Let us mention only that the "savage philosopher" speculates on the "difference between a living body and a dead one,"[11] while even in Homer the idea of a living body does not yet exist; or, that the "personal soul or spirit" possesses "the personal consciousness and volition of its corporeal owner,"[12] while again

---

[6] For the appearance of the problem of the *analogia entis* within the compact form of the cosmological myth cf. *Order and History* I, 87.

[7] Sir Edward B. Tylor, *Primitive Culture* (1871); references are to the Third American Edition, New York, 1889. Erwin Rohde, *Psyche. Seelenkult und Unsterblichkeitsglaube der Griechen* (Freiburg, 1891–94).

[8] Tylor, *Primitive Culture*, I, 427.

[9] *Ibid.*, 428.

[10] *Ibid.*, 428.

[11] *Ibid.*, 428.

[12] *Ibid.*, 429.

the Homeric figures have no personal soul or consciousness, and while even in Plato the meaning of volition (the Greek language, incidentally, has no word for it) is yet so undeveloped that the problems of ethics can become conscious only on occasion of concrete decisions (*proairesis*).[13]

3. *The Universality of the Divine*

The criticism of anthropomorphic representation will appear under a new aspect if one considers the Xenophantic alternative to the Homeric and Hesiodian myth. As long as men create gods in their own image on the comparatively undifferentiated level described and criticized by Xenophanes, there will be as many different gods as there are men who indulge in such creations. Only when this primitive symbolization is abandoned will it be possible to recognize the "one god who is greatest" as a common god for all men, correlative to the identical humanity in all human beings. Behind the critique of anthropomorphism there appears the experience of divine and human universality as the motivating force. Primitive symbolizations particularize and parochialize divinity along with humanity; a universal god for all men requires a different "type" of symbolization. When we speak of god analogically, as we must, not all analogies are equally suitable to the universality of his nature, nor to the universality of human nature. The concern about seemliness, thus, reveals itself as the concern about adequate representation of a universal god. In the pursuit of this problem Xenophanes opposed himself to Homer and Hesiod, while actually he continued the work of the earlier poets; for the Homeric and Hesiodian creation superseded the local myths by a Panhellenic myth, while Xenophanes took the next step toward the creation of a universal divinity.

I have stressed the universalism in Xenophanes' theology more strongly than is usually done because it seems to be an independent

---

[13] The criticisms should not detract from the merit which Tylor's theory had in its time. Tylor's Animism, as a theory of religion, was a distinct improvement over the crude assumptions entertained by anthropologists in the middle of the nineteenth century. It must be seen against the background of such views as revealed in Lang's assertion that the aborigines of Australia have "nothing whatever of the character of religion, or of religious observance, to distinguish them from the beasts that perish" (Tylor, *ibid.*, 418). The principles underlying our criticism do not substantially differ from those of Cassirer, *Philosophie der Symbolischen Formen*, Volume II: *Das Mythische Denken* (Berlin, 1925), 191ff. The neo-Kantian terminology, as well as the peculiar vagueness of Cassirer's philosophical style unfortunately deprive his argument of much of the effectiveness which in substance it has. I want to stress all the more that Cassirer's work is still the most serious attempt to deal with the problem of the myth on principle.

factor in the new type of symbolization, of equal rank with the oneness of divinity. The point is of importance for two reasons.

In the first place, while Xenophanes himself does not have a special term for predicating the universality of his divinity, the problem achieves terminological differentiation already in the work of his younger contemporary, Heraclitus. In Heraclitus' speculation on social order the factor in the divine-one which constitutes community among men is terminologically distinguished as the *xynon*, as that which is "common." The less articulate presence of the factor in Xenophanes should be noted as a matter of tracing the continuity of the problem.

The awareness of universality as an independent motif in the thought of Xenophanes will, secondly, aid us in understanding a problem that must remain puzzling as long as we fix our attention exclusively on the oneness of Xenophanes' god. The evocation of the One God who is greatest among gods and men (B 23) is an important event in the religious history of mankind, and as such it has occasioned a debate among scholars concerning the question whether Xenophanes was a monotheistic thinker. Some are inclined to answer the question in the affirmative. Others point to the fact that Xenophanes speaks of gods in the plural more than once and that, therefore, he should be considered a polytheist after all. Still others point to fragments like "She whom we call Iris, she too is a cloud, purple and scarlet and yellow to view" (B 32), and are ready to settle for pantheism. The debate on this question is, in our opinion, inapposite because it misconceives the symbolization of divinity as a matter of theoretical systems. It rests on the assumption that "religion" consists in adherence to a "system" of propositions concerning existence and nature of god. Moreover, it assumes that a thinker is obliged to make up his mind about his adherence to one or the other of the mutually exclusive systems—for, obviously, if one assumes the existence of many gods one cannot logically assume the existence of only one god at the same time; and if one assumes the existence of one personal, transcendental god, one cannot simultaneously assume one impersonal, world-immanent divinity. In opposition to this rationalistic attitude I should like to recall a dictum of Goethe: "As a moralist I am a monotheist; as an artist I am a polytheist; as a naturalist I am a pantheist."

Centuries of rational theological and secularized speculation have atrophied our awareness for the prespeculative complexity of the experiences in which transcendence is apprehended by man. The divine can be experienced as universal (or common in the Heraclitian sense) without necessarily being experienced as one; Xenophanes could evoke the One God as a universal god without attaching systematic importance to the attribute of oneness. He was a religious genius who discovered participation in a nameless realissimum as the essence of his humanity. Moreover, he understood the essentiality of his discovery at least to the extent that he could express it in the symbol of a "greatest god" for all men—with the implication that the realissimum was correlative to the experienced transcendence of existence common to all human beings. It was the universality of the realissimum that made all idiosyncratic representations of particular gods appear "unseemly." Nevertheless, the gods who were unseemly represented were still the gods; the unseemliness concerned their representation, it did not concern their divinity. Xenophanes could well accept for himself the saying attributed to Thales: "The world is full of gods." The universality of transcendence discovered by him did not abolish the old gods; it only improved their understanding.

We get a glimpse of this new religiousness in practice in the beautiful banquet elegy that begins:

"Now that the floor is clean and the hands of all
and the cups . . ."

When the preparations for the banquet are made and the altar is decked with flowers, first "joyful men must hymn the God with holy tales and pure words." And when the banquet is in progress, and the time has come for the men to show their memory of myths, then let them not tell "the battles of Titans or Giants, nor of Centaurs, these fictions [*plasmata*] of the men of old, nor of vehement discords, for in these things there is no worth; but ever to hold in reverence [*prometheia*] the gods, that is good" (B 1).[14]

4. The Divinity of the One

We have isolated one of the experiential components that went into the symbol of the "greatest god." But there is more expressed in it than the mere experience of transcendence. For the new god is unborn, he did not come into being like the Hesiodian gods (B 14), he always stays in the same place and does not move hither and thither (B 26), and from his unmoved position he sways all things through his mind (*noou phreni*)

---

[14] Cf. Plato, *Republic* 378b–c. The Xenophantic formulation has become a "type" of the new theology.

(B 25). In brief: he already bears a remarkable resemblance to the Aristotelian prime mover. The debate about a Xenophantic monotheism, while resting on erroneous assumptions, certainly is motivated by a real problem.

Fortunately we are informed about the nature of the problem through some observations of Aristotle. In *Metaphysics* I Aristotle surveys the variants of monistic philosophy. Parmenides understood the One "according to the logos"; Melissus understood it "according to matter" (*hyle*); Xenophanes, however, did not make any clear assertion and seemed not to have grasped the nature of either of these causes. Nevertheless, Xenophanes was the first of the thinkers about the One (*henizontes*), for "looking up at the expanse of the Heaven [*ten holon ouranon*], 'The One,' he said, 'is the God.' "[15] According to Aristotle, thus, Xenophanes is the first of a group of monistic thinkers. As distinguished from the later Eleatics he has not yet advanced speculation to the point of interpreting the One either as Logos or Hyle. His genius has a peculiar spiritual directness which can be sensed in the glance at the Heaven, followed by the assurance that the One is God. The most important part of this account is for us the formulation of the assurance. God is perhaps not one, but the One is the God. The experience is concerned with the One, and of this One divinity is predicated.

The attribution of divinity to the One suggests that the Milesian speculation on nature (*physis*) has influenced the thought of Xenophanes; and more specifically, one can sense the influence of certain ideas of Anaximander. The Milesians had divested the problem of origin of the mythical costume which it still wore in the Hesiodian *Theogony*. Hesiod had carefully distinguished his archaic trinity (Chaos, Gaea, Eros) from the generations of the gods; but his primordial divinities themselves still "came into being" because this was the "type" for the gods of the myth. In the Milesian speculation on becoming (*physis*) the medium of the myth was abandoned, and as a consequence, one of the things or substances that were given in sense experience could be posited as the something from which the world of experienced things originated. In this sense, Thales had posited water as the origin of things. Anaximander then took the decisive step to divest the originating something of all qualities that were given in finite experience, and to posit an infinite

---

[15] Aristotle, *Metaphysics* I, 986b18ff. Diels-Kranz, Xenophanes A 30. There is no reason to doubt the reliability of the information. Cf. Jaeger, *Theology*, 51ff.

something as the origin of the qualitatively differentiated content of the world. He called this something the Boundless, the *apeiron*.

It is again Aristotle who informs us about the speculation concerning the Apeiron. "Everything either is a beginning or is from a beginning; of the Boundless [*apeiron*], however, there is no beginning because otherwise it would have a boundary [*peras*]. In so far as it is a beginning [*arche*] it is imperishable. For what has come into being must of necessity come to an end; and there is also an end of all that is perishable. Therefore, as we say, it [the Boundless] has no beginning [*arche*], but is itself the beginning of all things." This Apeiron "encompasses and governs all things, as say those who do not posit other causes besides the Apeiron," as for instance the Nous of Anaxagoras or the Philia of Empedocles. And then Aristotle closes with the formulation that seems to have been the inspiration of Xenophanes: "And this is the Divine [*to theion*], for it is immortal and imperishable, as Anaximander and most of the natural philosophers [*physiologoi*] maintain." [16]

The meaning of the passage is clear enough, provided one avoids modernistic misconstructions. The *physis* of the Milesians is still close to the meaning of the verb *phynai* (to grow, to emerge); *physis* can, therefore, be synonymous with *genesis*.[17] Since nature is something that has grown, an inquiry into nature can attend either to the process or its result. And if the inquiry turns to the process, the problem of the beginning, as well as its dialectics, will come into view. The resulting speculation on *physis* will, then, be a symbolism intermediate between the Hesiodian theogony and the later speculation on time and creation as we find it, for instance, in St. Augustine. For the Milesians speculated on the origin in the manner of Hesiod, while their philosophizing was no longer bound by the form of the myth. They had achieved one of the great differentiating insights in the history of mankind when they discovered nature, as it is given in sense experience, as an autonomous realm; and their speculation moved in this new medium. Nevertheless, while the Milesians had differentiated the realm and process of nature, even they had not yet differentiated dialectics as a logic of process and the infinite; hence, their dialectics of the Apeiron could not separate from the specific speculation on the process of nature. In this intermediate situation, on

[16] Aristotle, *Physics* III, 4, 203b6ff.; Diels-Kranz, Anaximander A 15. The reliability of the passage as a correct rendering of Anaximander's ideas has been questioned. For the argument in its favor cf. Jaeger, *Theology*, Chapter III, especially the notes.

[17] Jaeger, *Theology*, 20ff.

the occasion of the Milesian discovery, emerged the experience of the process of nature as infinite. The openness of man toward nature, when it was experienced as a new type of transcendence into the boundlessness of the world, found its fit symbol in Anaximander's Apeiron. The Milesian transcendence into nature must be ranked as an independent experience by the side of the Xenophantic universal transcendence. The "physiologist" in the Aristotelian sense is a philosopher of transcendence in his own right, by the side of the "theologian." The two experiences of transcendence, represented in the fourth century by Aristotle and Plato respectively, have remained the motivating forces of two types of philosophizing to this day.

As soon, however, as the new type of transcendence was discovered, its relation to the transcendence of the gods became problematic. The Aristotelian report is revealing with regard to this question. The "boundless" that was experienced as the beginning (*arche*) of all things had to be "unborn and unperishable"; it was something that "encompassed all and governed all things." These, however, were the attributes of divinity. Hence Anaximander, reasoning that the something was "immortal and imperishable," endowed it with the predicate "the Divine." It is the first occasion on which the abstract *to theion* appeared. In Anaximander's formulation the "physiological" and "theological" experiences of transcendence converged toward the point where the One would become the God of the "monists." In the immanent logic of this process, there is no reason why the blending of the experiences should result in "monotheism" rather than in "pantheism." On the contrary, the analysis shows that a fixation of theological systems was improbable as long as the originating experiences were alive. Moreover, the experiences were capable of variations which do not fit into any theological "system"; and that was true in particular of the Xenophantic variety. For Xenophanes' "glance at the expanse of the Heaven" by which he recognized the One as the God, was neither a speculation on *physis,* nor the experience of universal transcendence, but an experience *sui generis* in which is prefigured the religiousness of the late Plato and of Philippus of Opus, and even of the Aristotelian *bios theoretikos.*[18]

[18] Through the mediation of Aristotle this complex of experiences and speculations has continued as a "type" of theologizing into Western Christianity. The Xenophantic formula "the One is the God" is still recognizable in the Thomistic *primum ens quod Deum dicimus* (*Contra Gentiles* I, 14). The reader should compare our analysis in the text with St. Thomas, *Contra Gentiles* I, 10–14, *i.e.,* with the classic example of the transposition of the pre-Socratic complex of experiences into the Christian medium of theologizing.

CHAPTER 7

The Aretai and the Polis

1. The Sophia of Xenophanes

The insights of Xenophanes were gained in opposition to the culture of the surrounding society. Fortunately there is preserved a fragment of an elegy (B 2) in which the poet himself dwells on the conflict and its nature:

> If a man through swiftness of foot should gain victory,
> Or through the pentathlon, in the precinct of Zeus
> By Pisa's stream at Olympia, or through wrestling,
> Or if he should hold his own in painful boxing,
> Or in that terrible contest that is called pancration—
> He would become glorious in the view of the citizens,
> He would gain a front-seat of honor at the games,
> He would receive food at the people's cost
> From the polis, and a gift for a keepsake—
> Or if he would win with the horses,
>   all this would be his share—
>
> And he would not be worthy to have it as I am!
>   For better than the strength
> Of men or of horses is our wisdom [*sophie*]!
>
> Senseless indeed is custom in such matter;
>   it is not right [*dikaion*]
> To judge strength higher than holy wisdom [*sophie*].
>
> Even if there arise a good boxer among the people,
> Or one good at the pentathlon, or at wrestling,
> Or at swiftness of foot—which is held highest in honor
> Among feats of men's strength in the games—
> Never for that would the polis be better in order [*eunomie*];
> And little joy would accrue to the polis
> If a man through his efforts conquer at the banks of Pisa,
> For that will not fatten the store-rooms of the polis.

The elegy is a precious document for the philosopher's consciousness of order at the time when his speculation enters into opposition to society. In the proud declaration of his own worth in the first person, Xenophanes follows the Hesiodian paradigm, fortified now by two centuries of development of personality through the lyric poets. Moreover, his self-consciousness is rooted in the authority of his *sophie*, in the same manner as Hesiod's was rooted in the authority of his specific *aletheia* (truth). What the precise meaning of the term *sophie* is, cannot be determined by a simple translation. We have rendered it as "wisdom" in order to preserve the terminological continuity from the Xenophantic to the Platonic *sophia*. Others render it as "art" or "skill"—but not much is gained by such interpretive translations which in their turn would require an elaboration of their meaning. The meaning of *sophie* can only be determined by reference to the whole of the Xenophantic work; it should be comprehensively understood as the differentiation of personality, together with the correlative body of knowledge, that has been studied in the preceding chapter, in the section "Xenophanes' Attack on the Myth." With this comprehensive meaning of *sophie* in mind we can approach the rebellion in the name of the new excellence (*arete*) of man against the aristocratic, agonal culture of the Hellenic polis in which the victor at Olympia has become the successor to the Homeric hero.

The attack on Homer and Hesiod is broadened in the elegy by the attack on the glory of panhellenic excellence. With regard to its theoretical structure, the new attack closely resembles the earlier one on the poets. The discovery of *sophie* is accompanied by an insight concerning the rank of the newly differentiated area of the soul; the philosopher knows that "it is not right" to judge strength higher in rank than his wisdom; the formula "it is not right," which appears on this occasion corresponds to the earlier "it is not seemly." Theoretically the new formula suffers, therefore, from the same fallacy as the first one in so far as those who hold in honor the Olympian excellences do not actually judge them higher in rank than the Xenophantic wisdom, for the good reason that they have no knowledge of the latter. The new wisdom as a "knowledge about" the things of which Xenophanes speaks is accessible only to those who have developed it existentially as an awareness and habituation of the soul. Hence Xenophanes rightly speaks of "our wisdom" possessively, for the others, who supposedly have no proper regard for it, indeed do not possess it at all.

Knowledge and existence depend on one another; the order of being becomes visible only to those whose souls are well ordered. The correlation, which becomes an issue on occasion of the Xenophantic attacks, developed into the fundamental problem of an epistemology of political science, that is, into the problem of the double status of types of cognition as (a) cognitive functions of the mind and (b) as excellences or virtues of the soul. In Plato we shall see the problem unfolding into the insight that the "true" science of man in society is accessible only to the philosophers who have seen the Agathon. And in Aristotle we shall find the types of cognition (wisdom, science, art, prudence, and intellection) as the dianoetic excellences which enable man to lead the *bios theoretikos*. In Xenophanes the problem appears still in a rudimentary form, embedded in the practical act of a rebellion of "holy wisdom" against a glory that contributes nothing to the right order (*eunomia*) of the polis.

The practical aspects of the rebellion set a further pattern which governed Hellenic politics down to Aristotle. The fallacy of berating people for their preferences, while in fact they live innocently in a tradition without knowledge of a preferable alternative, was more than a theoretical problem; as so frequently with fallacies of this type, there was a practical issue behind the façade of a theoretical mistake. Xenophanes was not satisfied with having gained his wisdom; he also wanted public recognition. This desire must not be understood in the cheap meaning of modern parlance. Xenophanes did not want attention for idiosyncrasies. He had discovered new areas of experience; and he knew that the differentiation of such experiences was an actualization of the common essence of man. The traditional culture of the polis had not yet risen to the new level of human actualization; but he sensed the rise as the duty of every human being individually, as well as of the community in general. The qualification of the cultural tradition as a "preference" (while indeed no such preference exists) must be understood, therefore, against the background of the implied postulate that knowledge with regard to the essentials of humanity is a duty and, consequently, that ignorance in such matters is preference.

The discovery of transcendence, of intellectual and spiritual order, while occurring in the souls of individual human beings, is not a matter of "subjective opinion"; once the discovery is made, it is endowed with the quality of an authoritative appeal to every man to actualize it in his own soul; the differentiation of man, the discovery of his nature, is a source of social authority. The assertion of such authority as well as the appeal to the ignorant to actualize the potentialities of their humanity, is a permanent factor in the dynamics of order. It is discernible as the justifying core even in such atrocious distortions as the colonization of "backward" peoples by the more "progressive" ones. While the objective authority of the appeal does not endow the prophet or discoverer from whom it emanates with a subjective right to maltreat his ignorant fellow men, there certainly is on the other side no subjective right to be ignorant. The unity of mankind is the community of the spirit. With the unfolding of the nature of man in history the men who actualize hitherto dormant potentialities in their souls live under the duty of communicating their insights to their fellow men; and on the others is incumbent the duty of living in openness to such communication.[1]

This fundamental structure of the progress of mankind in history must be presupposed in the Xenophantic attack on agonal culture. The attack is not a personal affair but a type-creating event. The critique of society with the authority of the spiritual appeal remains from now on a type for the expression of political thought. The awareness of this type created by Xenophanes will help us to understand certain aspects of the Platonic work which otherwise might remain puzzling. The peculiar tension of the *Republic*, for instance, stems from its character as an appeal, directed to the Athenians with the spiritual authority of the philosopher. It would be an unfortunate misunderstanding to interpret this intense call for spiritual reform as a rational blueprint of an "ideal constitution."

Moreover, even the specific limitation of the Xenophantic appeal has set a type for later Hellenic politics. On principle, the appeal might be directed to mankind at large; it might transcend the limits of the polis and even of Hellas. In fact, however, both rebellion and appeal of Xenophanes accept the polis as its social field. Agonal culture comes under attack because a victory at Olympia contributes nothing to the *eunomia*

---

[1] It should be noted that the violent assertion of the right to be ignorant with regard to essentials of humanity, which is characteristic of the contemporary movements of progressivism, positivism, communism, and national-socialism, is an epochal event in the history of order in so far as for the first time movements of worldwide effectiveness systematically propagate the destruction of the unity of mankind.

of the polis; and inversely, the new excellence of *sophia* is in search of recognition not by man but by the citizen. The Xenophantic limitation of the appeal has remained typical for the later speculation on the existence of man in society. Even Plato, in spite of his concern about the spiritual reform of Hellas, did not let his institutional imagination range beyond an Hellenic federation under the hegemony of a savior-polis. And Aristotle still considered man a *politikon zoon* in the strict sense, that is, a being that could actualize the excellence of the *bios theoretikos* only as the citizen of a polis. The process of spiritual and intellectual differentiation of man was conceived as bound up with the culture of the polis to the bitter end in the Macedonian conquest.

2. *The Savage Valor of Tyrtaeus*

Xenophanes wanted to have his *sophie* recognized by the polis; he was in rebellion against agonal culture, not against the polis itself. The latter he accepted, together with the virtues that created it and kept it in existence; and these creating and preserving virtues obviously were not exhausted by those excellences which carried a man to victory in Olympia. The Xenophantic exhortations are an effort at re-ordering a field of excellences already in existence. We must now examine this field as far as the extant fragments permit. We shall begin with an elegy by Tyrtaeus.

The elegy of Xenophanes created a new type only in so far as it articulated the opposition of the mystic-philosopher to the agonal culture of the polis; the literary form used for that purpose, however, was already a type in itself. The structure of the Tyrtaean elegy to which we now turn is the same as that of the later Xenophantic.[2] First comes the enumeration of excellences held in high traditional esteem; then follows the exhortation to live up to the new *arete*. Tyrtaeus begins: "I would not remember nor put in my tale a man for his excellence [*arete*] in racing or wrestling; not if he had the size and strength of Cyclops, nor if victoriously he could outrun the Thracian northwind; not if he were comelier of figure than Tithonus, or richer than Midas or Cinyras; not if he were more kingly than Pelops, or sweeter of tongue than Adrastus." This catalogue of excellences, not rejected but relegated to second place, is more archaic than the Xenophantic. While the opposition to the

[2] *Elegy and Iambus*, ed. and trans. by J. M. Edmonds (Loeb Classical Library), I, Tyrtaeus 12.

rank which the Olympian victories hold in public valuation already makes itself felt,[3] the list still includes comeliness, wealth, royalty, and persuasiveness, in other words, the Homeric excellences of the early aristocratic society. If a man were famous for all these traditional virtues, Tyrtaeus continues, he would not praise him unless he also had the new virtue, surpassing all others, the *thouris alke,* the "savage valor": "For a man is no good in war unless he can bear the sight of bloody slaughter and can reach out to his enemy, pressing close on him. This is virtue [*arete*]! The best and fairest prize to win for a youth among men! This is a common good [*xynon esthlon*] for the polis and all her people when a man perseveres among the foremost fighters, standing firm, forgetting all shameful flight, abiding with body and soul."

The structure of the Tyrtaean elegy (as far as we have related it), is the same as that of the Xenophantic. Nevertheless, on closer examination the elegy shows peculiarities that will permit a more intimate understanding of the relationship between Hellenic literary forms and the ideas which they convey. The origin of the elegiac form is obscure; Tyrtaeus did not invent it but he put it to a specific use. In the present case he used it for addressing a concrete audience of Lacedaemonian citizen-soldiers, exhorting them to practice the virtue of "savage valor." This raises the question on principle whether there is a connection between the lyric form of Tyrtaeus and its protreptic content. We have traced the problem of exhortation already through Homer and Hesiod. In the Homeric poems the exhortations were addressed by one person of the epic to another; the exhortatory relation lay entirely within the poem itself; the poet did not appear in person exhorting his audience—though we may take it for granted that the recitations not only of exhortatory passages but also of the feats of the heroes were experienced by the listeners as exhortations to live up to the great models. Hesiod's *Works and Days* brought the first great innovation in so far as the exhortation was no longer enacted within the story, thus reaching the audience only indirectly, but now was put into direct speech, addressed by the poet in person to specific other persons. That also is the case of the Tyrtaean elegy; and we need not doubt that Tyrtaeus followed the example of Hesiod. Again, however, we find an innovation in that the Paraenesis is now animated by the pathos of the polis. Tyrtaeus was neither a rhapsode who in his epic celebrated the feats and excellences of an aristocratic

[3] The Olympian record begins 776 B.C.; the elegy of Tyrtaeus must be placed c.640 B.C.

society like Homer; nor a humble farmer in a peaceably corrupt community who admonished his brother and the village oligarchs to cultivate the virtues of righteous conduct and hard work like Hesiod. While nothing is reliably known about his personal circumstances, he appears in his poems as the member of a society of citizen-soldiers who admonishes his companions to excel in the virtue of "savage valor" because on the practice of this excellence depends the existence of the polis in a mortal struggle against subjects and neighbors who curiously enough want to be free of Spartan domination.

The protreptic praise of "savage valor" as the specific excellence of the polis is a further new "type" in the history of order and its symbolization. It introduces a problem that plagues political speculation to this day—the pathos of the polis engenders the will to fight for the community regardless of the justice of its cause. The pathos of the polis splits its ethos. No questions must be asked whether or not the Messenian revolt was the quite justified struggle of an oppressed people for its freedom; no questions whether or not the Spartan so-called "polis and her people" was, militarily, a highly capable association of robbers who had descended on a country, plundered it, and made its people work as serfs on their former property. To raise the question of justice would be treason and desertion. The Tyrtaean inquiry into the nature of true Arete accepts the fact of conquest; it starts from the Spartan polis in unquestioned historical existence.[4] The pathos of communal existence, thus, appears as an independent factor in a theory of order and of the excellences that will maintain it, by the side of the Dike that was Hesiod's concern. A theory of politics, as a consequence, is not exhausted by a theory of justice or a philosophy of morals; the *mysterium iniquitatis* is part of human existence in society. With the Tyrtaean praise of unconditional "savage valor" this problem becomes articulate in Hellenic thought.

In the situation of a struggle for existence the protreptic poetry of Tyrtaeus acquires a peculiar poignancy. To be sure, the poet appears as the speaker who exhorts his audience—an exhortation always presupposes somebody in need of it—but Tyrtaeus neither speaks with the authority of truth like Hesiod, nor the authority of wisdom like Xenophanes. He is not a prophet in opposition to society, but rather the

---

[4] There is extant a fragment of a poem, entitled *Eunomia* (Tyrtaeus 2), in which "this polis" is praised as given by Zeus himself to "the Heraclides." Tyrtaeus, thus, seems to have been not quite unaware of the need for justification.

speaker *for* the community. While the external, literary form of the address implies the tension between speaker and audience, the substance of the poem annihilates it. For the poet identifies himself with his audience, he is the voice of the community itself; and by its inner form, therefore, his elegy is addressed to nobody at all. The songs of Tyrtaeus hold their stark appeal as the lyricism of existence in its glory and its horror, of life at the risk of death; and by virtue of this quality they have become immortal.

Nevertheless, the literary form of the exhortation is not without meaning. The Arete of Tyrtaeus is an excellence in historical formation in a community; it is by far not the unquestioned possession of every Lacedaemonian warrior. The question whether there will be a Lacedaemonian polis in continued historical existence at all hinges expressly on the point whether the excellence of "savage valor" is a living force in the soul of every individual Lacedaemonian or not; and its protreptic articulation by the poet is one of the factors that brings it to consciousness, forms it, and preserves it. The Tyrtaean Arete is a habituation of the soul that must be engendered in competition with other motivations. "Sweet is it and honorable to die for the country"—but no warrior who returned from battle has ever committed suicide in despair because such sweetness escaped him. If the human love for the sweetness of life is disregarded, the lyricism of "savage valor" and death in battle can reach the danger point of romantic nonsense. The exhorting Tyrtaeus, however, is not a romantic; on the contrary, he is quite willing to fortify his praise of deadly Arete by an appeal to the desire for survival. In another elegy he admonishes the young men not to be afraid of the multitude of enemies (as apparently they are), to fight in the front line (which they are not particularly eager to do), not to hide behind their shields out of the range of missiles (what they seem to prefer), and to make Life their enemy and to hold the black spirits of Death dearer than the rays of the sun (a psychological perversion for which they have little taste). And after such admonitions, apparently addressed to a demoralized army, he drily explains that fighting in the front line, shoulder to shoulder with comrades, provides a better chance of survival than running away and thereby inviting the pursuit of an enemy for an easy kill (11).

Tyrtaeus, thus, is not a romantic. But it is precisely his common-sense speculation on the chance of survival that would ultimately corrode his praise of valor unless the *arete* had an appeal of its own. This specific appeal the poet reveals in the second part of the great elegy. Valor in battle is the "common good" of the polis—and the polis has to offer something in return for valorous service, even to the dead. For, when a man loses his "dear life" in battle, thus gaining glory "for the city, its people and his father," he will be lamented alike by young and old and the whole polis will mourn for him in sad grief. "His tomb and his children will be honored among men, and his children's children and his race in all future; never will his good fame [*kleros*] perish nor his name [*onoma*]; and though he lie beneath the earth he becomes immortal [*athanatos*]" (12, 20–44).

In order to gauge the full weight of the Tyrtaean appeal one must remember that men of the seventh century B.C. had no soul, immortal or otherwise. The terms immortal and mortal simply meant gods and men. A man could become immortal only by becoming a god. The Tyrtaean promise of transfiguration through death into the eternal memory of the polis reveals the desire for immortality as a motivating experience of its order. The immortality of the aristocratic society, through the Mnemosyne of the poets, has become the citizen's immortality through survival in the memory of the grateful polis. Other factors, to be sure, have entered into the making of the polis and the Tyrtaean promise is not the key to all of its riddles. Nevertheless, here we touch upon the experience which decisively determined the pathos of the polis, the passionate character of its existence that could not be broken by the most obvious exigencies of rational politics. Life in the polis was truly life in a sense which Christians will have difficulty in reconstructing imaginatively because it presupposes an undifferentiated compactness of experience that we no longer have. It is a compactness just becoming luminous with transcendence through the prefiguring immortality of fame and name. The tenacity of the polis becomes intelligible if we understand it as the immortalizing faith of men whose differentiating self-consciousness has reached the stage of the "name" but not yet of the soul. Its strength should be measured by the fact that it remained the ultimately limiting faith even for Plato and Aristotle.

If now the Tyrtaean answer to the problem of Arete be held by the side of the Xenophantic, a pattern both theoretical and historical begins to emerge. The Hellenic poets and thinkers were engaged in the search for Arete. What they found was not the one true Arete but a whole series of Aretai. With each new discovery the claim for superior rank of the previous discovery was broken; and in the end the problem had to arise whether the latest discovery invalidated all previous ones, or whether each discovery differentiated a certain sector of human experience so that only a balanced practice of all the Aretai fully expressed the potentialities of man. That ultimate phase of a systematic, ordering survey of Aretai was reached in the work of Plato, in particular in the *Republic* with its hierarchic order of the excellences from wisdom to temperance.

The transition from the discovery of new Aretai to their systematic ordering, however, must not be misunderstood as some mysterious awakening of a "scientific spirit" or as the beginning of a "science" of ethics; rather, it indicates that the search has reached its end. The search for the true Arete ends in the discovery that the Aretai are habituations of the soul which attune the life of man with transcendent reality; with the full differentiation of the field of Aretai there emerges the "true self" of man, the center at which he lives in openness toward the transcendental highest good, the Platonic Agathon. The transition to the ordering survey of Aretai means that the Agathon has been discovered as the principle of order in the soul.

When the whole range of Aretai is understood as the transparency of life for the realissimum, the single Aretai must undergo a revaluation through relativation. The compactness which an Arete has in the experience of its discovery must dissolve under the impact of further differentiating discoveries and, in particular, under the impact of the discovery of the Agathon. The compelling force of the Tyrtaean elegy is due to the fact that the experience of the new Arete carries the full weight of the experience of transcendence. With the further differentiation of the soul, with the discovery of wisdom and the nous, the transcendence through "savage valor," while retaining such truth as it has, will sink to comparatively low rank. This is the fate which the Arete of Tyrtaeus experienced at the hand of the all-weighing Plato. In the *Laws* (629f.) he reflected on the Tyrtaean elegy. He found that "savage valor" had its merits as a virtue in wars against aliens but that it would not contribute much to the just order of the polis. What the citizen-soldier can do as a warrior can also be done by mercenaries who are ready to die at their post; and yet, with few exceptions, they are insolent, unjust, brutal, and rather senseless individuals. The courage of Tyrtaeus will rank only fourth in the order of excellences, preceded by wisdom, justice, and temperance.

3. *The Eunomia of Solon*

The Tyrtaean valor will maintain the polis in existence in a deadly crisis but it is not a virtue of civic order. To be sure, it is not entirely void of ordering content; for the valor of the citizen-soldier already presupposes a democratization of society in comparison with the Homeric aristocracy. Nevertheless, the Spartan democratization was limited to the freemen of the clans; the people at large remained a subject population under the Lacedaemonian ruling group. Sparta never developed a political order of the people; its constitution, as we said, was the fossilized order of conquest. The symbols of order for a whole people with its conflicts of interests were developed in Athens, through Solon. He was a statesman as well as a thinker and a poet; and enough of his poems are extant to inform us about the development of his ideas from the crisis preceding the Reform of 594 B.C. to the tyranny of Peisistratus after 561 B.C.

In an elegy antedating the Reform Solon reflects on the probable fate of "our polis." [5] She will never perish by the will of the gods but only by the folly of her own citizens. Unrighteous is the mind of the leaders of the people; without respect for sacred or public possessions they steal right and left; and they have no regard for the venerable foundations of Dike. But Dike, in her silence, is well aware of such doings and her revenge always comes in the end. Ineluctably (*aphyktos*) the consequences of the violation of Dike will manifest themselves in civil strife. Conventicles (*synodoi*), so dear to the unrighteous, will be formed and the government will fall into the hands of its enemies, while the poor people will be sold into slavery in foreign lands. The public evil (*demosion kakon*) will penetrate into every private house; locking of doors will not keep it out, for it jumps over high walls; and it finds every man in the innermost recess of his house. Filled with the sorrow of such prospects, Solon concludes: "My heart [*thymos*] commands me to teach the Athenians this"—that unrighteousness (*dysnomia*) will create much evil for the polis, while righteousness (*eunomia*) will make things well-

---

[5] *Elegy and Iambus*, I, Solon 4.

ordered and proper (*eukosma kai artia*). Eunomia will restrain the unrighteous, check excess, reduce hybris, straighten crooked judgments,
stop factions and civil strife, and will make "all things proper and sensible in the affairs of men."

The elegy is carefully constructed and contains the principal ideas
which Solon elaborates in other poems. We can follow its guidance and
consider the topics in succession.

The elegy opens with a reflection on the causes of the Athenian crisis.
The responsibility rests not with the gods, but with the folly of men. It
is the great theme of theodicy, following the paradigm of the *Odyssey*.
Solon, however, goes far beyond Homer in the exploration of the problem. Later, when the tyranny of Peisistratus is established, he chides his
countrymen not to blame the gods when they suffer through their own
cowardice. The Athenians themselves have given the tyrant the guards
that now keep them in servitude; they step like foxes but they have no
brains; they trust a man's talk and don't look at his deeds (10). For the
first time, the historico-political process appears as a chain of cause and
effect; human action is the cause of order or disorder in the polis. The
source of the new aetiology becomes apparent in the following fragment:
"From the cloud comes the strength of snow and hail, and thunder is
born from bright lightning; a polis is ruined by its great men, and the
people falls into the servitude of a tyrant through its simple-mindedness"
(9). The historical causality is modeled on the causality of nature that
was being discovered at the time by the Ionian physicists.

Nevertheless, we are yet far from a Thucydidean causality of politics.
The actions of man are still embedded in a cosmic order that is governed
by the gods. Evil conduct will lead to evil results because offended Dike
will have her revenge. This is the aspect of theodicy which Solon explores
thoroughly in the great Prayer to the Muses (13). Grant me wealth (the
Homeric *olbos*), he prays to the Muses, as well as good fame among men;
and with wealth will come the power, for which he prays, to be "sweet
to my friends, and a bitter taste to my foes." But the prayer for the excellences of an Homeric aristocrat is softened by concern for the Hesiodian Dike: "Wealth I desire to possess—but I would not have it unrighteously; for Dike always catches up." Zeus himself, through his Dike,
watches over the actions of man; the works of hybris and force will
arouse his wrath slowly but surely; the one will pay earlier, the other

later; and if he escape himself, his guiltless children and their offspring will pay for his misdeeds. Then the poem broadens into a grandiose meditation on the delusions of man. Each of us, whether good or bad, lives engrossed in his own illusion (*doxa*) until he suffers. The sick hope to be healthy, and the poor to be rich; the cowards believe they are brave, and the ugly man believes himself good-looking. Each, furthermore, follows his business and hopes to gain by it—whether as a fisherman, a peasant, a craftsman, a physician, or a seer; and he will not be deterred by hard work, failure, and little profit. But the goods of comeliness and health, of success and riches, are not at the disposition of mortal action. Moira, Fate, brings good and ill to the mortals; and the gifts of the immortals must be accepted. Honest endeavor may fail, and the wicked ones may succeed. Nevertheless, this order of things is not senseless; it appears devoid of sense only if the illusionary wishes and pursuits of man are substituted for the sense of the gods. The source of senselessness is the illusion (*doxa*) of man. And, in particular, the striving for wealth, the highest aim of all effort, cannot be a principle of order. There is no clear end (*terma*) to such striving; for the richest among us are twice as eager to have more than the others; and who could let them all have their fill? Possessions, to be sure, come from the gods; but there is a fatality attached to them, which passes along with them, from hand to hand.

In the meditative prayer of Solon, as in the elegy of Tyrtaeus, the polis asserts itself against the excellences of the old aristocracy. The citizen of a polis cannot lead the heroic life of an Homeric prince. If everybody wants to play Agamemnon or Achilles, the result will not be an aristocratic culture but a war of all against all and the destruction of the polis. In a polis heroic existence degenerates into exploitation and tyranny. The conflict becomes the occasion for a profound reconsideration of political ethics on the part of Solon. If the Athenian aristocrats use the advantages of their economic position to the full, the danger is imminent that Athens will perish and Homeric conditions will be restored, indeed. Thucydides, in his *History*, shrewdly discerned that the most backward regions of Hellas gave an idea of conditions in the age depicted by Homer. Solon recognized the truth of the Homeric excellences; but he also knew that the polis required a new temperance. The naive prosperity and magnificence of the hero could no longer be the Arete of man. "Many bad men are rich, many good men are poor; but we for our part shall not exchange Arete for riches; for Arete lasts forever, while possessions are in the hands now of one man, then of another" (15). The true Arete of man is distinguished as something less tangible than the possessions in which the hero finds confirmation of his worth. But wherein precisely does the newly discovered Arete consist? The religious genius of Solon reveals itself in the refusal of a positive answer. The excellence of man cannot find its fulfillment in the possession of finite goods. The goods at which man aims through his action are apparent only; they belong to the *doxa* of his wishes and pursuits. The true Arete consists in man's obedience to a universal order which in its fullness is known only to the gods. "It is very hard to know the unseen measure of right judgment; and yet it alone contains the right boundaries [*peirata*] of all things" (16). The true Arete is an act of faith in the unknown order of the gods who will see to it that the man who renounces his *doxa* will act in accordance with Dike. On the one hand, "The mind of the immortals is all unseen to men" (17); on the other hand, "At the behest of the gods have I done what I said" (34, 6). We are already very close to the Platonic Agathon about which nothing can be said positively, although it is the source of order in the Politeia.

The Doxa is the source of disorder; renunciation of Doxa is the condition of right order, Eunomia. When man overcomes the obsession of his Doxa and fits his action into the unseen measure of the gods, then life in community will become possible. This is the Solonic discovery. At the core of his Eunomia, as its animating experience, we find the religiousness of a life in tension between the passionate, human desire for the goods of exuberant existence and the measure imposed on such desire by the ultimately inscrutable will of the gods. Neither of the two components of life is invalidated by the other. Solon is neither a middle-class type who finds virtue in a medium situation because it fits his medium stature; nor is he a broken Titan, resigned to the frustration of his desires by Fate. He passionately loves the magnificence and exuberance of life; but he experiences it as a gift of the gods, not as an aim to be realized by crooked means against the divine order. Through openness toward transcendence, the passion of life is revealed as the Doxa that must be curbed for the sake of order.

The concretization of this unseen measure, its translation into rules of conduct, is determined by the existence of the polis. Concretely the politics of Solon becomes the appeal, and the statesman's practice, of balancing the conflicting desires of the social groups so that their co-existence within the polis, and thereby the existence of the polis itself, will be possible. The following fragment of an appeal is typical:

> Calm the hard-burning heart in your breast,
> You who have had surfeit of many good things,
> And put within limits
>   your great-mindedness [*megan noon*] (28c).

And the same principle of restraining the excess of passion underlies his advice for treating the masses:

> For abundance breeds hybris
>   when too much prosperity [*olbos*] comes
> To men whose mind is not fit for it. (6)

Standing between the two factions of the landed aristocrats who did not want to surrender any of their privileges and of the poor people who were greedy for more than their personal caliber could bear, Solon had to strike a balance. And he prided himself that to the people he gave such privilege as was enough for them, and that the wealthy and powerful did not suffer undue hardship through his Reform: "Holding a strong shield I protected them both, and would not let either gain unrighteously over the other" (5).

The most important part of Solon's politics, however, was the conduct of the man himself. Not only did he have to function as the arbiter and lawgiver for the conflicting social groups; he also had to resist the temptation of using his enormous power for his own advantage and of imposing himself as tyrant on the polis. In his justification, in the iambic poem, he reminds his critics that another man "had he taken the goad in his hand, a man unwise and covetous, would not have restrained the people." The upper class might well praise him as a friend for, "had another man won such honor, he would not have restrained the people until he had done his churning and taken the cream off the milk" (36 and 37). The temptation must have been great because the people more or less expected him to assume the tyrant's role; not only would they have condoned it, but they considered him rather a fool because he did not avail himself of the opportunity. There were the many who sneered at him because he had not taken his chance, and who loudly proclaimed that they would gladly have submitted to any punishment afterwards if only they had first gained riches and exercised the tyranny of Athens for a single day (33). Against such popular opinion Solon professed not to be ashamed because he did not seize tyranny and thereby disgrace his good name (32). Criticisms and sneers of this kind must have been trying, for on occasion he sighed: "In great matters it is hard to please all" (7). He left Athens for ten years in order to escape such molestation; and from the judgment of the citizenry he proudly appealed to "the tribunal of Time" (36).

Sweeping judgments in such matters are as easy as they are dangerous. Nevertheless, we risk to say that, through his restraint and its motivation, Solon was the most important single personality in Hellenic politics. Very few individuals in the history of mankind, like Alexander or Caesar, have had the privilege of creating a new personal type. Solon was one of them. He created the type of the lawgiver, the *nomothetes,* in the classical sense, not for Hellas only, but as a model for mankind. He was a statesman, not above the parties, but between them; he shared the passions *of* the people and, thus, could make himself accepted as one of them in politics; and he could act with authority as the statesman *for* the people, because in his soul these passions had submitted to universal order. The Eunomia he created in the polis was the Eunomia of his soul. In his person came to life the prototype of the spiritual statesman. His soul had a unique amplitude and elasticity. He could share the pessimism of the Ionians when he wrote: "No man is happy; all mortals on whom the Sun gazes are wretched" (14); and he could wish to live to the age of eighty (20) because he felt his mind still growing: "As I grow old I learn many things" (18). Moreover, the miracle of his life has determined the later concern with order inestimably in so far as the work of Plato is hardly conceivable, and certainly not intelligible, without the paradigmatic life of Solon. In the *Timaeus,* in retrospect, Plato interprets the *Republic* as the Solonic phase of his own life. The conception of the Politeia as "man written large" is fundamentally the Solonic conception of the polis whose order embodies the Eunomia of the soul; while the conception of the philosopher-king as the substance of order hearkens back to the paradigm of Solon as the substantive source of Athenian order. Between Solon and Plato lies the history of the Athenian polis—from the creation of its order through the soul of Solon to its disintegration when the renovation of order through the soul of Socrates and Plato was rejected. The union of human passions and divine order in the Eunomia dissociated into the passions of the demos and the order that lives through the work of Plato.

4. "But I say unto you . . ."

The subject of the Aretai is by far not exhausted by the preceding analysis. A considerable amount of detail would have to be added in order to complete the picture. We have not mentioned, for instance, the first appearance of the excellence of *andreia,* manliness, in a poem of Simonides of Ceos,[6] although it is the excellence which later plays an important rôle in the Platonic hierarchy of virtues. Neither have we dealt with the Pindaric glorification of aristocratic excellences at the time when politically the aristocracy of the Hellenic polis finally succumbed to the rising democracy, while again the aristocratism of Plato is hardly conceivable without the living force of Pindar's *Odes* in the consciousness of the people. Nor have we dealt with the poems of Theognis which show the aristocracy in the crisis of its transformation from a ruling estate into a political party within the polis, and its excellences on the point of their transformation into the loyalties and rules of conduct of a political club with conspiratorial touches. But we must resist the temptation to expand a study of order and history into a study of Hellenic political culture—the analysis must be restricted to the representative thinkers whose discoveries decisively advanced the understanding of the order of man and society.

Nevertheless, the subject of the Aretai and the Polis requires a few concluding reflections on a type of experience that was fully articulated only by the Platonic-Aristotelian and Christian theoretizations, as well as on the symbolic form that was developed for its expression at the time.

In the Xenophantic elegy on Sophia the enumeration of the excellences held in popular esteem was followed by the opposition of the new excellence that from now on will hold the higher rank. The Tyrtaean elegy on "savage valor," then, proved to be the prototype of the Xenophantic form of expression. And the poems of Solon, finally, displayed the same opposition of the new Arete to the older aristocratic excellences. The recurrence of this form is not simply a matter of imitation, not even when one of the elegies serves as the literary model for the other; its repetition rather suggests itself because the experiential situation recurs. The precise nature of this situation becomes more clearly visible in the non-

[6] *Lyra Graeca,* ed. and trans. by J. M. Edmonds (Loeb Classical Library), II, Simonides 65. Simonides lived *c.*556–468 B.C.

political lyrics than in the formal, political professions. It reveals itself in
its purity on the occasion of its emergence in the poetry of Sappho. Let
us consider, therefore, the following Sapphic stanza:

> Some say a parade of the horse, some of the marchers,
> Some say a naval display is on the dark earth
> The most splendid thing: But I say it is
> What one ardently loves.[7]

The stanza has the same formal structure as the elegies of Tyrtaeus
and Xenophanes; but here we can see more clearly that a popular form
for expressing preference of one thing over another (the so-called "preamble") is used for the specific purpose of opposing an authoritative
judgment to commonly accepted opinions.[8] With such utilization the
meaning of preference undergoes a radical change. For Sappho does not
indulge her personal fancy; on the contrary, she enumerates a number of
predilections in order to pool them in what might be called a conventional
range of preferences; and over and against this whole conventional range
she defines: "The most beautiful [kalliston] is what one loves [eratai]."
Eros is the passion that authenticates the "really" beautiful against the
mere subjectivity of conventional preferences. With the differentiation
of Eros as the source of objectivity in judgment, convention acquires
the characteristic of "subjectivity."

The problem of subjectivity arises when the unquestioned values of
archaic society are challenged by the new authority of the differentiating
soul. In the course of this process there arises an awareness of the qualitative differences between men as expressed in their preferences. In the
Iliad this awareness is not yet strongly developed; but in the *Odyssey*
already the hero sets forth his taste for war in preference to cultivating
one's land or caring for a household—"for different men take joy in
different works." [9] And Archilochus, resuming the Homeric line, says:
"Another thing warms another man's heart." [10] It is in the poems of
Archilochus that the insight into the variety of preferences acquires a
touch of "debunking"; the conventional preferences appear as illusionary, if not hypocritical, and are opposed by sounder judgment, as for
instance in the verses:

---

[7] *Lyra Graeca*, I, Sappho 38.

[8] On the questions of the present as well as the following paragraph cf. Snell, *Entdeckung des
Geistes*, 6off.

[9] *Odyssey* XIV, 228.   [10] *Elegy and Iambus* II, Archilochus 36.

> I don't like a tall general, nor a long-legged, wide-striding one,
> Nor one who is proud of his curls, or sports a dandy-shave;
> Rather give me a short one, and even with bow-legs,
> If he be sturdy on his feet and full of heart.[11]

The preference for the military "figure of a man" is couched in such terms that the tall general looks rather like a poseur whose wide strides may accelerate to running. The contrast between the two types prefigures the theoretical conflict between appearance and reality. In the previously quoted Sapphic stanza the contrast is further articulated to the point where the passion of Eros is understood as the source of knowledge about true reality. And in the meditative Prayer of Solon, finally, the term Doxa is introduced for designating the delusionary character of common opinion in contrast with the truth of the unseen Measure.

The recurrence of the literary form, thus, is not an imitative play. The form is recurrently determined by the experience of a truth, gained through the differentiation of the soul, in opposition to the delusions of commonly accepted opinion. And since the differentiation of the soul is not a collective process but occurs in the individual souls of specifically gifted persons, the expression will become more pointed the more the universality of truth becomes understood as mediated through individuals in opposition to the community. The closer we approach the revelation of a transcendental truth valid for all mankind, the more intense becomes the solitude of the mediators. In the Xenophantic elegy the Sophia is still "our" possession. In the Socratic apology the formulae of Xenophanes are repeated, but the isolation has become fatal. Socrates demands as his reward maintenance in the Prytaneum; like Xenophanes he proudly claims that he would deserve the honor rather than the Olympic victor; and then he continues: "For the victor gives you the illusion of happiness, but I give you its reality." [12] The Xenophantic revolt against the unrighteous judgments of custom has sharpened to the deadly rejection of the mediator by his people. Plato articulates his own position still further in the *Gorgias* by claiming the authoritative statesmanship of Athens against the renowned leaders who only in appearance are representative of the polis,[13] until in the fullness of time this formula becomes the vessel for the assertion of the authority of Christ against the Old Law in the powerful repetitions:

> You have heard it said by those of old. . . .
> But I say unto you . . .

[11] *Ibid.*, Archilochus 58.   [12] Plato, *Apology* 36d–e.   [13] Plato, *Gorgias* 517–21.

CHAPTER 8

Parmenides

With Tyrtaeus, valorous man is immortalized through the commemorating pathos of the polis; with Solon, the Doxa of man is assuaged to Eunomia within the polis through the experience of the "unseen Measure"; and with Xenophanes, the Sophia of the mystic-philosopher reaches beyond the polis toward a universal realissimum for mankind. Even with Xenophanes, however, the polis itself is not transcended; even the mystic-philosopher is a figure in the competitive struggle for the formation of the polis. And this, as we have pointed out, remains the limiting structure of Hellenic philosophizing on order down to the Macedonian conquest. Nevertheless, in the succession of discoveries the experiential trend can be discerned which, by its inner logic, will articulate the soul to the point where its supranatural destiny achieves consciousness. In the generation following Xenophanes (though still within his lifetime, as Xenophanes grew very old) this phase of articulation was reached through Parmenides.

In his didactic poem, *c.*485, the Eleatic philosopher created the symbol of the "Way of Truth" that leads man beyond the deafness and blindness of Doxa toward his fulfillment. The Way of Truth was a "type" in the Platonic sense. This way, from the immortalizing pathos of the polis to the truth for the individual soul, runs parallel in time to the way, in Israelite history, from the Chosen People to the Suffering Servant of Deutero-Isaiah. The process in which the soul disengages itself from collective existence and achieves its attunement with transcendent-divine reality, was in both instances on principle the same—with the important difference, however, that in no period of Jewish history before the appearance of Christ had the articulation of the life of the soul, as well as of the way of truth, reached an intenseness and a precision of symbolism comparable with the Hellenic of the fifth and fourth centuries B.C. Only with Jesus does the symbol of the Way of Truth appear in the Jewish orbit. But when Jesus answers the question of the apostle with his

"I am the way, the truth, and the life" (John 14:6), he firmly takes the symbol away from the philosophers. From then onward the redemption of the soul goes through Christ; the component of redemption, which is still present in the compact philosophizing of Parmenides, has been revealed in its true meaning; and philosophy, the sole source of transcendent order for the polis, has become one of the two sources of order for mankind, that of Reason by the side of Revelation.

The poem of Parmenides is organized in a Prologue, which tells the philosopher's transport into the presence of the nameless goddess of light, and in two parts, which report the knowledge received from the goddess concerning Truth (*aletheia*) and Delusion (*doxa*). The Prologue and the major portion of the part on Truth are preserved; of the part on Delusion only fragments survive which are estimated to represent about one-tenth of the text.[1]

1. *The Way*

The Prologue gives an account, in mythical symbols, of the philosopher's transport. It probably expresses an experience which Parmenides had in his younger years for he lets the goddess address him as "O youth." [2] He describes it as a journey on a horse-drawn chariot. The "much-knowing horses," guided by the maidens of the Sun, carry him on the "renowned way" to the goddess. It is the way that will be traveled "unscathed by the knowing man as far as his heart will allow [or: desire]." As the ride proceeds, the sun-maidens quicken it; and, having forsaken the House of Night, they throw their veils back as the train approaches the Light. The gate at which the pathways of night and day separate is reached; and the guardian Dike opens it to the persuasion of the sun-maidens. The chariot and its escorts enter. At this point, when the light-vision itself begins, all imagery ceases. We only hear of a goddess (undescribed and unnamed) who receives the youth graciously: "No evil Moira leads you this way (for it lies far away indeed from the pathways of men) but Themis and Dike. Meet is it for you to learn all things: the unshaken heart of well-rounded Truth [*aletheia*] as well as the Delusion [*doxa*] of the mortals in which there is no true reliance

---

[1] Still basic is the edition, with translation, introduction, and commentary by Hermann Diels, *Parmenides. Lehrgedicht* (Berlin, 1897). The following interpretation owes most to Francis M. Cornford, *Plato and Parmenides* (London, 1939), as well to the chapters on Parmenides in Gigon, *Der Ursprung der griechischen Philosophie*, and Jaeger, *Theology* (Oxford, 1947).

[2] Diels-Kranz, *Fragmente der Vorsokratiker* (7th ed.), Parmenides B 1, 24. All further references are to this edition.

at all. And this you will also learn thoroughly—how going through all things one shall discern clearly the delusions [*dokounta*]." After these introductory remarks the instruction proper begins (B 1).

The Prologue resumes a number of themes that we know already from earlier contexts. We can sense the paradigm of Hesiod in the search for a truth opposed to commonly accepted falsehoods, as well as in the imagery of the two ways leading to misery and true *arete* respectively. And the whole construction of the poem, with its authentication of the truth through the unnamed goddess, follows Hesiod's model of authenticating his new myth through the Heliconian Muses. Moreover, the Solonic opposition of the unseen Measure to the Doxa of man is now sharpened to the opposition of a mystical vision of the truth to the delusions of the mortals. These traditional themes, however, are subordinated to a new type of imagery. We hear of the "renowned way" of the goddess that leads far away from the "pathways of men"; we learn that this way is not safe for everybody but only for the "knowing man"; that others may not travel it "unscathed"; [3] that man is partly driven on it by his "heart's desire," partly guided by Themis and Dike; and, finally, that it is a way that leads from Night to Light. In such imagery we can recognize the symbolism of a mystery religion, expressing the ascent of the initiate to the full revelation of truth; and we can be sure that it stems from the Orphism and Pythagoreanism of the sixth century. Unfortunately, however, we know very little about its sources; the extant fragments of these movements are so scanty that the development of symbols cannot be traced in continuity.[4] All we know for certain is that in the mystery religions of this period the essential divinity of the soul was experienced, and the experience was expressed in the belief in the immortality of the soul.[5]

Since an understanding of the new conception of the soul is of importance for the interpretation of Parmenides, and since the early sources are insufficient, we shall supply a later formulation which most probably renders it accurately; it is a passage from Plato.[6] In *Timaeus* 90 a–b Plato says:

> With regard to the kind of soul which is dominant in us we should
> consider that God has given it to each of us as a *daimon*, dwelling
> as we said at the top of the body; and because of its affinity with

[3] I am following the emendation of Meineke and Jaeger.

[4] On the ancestry of the Parmenidean transport cf. the survey in Diels, *Parmenides*, 13 ff.

[5] For a survey of this problem, and bibliography, cf. Jaeger, *Theology*, the chapter "Origin of the Doctrine of the Soul's Divinity."

[6] I am following a suggestion by Cornford, *Plato and Parmenides*, 27.

Heaven it draws us away from Earth, for most truly we are a heavenly growth, not an earthly one. The Divine [*to theion*], indeed, has placed our head in the direction from where the soul had its first origin, as it were as its root, thus making the body upright. Now, when a man abandons himself to his desires [*epithymia*] and ambitions [*philonikia*], indulging them incontinently, all his thoughts [*dogmata*] of necessity become mortal, and as a consequence he must become mortal every bit, as far as that is possible, because he has nourished his mortal part. When on the contrary he has earnestly cultivated his love of knowledge and of true wisdom, when he has primarily exercised his faculty to think immortal and divine things, he will—since in that manner he is touching the truth—become immortal of necessity, as far as it is possible for human nature to participate in immortality. For incessantly he is engaged in the cult of the Divine; and since he keeps in good order [*eu kekosmemenon*] the *daimon* that lives in him he will himself become thoroughly *eudaimon* [blessed].

The passage articulates a conception of the soul that must be presupposed not only in the work of Parmenides, but also of Xenophanes and Heraclitus. The articulation is concise in the sense that it brings out the essentials of a doctrine of the soul but hardly goes beyond the bare essentials. Because of this conciseness, developing as it were a minimum dogma of the soul, we feel justified in introducing it at this point as an instrument for interpreting the Parmenidean poem.

In the first place, the passage accentuates the connection between divinity and immortality. In archaic Greek thought men are mortal, gods are immortal; if man becomes immortal he will attain such immortality through what is divine in him. The attribution of divinity and immortality to the soul, however, must not be understood as the futile indulgence of a "desire for immortality," perhaps as a "rationalization" in the sense of contemporary, ideologizing psychology. The experience of immortality is a fundamental human experience which historically precedes the discovery of the soul as the source of such knowledge. Immortality is predicated of the gods long before the soul is differentiated as the subject of which also, with certain qualifications, immortality might be predicated. We might say that the experience of immortality advances from archaic opacity to the lucidity of consciousness in which it becomes clear that the divine can be experienced as immortal because the experiencing soul shares or participates (*metaschesis*) in the divine. This participation, however, is experienced as precarious; it is something that may increase or decrease, that may be gained or lost. Hence, the practice of the soul will either nourish the mortal or the immortal element in it. The cultivation of the immortal part through occupation of the mind with things immortal and divine is understood as a "cult" of the divine, symbolized as the *daimon;* and through a life of such cult practice the soul itself will become *eudaimon.*

The metaphor of man as a heavenly growth (*phyton ouranion*) deserves particular attention. The setting of the metaphor is still Hesiodian; man lives in the tension between Gaea and Ouranos. But subtly the meanings of the symbols are shifting, due to the introduction of the idea of growth, of *physis.* Under the "type" of the Hesiodian myth gods and men "come into being," or "are made"; and there they stand side by side as static figures. Now man is conceived as a "growth"; the earthly and heavenly, the mortal and immortal qualities are internalized in a "soul" which is the subject that can grow in one or the other direction. Life is the cult of the divine within the soul, and through this cult the soul will grow into its own divinity. In the Parmenidean poem we also find the Hesiodian apparatus of mythical symbols with the tension of the soul between Night and Light; and we, furthermore, find a designation, if not description, of the forces in the soul which provide motive power and direction for the growth. The *thymos* (heart) which urges the thinker on is the force in the soul that later, in the Platonic work, becomes the Eros of the philosopher; and the direction is given through Themis and Dike, the goddesses of right order and justice, which also reappear in Plato's *Republic* as the Dike that is the proportioning force of order in the soul. The third Platonic force of the soul, Thanatos, is not directly named in the poem of Parmenides but it is pervasively present in the conception of the cathartic way that will lead man from the Night of the mortals (the submarine existence of Plato) to the Light of eternal truth.

2. The Truth of Being

What is the truth of being? With this question we turn from the experience of mystical transport to the philosophical articulation of the vision.[7]

---

[7] We are concerned only with those aspects of Parmenides' work that have a bearing on the genesis of speculation on order. For a fuller exposition the reader should refer to Gigon, *Ursprung.*

First to be considered is the intimate connection between the content of truth and the mystical transport. Parmenides' philosophy is a speculation on the *Eon*, on Being. The symbol "Being" appears for the first time; and without exaggeration it can be said that with Parmenides the history of philosophy proper, as the exploration of the constitution of Being, begins. The Being of Parmenides is not an origin of sensually perceived entities (*ta onta*), as in Ionian speculation. It is the something that is given in the experience of the transport. Hence, its existence cannot be derived speculatively as the *arche*, as the beginning of the stream of experienced entities (which, as a stream, is at the same time a becoming), but is given to speculation as an immediate datum of experience. The experiential origin of Being in the mystical transport must be well understood, for otherwise the historical appearance of the new object of speculation will remain enigmatic. Parmenides has no predecessors, and his concept of Being has no prehistory.[8] The historical process which results in the concept of Being does not itself move on the level of philosophical speculation; it rather is the process of the soul in which Being as absolute transcendence comes ultimately into experiential grasp. If we search for the antecedents of Parmenides, we must look, not for an earlier, more primitive philosophy of Being, but for a less differentiated experience of transcendence, as we find it for instance in the universalism of Xenophanes.

The visionary philosopher, since he has gone beyond the realm of sense perception, does not speculate on the plurality of things as given to the senses. His vision has a specific content and in order to apperceive it he needs a specific faculty of the Soul. Parmenides called this faculty the *nous*: "Look with the Nous as it makes present with certainty the absent" (B 4). The Nous is discovered as the organ of cognition that will bring nonsensual, intelligible reality into the grasp of man. At this point, however, some caution is necessary; for the Nous is a rather compact symbol, and even in Aristotle it still has an amplitude of meaning from intellection to faith. In order not to read later, more differentiated meanings into the term, we should understand it strictly as the organ of the soul that brings "Being" into grasp, so that its further determination will depend on the meaning of "Being." Moreover, the Nous, while it

---

[8] Cf. Gigon, *ibid.*, 270f.: "Der Ursprung des Begriffs des Seienden bei Parmenides bleibt ein Raetsel. Es ist zwischen ihm und den unmittelbaren Vorgaengern des Parmenides eine Luecke, die historisch nicht zu ueberbruecken ist."

brings Being into grasp, does not articulate its content. The content of Being is articulated by a further faculty that appears on this occasion for the first time, by the *logos* in the narrower sense of logical argumentation. The Nous, together with the Logos, is the Parmenidean cognitive organ for determining the nature of Being.

The revelation of the truth about Being assumes the form of a classification of the various ways of inquiry. Spinning out the metaphor of the "Way," the goddess informs Parmenides about the "ways of inquiry" that alone are thinkable. The meaning of way, of the *hodos*, shifts in this opening from the mystical to the logical way, foreshadowing the meaning of *methodos*, of the method of scientific inquiry. There are two such ways: "The one way, that *Is* and that *Not is* cannot be,[9] is the path of Persuasion [*Peitho*] which is attendant upon Truth [*Aletheia*]. But the other path is utterly undiscernible; for, Notbeing you can neither know nor pronounce; for, what is, is the same [*auto*] to thinking and being" (B 2 and 3). The goddess warns Parmenides away from this second path. And then she informs him about the third path, equally to be shunned, that is, the assumption that both Being and Notbeing exist. This is the way on which "mortals wander who know nothing, the doubleheads. Perplexity guides the wandering mind in their breasts. They are borne along, deaf and blind, a bemused, undiscerning crowd, by whom Being and Notbeing is reckoned [*nenomistai*] the same and not the same, for whom in all things there is a way that turns upon itself" (B 6).

These terse lines contain the first piece of methodical philosophizing in Western history. The truth about Being is the object of inquiry. The inquiry is conducted through (1) a logically exhaustive enumeration of theses concerning the nature of Being, and (2) the elimination of the wrong theses. In the present context we cannot go through the technical details of the process of elimination; we should merely like to draw attention to one point. The philosopher is warned against the second way (that Notbeing exists): "Restrain your thought [*noema*] from this way of inquiry; let not much-experienced habit force you on this way, giving reign to the unseeing eye and the droning ear and the tongue, but make your decision in the much-disputed inquiry by means of argument [*logos*]" (B 7). The Logos is the instrument for ascertaining the truth; and parallel with the Logos appears the source of error, that is, the habit, or custom (*ethos*) of "much-experience," as transmitted uncritically

[9] Or, more discursively: "that Being is and that Not-Being is not."

by ear, eye, and tongue. The commonly accepted "experience" (*poly-peiria*) moves, on the epistemological level, into the position of the commonly accepted valuations against which the new insight asserted itself from Sappho to Xenophanes. A further shade of meaning is added to this common experience through the characterization of the third way on which Being and Notbeing are "reckoned" or "considered" (*nenomistai*) the same, with the implication (in the Greek term) that the *nomos,* the custom, is the source of confusion. This Parmenidean meaning of *nomos* enters as an important component into the later Sophistic concepts of *physis* and *nomos.*

In the description of the one true way of inquiry into Being, there appears a peculiarity of expression that is much debated among philosophers. The reader will have noticed that in the description of the way "that *Is* and that *Not is* cannot be" the "Is" has no subject in the grammatical sense. Translators frequently supply a subject, such as "It is," or "Being is." As far as the sense of the passage is concerned the supplementing of "Being" as the grammatical subject is perfectly legitimate; and the *Eon* indeed appears in other passages in this function. Nevertheless, it does not appear in these preliminary formulations, and we are not satisfied with the explanation (so ready at hand in dealing with early Greek thinkers) that the good man was "clumsy" and did not quite know yet how to handle the philosophical vocabulary that he was just about to create. Rather, we suspect that there was a good reason for the hesitation to use the subject *Eon* and that in this hesitation the true philosophical genius of Parmenides reveals itself. For the "Being" which becomes the object of inquiry can be grasped in the mystical transport, and the area of the soul in which the object is experienced can be named Nous; but that does not make "Being" a datum in the immanent sense, a thing with a form that can be discerned by noesis. To speak of such an object, which is not an object, in propositions with subject and predicate ought to give pause. As far as the predicates of a transcendental subject are concerned, the matter has been cleared up on principle by the Thomistic *analogia entis;* but even the Thomistic exposition of the problem leaves the question of the subject wide open. To name the subject "God," as is done in Christian theology, is a convenience, but quite unsatisfactory in critical philosophy. With great circumspection Parmenides has resisted the temptation of calling his Being God—a temptation which must have been great in the face of the preceding Ionian and Italian

speculation; and it seems that he even hesitated to call it by the name of
"Being." [10] That which comes into grasp through the Nous does not come
into grasp in the manner of an object for discourse. The progress on the
way toward the Light culminates in an experience of a supreme reality
that can only be expressed in the exclamatory "Is!" When the philosopher is confronted with this overpowering reality the "Not is" becomes
devoid of meaning for him. With the exclamation "Is!", we come closest
to the core of the Parmenidean experience. The propositional expressions
"Being is," and "Notbeing cannot be," are already "clumsy" circum-
scriptions.

A clear understanding of this point is of special importance because
its misunderstanding lies at the root of a good deal of Greek philosophizing for the next three generations. The experiential conviction of the
"Is!", as grasped by the Nous, was expressed by Parmenides in the
formulae already quoted that thinking and being are the same, that
Notbeing cannot be because it cannot be thought (*noein*), and so forth.
If such formulations are not understood as true only in the context of
an inquiry into the "Is!", if they are generalized into logical theories ap-
plicable to propositions concerning immanent objects, fantastic consequences will ensue. If we assume that all that is thinkable is, we can
arrive at the conclusion that error is impossible; if error refers to Notbeing, error is impossible because Notbeing does not exist—and this was
indeed the theory of Antisthenes. Since the result is absurd, others may
arrive at the opposite conclusion that Being is unthinkable, and only
Notbeing is thinkable—as did Gorgias or Aristippus. And if the thesis
that the thinkable is receives a subjective slant, we arrive at the Protagorean principle of man as the measure of things.[11] The problem remains
one of the unresolved components in Plato's *Parmenides,* and, through
the mediation of Plato it has codetermined Neoplatonic speculation. The
inability to achieve clearness about it still determines Aristotle's attack
on the Platonic conception of ideas as forms in separate existence.

Let us now turn from the subject to the predicates of Parmenides'
propositions about Being:

(1) A first group of predicates continues and elaborates the nega-
tions of earlier speculation. Parmenides speaks of the many signs (*semata*)

[10] In other contexts, as for instance in Parmenides B 8, 53, the "giving of names" appears as
a source of error.
[11] For a tentative classification of the consequences of the Parmenidean principle in Sophistic
and Socratic philosophy cf. Gigon, *Ursprung,* 253ff.

of Being on the one true way of inquiry. They are: uncreated, imperishable, whole (or complete), unmoved (or immovable), and without end (*ateleston*) (B 8, 1–4). The last of the predicates seems to mean that Being cannot exist toward an end because an end, however understood, would imply a becoming or a ceasing.

(2) The enumeration is followed by a new type of predication with regard to time: "And it was not and it will not be, for it is altogether Now [*nyn*]" (B 8, 5). Being is not a flux with a past and a future. The predication expresses what we considered the primary experience of Parmenides, the "Is!" In exclamatory form he repeats the question: "*Is* or *Is not*" (B 8, 16). When we decide for *Is* it cannot have a becoming. "Thus is 'becoming' extinguished and 'passing away' not to be heard of" (B 8, 21). The predication accomplishes by this first speculative stroke the philosophy of time which Plato and St. Augustine have further elaborated; that is, the philosophy of a ground of being that exists in the eternity of the *nunc stans*. Parmenides arrives at it by means of argumentation on the "Is." "Dike has not set free [*sc.* the "Is"] for becoming or passing, releasing her fetters, but holds fast" (B 8, 13–15). If it were otherwise, the present of the "Is" would be negated, since Parmenides equates becoming or passing away, in past or future tense, with "it was" or "it will be." The conception of the *Nyn*, the Now, as the predicate of Being follows from the meaning of the "Is."

(3) A similar argument is used to establish the continuum of Being as one, homogeneous, and indivisible (B 8, 6 and 22ff.). As the same in the same it rests in the selfsame place, abiding in itself. Powerful Ananke (Necessity) keeps it in the bonds of the boundary that surrounds it on every side, because Being must not be unbounded (*ateleuteton*). For Being is in need of nothing; but, if it were unbounded it would be in need of everything (B 8, 29–33). The self-contained, homogeneous continuum is the spatial predicate of Being, corresponding to the temporal Now. Like the Now, it has a rich later development in philosophy, beginning with its elaboration into the theory of the continuum of being of Anaxagoras and with the conception of homogeneous, indivisible (*atomos*) particles of matter in the atomic theory of Democritus.

(4) Of special interest is the concluding metaphorical description of Being as a "well-rounded sphere" (B 8, 42–49). The idea of a boundary of Being, thus, is elaborated by the idea of a spatial form which, by its limitation, would transform Being into a shape in an environment of

Notbeing. To the Eleatic succession, already to Melissus, this conception of the boundary of Being seemed inadmissible; and both Anaxogoras and Democritus returned to the idea of the infinity of Being. Parmenides, however, is specific on the point that Being is "comparable" to such a sphere, that it is not really one. The image of the sphere is introduced in order to predicate of Being a homogeneousness of extension in all directions, comparable to the equidistance of all the points of a spherical surface from its center. In modern terminology we may say that Parmenides tried to express in symbols of Euclidian geometry a quality of extension which can adequately be expressed only in symbols of non-Euclidian curved space.

The reader should be aware that our analysis presents not much more than the bare skeleton of a rich body of argumentation. Even in such abbreviation, however, it will have become clear that in the poem of Parmenides we are witnessing the outbreak of a new force. The autonomy of the Logos asserts itself; critical speculation, in the pregnant Parmenidean sense of logical distinctions and decisions (*krinein*), not only develops a method but, what is equally important, an ethos. The relentlessness of the course of argument is a most impressive characteristic of Parmenides' philosophizing. That outbreak has a specific occasion, in so far as the logical operations are not performed on an indifferent subject matter but on the reality that is grasped through the Nous. Critical speculation, philosophy in a technical sense, arises as a logical operation on the experience of "Is!"

In the speculation of Parmenides the two components, the experiential and the operational, are inseparable. What results from this combination is for Parmenides the Truth about Being as distinguished from uncritical Doxa. In the Prologue the goddess assures the philosopher that she will divulge to him the "immovable" heart of "well-rounded" Truth (B 1, 29). The attributes of Truth which appear in this assurance are the same (*atremes, eukyklos*) that appear later as the predicates of Being (B 8, 4 and 43). The result of the speculation, thus, is not only a truth *about* Being; it is the Truth *of* Being voiced through the "knowing man." In the medium of speculation the philosopher reproduces Being itself; the well-rounded sphere of Being becomes the well-rounded sphere of speculative order. Philosophical speculation is an incarnation of the Truth of Being. This hieratic compactness of philosophizing is the greatness of Parmenides.

The hieratic tension of Parmenides could not be retained by his successors. With the expansion of the logical operations to the immanent realms of being, as we have hinted, a good deal of confusion ensued. The equivocations between immanent being and the Being which grammatically explicated the experience of "Is!" led to the logical puzzles that we know as the Eleatic paradoxa, to the epistemological fallacies of Protagoras, and to the theory of atoms. In the eristic logic of the Sophists, the operational Logos separated completely from the substance of Truth. Nevertheless, the effectiveness of Parmenides even in such derailments would be unintelligible without the initial meaning of his work. This meaning was recovered, and magnificently enriched, in the work of Plato. The *Republic* is animated by the Parmenidean conception of the light-vision, giving the philosopher his grasp on the Truth of Being, and of the incarnation of the paradigmatic order in the work of the philosopher, that is, in the order of his Politeia. Philosophy in the strict sense, as the tree of speculation that grows from the heavenly root, is the creation of Parmenides and Plato.

3. *Doxa*

By tradition Parmenides is accorded the place of the philosopher of Being, and this position is accentuated by opposing him to Heraclitus as the philosopher of Becoming. In fact, we do not know whether either of the two philosophers knew of the work of the other; and the traditional characterization of the two opposing types, though it is backed by the authority of Plato, is of doubtful value. To be sure, Parmenides speculated on the experience of the "Is!"; in the *Eon* he found the realissimum, in self-contained, homogeneous existence in the eternal Now, beyond the reality of sense-experience and custom. Moreover he understood the Ananke of this Being as the Ananke of the Logos which determined its predicates. Nevertheless, he could not have the experience of the "Is!" without the experience of the Way that must be travelled toward it; and he could not have the experience of the Way without the experience of its starting point in the world *kata doxan*, that is, according to the Delusion of the mortals. He could not gain the Truth of Being without understanding the realm of Delusion. Hence, the second part of his didactic poem, the part on the delusions (*doxai*), in the plural, of men, is quite as essential to the philosophy of Parmenides as the first part on Aletheia.

The meaning of Parmenidean Doxa, as well as its relation with his

Truth, is the subject of a millennial debate. The main points have been
cleared up at one time or another; but with regard to the problem as a
whole we still have no convincing picture. The principal reason for this
state of things seems to be the fallacy which distorted the great discovery
already in the immediate succession of Parmenides, that is, the latent or
open equivocation between the pair of concepts Truth-Delusion in the
Parmenidean sense and the pair true-false in the sense in which we speak
of true or false propositions with regard to objects of immanent experience. If the philosophy of Being is a body of true propositions, runs the
argument, then the *doxai* must be false propositions about the nature of
Being. Such errors of argument can be avoided only if we ascertain the
meaning of Doxa in the context of the poem itself and do not indulge
in speculative guesses about the meaning which such a term must have
on the basis of general usage.

In the context of the poem itself the Doxa is simply a cosmology in
the Ionian sense. It is dualistic in conception, assuming Light and Night
as the two principles (or forms) from whose interactions and mixtures
the phenomena of the world of experience, including the world of man,
arise. This cosmos has a beginning, a growth into the future, and it will
have an end. The complicated details are not our concern. We are, rather,
interested in the question why this cosmology—which could stand quite
well for itself—is placed as the second part in a didactic poem of which
the first part is called "Truth," and why it is called "Delusion." The
meaning of Delusion obviously cannot be found in the content of the
second part itself; it can only be found by relating this second part to
the meaning of Truth in the first part. Only because the exposition of
the first part is "Truth" can the content of the second part be called
"Delusion." We must return to the core of this Truth, that is, to the
experience of the "Is!"

The philosopher in his transport experiences the presence of a supreme
reality; we may call it, as we have done before, the realissimum. The
Parmenidean argument now takes the following course:

(1) If what is given in the experience of the "Is!" be called Being,
then whatever is not given in this experience of a homogeneous presence
must be called Notbeing by definition.

(2) If the Logos is applied to this initial situation we arrive at a
body of predicates about Being; and that body will be the "Truth" about
Being.

(3) All propositions which disregard the initial situation, which draw into the orbit of speculation materials that are not to be found in the experience of the "Is!", will be compelled to treat as Being what according to the initial definition is Notbeing. All such propositions are "Delusion."

The conflict of Truth and Delusion, thus, is not a conflict between true and false propositions. In fact, the Delusion is quite as true as the Truth, if by truth we mean an adequate and consistent articulation of an experience. The conflict occurs between two types of experience. Truth is the philosophy of the realissimum that we experience if we follow the way of immortalization in the soul; Delusion is the philosophy of the reality that we experience as men who live and die in a world that itself is distended in time with a beginning and an end. The characterization of this philosophy of reality as a Delusion derives its justification from the experience of a superior reality, of an immortal ground of the mortal world. The conflict goes ultimately back to the experience of the mortal and immortal component parts of the soul.

The Truth is one, the *doxai* are many. Nevertheless, the multiplicity of *doxai* does not mean that the philosophy of mortal reality is an anarchic field of flights of fancy. The experience of the world is common to all mortals, and the articulation of the experience can be more or less adequate, complete and consistent. The part on Doxa, therefore, is not, as sometimes has been assumed, an account of the opinions of other philosophers but contains Parmenides' own cosmology. The light-goddess herself gives him the information, just as she gave him the information on Truth; and she promises to tell him of the arrangement of the world (*diakosmos*) as all is likely (*eoikota panta*) (B 8, 60), so that the thought of other mortals will not surpass his account (B 8, 61). This conception of a "likely" account, an account that can be more or less true, of a specifically contingent truth as compared with the strict truth of the Logos, had a momentous consequence in the history of ideas in that it was continued and elaborated in the Platonic conception of the *eikos mythos,* the "likely" mythos or story in the *Timaeus.* Especially in the late work of Plato the myth became the instrument of expression for certain areas of experience which Parmenides had assigned to the Doxa.

The peculiar development from the secondary position of the Doxa in Parmenides to the primary importance of the Myth in the late work of Plato is accompanied by an enrichment of the subject matter of phi-

losophizing on which we must dwell for a moment. Parmenides juxta-
poses Being and Delusion without touching the problem that the reality
as given in the "Is!" and the reality of Delusion must somehow be ontologically connected.[12] Being and Delusion are not two different worlds;
they are two aspects of one world that is given in two kinds of cognitive
experiences of the same human being. Parmenides, however, simply describes the delusionary cosmos. The component factors of Light and
Darkness pervade it all through; and because man participates in the
mixture he experiences the cosmos in its delusionary dualism. Moreover,
Parmenides places the gods into the delusion. At the center of the physical cosmos is a female daimon who rules its order; and this central goddess creates the other gods, Eros as "the first of them all" (B 12 and B
13). How the Being, which apparently is not God or *a* god, ever came
by the world of Delusion including the gods remains a mystery. This
mystery becomes the concern of Plato. In his myth of the cosmos he fills
the empty space in the philosophy of Parmenides with the symbol of the
creator-god, of the Demiurge. The Demiurge is the mediator between
Being and the cosmos; he incarnates the eternal paradigm in the world.
The likely Myth provides the link between Being and the world of the
likely Doxa. We may venture the generalization that the late Platonic
myth is primarily the instrument for expressing the incarnation of Being—and not the incarnation of Being in the physical cosmos only, but
also (and this is our special interest) in the order of society and history.
The Part on *Plato* in the present study will bring a full exposition of this
problem.

4. The Rivalry between the Ways of Truth

We have opened our study of Parmenides with reflections on the
symbolism of Way and Truth and its fulfillment in the Johannine symbolism of Christ as the Way and the Truth. Our last reflections on the
evolution from Doxa to Myth open an entirely different historical perspective. The Way of Parmenides leads from the darkness of the world
as experienced by mortals to the beyond of a light-vision in which man
through his Nous experiences the immortal presence of the "Is!" This
immortal Being is determined as to its nature by the necessity of the

---

[12] The fragments from the part on Doxa are scanty; but they seem sufficient to permit the
conclusion that the ontological connection between homogeneous being and dualistic world was
indeed not touched.

Logos; and the same necessity determines its cognitive articulation. It is pure logical structure, resting in itself; it has neither soul, nor will, nor creative power; and, what is most characteristic, it cannot even reveal itself but must be revealed by a light-goddess. The experience of the "Is!" as well as its logical articulation, are surrounded by a symbolism of revelation through divine powers. This setting of the revelation raises interesting questions because in the revelation itself the gods are placed in the world of Delusion. What are the relations between the gods that appear in the revelation concerning Delusion and the goddess who reveals the gods as delusionary? Could it be that we, after all, do not emerge from the Doxa into the Truth of Being, but that the Truth of Being is embraced by the Doxa? Or are there nondelusionary gods beyond Being? Or is the revelation of the Truth, coming from a goddess, perhaps itself a Delusion? The poem offers no answers to such questions; we have reached the limits and the limitations of Parmenidean philosophizing.

Nevertheless, these questions, while not answered by the poem, are raised by its very structure. The revelatory setting is as much an expression of Parmenidean experiences as the content of the revelation. Hence, as a poet Parmenides has a much wider range of sensitiveness than as a philosopher of Being. This wider range must be taken into account if we want to arrive at a full understanding of the historical position of Parmenides and the secret of his effectiveness. The doxa and the revelatory Prologue, as we see, are pregnant with problems pressing toward articulation. In the evolution from the likely Doxa to the likely Myth we recognize a first step of such articulation, bridging the gap between Delusion and Truth; the Myth expands the realm of Doxa to include the incarnation of Truth. If the articulation of the Parmenidean range of problems would proceed in the same direction beyond Plato, we might anticipate an expansion of the Doxa to include the revelatory sphere itself; the Doxa as Revelation would be a truth beyond the Parmenidean truth of Being. This final step was taken, not within Hellenic philosophy, although its logic was immanent in its course, but only in the Hebrew-Christian revelation.

In Revelation the Doxa has expanded into a Truth beyond the Truth and Delusion of Parmenides. In order to arrive at this higher Truth, however, man had to discover the cognition of faith; and the way of Pistis (Faith) is not the way of the Logos that speculates on the experience of "Is!" Again, as in the analysis of Xenophanes, we are confronted with the problem of a plurality of experiences in which transcendence comes into grasp. In Faith and Revelation levels of transcendence beyond the Truth of Being become accessible—but the symbolism of Faith and Revelation retains the qualities of "likeliness" that characterized Doxa and Myth, as distinguished from the Ananke of the Logos. Revelation does not abolish the Truth of Being. Hence, with the entrance of Revelation into history we enter into the history of permanent rivalry between the two sources of Truth. It is a rivalry which occupied Jewish, Christian, and Islamic thinkers. It could express itself in the demand that the Truth of the philosopher be subordinated to revealed Truth, that philosophy should serve as the handmaid of Scripture or theology; or in the demand of allegorical interpretation of Scripture in order to conform its meaning to philosophy; or in the theory of a harmony between Faith and Reason; or in the Arabic conception of Scripture as giving to the people the same Truth in doxic form that speculation gives to the philosopher in logical form. Or, finally, the intellect could take the offensive and substitute the truth of speculation for the truth of faith, as it has happened in the modern gnostic movements of Progressivism, Hegelianism, Comtism, and Marxism.

The struggle between the Ways of Truth is the fundamental issue of Western intellectual history from the blending of Hellenism and Christianity to the present. And Parmenides is the thinker who has created the "type" for this world-historic struggle through his unshakable establishment of the Way of the Logos.

CHAPTER 9

Heraclitus

The speculation of Parmenides intensely concentrates on the experience of the "Is!" The light of the Logos is focussed, within the much wider revelatory range of the poem, on the one experience which relegates everything else into Notbeing. If one breaks, therefore, with the historiographic tradition of classifying Parmenides as "the philosopher of Being," and recognizes the non-logified sectors of his work as quite as essential as his logification of the "Is!", several areas of subject matter can be distinguished and arranged on a scale of diminishing logical penetration. The area of maximal penetration is the experience of the "Is!"; the second area is the realm of Doxa where Parmenides recognizes the possibility of more or less "likely" symbolizations, without arriving at clearness about the criterion; the third area is the revelatory sphere of the Prologue where even the question of doxic likelihood disappears; and the fourth area (if one may call it by that name) is the ontological gap between the realms of Being and Notbeing where not even an attempt at symbolization is made. The experience of the way from darkness to light, and of the light-vision itself, has absorbed the speculative powers of Parmenides to the point of neglecting all other experiential areas as sources of cognition that would merit an equally careful speculative articulation. In particular, we noted the purely logical structure of Being, excluding not only matter but mind, will, and creativeness as well. One component of the life of the soul has asserted itself with blinding force. This is the strength of Parmenides; he has fully experienced the inner dimension of the soul, as it were its height that is domed by transcendental Being. And the paradigmatic articulation of this inner dimension has become part of the *philosophia perennis*.[1]

If, thus, we place the philosophy of Being into the wider context of Parmenides' poem, the direction becomes visible in which the further

---

[1] The Platonic myth in the *Phaedrus* continues and develops this Parmenidean experience.

exploration of the soul was bound to advance. Being comes into grasp because the thinker has achieved consciousness of the inner dimension of his soul; with the understanding of the soul as a something that has an inner dimension, there is correlatively given the consciousness of a border of this something and of a Beyond of this border. Being is not discovered by a static man, for in the act of discovery the soul of man itself differentiates and gains consciousness of its dimension. With the Parmenidean consciousness of the way that leads toward the border of transcendence, the soul itself moves into the field of philosophical speculation. We can speculate about transcendent Being because the soul is a sensorium of transcendence. The light of Parmenides cannot be seen without a light in the soul that illuminates the way toward its border. Hence, the further advance of speculation had to be intimately bound up with a systematic exploration of the inner dimension of the soul, of the manifold of the experiential sources of knowledge which alone can authenticate speculation and raise it above mere "likelihood." Such an exploration of the soul was the work of Heraclitus.

1. The Pythagorean Destiny of the Soul

We again must deal with the vexing problem of the soul—vexing because the extant literary documents are so scanty that the development towards the self-understanding of the soul cannot be traced in continuity. There is a period in which a knowledge of the soul does not yet exist, and we may roughly call this period "Homeric"; and then, all of a sudden, the meaning of the soul is present in the work of Xenophanes, Parmenides, and Heraclitus, probably under the influence of the Pythagorean movement.

In the Homeric period we have yet no "life of the soul." The term which later designates the soul, *psyche*, does exist but it designates the life-force which departs from man in death. The Homeric *psyche* has the peculiar existence of the "shadow" that also can appear in dreams, but it is no immortal soul with an afterlife. What we would call the "person" of a man, in Homeric language his *thymos*, dies with him. Since there is no conception of a soul, of an *anima* in the Christian sense, there also cannot be an animated "body." The term which later designates the body of the living person, *soma*, also appears in Homer but there it has the strict meaning of "corpse"; we have no Homeric term for "body." In Xenophanes, then, the terms appear in their new meaning. In one of the fragments he tells an anecdote of Pythagoras: "Once he passed by when a dog was being beaten. He took pity and spoke this word: Stop! Don't beat him, for it is the soul [*psyche*] of a man, of a friend whom I recognized when I heard his voice crying out!" And in the previously quoted fragment on the animals who would give their gods their respective animal shapes if they could make works of art, the shapes are *somata*.[2] Here we have living bodies of animals, men and gods; and we have a psyche which can migrate into an animal, preserving its identity.

In Fragment B 7 Pythagoreanism is suggested as the source of the new conception. In the absence of direct Pythagorean sources we have already, in the section on Parmenides, supplied a passage from Plato on the demon in man. We shall now follow the same procedure and supply the Pythagorean ideas concerning the destiny of the soul, which must be presupposed as the background of Heraclitus' philosophizing, from a later source, the *Katharmoi* (*Purifications*) of Empedocles (*fl. c.*450 B.C.)

Empedocles speaks of an old oracle of Ananke (Necessity), an ordinance of the gods: Whenever one of the demons, whose portion is long life, has sinfully polluted himself with blood or committed perjury, he will have to wander apart from the dwellings of the blessed for three myriads of years, born into all kinds of mortal forms, changing one path of life for another.[3] The *daimon* (whom we already know from the *Timaeus* passage) once had a blessed existence and forfeited it through some polluting action. The misdeed was followed by the fall into mortality and the transmigration from one mortal body into the next. From the abode of the blessed "we have come into this over-roofed cave."[4] "From what honor and what height of bliss have I fallen to go here on earth among mortal beings" (B 119). "I wept and I wailed when I saw the unfamiliar land" of death and wrath and of putrefaction (B 118, B 121). The demons, however, will not of necessity become men; they may become beasts or trees (B 127); but at last they will become prophets, poets, physicians, or princes among the mortals;

---

[2] Diels-Kranz, Xenophanes B 7 and B 15.   [3] Diels-Kranz, Empedocles B 115.
[4] Empedocles B 120. The symbolism of the world of the mortals as the cave under the roof of the sky is developed by Plato, in the *Republic*, into the Parable of the Cave.

and from such final incarnation they will rise to the immortals and again join the company of the gods (B 146, B 147).

From the general conception of the soul as a *daimon* that has fallen from blessedness, and is now imprisoned successively in a series of mortal bodies, follow the Pythagorean rules for purity and purification of life.[5] Of the manifold of detail we mention only the abhorrence of "slaughter" for sacrificial purposes as well as for the consumption of meat, as one of the roots of vegetarianism.

Of greater interest for us is the question: Whence do Pythagoras and Empedocles derive their knowledge of metempsychosis? With regard to this question we have no more than the barest indications of an answer. In a fragment which even in Hellenic antiquity was understood as referring to Pythagoras, Empedocles speaks of a man of unusual knowledge who, when he strained with all his mind, could see all things that are "for ten or twenty life-times of men" (B 129). Of himself he has to say that before his present life he had been a boy and a girl, a plant and a bird and a fish (B 117). Such fragments seem to point to an ecstatic experience in which the mind "reaches out" or "strains" to the utmost (*orexaito* in B 129). From an ecstasis of this kind, which (as the formulations suggest) may have been induced by a discipline, probably stems the sure conviction which Empedocles expresses in his address to the citizens of Akragas: "I go about among you, an immortal god, no longer a mortal" (B 112). This assurance of essential divinity, combined with the experience of the fall into mortal embodiment, and with a high degree of empathy for the psyche in plant and animal life, seems to be the experiential aggregate which, on the doctrinal level, results in the conception of metempsychosis.[6]

2. The Exploration of the Soul

The conception of the immortal soul, of its origin, fall, wanderings, and ultimate bliss, which we just have assembled from the fragments

---

[5] The conception of the body (*soma*) as the prison or tomb (*sema*) of the soul is Pythagorean. It appears in Plato's *Phaedo* (62), attributed to Philolaus but with the implication of an older origin. Cf. Plato's *Gorgias* (493) where the *soma-sema* conception is attributed to a "sage"; and Phaedrus (250c) where Plato speaks of the state in which the souls are still "pure and untombed."

[6] The Pythagorean metempsychosis was further developed by Plato into the Judgment of the Dead.

of Empedocles, must be presupposed in the thinkers of the generation around 500 B.C. In particular, it must be presupposed in Heraclitus who consciously explores the dimensions of this soul.[7]

The new deliberateness and radicalism of the inquiry can perhaps be sensed most clearly in the famous fragment: "Character—to man—demon" (B 119). It is not easy to gauge the full importance of the fragment because it is isolated. In a first approach one might attribute to it as little technical meaning as possible and consider it no more than a formulation in opposition to conventional opinions about character as the inner and demon as the external factor of human fate. Even if we exert such caution, there still remains the important fact that the demon is immanentized and identified with character (*ethos*). If, however, we put the fragment into the context of the Pythagorean conception of the soul (a procedure that seems to us well justified), then it identifies the *daimon* in the Pythagorean sense with that structure of the soul which Heraclitus designates by the term *ethos*. This identification would imply the momentous break with the archaic inseparable connection of immortality with divinity. The soul, in order to be immortal, would not have to be a *daimon;* we would advance from a theomorphic conception of the soul to a truly human one. The basis for a critical, philosophical anthropology would be created.[8]

We believe, indeed, that this is the great achievement of Heraclitus. And we find our interpretation supported when we place the fragment into the context of Heraclitean meanings. For even if B 119 is understood to identify *daimon* and *ethos,* we have not advanced very far as long as we do not know what Heraclitus means by *ethos* and the conventional translation as "character" does not help. The needed help comes from B 78: "Human *ethos* has no insights, but divine has." Human *ethos* is distinguished from divine through the absence of insight (*gnome*). Hence, the term *ethos* must have a range of meaning beyond

---

[7] The following interpretation of Heraclitus is principally guided by Olof Gigon, *Untersuchungen zu Heraklit* (Leipzig, 1935); by the same author's *Der Ursprung der griechischen Philosophie;* and by Jaeger, *The Theology of the Early Greek Philosophers.* Of great value were the pages on Heraclitus in Bruno Snell, *Die Entdeckung des Geistes* (2d ed., Hamburg, 1948), 32ff. The works just enumerated have put the understanding of Heraclitus on a new basis.

[8] The term "theomorphic" has theoretical implications which cannot be elaborated on this occasion. The so-called "anthropomorphism" of archaic symbolization is indeed not a symbolization of gods in human shape but, on the contrary, a symbolization of areas and forces of the soul by means of divinities. "Anthropomorphism" disappears when the divinities are absorbed into the soul.

character; it must designate the "nature" of a being in general, whether human or divine (*theion*). Moreover, the difference between human and divine *ethos* is very considerable. The proportion is expressed in B 79: "Man is called a baby by the divinity [*daimon*], as a child is by man." *Daimon* is used in this fragment specifically in order to distinguish god and man. Beyond this point, unfortunately, we run into certain difficulties because the texts are not too well preserved. It seems that Heraclitus used of his divinity the predicate "the alone wise," as in B 32: "One, the alone wise [*to sophon mounon*], wants and wants not to be called by the name of Zeus." Moreover, in B 108 he considers as the distinguishing feature of his philosophizing the recognition "that the Wise is apart from all things." But in B 41 he speaks of the *hen to sophon*, of the One that is Wise, as "the understanding of the insight [*gnome*] that steers all things through all things [that is, rules the universe]." The *sophon* seems to designate a human wisdom concerning the *gnome* that rules the world.[9] If we accept both fragments as they stand, the term *sophon* would be used of god as well as of man—with the distinction, however, that the predicate the "Alone Wise" is reserved for god. Human wisdom would then consist in the understanding that it has no wisdom of its own; human nature (*ethos*) is wise when it has understood the *gnome* that governs the cosmos as god's alone.

Human and divine natures, thus, are distinguished by the "types" of wisdom, and related with each other in so far as human wisdom consists in the consciousness of a limitation in comparison with the divine. We know about the divine wisdom but we do not have it; we participate in it far enough to touch it with our understanding, but we cannot hold it as a possession. The Heraclitean experience resembles the Parmenidean. But Heraclitus does not attempt to articulate "Being" through logical explication; he is rather concerned with the relation between

[9] On the meaning of the corrupt text, as well as on the various attempts at reconstruction, cf. Zeller, *Die Philosophie der Griechen*, I/2 (Leipzig, 1920), 839ff. Heidel (1913) and Reinhardt (1916) have suggested reconstructions that would result in substantially the following meaning: "One, the Wise, alone has the insight to govern through all." Recent opinion is divided on the question. Jaeger, *Theology*, 125, n. 58 makes the "one, the Wise" of B 41 refer to the divinity as the same phrase in B 32; Gigon, *Ursprung*, 258, interprets it as human wisdom. The reconstructions as an attribute of divinity are motivated by the sound conviction that the phrase *hen to sophon* so clearly refers to the divinity that the text must have suffered. The acceptance as human wisdom takes into account that the fragment appears in Diogenes Laertius IX, 1 in a context which proves that the ancient author understood it without hesitation as human wisdom. In our opinion a final decision is impossible at present.

the two natures and their types of wisdom. On the level of logic, as a consequence, we find "contradictory" formulations which by their very contradiction express a wisdom that partakes of true wisdom without possessing it fully. Thus, in the previously quoted B 108 Heraclitus praises as the specific result of his logos (discourse), as distinguished from the logoi of all other thinkers, the insight that the "sophon is apart from all things." In B 50, on the other hand, he insists that it is wise (sophon) for all who hear his logos to agree (homologeein) that "all is one." The One that is wise is apart from all things; but for the man who is wise all things are the One. The meaning is elucidated by another pair of contradictory fragments. In B 40 (to which we referred already in the section on Xenophanes) Heraclitus speaks of the polymathie, the "much-knowing," which does not teach "understanding"; and more specifically in B 129 he speaks of Pythagoras who pursued scientific inquiries (historie) more than any other man, and only arrived at a wisdom (sophie) of his own, at a polymathie, a "bad art." In B 35, on the other hand, he insists that the "lover of wisdom" (philosophos) must of necessity have inquired (historein) into many things. The intention of Heraclitus comes now more clearly into view. Human wisdom is not a completed possession but a process. The participation in the divine wisdom that is apart from all things, cannot be achieved through a leap beyond all things; it is the result of the occupation with these very things, ascending from the manifold to the One that is to be found in them all. The attempt may fail; and the lover of wisdom, the philosopher, may end as a polyhistor.

The first appearance of the term "philosopher" in this context suggests the passages in the *Phaedrus* where Plato—undoubtedly following Heraclitus—contemplates a new term for the poets, orators, and legislators who can go beyond the written word of their compositions and prove through oral defense and elaboration that their work indeed is based on knowledge of "truth." The new term for the man of such higher knowledge should not be *sophos*—for that is a great name "seemly to God alone"—but the more humble and befitting *philosophos* (278d). And those who cannot rise beyond their compilation and composition, the patching and piecing, they by right will be called poets, orators, and lawmakers (278d–e). The Platonic opposition of the living, spoken word to the merely written—which is still a subject of debate—illuminates the Heraclitean intention, and in its turn receives light from it.

Literary composition in itself seems to be fraught with danger because it engenders the illusion that "truth" or "wisdom" can be fully expressed and stored away in the work. The living truth, however, is a movement of the soul in the direction of the divine *sophon,* and such movement can never be banned completely into form. Hence, the work has quality only in so far as it has banned this movement so that the formulations will stimulate the corresponding movement in the soul of the reader; and the acid test of such quality is the ability of the creator to elaborate on his subject matter orally from the resources of his soul. By such free oral expression in conversation the creator will prove that he is a creator indeed, and not merely a skilled polyhistor or craftsman who has done a piece of patchwork with instruments supplied by tradition. The Heraclitean attack is primarily directed against the polyhistoric collector of facts, the Platonic primarily against the poetic, legal, and oratorical craftsmen. Both Heraclitus and Plato, however, agree that no composition can lay claim to "truth" unless it is authenticated by the movement of the psyche toward the *sophon.* The problem of truth now is differentiated so far that the loving movement of the soul toward the "Alone Wise" is recognized as the source of such truth as the production of the thinker or poet may have. In so far as this recognition implies a clear distinction between the divinity of "wisdom" and the humanity of "love for wisdom," the philosophical orientation of the soul becomes the essential criterion of "true" humanity. The soul of man is a source of truth only when it is oriented toward god through the love of wisdom. In Heraclitus the idea of an order of the soul begins to form which in Plato unfolds into the perennial principle of political science that the right order of the soul through philosophy furnishes the standards for the right order of human society.

If the nature, the *ethos,* of man is to be found in a process or movement that will result either in an increase of wisdom or in a failure of achievement, we may expect at least an attempt to describe the dynamics of the psyche. A few of the preserved fragments show that Heraclitus was, indeed, occupied by this question. In B 45 he says: "You could not find the limits of the soul, even if you travelled every path; so deep is its logos." Whether "logos" in this fragment simply means extension or measure (as suggested by Burnet), or whether logos means an intelligent substance with a depth of understanding, cannot be decided on the basis of this sentence alone. We prefer the second assumption because the Logos reappears in B 115: "The soul has a logos that augments itself." Such self-augmentation or increase is due to the exploratory activity of the thinker. B 101 emphatically says: "I explored [or: searched into] myself"—and this sentence is certainly not a confession of introspective activities in the modern sense but hints, rather, at an inquiry into hitherto unsuspected depths of the soul, thereby increasing its self-understanding.[10] The polarity of this exploratory movement is again expressed by means of "contradictions." On the one hand: "What comes within the range of eye, ear and learning, that I prize most highly" (B 55); but on the other hand: "The invisible harmony is better [or: greater, more powerful] than the visible" (B 54). The movement, thus, goes from the visible to the invisible truth. The invisible truth, however, is difficult to find, and it will not be found at all unless the soul be animated by an anticipating urge in the right direction. "If you do not hope, you will not find the unhoped-for, since it is hard to be found and the way is all but impassable" (B 18). "Nature loves to hide" (B 123) and "Through lack of faith [apistie] the divine [?] escapes being known" (B 86). When the soul has no direction through the anticipating urges of hope (elpis) and faith (pistis), then there will be no movement from the visible to the invisible. The ordinary experiences will remain undeciphered, and even may become misleading: "Fools [asynetoi], even when they hear it, are like the deaf; of them it is said: 'Present, they are absent'" (B 34); and: "Eyes and ears are bad witnesses for men whose souls are barbarous" (B 107). And above all, the destiny of the soul is hidden to the "fools": "There awaits men at death what they neither hope nor surmise" (B 27).

The language of Heraclitus is very close to the symbolism of Pauline Christianity. Love, hope, and faith are the orienting forces in the soul; the invisible attunement is hard to find unless it is hoped for; and the divine escapes being known unless we have faith. We are forcibly reminded of Hebrews 11:1: "Faith is the substance of things hoped for, and the proof of things unseen." There is no reason to diminish the importance of such parallels; they should be given full weight (though

---

[10] B 101 is also preserved in other versions, allowing the interpretation that Heraclitus insisted on his independence from any teacher. I prefer the interpretation given in the text because it fits into the Delphic style of Heraclitus' thought. It is quite possible that the fragment expresses an obedience to the Delphic command "know thyself." As a matter of principle, whenever I must decide between two interpretations which both can be supported philologically I prefer the profounder to the flatter meaning.

this is rarely done) in appraising the length of preparation for the irruption of transcendental reality in Christianity, as well as the historical
momentum which the life of the soul had gathered when it debouched
into the experience of Revelation. On the other hand, the parallels
should not be overrated. Heraclitus is far from being an *anima naturali-
ter Christiana*. The exploration of the soul in the Christian direction is
one strand in his far-flung philosophizing; and it is deeply embedded
in the experiences of infinite flux and cosmic cycles. There is no touch
of Revelation in his work; the divine is hidden indeed and does not reveal itself clearly in the soul. "The Lord at Delphi neither speaks nor
conceals; he rather gives a sign" (B 93). And when he manifests himself through the word, he uses the language of the oracle: "The Sibyl
with raving mouth, uttering mirthless and unadorned and unscented
sounds, reaches through a thousand years with her voice because it is
full of the God" (B 92). The oracular form, deliberately adopted by
Heraclitus as most suitable for a human utterance that is full of the
God, carries his wisdom through the ages. This form is his achievement
and his limit; it lies about halfway between the myth of the poets and
the Platonic myth of the soul.[11]

3. *The Philosophy of Order*

The work of Heraclitus is preserved only in fragments. They are
parts of what once was a "book." Considering the oracular form of the
extant sentences, the "book" can hardly have been an argumentative,
philosophical discourse but must, rather, have been a carefully considered
concatenation of Delphic "hints" or "signs." Hence, it is not to be won-
dered that even in antiquity the thinkers who had the "book" under
their eyes expressed widely differing opinions concerning the nature of
its content. Diogenes Laertius calls it a treatise *On Nature,* but relates
its contents as three logoi (discourses) on the universe, on politics, and
on theology. A "systematic" division of subject matter of this kind is
in itself hardly probable at the time; and it is, furthermore, in conflict
with the compactness of the fragments preserved. We may even doubt

---

[11] Heraclitus is by tradition "obscure." In fact, he is not quite as obscure as tradition would
make him. Level and form of his mysticism would become more intelligible through comparison
with parallel Eastern phenomena, in particular with Zen mysticism. The plan of our study does
not allow us to explore such possibilities on the present occasion.

that the title *On Nature* was given by Heraclitus himself; from its ascription we can only conclude that the work must have contained a sufficient number of pronouncements to allow anybody who was so minded to classify Heraclitus as a "physiologist" of the Milesian type and to extract a cosmology from the "book." [12] On the other hand, we have the opinion of the grammarian Diodotus who insisted that the book was not on nature but on government (*peri politeias*) and that the part on natural matters served only "by way of paradigm." [13] The extant fragments suggest that Diodotus comes considerably closer to the truth than the naturalist opinion. It seems to us that Heraclitus was concerned with a philosophy of order which had as its experiential center the order of the soul and from there branched out into the order of society and the cosmos. The three types of order would be related with each other ontologically in so far as the ordering principle of the cosmos was conceived as an intelligent substance, and the order of the soul as part of cosmic order. It would be a conception very near to the late Plato in *Timaeus* and *Critias*. The question what the subject matter actually was, if it can be answered at all at this date, must be decided through an analysis of the extant fragments, under the assumption that Heraclitus was a thinker of the first rank and that the lines of meaning to be found in the preserved pieces can, therefore, legitimately be used in reconstructing his thought. Such a reconstruction, we believe, will bear out the opinion of Diodotus rather than that of the "physiologists."

Fortunately there are preserved the opening sentences of the work, presumably setting the theme:

> This Logos here, though it is eternal, men are unable to understand before they hear it as well as when they hear it first. For, though all things come to pass in accordance with this Logos, they are like untried [*sc.* inexperienced] men when they try words and deeds such as I set forth, explaining each thing according to its nature and showing what the real state of the case is. But as to these other men, it escapes their notice what they do when awake, as it escapes their memory what they do when asleep (B 1).

Into the oracular compactness of these sentences Heraclitus has woven a considerable number of his principal motifs. He speaks of the Logos, meaning his discourse; but this Logos is at the same time a sense or meaning, existing from eternity, whether proclaimed by the Heraclitean

---

[12] Diogenes Laertius IX, 5.   [13] *Ibid.*, IX, 15.

literary Logos or not. Men at large will not understand it, with or without its exposition by the philosopher. Then Heraclitus hints that this Logos is a law or order of the cosmos; for all things come to pass in accordance with it. Since it is the all-pervading order of things, men should be thoroughly acquainted with it; but in fact they act as if they had no experience of it at all and hence, when they examine his discourse, with its exposition of the true nature of things, it will be strange to them. The mass of men are sleepwalkers who can experience without becoming aware of the meaning of their experience.

Before we follow the single strands of the intricate weave we must reflect on the social situation that is presupposed. If the logos governs all things whether men know it or not, and if men will not understand it even when set forth by Heraclitus, we may ask, what is the purpose in setting it forth? The protreptic situation that had become difficult for Xenophanes now shows further complications. In the case of the earlier thinker we had to reflect on the obligation of the mystic-philosopher to promulgate his insights and on the corresponding obligation of the hearers to live in openness to such wisdom; the sense of a common bond of humanity through the spirit was in formation. With Heraclitus the gulf between the philosopher and the mass has widened, while the sense of the common bond and of spiritual obligation has deepened. The sentence: "It is not meet to act and speak like men asleep" (B 73), may be primarily a reflection addressed by Heraclitus to himself,[14] but it also may be understood as a precept addressed to men at large involving an obligation of the philosopher to arouse the sleepwalkers from their slumber. In this direction at least point B 71: "Think also of the traveller who does not know where the way goes"; and B 75: "The sleepers too are workers, and collaborate in what is happening in the world."[15] While Heraclitus, thus, may be skeptical about the ability of the sleepers to wake up, he nevertheless invites them to participate in his Logos. The previously quoted B 50 exhorts them to agree (*homologeein*) with him, not hearing him but the *logos*. Agreement with his *logos* will produce *homologia*, a conception of community that prefigures the *homonoia* of Aristotle, of Alexander, and of St. Paul.

[14] It is worth noting that this fragment was preserved through Marcus Aurelius in his reflections addressed *To Himself*, IV, 46.

[15] B 75 also was preserved by Marcus, VI, 42, in the context of a reflection that we all co-operate in the fulfilment of the same plan, some knowing and understanding, others without knowing it.

Since the Heraclitean mode of expression is not discursive but oracular we shall employ the method of pursuing the word-pattern through the fragments in order to reconstruct a more comprehensive body of meanings:

(1) If the opening sentences (B 1) be used as a starting point, we can move in the direction indicated by the term Logos. In B 2 Heraclitus makes it a duty for all men to "follow the common [*xynon*]." And then he continues with the complaint: "But though the Logos is common, the many live as if they had a wisdom of their own [*idian phronesin*]." The Logos is what men have in common, and when they are in agreement with regard to the Logos (*homologia*) then they are truly in community.

(2) The pair common-private is then identified with the pair wake-asleep (B 1) in B 89: "Those who are awake have a world [*kosmos*] one and common, but those who are asleep each turn aside into their private worlds."

(3) On the occasion of B 2 there appears the term Phronesis in specific relation with the community-creating quality of the Logos, further supported by B 113: "It is common to all men to understand [*phroneein*]." The tendency toward the meaning of Phronesis as the prudential wisdom in matters ethical and political, as we find it fully developed in Aristotle, is unmistakable.

(4) Phronesis, however, has to share this function with the Nous that we know from Xenophanes and Parmenides. For, playing with a phonetic association, Heraclitus says in B 114: "Those who speak with the mind [*xyn nooi*] must strengthen themselves with that which is common [*xynoi*] to all." The community of the Logos, thus, moves also into opposition to the "much-knowing" (B 40), which does not teach understanding (*noon*), while the *polymathie* of Hesiod, Pythagoras, Xenophanes, and Hecataeus moves to the side of the sleepwalkers.

(5) Moreover, the phonetic play of B 114 carries the meaning of the common Nous over into the common Nomos: "Those who speak with the mind [*nooi*] must strengthen themselves with that which is common to all, as the polis does with the law [*nomoi*] and more strongly so. For all human laws nourish themselves from the one divine—which prevails as it will, and suffices for all things and more than suffices." It is probable that the later Platonic play with Nous and Nomos hearkens back to this Heraclitean sentence.

(6) Following the term *xynon* further one arrives at the content of the common order, or law, or logos. B 80 says: "One must know that war is the common [*xynon*], and justice [*dike*] is strife [*eris*], and that all things come into being according to strife and need [or: necessity]." War (*polemos*) is Heraclitus' dominating symbol for the order of the world in which man finds himself: "War is of all things the father, and of all things the king; some he makes gods and some again men; some he makes slaves and some again free-men" (B 53). The rule of war prevails over men as well as gods: "Immortals—mortals, mortals—immortals, they live each other's death and die each other's life" (B 62). And it also prevails over the celestial bodies: "The Sun will not overstep his measure; if he does, the Erinyes, the handmaids of Dike, will find him out" (B 94).

(7) Beyond this cosmos, which according to B 89 is "one and common" for all men who are awake, lies the principle that lives in it. "This order [*kosmos*], which is the same for all, no one of gods or men has made; but it was for ever [*aei*], and is and will be, ever-living [*aeizoon*] fire, flaring up [in the rising] measures and dying down [in the falling] measures" (B 30). The ruler of the cosmos determines the order by which things come into being and pass away. "The thunderbolt steers all things" (B 64). "The advancing fire will judge and convict all things" (B 66). This fire is beyond all fires within the cosmos and even beyond the sun: "How could one escape the notice of that which never sets" (B 16). And, finally, this fire is *phronimon*, that is, endowed with intelligence or wisdom (B 64).

This nucleus of interrelated meanings, all depending from the opening sentences of the work, obviously is an attempt at a philosophy of order. The term "common" is used as the overall designation of the community-creating function of the Logos. And the "common" is identified, successively, with the order of the cosmos, with divine law, and with the rule of war that governs the coming-into-being and the passing-away of all things.

In order to arrive at a closer understanding of these symbols, one must be aware that they have a prehistory in Milesian philosophy, and that their meanings contain a probably conscious differentiation beyond earlier attempts. In particular, there is preserved a fragment from Anaximander: "The origin of things is the Apeiron. . . . It is necessary that things should perish into that from which they were born;

for they pay one another penalty [*dike*] and compensation for their injustice [*adikia*] according to the ordinance [or: decree, *taxis*] of Time." [16] While the term *kosmos* does not appear in this passage, "the things" are clearly conceived as a universe with an ordered process. And the order, as the legal terminology shows, is conceived after the model of a lawsuit in which justice is administered—the decree of Time rules "the things" out of existence, back to where they came from, so that other things may have being for their allotted time. The "cosmos" is not something that is found through observation of the external world; it rather is the projection of a human order into the universe. This is fundamentally already the experience which Heraclitus expressed in the formula: "they live each other's death and die each other's life." With their projection of order from society into the cosmos Anaximander and Heraclitus have created a "type" that has determined the whole later course of Greek and Western political theory in so far as the paradigm of this projection (as Jaeger has recognized) was followed by Plato in his conception of the Polis of the Idea as "man writ large" and further (as we may add) in his conception of the cosmos as a psyche.

The line that is running from Anaximander to Heraclitus is unmistakable. Nevertheless, Heraclitus is not simply a continuator of the Milesian naturalists. On occasion of our analysis of Xenophanes we distinguished between the two experiences of transcendence leading to the respective symbols of an *arche* of "things" and of a universal divinity. In the first of these experiences nature in its infinite flow became transparent for an origin of the flow itself; in the second of these experiences the transcendence of the soul toward the realissimum was understood as the universal characteristic of all men. The two experiences were then interpreted as pointing toward the same transcendental reality, and the identity found its expression in the formula "the One is God." This identity, still at the stage of discovery and tentative expression in Anaximander, and even in Xenophanes, is presupposed as established in Heraclitus; the Ephesian thinker takes it for granted and elaborates its speculative consequences. The cosmos now is nature in the Milesian sense and, at the same time, it is the manifesta-

---

[16] Diels-Kranz, Anaximander 9. For the interpretation cf. Jaeger, *Paideia* I, 158ff. and *Theology*, 34ff.

tion of the invisible, universal divinity; it is a universe given to the senses and, at the same time, the "sign" of the invisible God.

The preliminary formulation of the problem may serve as a guide through a group of fragments, not all of which can be deciphered easily when taken in isolation without such guidance. There is, first of all, a plain statement concerning the identity of the visible world and its invisible ground in B 10: "From all is One, and from One is all." But the same thought may also be expressed through "contradictions." There are, on the one hand, the previously quoted fragments on the *kosmos* that is one, and common, and animated by the ever-living order of the fire; and there is, on the other hand, B 124: "The most beautiful *kosmos* is like a garbage-heap strewn at random." The cosmos, thus, is order only as far as it is transparent for the invisible ordering force, while it is disorder when seen as an opaque, external arrangement of "things." Then there are two fragments which seem to "hint" at the two dimensions of transcendental experience separately. There is the deceptively simple B 103: "Common [*xynon*]—beginning and end [*arche kai peras*]—in the periphery of the circle." Most probably this sentence does not betray an interest in geometry, but uses the circle as a symbol for the identity of beginning and end in the *xynon*, articulating more adequately the Anaximandrian thought that "the things" perish into that from which they were born. The Milesian search for the beginning in the horizontal line of the flux of things is now bent back, through the symbol of the circle, so that the beginning and the end will meet in the permanent presence of the *xynon* that is experienced in the vertical direction of the soul toward the "All-Wise." And this vertical direction itself is expressed in B 60: "The way [*hodos*]—upward and downward—one and the same"—a sentence which almost sounds like an answer to the one-way speculation of Parmenides, bridging the ontological gap of the Eleatic thinker. And, finally, we must in this context consider one of the most enigmatic pronouncements of Heraclitus, the B 52: "Aion is a child playing draughts; the royal rule [or: kingdom, *basileie*] is a child's." The conventional translations of Aion as "time" (Diels, Bywater, Nestle, Burnet) do not help, for Aion is a divinity and was understood as such in antiquity. Even Clement of Alexandria still took it for granted that the playing child was Zeus.[17]

---

[17] Clement, *Paedagogus* 22, 1.

And Euripides associated Aion, "the child of Kronos," with Moira in bringing on and ripening "many things." [18] Moreover, there is quite probably an Orphic and Cretan background to the "playing child." [19] Whatever the mythological ancestry of the Heraclitean Aion may be, it seems to us fairly certain that the Ephesian wanted to create a symbol expressing the ambiguity of order and disorder in the *kosmos,* the ambiguity which is made explicit in B 102: "To God all things are beautiful and good and just, but men hold some things just and some unjust." Certainly this was the sense in which Plato understood the symbol when he developed the child playing draughts (*paizon, petteuon*) into the God of the *Laws* (903d), the player (*petteutes*) who shifts the pieces according to an order that appears as disorder to man. [20]

The tension between the experience of the flow of "things" and the experience of a direction in the soul toward the divine "All-Wise," as well as the tension between the symbols expressing these experiences, will remain from now on, in varying degrees of consciousness, a dominant type of Hellenic speculation on order into the late work of Plato and into Aristotle. The tension did not break. Neither did the erotic orientation of the soul toward the *sophon* grow into an eschatological desire to escape the world; nor did the passionate participation in the flux and strife of "things" degenerate into a romantic surrender to the flux of history or to eternal recurrence. The emotional balance between the two possibilities was precarious, and in the generation of sophists after Heraclitus the strain began to show; lesser figures would break under it, but the great thinkers maintained the balance. A good deal of misinterpretation of Plato and Aristotle could be avoided if this problem were understood; and we must be aware of it now when we interpret the delicately shaded meanings of the all-too-few fragments of Heraclitus which carry his philosophy of order to the more concrete level of human destiny and political conduct.

We shall start with the flux of things. Heraclitus has expressed his experience of flux in such famous sentences as: "You cannot step twice into the same river" (B 91) and "You step into the same rivers, and

---

[18] Euripides, *Heraclidae* 898–900.

[19] Persson, *The Religion of Greece in Prehistoric Times,* 136ff., and Vittorio D. Macchioro, *From Orpheus to Paul* (New York, 1930), 171ff.

[20] We suspect that the "royal ruler" of Plato's *Statesman* also finds part of his ancestry in the Heraclitean Aion.

other and other waters will flow on" (B 12). Man participates in the
flux, and the feat of stepping into the same river twice is impossible
also because man has changed in the meantime and is no longer the
same: "Into the same waves we step and do not step: we are it and we
are not it" (B 49a). The permanent change may even become mo-
notonous: "One day is like every other" (B 106). The aimless monotony
of the flux, then, is broken through a desire to participate in it, through
something like an animal urge: "When they are born, they desire to
live, and to meet their fate; and they leave children behind also to suffer
their fate [morous]" (B 20). And this animal urge to live at the price
of death has even deeper roots in the cosmic urge of the Eris (B 80)
that brings all things into being.

Eris and the desire to live symbolize the passion to participate in the
flux, but they do not suggest a purpose. The question of the end is
raised, in the most general form, in an account of Heraclitus' philosophy
given by Diogenes Laertius. The reporter says: "Of the opposites that
which urges toward birth [genesis] is called war and strife, and that
which urges toward destruction by fire [ekpyrosis] is called homologia
and peace." [21] The Stoic ekpyrosis is a doubtful item in this account but,
for the rest, the language sounds genuine enough to justify the assumption that Heraclitus had indeed conceived the end of being as a liberation
from the war of existence and a transfiguration into the peace of the
homologia. The direction toward the peace of the Logos, however, is
counterbalanced by the reflection that Homer was wrong in wishing
"that strife [eris] might perish from among gods and men" for then
life, which is existence in strife, would disappear altogether.[22] On the
level of the animal and cosmic urge, death is the price that must be
paid for life; on the level of the reflection on the end, life is the price
that must be paid for the transfiguration in death. The tension is mas-
terfully expressed in the symbol: "The name of the bow [biós] is life
[bíos], but its work is death" (B 48).

Life, thus, becomes the arena for the struggle in which union with
the Logos is achieved, or rather should be achieved, for not all men are
willing to undertake it. "The many do not understand such things, even
though they run into them; and when learning they do not experience
them, though they believe they do" (B 17). "For what thought or wis-

[21] Diogenes Laertius IX, 8. Diels-Kranz, Heraclitus A 1.
[22] Diels-Kranz, Heraclitus A 22.

dom have they? They believe the singer in the street and take the vulgar as their teacher; not knowing that 'the many are bad, and few are the good' " (B 104). The ways divide sharply: "The best choose one thing before all others: eternal fame among mortals; the many eat their fill like cattle" (B 29). And the way of the few is not easy to walk; it is a continuous struggle, as suggested by the elliptic B 85: "It is hard to fight with one's heart desire [*thymos*]" and nevertheless it must be done because "whatever it wishes to get, it buys at the price of the soul." The soul, the psyche, appears for the first time as the object of human concern; its well-being must be sought through the repression of desires. "For men to gain whatever they desire is not good" (B 110); and when the desires become exuberant then "Hybris must be put out, more than a fire" (B 43). The soul should burn, but with the divine fire of the cosmos: "The dry soul is wisest and best" (B 118); on the other side: "When a man gets drunk, he is led by a beardless boy; he stumbles, not knowing where he steps; for his soul is moist" (B 117); but unfortunately: "It is a delight to souls to become moist" (B 77).[23] The discipline which creates and preserves the health of the soul, however, is not theoretical like the later Aristotelian; it is the discipline of a warrior and aristocrat in obedience to the War that is father and king of all things: "Gods and men honor those who are slain in battle" (B 24). The peace of the Logos can be reached only through participation in the war of existence; and there is held out the promise that "Greater fates will gain greater portions" (B 25).[24]

A final group of fragments has most intensely absorbed the experiences which Heraclitus had with his Ephesians. "The Ephesians would do well to hang themselves, every grown man, and leave their polis to the beardless boys, for they have banned Hermodorus, the best man among them, saying: 'None of us will be the best, and if he is, he will have to be it elsewhere and among others' " (B 121). Hermodorus went to Rome and, according to tradition, his advice was taken in giving the law of the Twelve Tables. To a sensitive witness an event of this kind might well reveal the fundamental foulness of a society and open his eyes to the possibility that one man might be right and the whole

---

[23] Into this context of the health of the soul also belongs the indirect report B 46 that Heraclitus called common opinion or self-conceit (*oiesis*) a "sacred disease." If the report (in Diogenes Laertius IX, 7) is authentic, Heraclitus would have used the concept of a disease of the soul (*nosos*) in the same sense as Plato in the *Laws*.

[24] With regard to the connection between love of the All-Wise and *askesis* of the warrior, a comparison with Zen mysticism would be especially helpful for the understanding of Heraclitus.

people wrong. From such experience may have sprung the pointed B 39: "In Priene lives Bias, the son of Teutamas, who is of greater account [*logos*] than the rest," as well as the grim B 49: "One man is to me ten-thousand if he be the best." In a corrupt society there may be only one man in whose soul burns the cosmic fire, who lives in love to the divine *nomos;* then the situation envisaged by B 33 may arise: "It may be law [*nomos*] to obey the will [or: counsel] of one." In the light of this sentence must also be read B 44: "The people [*demos*] must fight for its law as for its walls"—with the implication that the actual people is not desirous to engage in the fight for the law that nourishes itself from the divine (B 114).

4. *Conclusions*

The mystic-philosophers break with the myth because they have discovered a new source of truth in their souls. The "unseemly" gods of Homer and Hesiod must pale before the invisible harmony of the transcendental realissimum; and the magnificent Homeric epic that was enacted on the two planes of gods and men must sink to the level of "poetry" when the drama of the soul with its intangible, silent movements of love, hope, and faith toward the *sophon* is discovered. The order of the polis cannot remain the unquestioned, ultimate order of society when an idea of man is in formation that identifies humanity with the life of the common Logos in every soul. What appears negatively as the break with the myth is positively the transition from a theomorphic symbolization of experiences to their understanding as movements of the human soul itself. The true range of humanity comes into view correlatively with the radical transcendence of the divine realissimum. It is a process that may overshoot its mark—and actually did so in the century after Heraclitus—in so far as the recognition of the invisible God may degenerate into the denial of the existence of God when visibility becomes the criterion of existence. The movements of the soul which animate the speculation of a Xenophanes, Parmenides, and Heraclitus are not everybody's affair—as Heraclitus had diagnosed rightly. The many need gods with "shapes." When the "shapes" of the gods are destroyed with social effectiveness, the many will not become mystics but agnostics. The agnostic empiricist, if we may define him historically, is an enlightened polytheist who is spiritually not strong enough for faith.

The transcendental irruption which makes the generation of the mystic-philosophers an epoch in the history of mankind has profoundly affected the problem of social order up to the present because the old collective order on the less differentiated level of consciousness is under permanent judgment (*krisis*) by the new authority, while the new order of the spirit is socially an aristocratic achievement of charismatic individuals, of the "dry souls" who can say: "I have come to throw fire on the earth. . . . Do you believe I have come to bring peace to the earth? No, I tell you, rather division" (Luke 12:49, 51). As a consequence, entirely new problems of social organization appear. Neither can the Hellenic manifestation (or the Christian revelation) of the spirit be removed from history because, on the human side, they are structures of the soul; nor can the problem of the Heraclitean sleepwalkers be removed from history through human agencies, however much of a fire the mystics and saints may build under them to arouse them from slumber or at least to fits of wakefulness. Social order will from now on depend on the hierarchical structure that is foreshadowed in the authoritative self-assertion of the charismatic souls ever since Hesiod and Sappho, as well as in the Heraclitean insight that it may be law to obey the counsel of one man. And in order to make this hierarchical structure effective in social practice, institutions will be required for continuing and transmitting spiritual insights, as well as the intellectual culture that is necessary for their exposition and communication, through the generations, and for mediating them to the many thorough processes of education appropriate to their receptiveness.

This is the problem that was seen by Plato. In his philosopher-king he has created the symbol of the new order: that the spirit must be linked with power in order to become socially effective. And this demand is not a protective reflex under the impression of the fate of Socrates, which demonstrated that the sleepwalkers can solve their problem of order in the short run by the simple means of killing a disturbing "dry soul"; it springs from the insight of the patriot who sees the power of his polis disintegrating because it is not linked with the spirit. The work of Plato, however, the creation of the science of order under the conditions of the new epoch, did not get underway before the grandeur and catastrophe of Athens had furnished the object lesson that made it compelling and convincing.

PART THREE

The Athenian Century

The tension between the polis and the spiritual adventure of the poets and philosophers was the civilizational form of Hellas. The potentialities of the adventure had been fully actualized, however, and perhaps were exhausted, with the generation of Heraclitus and Parmenides. The myth, the *terminus a quo* of the movement toward transcendence, had been disintegrated through the discovery of the soul and its authority; and a *terminus ad quem*, a people that would live by the insights of the mystic-philosophers, had not been found. The authoritative "But I say unto you . . ." required a social response if it was not to peter out into repetitions, from time to time, by solitary individuals.[1] The Heraclitean reflections on the "sleepwalkers" ominously illuminate the social impasse of the magnificent adventure. In order to become truly the form of a civilization, the tension had to be something more than an irritation of the polis by odd individuals. Something like a Great Awakening was required to create a society in wakeful response to the depth of the soul, to the new humanity in love of the *sophon*, discovered by the philosophers.

The Great Awakening was the feat of the Athenian people in the fifth century B.C.—with consequences for the history of mankind which have not been exhausted to this day. For without the paradigmatic existence of the Athens of Marathon, the spiritual and intellectual community substance from which the political philosophy of Plato and Aristotle nourished itself would not have existed. Only with the paradigm of such a society in historical existence could a philosophy of order for a society of mature men be developed with conviction.

A history of Athens under the aspect just indicated has yet to be

---

[1] The problem of communal growth through response to solitary individuals, at which I can only hint in the text, is the great topic, under the title of transition from the closed to the open society, of Bergson's *Les deux sources de la morale et de la religion* (Paris, 1932).

written. That gap, however, cannot be filled by the present study, since more than one volume would be required for a moderately adequate treatment of the major topics. The following pages will give no more than a catalog of essential problems. The problems will be classified by three main groups and one chapter will be devoted to each of the groups. The three groups are: (1) Problems connected with the rise and end of tragedy; (2) problems connected with the so-called sophistic movement; and (3) problems connected with the historical rise and fall of Athens as a political power.

CHAPTER 10

Tragedy

1. The Truth of Tragedy

The awakening from the sleep was an awakening to a new consciousness. The Athenians were supremely aware of the historic rôle that had become their fate in its glory and its bitter end. In the great funeral oration the Thucydidean Pericles praised Athens as the "school [*paideusis*] of Hellas." In the pathos of the polis, as voiced by its leading statesman, the consciousness of power had merged with the consciousness of highest human rank; the people had reached the rank of the adventurous individuals; and the people of Athens collectively had become the school-head of the Hellenes. Power and spirit were linked in history for one golden hour through the inseparable events of the Athenian victory in the Persian War and the Aeschylean creation of the tragedy.

The setting of the scene goes back to Solon. His conception of the Eunomia of the polis set the pattern for the rough but sure evolution toward constitutional democracy, drawing the people into the culture of the aristocracy and bending the old nobility under the principle of isonomy.[2] Solon's faith in Dike and the unseen measure was fundamentally the faith of Aeschylus. The principal intermediate events were the tyranny of Peisistratus and the reform of Cleisthenes.

The reform of Solon had been unsatisfactory in detail, and a period of civil strife was followed in 561 by the rule of Peisistratus as the leader of the poor people from the hills. Under his rule the cult of Dionysus was introduced as a state-cult in order to break the power of the hereditary priesthoods of the noble clans. For the first time, at the Dionysian festivals of 535 (or one of the two following years) Thespis appeared with his chorus of *tragodoi*, the goat-singers, the archaic form out of which a generation later the tragedy was to grow.

[2] "Isonomy" is the older term. "Democracy" appears only in the fifth century.

From its very beginning the tragedy was established as a cult-institution of the people.

After the expulsion of the Peisistratides and a short interlude of party strife, Cleisthenes could effect the great democratic reform of 508 that we have described in an earlier chapter. With the reorganization of Athens on a territorial basis, the power of the noble clans was broken on principle, and immediately afterwards the style of the new democracy made itself felt in the conduct of politics—in the beginning friction with aristocratic Sparta, the expansion into Euboea, the naval support of the Ionians in their struggle with Persia which precipitated the Persian expedition against Athens, the development of the Piraeus, the great military quality displayed at Marathon, and the hysterical punishment of the victorious general Miltiades because he failed to capture Paros in addition. Most illuminating for the new nervousness of politics was the decade between Marathon and Salamis. Everybody knew that the Persian defeat of 490 would be followed by a full-scale major war in due course. But instead of systematically preparing for the great onslaught, Athens conducted an inconclusive war with Aegina (489–483), had a major constitutional reform in 488/7, introduced the institution of ostracism, practiced it by banishing successively Hipparchus, Megacles, Xanthippus, and Aristides, and in spite of such messy activity was able to propel to the decisive position of *strategos autocrator* Themistocles, the new leader of the people, the first genuinely "modern" Athenian, who prefigured in his complex personality the qualities that were to determine the greatness and fall of Athens through Pericles and Alcibiades.

What the tragedy meant in the life of the Athenian democracy can be gathered—in no more than a first approach, however—from the confrontation of Aeschylus and Euripides in the *Frogs* of Aristophanes. The poets appear as the educators of the people, holding up to them a model humanity; the quality of the people will depend on the type of humanity that is presented in the great performances at the Dionysian festivals. Aeschylus appears as the educator, the moulder of the generation of the Persian Wars; Euripides as the corrupter, responsible for a generation of effeminate indulgence without warlike vigor, of sophistic frauds and rhetors, of incestuous relationships, crimes of passion, general loose living, weakening of morale in the navy and discipline in the army, and loss of excellence even in gymnastic exercises. The idea of elevating the poets into the causes of Athenian greatness and decline certainly was far-fetched. Whatever effects the conduct of a Phaedra on the stage may have had on the love-life of a naturalistically experiencing lady in the audience, the problem of the tragedy did not lie on this level. Nevertheless, the excitement of Aristophanes reveals the evolution of tragedy from Aeschylus to Euripides as the representative expression of the political decline of Athens.

While the accusation against Euripides is hardly tenable, the nature of the charge is of interest. For the form which the criticism assumes is in itself an intellectual form of political decay. The Aeschylus of the comedy insists that the poet has, with regard to grown-up men, the function which the schoolteacher has with regard to boys. The poet is the teacher (*didaskalos*) of the people, apparently in the elementary form of straight information concerning right and wrong in matters of politics and morals. If we understand Aristophanes rightly, he accepts what we may call the "naturalistic" attitude toward complex works of art, that is, the attitude in which the many-storied edifice of meaning is disregarded and nothing extracted from the work but the "story." It is the attitude of contemporary literary critics who classify Thomas Mann's *Magic Mountain* as a story about life in a sanitarium, or condemn James Joyce's *Ulysses* as "immoral" or "indecent." Aristophanes takes the attitude of the audience for granted—and Euripidean tragedies performed before an audience of this kind may, indeed, have had unwholesome effects. But when communication through indirection has become impossible because the audience can understand only direct speech, the time for such complex structures as the great tragedies has run its course. It is symptomatic that the *Frogs* netted rare honors for Aristophanes, as well as the unusual distinction of a second performance, not because of the great qualities of the comedy, but because of a direct political exhortation to the Athenians (vv.686–705) to restore civic rights to the persons who had participated in the plottings of the period of The Four Hundred, in 411 B.C. The exhortation was considered a patriotic feat meriting rewards. To be sure, it is an afterglow of a great period that a political speech can have a particularly strong effect if presented incidental to a literary work of distinction, but it is no more than an afterglow, and the time is ripe for "teaching" through direct, discursive treatment of politics.

The disintegration of tragedy is complete when we reach the standard treatise on the subject, the *Poetics* of Aristotle. Tragedy has become a literary genus, to be dissected with regard to its formal characteristics, its "parts." It is the most important genus because of its formal complexity; he who understands tragedy has understood all other literary forms. As far as the substance and historical function of tragedy is concerned, however, there is barely an elusive hint in the *Poetics;* obviously the problem had moved for Aristotle entirely beyond his horizon of interests. The situation is illuminated by the famous definition of tragedy as "a representation of an action that is serious, coming to an end, and of a certain magnitude—enriched by language of all kind, used appropriately in the various parts of the play—representing through action, not through narrative—and through pity and fear effecting catharsis of these and other emotions." [3] We take Aristotle by his word, as we did Aristophanes; and we assume that he described to the best of his knowledge what an audience of the fourth century experienced when attending the performance of a tragedy. In its effect on the spectators, tragedy has now become something like a psychological therapy. The events on the stage arouse pity and fear, and other emotions, in the spectators and thereby give relief to pent-up quantities of passion. If again we may venture a comparison with contemporary phenomena, the theory of Aristotle resembles the theory of certain modern psychologists who consider football games and similar sportive events a good thing because they provide the spectators with virtual satisfaction of their aggressiveness. To be sure, it is a considerable cultural difference whether such relief is furnished by a Greek tragedy, or by games and movies, but the principle is the same; the spirit of the tragedy is gone.

Nevertheless, Aristotle hints at the real problem when he compares the object of the poet with the object of the historian. The poet does not tell what actually happened, as does the historian (*historikos*), but what happens "according to likelihood and necessity." For that reason, poetry is something "more philosophical and serious" than history; it does not relate mere facts, but it conveys what is "general"; we may say, perhaps, what is "essential." [4] Elusive as these hints are, we hear in them nevertheless an echo of the problems of the time of Heraclitus and Aeschylus. The "much-knowing" of the historian is opposed to the "deep-knowing" of the philosopher. The poet creates an action which conveys a

---

[3] Aristotle, *Poetics* VI, 2.   [4] *Ibid.,* IX, 1–4.

"general" insight; he participates in the great search for truth from Hesiod to the mystic-philosophers.

The tragedy continues the search for truth; and Aristotle has seen rightly that there is something "general" about this truth. The action of tragedy, its *drama,* is neither information about particular events, nor amusing fiction. The material used for the action is drawn from the stock of myths, but the tragedy neither narrates it in the manner of the Homeric epic, with the yet unreflected intention of telling a "true" story, nor does it recast the material into speculative form in the manner of Hesiod, with the intention of opposing the new truth to the old falsehood. The tragedy from Aeschylus to Euripides is quite deliberately a play. Neither the poet nor his audience is in doubt that the action is invented, that it uses the mythical materials quite freely, rearranges them to meet exigencies of literary form, and adds numerous imaginative details. There is not even that element of reality which was attached to the older cult dances and choric lyrics, of reenacting a paradigmatic mythical event. For chorus and audience have separated; the chorus has become part of the play, acting on the stage, and the audience does not participate in the action. Only when all erroneous associations are eliminated do we arrive at the true core of the problem: The truth of the tragedy is action itself, that is, action on the new, differentiated level of a movement in the soul that culminates in the decision (*proairesis*) of a mature, responsible man. The newly discovered humanity of the soul expands into the realm of action. Tragedy as a form is the study of the human soul in the process of making decisions, while the single tragedies construct conditions and experimental situations, in which a fully developed, self-conscious soul is forced into action.

2. The Meaning of Action

The character of the tragedy as an experimental study, as well as its search for the truth of decision, will become clear through an analysis of the *Suppliants* of Aeschylus. We shall not analyze the whole tragedy, however, but confine ourselves to the exposition of the argument that leads to the decision and subsequently to action. [5]

[5] The *Suppliants* was supposed to be the earliest extant tragedy of Aeschylus, but the recent analysis of a papyrus fragment by Albin Lesky, "Die Datierung der Hiketiden und der Tragiker

Danaus was defeated by his brother Aegyptus in the struggle for rule over the Nile valley, and the fifty sons of Aegyptus wanted to possess the fifty daughters of Danaus in marriage. Since the warrior-virgins had no taste for the union with the violent Aegyptians, they fled with their father from the Nile and sought refuge in Argos, the home of their ancestor Io. The drama opens with the appearance of the Danaides on the shores of Argos.

Pelasgus, the king of the polis, appears, and the request of the fugitives is presented to him. He is not pleased at all. The more he ponders the legal complications of the case, the clearer becomes the predicament of his situation. The Danaides are neither citizens of Argos, nor Hellenes who could claim *proxenia* (237–40), and hence cannot be received rightly into the polis. Moreover, their flight from the Aegyptians is not entirely justified. By the *nomos,* the law of their country, they should submit to the marriage with their kinsmen (387–91). It would be best to abandon the suppliant maidens to their Aegyptian pursuers and suitors, in order to avoid a war that at best would be a costly affair for the polis.

Unfortunately, there are arguments on the other side. The Danaides come as suppliants and are under the protection of Zeus under his various aspects. First of all, they can appeal to Zeus their begettor through Io (206), who perhaps is also the Zeus of their Aegyptian homeland (4, 558). They, furthermore, approach Argos with a prayer to Zeus Soter, the "guardian of the households of pious men" (26–27). Then, there is Zeus whose daughter is Themis, "the protector of suppliants" (359–60)—a predicate which also applies to Zeus himself (347). And, finally, there is the "other Zeus" (231), "the most hospitable" (157), who receives the dead and sits in last judgment (231). To him will go the last appeal of the suppliants, who are ready to commit suicide, unless they find justice, by hanging themselves from the statues of the gods (465). That will expose the Zeus of Olympus to the charge of

---

Mesatos," *Hermes,* Vol. 82 (Wiesbaden, 1954), 1–13, has made the late date of 463 practically certain. For a fuller analysis of the *Suppliants* with regard to the problems of law and justice cf. Erik Wolf, *Griechisches Rechtsdenken I: Vorsokratiker und Fruehe Dichter* (Frankfurt, 1950). Cf. further the chapter on Aeschylus in Jaeger, *Paideia* I, 1945; the chapter "Mythus und Wirklichkeit in der griechischen Tragoedie" in Snell, *Die Entdeckung des Geistes,* 1948. Of considerable interest, though to be used with caution, is Alfred Weber, *Das Tragische und die Geschichte* (Hamburg, 1943). For the older literature on Aeschylus cf. Wolf, *Griechisches Rechtsdenken,* 340.

injustice (168–69), and will bring ruin on Pelasgus and his polis (468ff.).

Aeschylus carefully constructs an unpleasant situation. The right order of *themis* is not free of conflicts. Themis governs the order of marriage. The Aegyptians have legal control over the Danaides and can demand them in marriage. Only if the marriage is abhorrent to the women is its enforcement *me themis,* unrighteous (336). That is the case which the Danaides plead for themselves. Their plea, however, is not quite sincere, because they dislike not only the Aegyptians but the bond of marriage on principle (1030–34). While the rejection of a specific man is justified, the rejection of marriage on principle is not *themis.* The order of Themis, furthermore, protects suppliants, especially when they are relatives (through Io). Hence, the supplication cannot be simply rejected, even if its justice is not beyond doubt. And, finally, Themis governs piety toward the gods. The pollution of the statues through suicide will have terrible consequences for Argos, even though the threat of suicide is a clear case of blackmail against Pelasgus, as well as of *hybris* against Zeus. What then shall the King do, threatened by the conflicts of *themis,* and forced to violate either the *nomos* of the Aegyptians with the consequence of war, or to bring the wrath of the gods on himself and his polis?

The King is in a state of indecision and formulates his dilemma: "Without harm I do not know how to help you; and yet again it is not advisable to slight such supplications." He is gripped by helpless confusion (*amechanos*); and his soul (*phren*) is fearful whether "to act, or not to act and take what fortune brings" (376–80). Gravely he reflects: "There is need of deep and saving counsel, like a diver's, descending to the depth, with keen eye and not too much perturbed" (407ff.). Clearly the lines recall the Heraclitean "deep-knowing" of the soul whose border cannot be measured because its Logos is too deep. The Heraclitean dimension of the soul in depth is dramatized by Aeschylus into the actual descent of a soul in a concrete situation that requires a decision.[6]

From the depth the King is supposed to bring up a decision in accordance with *dike.* The Chorus admonishes him to make Dike his ally (395) and assures him that Dike protects her allies powerfully (343). Beyond the order of *themis* with its conflicts, there lies an order of

---

[6] The Aeschylean simile points to a dictum attributed to Socrates that it requires a Delphic diver to descend to the meaning of Heraclitean formulations.

dike, in the double sense of a higher law and of concrete decisions. The situation that is not covered by *themis* will have to be ordered by a concrete decision, a *dike,* of ultimate rightness. That *dike* beyond *themis* has its source in the depth of reflection into which the King is ready to descend. At this point, when the actual descent should occur, however, it becomes clear that Aeschylus has moved far beyond the situation of the solitary Heraclitus into the community of a polis whose citizens are willing to descend into the soul as a people. For the King informs the Danaides that they are not taking refuge at the hearth of his private home, but in a polis. "The common" (*to koinon*) of the polis is threatened by them; and "in common" (*xyne*) the people will have to find a solution. The King can make no promise before he has "communicated" (*koinosas*) with all the citizens (365–69). The *xynon* of Heraclitus is institutionalized as the community of citizens in council. The Chorus protests vehemently with an appeal to his absolute kingship: "*You* are the polis! *You* are the people!" (370). But Pelasgus is not a mystic-philosopher; he has a people, and energetically he tells the Chorus: "Nothing without the people [*demos*]" (398). He leaves the suppliants in order to assemble the people and to submit the case to the general body (*koinon*) of the citizens (518), and he hopes that Persuasion (*peitho*) will aid him (523). The speech of the King is indeed successful. The decrees extending *proxenia* to the suppliants are passed. "It was the Pelasgian people that willingly heard the subtle windings of the speech; but it was Zeus who brought the end to pass" (623–24). The descent into the depth was taken in common and what the people found was the Dike of Zeus.

We have assembled the main elements of the Aeschylean theory of action. The order of Themis still governs the gods, the world, and society, as in the Homeric epics. But the existence of man under the order has become difficult, in so far as *themis* is no longer a guide for decisions in the concrete situation. In the Homeric epic a decision could be reached either by weighing the consequences of action on the utilitarian level, or by following counsel, divine or human. That was the burden of the great, paraenetic speech of Phoenix to Achilles. With Aeschylus both possibilities are excluded. The utilitarian weighing is expressly rejected as a motive (443–54); and Aeschylus, in order to prepare the case in experimental purity, even resorts to the technique of building up sound reasons which man must reject in order to arrive at the right decision (477). And no external counsel through the helpful appearance of an Homeric god or man is available. The decision must be reached, without such counsel, from a searching of the soul. The leap in being does not assume the form of an Israelite revelation of God, but of the Dionysiac descent into man, to the depth where Dike is to be found. Not every type of conduct, therefore, is action. We can speak of action only when the decision was reached through the Dionysiac descent into the divine depth. And conversely, not every situation is tragic. We can speak of tragedy only when man is forced into the recourse to Dike. Only in that case is he faced with the dilemma expressed by the line "to act or not to act." Apparently Aeschylus considered as action only the decision in favor of Dike. A negative decision, an evasion through utilitarian calculus, or a mere insensitiveness toward the issue, would not be considered action.

The Aeschylean meaning of *drama,* of action, symbolizes the Dionysiac order of Dike. The great symbol raises serious questions with regard to the history both of Athens and of tragedy. The action, experienced and expressed by Aeschylus, requires a certain human stature. There may arise a tragic situation without a tragic actor. If the soul is not responsive to Dike, and man is not willing to descend into its depth, an easy way out may be found by weighing present losses against uncertain future profits. The passion of the moment, utilitarian calculation, or plain cowardice, may blur, or completely obfuscate, the tragic issue. Tragedy of the Aeschylean type, in order to be socially possible as an expensive state-cult in a democracy, requires a citizenry that willingly opens its soul to the tragic conflict. Even if the audience is not an assembly of heroes, the spectators must at least be disposed to recognize tragic action as paradigmatic. The heroic soul-searching and suffering of consequences must be experienced as the cult of Dike and the fate of the hero must arouse the shudder of his own fate in the soul of the spectator—even if he himself should succumb to his weakness in a similar situation. The meaning of tragedy as a state-cult must be sought in such representative suffering. The binding of the soul to its own fate through representative suffering, rather than the Aristotelian catharsis through pity and fear, is the function of tragedy. The Epitaph, according to tradition written by Aeschylus himself, unmistakably speaks to us:

"His glorious valor [*alke*] the precinct of Marathon may proclaim,
And the long-haired Medes who knew it well."

To have proven his worth as the soldier of the polis in action is his proud
title to fame rather than his work as a poet; Marathon is the test of
tragedy.

With the spirit of Marathon the tragedy would have to die. The
shouldering of fate would become too heavy a burden. In the full
unfolding of tragedy, in the grandiose personalities of Sophocles, one
can sense the exceptional character of such suffering; a solitude begins to
spread around the hero that makes his suffering unrepresentative for the
common man. And Euripides, as we shall see, was preoccupied already
with the problem of the hero who breaks under his fate. A sense of
demonic capriciousness of the gods becomes stronger than the faith in the
ultimately harmonizing order of Dike. Under such conditions the social
function of tragedy will become problematic and, finally, impossible.
The *Suppliants* has its distinctive place in the history of order because
the line along which the tragedy as an institution of the polis will break
emerges from the action itself. Pelasgus, the King, as we have seen,
has gone through the decision in his own soul; and then he must induce
the same process in the soul of the citizens through his speech, re-acting
his own argument and that of the Chorus before the assembly. Through
Peitho (persuasion) the paradigmatic action of the hero must expand
into the soul of the people, binding it to the communal purpose. In the
last work of Aeschylus, the *Oresteia*, Peitho becomes the great instrument
of the order of Zeus by which the demonic divinities of the old law,
the Erinyes, are themselves bent to Dike and are transformed into the
Eumenides. In the *Suppliants* this meaning of Peitho as the persuasion
of Jovian Dike (not perhaps as psychological management) is suggested
in the lines of the Chorus that the people made the decision but that
"Zeus brought the end to pass" (623–24). When Peitho, persuasion in
this pregnant sense, is no longer socially effective, the political order of
the democracy which must rest on Dike will disintegrate and give way
to the nightmarish disorder that we find described by Thucydides. The
restoration of social order in the polis, when it is to rest on spirit and not
on fearful subservience to power, will then require the restoration of
spiritual persuasion. And this has, indeed, become one of the great themes
of Platonic politics, with increasing intenseness in the later works, until

in the *Timaeus* Peitho appears as the force of the psyche that imposes order on the recalcitrant Ananke of the cosmos.

3. *Tragedy and History*

The *Suppliants* is the finest study of the essence of tragic action, but of no more than this very essence. The central action is surrounded by an area of issues, some of them of a rather disquieting nature. The hero follows Dike, the highest ordering principle of cosmos and polis—and woe to him if he does not—but the situation as a whole does not show the ordering principle as a particularly effective one. There is the beastly conduct of the Aegyptians and the corresponding misery of the Danaides; in the background of this affair lies the equally unjust fate of the ancestress of the cousins, Io, who was loved by Zeus, metamorphosed into a cow by Hera, and driven over the earth in madness by a gadfly, all without any guilt of her own; and Pelasgus rightly does some cursing about a situation that involves him in all sorts of peril though he would much prefer to mind his own business. The only point in the universe at which Dike really dwells seems to be the soul of the King, while the surroundings look rather like a world of demonic mischief. Moreover, the Dike in the heroic soul would not help the Danaides much unless it were the soul of a king who can use his persuasion on his soldier-citizens so that his decision will be implemented by an army when the clash with the Aegyptians comes. The King does not consider for a moment using his powers of persuasion on the Aegyptians—though he engages in legal argument with their herald. The Hellenic polis thus appears, through its combination of Dike and Valor in the body of its militant citizenry, as a shining bulwark of order in a very disorderly world.

The disquieting background of tragic action must be clear, when now we approach *Prometheus Bound,* the work of Aeschylus in which the morass of demonic evil surrounding the island of order becomes the great problem.

The interpretation is faced with the difficulty that the extant *Prometheus* is one part of a trilogy, probably its middle part (though even that is contested), so that one cannot always be certain where the lines of meaning running through the play have their beginning and their end. Moreover, the isolation of the extant *Prometheus* has become the occasion for an overgrowth of modern Promethean symbolism which is at variance with the intentions of Aeschylus. The Promethean symbols of Shaftesbury and Goethe, of Shelley and the young Marx, belong to the age of enlightened, human self-reliance, of the titanism of the artist, and of the defiant revolutionary who will take the destiny of mankind into his own hands. All that has nothing to do with Aeschylus, but it has become an additional obstacle to understanding him in our time.[7]

As far as its subject matter is concerned, the *Prometheus* is a story about gods, not about men. It is an episode of the Titanomachia in the Hesiodian sense. When Zeus engaged in his battle against the Cronian generation of gods, one of the Titans, distinguished by his "Fore-Thought" (Prometheus), knew that victory would lie with brains, not brawn, and joined the coming powers. As an ally of Zeus he could persuade him not to extinguish the unsatisfactory race of men and replace it by a new one; and when he had saved them from extermination he aided them, motivated by his *philanthropia,* in various ways through inventions to improve their sad lot. In his humanitarian endeavors, however, he went so far as to transgress the new order established by Zeus; he stole the divine fire and gave it to man. For his transgression he must now suffer the punishment that he knew would come to him when he violated the Jovian order, though he did not expect it to be quite as horrible as it turned out to be. The *Prometheus* opens on the scene of the Titan held by Power and Force (*Kratos kai Bia*), ready to be fettered by Hephaestus to the rock overhanging the northern ocean.

At first sight, it would seem that the choice of subject matter throws us back to the Hesiodian theogony and anthropogony. The *dramatis personae* are divinities—Prometheus, Oceanus, the Oceanids as Chorus, and Zeus himself, though he does not appear on the stage but acts through his messengers and agents, Hephaestus, Hermes, Cratos, and Bia. How can tragic action, the action of the mature man faced by decision, be studied in the conflicts of gods? Are we dealing with a serious reversion to the pre-philosophic "anthropomorphism" of Hesiod? The question can be asked only to be denied. But it must be raised in order to bring out in proper relief the Aeschylean achievement in penetrating the demonic background of tragic action.

[7] "Modern" Prometheanism is in fact a form of Gnosis. The reinterpretation of the Hesiodian and Aeschylean Prometheus as the symbol of the philosopher who is superior to destiny goes back to the gnostic alchemist Zosimos. Cf. Hans Jonas, *Gnosis und Spaetantiker Geist,* I (Goettingen, 1954), 218ff.

The movement of philosophical speculation from the Milesians to Heraclitus, we may say, is a movement away from the experience of actual disorder in the direction of a principle of meaningful order. The discovery of the Solonic unseen measure, or of the Parmenidean Being, or the orientation of the soul through love, hope, and faith toward the *sophon*, are truly great discoveries; in fact, they are the foundation of philosophical speculation as a critical exploration of the constitution of being. Nevertheless, this movement and its discoveries are beset by a grave danger. The occupation with transcendental being and with the orientation of the soul toward the unseen measure may become a preoccupation which lets man forget that he lives in a world of unoriented souls. The movement of a soul toward the truth of being does not abolish the demonic reality from which it moves away. The order of the soul is nothing on which one can sit down and be happy ever after. The discovery of truth by the mystic-philosophers, and still more the Christian revelation, can become a source of serious disorder if it is misunderstood as an ordering force that effectively governs society and history. From such misunderstandings result the psychologically understandable, but intellectually deplorable, "great" problems of theodicy, such as the reconciliation of the all-too-present evil in the world with the omnipotence and goodness of God. In problems of this kind there is implied the speculative fallacy that the transcendental order, which is sensed in the orienting movements of the soul, is a world-immanent order, realizing itself in society independent of the life of the soul. In brief: the discovery may produce an intoxication which lets man forget that the world is what it is.

It was the greatness of Aeschylus that he understood the order of Dike in society as a precarious incarnation of divine order, as a passing realization wrung from the forces of disorder through tragic action by sacrifices and risks, and—even if momentarily successful—under the shadow that ultimately will envelop it. The *Prometheus* is not a return to the Hesiodian type of speculation on the myth. It is not a "true story" about a theogonic episode, but quite consciously a study of the forces in the human soul that will create social order when they are properly balanced, and will destroy this order when the balance is disturbed. It was the good fortune of Aeschylus the artist that the theomorphic symbolization of the soul in the myth provided him with a divine personnel which could credibly act out the tragedy of the soul.

The problem of the balance and struggle of forces is carefully built up. The victory of Zeus in the Titanomachia has resulted in the order of Dike. It is a rule of law replacing the ancient horrors. The victory was not gained by sweetness and reason but in a violent struggle; and the forces that were overcome are not dead, but are held in the nether world by the continued application of main strength. In the historical struggle the realization of order is inseparable from force; Zeus and his Dike appear now accompanied by the sinister executioners Cratos and Bia, who will see to it that the hard-won order will not be immediately endangered by trangression. Under this aspect of the force that has gained, and is resolved to maintain, the new order, the rule of Zeus is a "tyrannis" (10). The precise meaning of the term "tyranny" in this context must be understood in order to avoid conventional misinterpretations. The Zeus who rules by Dike has not suddenly become a tyrant who indulges in personal, lawless whims. There is no doubt about the legal situation: Prometheus has committed a transgression, he knew that he would be punished by right, and Zeus inflicts the punishment in order to uphold Dike. The tyrannical character of the action is due to the exaggerated harshness of the punishment, and this harshness is expressly declared an aspect of the newness of the régime (35); if the power were firmly established for a longer time the punishment would be less crushing. The time factor, the history of the order, is introduced into the argument. Moreover, we are left to suspect that under less raw conditions the transgression might not have occurred—either because Zeus could have persuaded Prometheus to abandon his wilful action, or because Prometheus could have persuaded Zeus to permit and thereby to legalize it. Dike itself has a history and may become more equitable with age; and in the last part of the trilogy, *Prometheus Unbound*, the old enemies will become reconciled.

The problem must have occupied Aeschylus permanently, for it reappears in the last work, the *Oresteia*. Orestes, at the behest of Apollo, murders his mother in order to avenge her murder of his father, and now the Erinyes pursue him. The father had to be avenged by divine law, and the matricide cannot go unpunished; everything is perfectly legal. But this horrible legality, begetting crime on crime, must be broken by some sense and equity. The solution is brought about by Athena who induces Apollo and the Erinyes to submit the case to arbitration by herself and a tribunal of Athenian citizens, the Areopagus, instituted on this occasion. The judges tie, Orestes is acquitted; but this acquittal of the

man Orestes by the neat device of a tie between his human judges does
not satisfy the Erinyes whose *time*, their allotted right and honor, is
slighted. And now Athena must subdue the muttering Erinyes through
her persuasive argument, offering them compensating honors. Peitho
is used for settling a difficulty that has arisen under the régime of Zeus;
the Erinyes with their claims belonging to the older generation of gods
are not simply beaten down—but even now, when an older and wiser
Zeus prefers gentler means, the threat of force is in the background
and Athena reminds the Erinyes (827f.) that she holds the key to the
armory wherein the thunderbolt is sealed. Dike, thus, evolves from rigid
enforcement to flexibility and persuasion; and in the *Oresteia,* as in the
Suppliants, the development is underlined by the institution of a court
of citizens who will decide the case (literally: diagnose Dike), not
giving way to "anarchy or despotism," inspired by "reverence and fear."

The analysis of the Prometheus figure must avoid the traps of romantic Titanism. To be sure, there is something like a revolt of man
against God in the conduct of Prometheus, but the formula does not
mean much as long as the terms God and man are not defined. We must
start from the firm basis that Prometheus is not a man but a god himself
like Zeus; both are generically co-ordinated; both equally stand for
forces that are experienced in the soul of man. The divinity of Prometheus is especially stressed by the executioner (29); the god should have
had more sense of loyalty toward his fellow gods, he should not have
aroused their wrath by indulging his philanthropic inclination (*philanthropos tropos*) (28). There is, thus, a divine force in man which can
ally itself with the order of Dike, as Prometheus did in the Titanomachia
with Zeus; but it nevertheless belongs to the conquered race of gods
and is apt to assert itself disloyally against the new order. And its philanthropic inclination is probably not quite accidental. For the race of
men itself was not created by Zeus, but found by him as part of the
older world; the race of men shares with Prometheus the character of a
relic of the old dispensation, accepted into the new one, but apparently
still partaking of the demonic, disorderly qualities of the older period.[8]

With regard to the nature of the divine-demonic force one must
again cling as closely as possible to the Aeschylean text. Prometheus is

---

[8] The characterization cannot go beyond probabilities because the first part of the trilogy, in
which questions of this type must have been clarified, is lost.

a *sophistes*. He is riveted to the rock in order to learn that for all his being a *sophistes* he is a dullard compared with Zeus (62); and again Hermes addresses himself to "You, the *sophistes*, bitter beyond all bitterness," and so forth (944). The wisdom or knowledge to which he owes the title *sophistes* has a considerable amplitude of meaning. He is a sophist because he has brought science to man, and especially mathematics, the "chiefest of sciences" (*sophismata*). But *sophisma* may also have the meaning of plan, device, or trick, when he complains that he has no *sophisma* for extricating himself from the present predicament in spite of all the inventions (*mechanemata*) which he devised for the mortals (469–71). And a further facet of meaning appears in the passages which reflect on his lack of wisdom. The deficiency expresses itself in his *authadia* (1012, 1037), a term that cannot be translated by a single word, but may be circumscribed as a brazen, shameless, conceited, self-reliant self-satisfaction. To persist in this attitude is shameful and dishonorable; it is not worthy of a *sophos;* and the Chorus admonishes him to take "good and wise [*sophen*] counsel" (1036–39).

From the various passages the sophist emerges as a complex figure. There is no doubt about his inventiveness and his discovery of the sciences; but such wisdom still leaves him incomparably the inferior to the wisdom of Zeus. The *polymathie* in the Heraclitean sense is no true *sophia*. Nevertheless, at least potentially he is more than a sophist; he is "wise" in the sense of being capable of taking "wise" counsel; if he does not take it, he is prevented by his *authadia*. This *authadia* is an ambiguous mood of existence. It manifests itself in the self-willed disloyalty to the order of the gods. Zeus wanted to abolish the race of men but Prometheus intervened on their behalf because he had "pity" on them. When he had saved them, however, he experienced more pity and tried to improve their miserable lot in various ways. At this point, the pity with man and the philanthropy begin to be pervaded by the pride of inventiveness. Aeschylus lets his Prometheus give the magnificent catalogue of civilizational history: Man received the art of housing, of observing the seasons and the stars, the science of numbers, the domestication of animals, the art of shipbuilding and sailing, medicine, the art of reading omina, metallurgy, and above all he received fire. In brief, the catalogue concludes: "All arts came to mortals from Prometheus" (506). The pride of civilizational achievement breaks through; and we may suspect that this showering of gifts on the mortals was not all due to pity but in part at least to the joy of creative invention, and that creative exuberance led to the final act of transgression.

There is a still deeper stratum in the *authadia*. In the dialogue with Oceanus it appears that Prometheus has omitted a few points in his great confession. We hear Oceanus counsel Prometheus to be a bit less bitter and loud in his complaints about his fate at the hands of Zeus because the angered tyrant might inflict even worse punishment on him. His present plight has come to him as a consequence of his former overbearing language (320–21), but not even now has he learned humility. The "overbearing language" is the cause of punishment; the theft of the fire is not mentioned at all. Besides philanthropy and the pride in civilizational inventiveness, so it would seem, there was a more primordial defiance at work of which the theft was only the most tangible symptom. The nature of this sentiment is perhaps revealed in the admonition: "Learn to know yourself and to acquire new ways; for the tyrant is also new among the gods" (311–12). The Delphic "Know thyself!" is recommended as the cure for the Promethean trouble; and this self-knowledge, significantly, is required as a correlate to the rulership of Zeus. The *authadia* belongs to the pre-Jovian period, it is a survival of demonic dynamism, not yet improved (*metharmozein*) by the reflective self-knowledge that makes one aware of limitations and obligations under order. The self-willed defiance of Prometheus (see especially 268) is not the assertion of a righteous claim against despotism. The selfhood of Prometheus is not endangered by the gods; on the contrary, the absence of a self in the Delphic sense is the source of the difficulty. The new order requires maturity and humility of "deeply" reflected action. The Prometheus of the extant tragedy is yet far from being a tragic hero; he is punished for his pre-tragic, demonic action.

The theme that appears in the scene with Oceanus is, then, made the center of the later scene with Hermes. Again Prometheus proclaims in no uncertain terms his contempt for the new, the upstart gods. The Titan of the old order remembers two tyrants being cast from power. He will outlast the third one and see him in the distress that changing fortune will bring on him. The struggle has become clearly the case of the old gods against the new ones. And he summarizes his feelings in the lines: "In one word, I hate all the gods who received good from me and wrongfully returned evil" (975–76).[9] The diagnosis of the trouble that was begun by Oceanus is now continued by Hermes in his answer: "I hear it, and it strikes me as no small madness" (977). The *authadia* is a madness, a *nosos*, a disease. The same term appears here in Aeschylus as in the Heraclitean characterization of conceit as a "sacred disease." It is a spiritual disease that can be healed only by self-conquering submission (999f.); and if that should prove impossible as a personal act, the redemption would have to come from another source, announced by Hermes: "Look for no end of this your agony, until a god appear to take upon himself your suffering, who willingly descends to unlighted Hades and the dark depth of Tartarus" (1026ff.). The tragic action in which the demonic Prometheus failed will have to be completed by the representative suffering of the divine descent to the "depth."

The complexities of the *Prometheus* are by far not exhausted, but it will have become sufficiently clear that we are dealing with the evolution of the soul toward the level of matureness on which tragic action is possible, as well as with the ramifications of the process in society and history. The order of Dike struggles into existence with the dynamic aid of the forces represented by Prometheus. On these forces depends civilizational progress through inventions, through the imaginativeness of pragmatic intellect and the sciences of the external world, and through the creation of a sense of security that comes with predictability of events. The civilizing force, however, does not by itself create an order of the soul or of society. Aeschylus has advanced beyond the Heraclitean deprecation of *polymathie* to a critique of civilization. Before the Age of the Sophists proper had begun, he understood power and achievement of the sophistic intellect as well as its danger of overreaching itself and destroying the order of Dike through the unmeasured, demonic pursuit of its possibilities. The concepts used in the psychological diagnosis of the disease are highly developed. Prometheus has given "first place in his pity" to man (241), and he could indulge in this sentiment because he had "no fear of Zeus" (542). When reading such lines we can only admire the Aeschylean insight into the connection between excess of pity and a deficiency in fear of God. For the excess of pity distorts the sense of the place of man in his relation to God, of his *conditio humana*: Prometheus tried to bestow honors (*timas*) on man "beyond

[9] The line "In one word, I hate all the gods" deeply impressed the young Marx. He quoted it as the confession of philosophy and made it the carrier of his own antitheistic revolt.

his true portion" (30), and he replaced the divine decision with regard to the fate of man by his "private opinion or decision" (*idia gnome*) (544).[10] In a fascinating passage Aeschylus, finally, identifies the Prometheus of the tragedy with the Promethean drive in man in an explicit declaration. The indulgence of *philanthropia* and *authadia* has resulted in grief: "See now, my friend, how unblessed are your blessings!" (545). When the civilizational drive has disrupted the order of Dike and caused a social catastrophe, then man is helpless: "What succour do you have now, what help, from the creatures of a day?" (546–47). Was Prometheus unaware of the infirmity of man? And in direct speech Aeschylus concludes: "Never shall the counsels of mortals disturb the harmony of Zeus" (550–51).

Prometheus symbolizes the demonic drive of human existence in its self-assertion and expansiveness. Since he represents only this one force in the soul, he is not the tragic hero; for only the soul as a whole is capable of tragic action. The tragedy of order in history comes into view in the interplay of Jovian Dike with the Promethean drive. On the one hand, Prometheus is more than a villain who breaks the law; and on the other hand, Zeus is less than a pure force of goodness and right. As far as Prometheus is concerned, the tone of sympathy with the fate of the sufferer is unmistakable throughout the play. Sea, heaven, earth, and the stars are stirred up by the execution and nature responds to the clang of the fettering with the appearance of the Oceanids. Man and his Promethean drive are part of the order of things; the mortals, to be sure, are wretched creatures of a day, but all the more are they in need of pity, of inventiveness, and imaginative self-help. Prometheus has sinned through excess, but short of excess his pity is a legitimate element of order. Zeus appears in a dubious light because he fails in pity himself when he refuses to consider the pity in the Promethean transgression as an extenuating circumstance (241f.). As far as Zeus is concerned, his order is not a divine, eternal order in the Christian sense. It has come into existence and will pass away, being no more than a phase in the life of the cosmos. And Zeus himself is not the God beyond the world, but a god within it. The traits that mark the historicity of his order, traits that will bring about its fall, are visible even now. Zeus had

---

[10] In his opposition of divine allotment of *time* to gods and men to private opinion Aeschylus again is very close to the Heraclitean opposition of the Logos that is common for all to the "private worlds."

to rely on the help of some of the Titans for conquering the others. As a consequence there is something demonic in the foundation of his own rule, represented in the victimization of Prometheus by Power and Force. Moreover, he is the Zeus who by his philandering has brought the terrible fate on Io, and Io appears on the stage to give an object lesson of the demonic component in Zeus that strikes the innocent with misery. One of the most impressive features in the performance of the play must have been the sinister scene in which Prometheus is fettered, immovable, high up on the rock, while down on the beach-strip Io writhes in the madness of her dance, stung by the gadfly, both related in fate through the prediction of the foreknowing sufferer on the rock that an offspring of Jovian licentiousness will do to his father what Zeus did to Cronos. The executioner believed that "Nobody is free save Zeus" (50) but Prometheus knows better. Even Zeus is enmeshed in the network of Ananke (Necessity) against which no art is of avail (514), and Ananke herself is steered by the Moirae and Erinyes (515ff.). The rule of Zeus will not last forever; and Prometheus, the immortal, can wait until it has run its "short time" (939). The loss of the *Prometheus Unbound* makes it impossible to know how Aeschylus carried these problems to their conclusion. The antagonists, it appears, would have come to an agreement, and the surrender of Prometheus' foreknowledge of the doom of Zeus would have played a rôle in it. A considerable theme would certainly have been the growth of wisdom through suffering on both sides—for "ever-aging time teaches all things" (982). But whether the revelation of the secret would have forestalled the doom of Zeus only for a time or forever, we do not know. It is certain only that the tragic "action" would have been completed by securing the balance of wisdom for the present aeon.

In the *Prometheus* Aeschylus has used the form of tragedy for presenting the historical drama of the soul. The order of the soul in historical evolution is the "hero" of the trilogy, not any of the dramatis personae. Such formulations, however, do not mean that Aeschylus attempted a tour de force, that he used the form of tragedy for treating an unsuitable subject. On the contrary, the experience of history grows out of tragedy. Only when the ideas of a completely human soul, of the reflective descent into its depth, of a decision that is drawn from its depth, and of an action that is the responsibility of man, are fully developed, can the meaning

of tragic action radiate over, and illuminate, the order of human existence in society. The social order itself acquires the hue of tragedy
when it is understood as the work of man, as an order wrested by man
from the demonic forces of disorder, as a precarious incarnation of Dike
achieved and preserved by the efforts of tragic action. The course of
human affairs becomes a course of history when the order of the soul
becomes the ordering force of society. For only then can the rise and
fall of a polity be experienced in terms of a growing or disintegrating
psyche.

The formulations of the preceding paragraph must be qualified,
however, by comparison with the genesis of history in other civilizations.
History was born from tragedy in Hellas, but nowhere else. The Hellenic
experience of history, as well as its symbolization, can be determined
more precisely by comparing it with the more compact Chinese, as well
as with the less compact Israelite forms. The Chinese meaning of history
grew, not from the experience of tragedy, but from the experience of
the flowering, decay, and extinction of organically conceived forces. Such
a force might live in a family and make it, for a limited time, the carrier
of cosmic order in society. Historiography, then, was the account of an
indefinite series of such life-forces, the "dynasties." Moreover, the symbolism of the dynasties was embedded in the wider symbolic form of
society as a universal organization of mankind analogous to the order of
the cosmos, that is, in the stratum of symbolization common to all
cosmological civilizations, Far Eastern as well as Near Eastern. The
tragedy of rise and fall, to be sure, was present in Chinese historiography,
but it was still compactly bound by the cosmological myth. The radical
break with the cosmological myth was achieved only by Israel. And
the break was so thorough that at once history was established as the
symbolic form of existence for the Chosen People in the present under
God. Israel, though, still had to carry the "mortgage" of its revelation
in so far as the universalism of existence under God was still narrowed
down to a particular people. The existence of the Chosen People, therefore, prefigured the universal history of mankind under God through
Christ. The Hellenic experience of tragic history has a degree of compactness in between the Chinese and the Israelite. Athenian tragedy is certainly no longer bound by the myth of a cosmological empire, but it
carries the "mortgage" of the polis, as Israel carried its "mortgage" of
the Chosen People. Moreover, the polis of Aeschylus, unlike the people

of Moses, does not exist freely under God through the leap in being, but approaches such existence through the tragic efforts of its people to descend into the divine depth of Dike. The Dionysiac component in tragic existence precludes the irruption of a divine revelation from above.

The qualifications should not detract from the greatness of Aeschylus. The revelation of God to man in history comes where God wills. If Aeschylus was no Moses for his people, he nevertheless discovered for it the psyche as the source of meaningful order for the polis in history. If he did not bring the law from Sinai, he laid the foundations for a philosophy of history. For Plato's philosophy of history derived from Aeschylean tragedy, and not on principle only but in such specific detail as the transformation of the trinity of the *Prometheus* (Prometheus, Zeus, Ananke) into the mythical trinity (Innate Desire, Demiurge, Heimarmene) of the *Statesman*. Moreover, Aeschylus had created a symbolic form when he used the theomorphic symbolizations of forces of the soul as the persons of his drama. And again this form was continued and further developed by Plato, for the Platonic myth as a symbolic form derives from the mythopoeia of Aeschylus' *Prometheus* and *Eumenides*.

4. The End of Tragedy

Tragedy as the representative action of the Athenian people had to die when the reality of Athens made heroic action incredible and the island of Dike was swallowed up by the sea of disorder. To follow the floundering and sinking of the polis through the extant tragedies would be a major study in itself. We can do no more than state the fact that the disintegration of Athenian democracy was faithfully reflected in the work of the great tragedians, and point to a few instances that will illustrate the process. Some typical examples, which betray the increasing devastation through the Peloponnesian War, can be gleaned from the work of Euripides after 428 B.C.

The *Hecuba* (c.425) studies the misery that befalls the queen after the fall of Troy. Up to a point she can sustain the burden of her suffering. And the sacrifice of Polyxena even opens new resources of dignity. When, however, the news of the death of her last son arrives, she breaks down under the knowledge of the extinction of her race. The order of her soul breaks down; she is now possessed by the demon of revenge that will draw the world into her own annihilation. With self-debasement and cunning she prepares the blinding of Polymnestor who had betrayed his trust and murdered her son for the treasure in his possession. And before the blinding she has killed his two innocent little children. The horror ends with the blind Polymnestor's information, received from Dionysus, that the queen will be metamorphosed into a red-eyed dog. The order of Dike has fallen apart; the soul no longer becomes wise through suffering but breaks under its fate; and the heroine becomes a dog.

Similarly devastating is the end of the *Madness of Heracles* (*c.*421). Heracles, like Io, is an offspring of Zeus, persecuted by Hera. The demonism of the gods governs the events of the tragedy without relief. In the absence of Heracles a usurpator has made himself the ruler of Thebes and prepares to extinguish the family of the hero. At the last moment Heracles returns, after the impending fate of his family has given occasion to characterize the invidious Zeus, saves his family, and kills the tyrant. The dissatisfied Hera sends the demon of madness, so that the stricken Heracles continues his butchery and kills his own family. When Heracles awakens to the realization of his deed, his first thought is the classic solution: "The first man of Hellas" cannot continue to live after such dishonor. And now comes the surprising turn. His friend Theseus persuades him to live, with the revealing argument that the gods have committed all sorts of misdeeds and still live merrily on. Does he, a man, want to be more exacting than the gods themselves? The work of the mystic-philosophers is undone by Euripides. The upsurge of the soul toward the *sophon* has fallen back; the gods have become a shameless vulgarity, and man should not try to be better than they are. Heracles is led off by Theseus into a resigned old age on the estate of his friend in Athens. Exit the hero into retirement with a pension.

In the *Troiades* (*c.*415), finally, Euripides holds up the mirror to Athens herself. The extant tragedy is the third part of a trilogy; the first two parts, the *Alexandros* and the *Palamedes* are lost. Of the *Palamedes* we know that the wise hero, a humanization of the civilizing Prometheus, falls a victim to the jealous treachery of Odysseus; the fourth century understood the tragedy as a prediction of the fate of Socrates at the hands of Athens. The issue of the *Troiades* is the suicide of the Greek soul in the hour of victory. What began as an heroic adventure, ends in the vulgarity and atrocity of the conquest. The morass of filth and abuse will suck down the Greeks themselves. Athena, the guardian of her people, will switch sides because her temple has been insulted. In the ominous scene which opens the drama she combines with Poseidon to destroy the victors on their homeward trip. The *Troiades* falls in the year after the slaughter at Melos that had revealed the corruption of Athenian ethos; and it falls into the very year of the Sicilian expedition that ended in disaster. That was the year in which the doom of Athens was sealed; the gods had indeed switched sides.

CHAPTER 11

The Sophists

The tragedy was eminently the creation of Athens in so far as the great poets were Athenians themselves, drawing for their work on the spiritual resources of their people; it was the gift of the new democracy to Hellas and to mankind. The people had awakened to the call for action in the tragic sense, and it had put its maturity to the test in the Persian Wars.

The victory brought a complete change in the intellectual and political atmosphere. Before the war Athens had been a politically rather insignificant town, and it hardly had participated in the intellectual adventures of Ionia and Italy. After the war, the city was propelled into political leadership in rivalry with Sparta, its hegemony in the Delian League was soon converted into the rule over a maritime empire held together by force, and Athens became the expanding, wealthy capital of this new political structure. Moreover, the Hellenic poleis emerged from the war as a much more tightly knit world, as an area of intense intercourse, and in Athens this world found a city that was able to play the rôle, not only of a political center, but of a cultural capital as well. The city played this rôle brilliantly—but in order to play it, the people had to leave the safe backwater of ancestral piety, from which the greatness of the generation of Marathon had come, and to merge its abilities with the intellectual life of Hellas. In order to become, in the proud words of Pericles, the school of Hellas, Athens had to be its schoolboy for two generations. The education of Athens through Hellas to the point where the pupil became the undoubted representative of Hellenic culture was the decisive event of the so-called Age of the Sophists. In this interpenetration of Athenian abilities with the older culture of the border regions came into being what in retrospect appears as classic Hellenic culture. It was the process from which, after the political disaster, Plato and Aristotle emerged.

§ 1. The Education of Athens .

Socially the process of education assumed the form of what can be described only as a descent on Athens of everybody who in Hellas was the possessor of some desirable knowledge, at one time or another in his life, to be received in the houses of statesmen and social leaders, sometimes for prolonged periods, in order to dispense his wisdom through individual instruction or public lectures, for high fees to those who could afford them and for smaller entrance prices to the less well-to-do audience. It is the period which Aristotle characterized succinctly in one sentence of his *Politics* (1341a28–32): When the Athenians "came to have more leisure because of their wealth and grew more great-minded in the measure of their excellence, even before but especially after the Persian Wars when they gained confidence because of their achievements, they began to engage in all branches of knowledge, not with discrimination but reaching out in every direction." To the "foreigners" who were willing to satisfy this Athenian thirst for knowledge may be applied the term sophists.

Not too much importance, however, should be attached to the term sophist and its definition. We are less interested in defining a term that has become a historiographic convenience than in the process that we characterized as the education of Athens. The scene changed rapidly and the differences in the concrete cases were frequently quite as important, if not more so, than the general characteristics of a foreign, migratory teacher. The term should be used, therefore, with the understanding that it has a center of sure application, surrounded by wide rings of cases to which it can be applied only with increasing qualifications.

In the first place, of course, the term applies to the men who by historiographic tradition are called sophists, and especially to the Great Four: Protagoras of Abdera, Gorgias of Leontini, Hippias of Elis, and Prodicus of Ceos. They represent the type in its purity; they all belong approximately to the same generation; and their mode of thought shows traces of effectiveness in Athens from the 440's onward. Beyond this center we must include among the relevant personnel the older generation of Zeno of Elea and Anaxagoras of Clazomenae, though conventionally they are not considered sophists. They certainly were "foreigners," they wandered, they taught at Athens, and the influence especially of Anaxag-

oras on the formation of Pericles was considerable. Moreover, they were
the mediating link between the philosophy of Parmenides and the
methods of argumentation developed by Protagoras and Gorgias. And
there must also be included the personnel which mediated Pythagorean
wisdom, especially after the disaster of Croton in 440, as well as the
men who mediated knowledge from the medical school of Cos.

Even if we stretch the term to the utmost, however, the category of the
migratory, foreign teacher will not cover all human aspects of the process
that are relevant to our purpose. We hesitate to speak of the Ionian
Herodotus as a sophist, though he lived for a time at Athens and his
History, with its information on customs of foreign civilizations, was
a splendid support of sophistic relativism with regard to ethics. We do
not apply the term to Democritus of Abdera, though he touched Athens
at one time on his travels and met the old Anaxagoras, because his
philosophical stature is too high to put him in the company even of a
Protagoras or Gorgias—and nevertheless he is one of the most interesting
figures in the education of Athens in so far as he found his way from
ancient piety to the new conscience and ataraxy unscathed by the relativism of the age, and inestimably affected the philosophies of conduct
that grew in Athens after 400 B.C. Difficulties in applying the term,
furthermore, arise when we approach the end of the fifth century and
Athenians themselves begin to show the effects of sophistic education in
their politics as well as in their intellectual achievements. Should we include among the sophists their products of education among Athenian
oligarchs of whom we have a composite picture in Plato's Callicles? Was
the tyrant Critias a sophist? And we hesitate to speak of Thucydides as
a sophist, although his *History of the Peloponnesian War* is the grandiose
epitaph of the age, in every accomplished sentence the product of sophistic culture at its best.

With Socrates and Plato, finally, we reach the opposition to the
sophists. Under the present aspect this opposition means that Athens had
come to the end of its ordeal of being educated by "foreigners." Athenians at last were able to articulate their problems for themselves, in their
own manner. The antiforeign sentiment of Socrates and Plato has deeply
colored their opposition to the sophists; but this opposition does not mean
that the achievements of the sophistic age were rejected; on the contrary,
the achievements were taken over, to an extent that is still not quite
recognized because our historiography of ideas pays more attention to

Plato's vociferous criticism of sophists than to his quiet acceptance of their work.

In characterizing the achievements we must proceed summarily. The sophists were migratory teachers. In order to find an audience and an income they had to dispense what their public needed. Nature and form of their teaching was inseparable from the needs of the new democracy and in particular of Athens. From our study of the tragedy we are acquainted with the meaning of action as well as with the necessity of translating the decision reached by the political leader into the will of the people through persuasive speech. The political supremacy of the aristocratic clans was broken, and while the aristocrats might transmit their traditional way of life to their sons through education, such transmission had become the private affair of a social class but did not lead by itself to political success in a polis of freemen. The old style was breaking down, as we have seen, in the time of Solon; and now, in the age of the democratizing constitutional reforms of Cleisthenes, Themistocles, and Pericles, it was dead as a political force. The leading statesmen, generals, and magistrates might still come from the old families but their political success depended on their ability to gain the favor of the people against competitors as well as to gain continued popular support for their policies in the face of the intense criticism, gossiping, and intriguing of a compact, comparatively small town. The mastery of typical situations and arguments in public debate, a stock of thorough knowledge with regard to the public affairs of the polis in domestic and imperial relations, a ready wit, a good memory improved by training, a disciplined intellect ready to grasp the essentials of an issue, the trained ability of marshalling arguments on the spur of the moment, a ready stock of anecdotes, paradigmata and sayings drawn from the poets for illustrating a point, general oratorical perfection, skill in debate leading to more or less graceful discomfiture of an opponent, a good deal of psychological knowledge in handling people, good appearance and bearing, natural and trained charm in conversation—all these were required for success in the competitive game of the polis. Anybody would be welcome who could train the mind in arriving at sound decisions and in imposing them on others in this new form of politics through debate, speech, argument, and persuasion.

Obviously, neither Milesian cosmological speculation nor the study of Heraclitean oracles could play an appreciable part in teaching that was calculated to satisfy such needs. A classified polyhistory of a quite different type was required. As far as the sources allow a judgment, the sophists in fact ordered the areas of knowledge that would be of service to a well-educated man in a cultivated, competitive society. They created something like a curriculum of liberal education and their efforts in this respect have stood the test of time in so far as their ordering of subject matters in education was retained through the ages as the Quadrivium and the Trivium. The Quadrivium of arithmetic, geometry, music, and astronomy met with certain misgivings at the time because the value of mathematical knowledge for a young gentleman who wanted to become a political leader seemed doubtful; but in Plato's *Republic* as well as in the practice of the Academy we find mathematics, and in particular geometry, already firmly established at the beginning of the curriculum, not only as a general instrument of intellectual training, but also as a convenient method for weaning the student from the fascination of concrete facts and making him aware of the importance of formal structures, ultimately of ideas. About the practical value of the Trivium of grammar, rhetoric, and dialectic there was never a doubt; the forms of language, speech, and thought had to be mastered under all circumstances.

Prodicus of Ceos seems to have been the most notable philologist among the major sophists. According to tradition Socrates at some time was his pupil and we still can sense a distinct sympathy for him in the dialogues of Plato. He was concerned with semantic problems, with ascertaining the precise meanings of words and distinguishing shades of meanings of related terms. Moreover, it seems that his concern about meanings led to occupation with the objects denoted. That would go far to explain the Socratic and Platonic interest in him for, under one aspect, Platonic and Aristotelian philosophizing is the arduous process of developing the terms, which in retrospect have become "philosophical vocabulary," out of the meanings which the words had in everyday parlance. Plato's sympathy for Prodicus may well have been rooted in a craftsman's respect for the valuable work of a predecessor.

Beyond the fundamentals of the Quadrivium and Trivium the sophists developed the *techne politike,* the art of politics, as a special new discipline. It was the theory of an education from early childhood that would fit a man into the customs and cultural patterns of his community. And since the laws were the embodiment of the ultimate principles on which the order of the community rested, the process was crowned by imparting to the young man a thorough knowledge of the laws of his polis. At this point the decisive difference between the old aristocratic and the new democratic education perhaps becomes most clearly visible. The appeal to authority in education no longer goes to the conduct of honorable ancestors and heroes, nor to the paradigmatic Aristeia or the paraenetic sections of the epic; it goes, rather, to the laws of the polis as the ultimately obligatory standards of conduct in command and obedience. The new education was bound by the horizon of the polis; its purpose was the formation of the responsible and successful citizen.

As far as the almost complete loss of primary sources permits a judgment in such matters, the most noteworthy contributions to the art of politics were due to Protagoras. If we accept the self-presentation of the great sophist in Plato's *Protagoras* as a substantially correct account of his ideas, he must have developed a rather detailed theory of education, history, and politics. Moreover, the ideas which appear in his profession (*epangelia*) are on the whole not at variance with the ideas that we know as Plato's own from his dialogues. It seems that the sophistic art of politics developed a body of theory that could pass as an important part into the politics of Plato. In his theory of education Protagoras arrived at the notion of the "nature" of a child or student, this nature and its gifts being the precondition of educational work. The educator will have to improve on the student's nature from as early an age as possible, by means of instruction that will impart knowledge, as well as by practice that will make this knowledge a second nature. The principles of Protagoras recur as the fundamentals of education in Plato, as indeed we find them ever since in every theory of education. Plato, furthermore, adopted the Protagorean conception of the law as the supreme teacher of the citizen and developed it, in the *Laws*, into the Proems of the laws with their educational, epodic function. In particular, Protagoras insisted that "reverence and justice" (*aidos, dike*) be living forces in the soul of every human being because without their presence the order of a community could not be maintained. The laws should provide that a man be put to death as a "disease of the polis" if he were found wanting in this respect. And this express Protagorean demand recurs in the *Laws* as the rule of Plato that a man who is spiritually diseased should be condemned to die when educational attempts, continued through five years, have proved ineffective.[1]

The sophistic art of politics dealt, finally, with the right principles of social order. The appeal to the laws as the ultimate educational authority inevitably led to questions of principle because the laws are given and changed, and the rules governing the giving and changing of laws rank higher than the content of the actually valid law. The budding statesmen among the students would need information on principles of justice and right conduct. We know more about the nature of this debate than about the conclusions reached. The debate was concerned with the manifold of Aretai as it had grown historically. The question was raised whether virtue was fundamentally one, or whether there was an irreducible plurality of virtues; and if there were a plurality of virtues, the further question whether their number was indefinite or limited had to be asked. From the debate resulted the attempts at establishing exhaustive lists of virtues, such as justice, wisdom, courage, and temperance, the group of four that we find in Plato's *Republic*. There may have been other such groups; and there was certainly no agreement on any particular list as the right one, for even in the dialogues of Plato we still can notice the hesitations about this or that virtue and its place in a "system." The ethical debates, furthermore, extended to the excellences of the somatic sphere, resulting in the list of health, beauty, and strength. And if, finally, we consider the debates on the arts (*technai*), on the various sciences on which the arts are based, as well as on political prudence, there must have existed fairly comprehensive surveys, if not actual lists, of the excellences which Aristotle classified as dianoetic virtues. Altogether the sophists must have left as their heritage a broad and solid inventory of the problems that later appear in the more highly theorized contexts of Plato and Aristotle.

The very considerable extent to which the politics of Plato rests on the achievements of the sophists, and in particular of Protagoras, should not obscure, however, the decisive difference between their worlds of thought. Plato opposed his "God is the Measure" deliberately as the counter-formula to Protagoras' "Man is the Measure." In sophistic

---

[1] Plato's agreement with Protagoras on this particular point deserves attention, as Plato is still maltreated, because of this rule, as an illiberal, authoritarian, if not "fascist" thinker by a good number of historians. That the liberal criticism of Plato would also have to be directed against the great sophist, should give some food for thought.

thought, we may say succinctly, there was missing the link between the well-observed and classified phenomena of ethics and politics and the "invisible measure" that radiates order into the soul. The opposition to a world of thought without spiritual order was repeatedly expressed by Plato at critical junctures of his work. In particular he quoted twice, as a target for criticism, a set of agnostic, if not atheistic, propositions that may well have come from a sophistic source.[2] They summarize an argument concerning the gods:

(1) It seems that no gods exist;
(2) Even if they do exist, they do not care about men;
(3) Even if they care, they can be propitiated by gifts.

Plato opposes to them his counter-propositions that the gods do exist, that they care about men, and that they cannot be appeased by prayer and sacrifice.

We are inclined to assume sophistic origin (perhaps Protagoras' book *On the Gods*) for these propositions, because the pattern of argument is authenticated as sophistic through Gorgias' essay *On Being,* the only work of a sophist that is preserved as a whole at least in an abstract.[3] For once we have an opportunity to study the organization of argument by a major sophist from a source that comes close to the original. The Gorgian tract was concerned with Parmenidean problems. It was organized into three parts defending successively the following propositions:

(1) Nothing exists;
(2) If anything exists, it is incomprehensible;
(3) If it is comprehensible, it is incommunicable.

In the first part of his tract Gorgias proved the nonexistence of Being. He proceeded by demonstrating the contradictions to which the Parmenidean predicates of Being will lead. We select as representative the argument on the predicate "everlasting":

> Being cannot be everlasting because in that case it would have no beginning; what has no beginning is boundless; and what is boundless is nowhere. For if it were anywhere it would have to be surrounded by something that is greater than itself; but there is nothing that is greater than the boundless; hence the boundless is nowhere; and what is nowhere does not exist.

[2] *Republic* 365 d–e and *Laws* 885b.   [3] Diels-Kranz, Gorgias B 3.

The abstract of the essay *On Being* is a priceless document because it has preserved one of the earliest, if not the very first, instance of the perennial type of enlightened philosophizing. The thinker operates on symbols that have been developed by mystic-philosophers for the expression of experiences of transcendence. He proceeds by ignoring the experiential basis, separates the symbols from this basis as if they had a meaning independent of the experience which they express, and with brilliant logic shows, what every philosopher knows, that they will lead to contradictions if they are misunderstood as propositions about objects in world-immanent experience. Gorgias applied his acumen to the Parmenidean Being; but the same type of argument could be applied to other symbols of transcendence, and the set of three propositions about the gods are probably the summary of such an argument.

If we assume the Gorgian tract to be representative of the sophistic attitude toward problems of transcendence, and if, furthermore, we define enlightenment by the type of philosophizing just characterized, we can arrive at some clearness with regard to the question whether the sophistic age can justly be labelled an age of enlightenment. We may say that the age indeed has a streak of enlightenment in so far as its representative thinkers show the same kind of insensitiveness toward experiences of transcendence that was characteristic of the Enlightenment of the eighteenth century A.D., and in so far as this insensitiveness has the same result of destroying philosophy—for philosophy by definition has its center in the experiences of transcendence. Moreover, the essentially unphilosophical character of sophistic writings may have been the most important cause of their almost complete disappearance in spite of the impressive collection and organization of materials which they must have contained. For the materials could be taken over by later writers and, stripped of the materials, the writings held no interest for philosophers. And, finally, we can understand more clearly why Plato concentrated the essence of his own philosophizing in an emphatic counter-formula to the Protagorean *homo—mensura*. After the destruction of philosophy through the sophists, its reconstruction had to stress the *Deus—mensura* of the philosophers; and the new philosophy had to be clearly a "type of theology."

The great achievement of the sophists in the material organization of the sciences of education, ethics, and politics must be recognized quite as much as their decisive philosophical deficiency unless the sudden magnificent unfolding of philosophy through Plato and Aristotle shall appear as a miracle beyond historical causality. The philosophic genius was Plato's very own but the materials to which he applied his genius must have broadly pre-existed. There is preserved a remark by Aristoxenus, the pupil of Aristotle, to the effect that Plato's *Republic* had substantially been anticipated by the *Antilogies* of Protagoras.[4] In this form the remark is a gross exaggeration because it ignores the philosophical difference. It must be considered one of the courtesies which Greek intellectuals extended to each other not infrequently. Nevertheless, there may be a solid core of truth in it as far as materials and their technical treatment are concerned.

Plausible conjectures have been made concerning the topics of the *Republic* to which Aristoxenus might have referred. One of the arguments developed by the early sophists was the argument from "likelihood." In application to politics one could develop such types as the "democrat" or the "oligarch" and then expand these types, through the argument of likelihood, to stand for social classes and for the character of institutions dominated by these classes; we know the individual psychological types and are ready to draw conclusions with regard to the "tendencies" or the historical development which the institutions associated with the individual types are likely to follow. This type of reasoning in the construction of forms of government is to be found in the *History* of Herodotus as well as in the pseudo-Xenophontic *Constitution of Athens* (the treatise of the "Old Oligarch"); it may have been used in other works which are lost; it certainly is present in Thucydides; and, finally, it appears in Plato's classification of forms of government in *Republic* VIII. Since even Herodotus and the Old Oligarch show the sophistic, probably Protagorean, influence it is quite possible that *Republic* VIII has absorbed a large body of classified materials which ultimately go back to Protagoras.[5]

It is also possible, however, that Aristoxenus thought of Protagoras' method of parallel demonstrations for thesis and antithesis. This problem goes back to Zeno of Elea and Parmenides. Zeno set himself the task of supporting, by a series of demonstrations, the thesis that Being is One.

[4] Diels-Kranz, Protagoras B 5. Diogenes Laertius III, 37.
[5] For the genealogy of the problem, further materials, and bibliography cf. John H. Finley, Jr., *Thucydides* (Cambridge, Mass., 1947), 46ff.

He proceeded by showing the contradictions that would follow from the opposite assumption that Being is Many. If Being is many then it would have to be at the same time large and small, moved and unmoved, and so forth. Zeno, according to tradition, developed no less than forty such couples that were to show the contradictory character of the world of delusion. Protagoras continued and elaborated this method—probably not for the purpose of showing that Being could be only One. He extended it to ethical problems and in long chains of argument he seems to have shown that the just at the same time is unjust, the courageous is the cowardly, the true is the false, and so on. There is no doubt that from such demonstrations of opposites an art of dialectic evolved, independent of the specific subject matter at hand; that the skill in such demonstrations was the basis for theoretical debates; and that the practice of school debates is one of the roots of the Socratic-Platonic dialogue. Hence, again it is quite possible that a dialogue like the *Republic* contains *passim* a vast amount of sophistic literary and school traditions of dialectical debate the presence of which escapes us because the older literature is lost.[6]

In conclusion we may say that the remark of Aristoxenus in spite of its deprecatory tendency deserves the serious attention of the historian because it suggests that the stream of continuity from the sophists to the philosophers of the fourth century was probably on the surface of materials very much broader than our historiographic conventions have accustomed us to believe.

§ 2. PLATO ON THE SOPHISTS. HIPPIAS

More than once in the preceding section we had to stress the almost complete loss of sophistic literature. With the exception of the abstract of Gorgias' essay *On Being* the extant primary sources consist of insufficient fragments. A coherent picture of the sophistic period can be gained only precariously through assumptions concerning the nature of the ideas which must have produced the effects that we can study in the secondary sources. If it be not always possible to attribute precisely formulated ideas to a specific sophist, there will nevertheless emerge typical problems and solutions. This method, however, runs into a serious difficulty because

[6] For the genealogy of the problem cf. Olof Gigon, *Sokrates. Sein Bild in Dichtung und Geschichte* (Bern, 1947), 204ff.

the most important secondary source is Plato. Not that the information tendered by Plato is untrustworthy in itself; on the contrary, it is most probably quite reliable; and we culled several pieces from the *Protagoras* because we saw no reason to distrust Plato when he expressly attributed to the great sophist an idea which he adopted for himself in his later work. The difficulty arises from the fact that Plato's dialogues are works of art. The information tendered is not meant as a historical report, and the form in which it is couched, more likely than not, serves the economy of Plato's own work. While the accounts may be substantially correct as far as the meanings of ideas are concerned, we have no assurance at all that any sophist ever gave them the specific form which they have in a Platonic dialogue. We shall illustrate this problem by an anecdote which Plato tells about Hippias of Elis.

In the *Hippias Minor* Socrates addresses the sophist as the wisest of all men in most of the arts. Hippias had proclaimed himself as such in the agora. As proof of his universal accomplishment, the sophist is supposed to have told a story about his appearance at the Olympic games. On that occasion, every article he had on his person was made by himself: There was a ring of his workmanship, and he boasted of having mastered the art of engraving; the seal he carried was made by himself, too, as was his strigil and his oil flask; his shoes, cloak, and tunic were self-made; and what attracted most attention was a girdle woven as finely as the most costly Persian fabric. In addition he had with him poems, epic, tragic and dithyrambic, as well as assorted prose writings; moreover he could pride himself on his mastery of mathematics, music, astronomy, grammar, and mnemotechnics. Here we have the picture of the many-sided, if not the all-sided, sophist; and this passage, together with supporting materials from the *Hippias Major,* is conventionally used in histories of political ideas as a piece of direct information. In particular the anecdote of his appearance in an outfit completely made by himself is considered a fine illustration of Hippias' character.

In order to arrive at an opinion with regard to the trustworthiness of this anecdote we shall confront it with a passage from the *Charmides* (161e–162a). Here Socrates asks his young interlocutor: "Would you think that a polis would be well-ordered under a law which enjoins everybody to weave and wash his own coat, and to make his own shoes, and his own flask and strigil, and so everything else on the principle of not touching the things of others but of everybody working and acting for himself?" The question is answered negatively and the principle of self-sufficiency is opposed by that of a division of functions, in the manner in which it is later elaborated in the vast discussion of the *Republic*.

The passages from the *Hippias Minor* and *Charmides* are closely related by their parallel formulation, and we suspect them to be also closely related with regard to their function in Plato's work. The insistence on the division of functions in a well-ordered polis has a polemical point against somebody's idea of radical self-sufficiency. We may safely assume that a sophist, quite possibly Hippias himself, had advanced it in some context. The passage in the *Charmides* may have been Plato's device for illustrating the absurdity (from the point of view of civilized life) to which the idea of self-sufficiency will lead if carried out to the letter; and the anecdote of the *Hippias Minor* may be a caricaturistic invention (by Plato or by somebody else), hung on Hippias as a well-known advocate of the idea.[7]

While it seems to us beyond doubt that the *Charmides* passage is connected with the Hippias anecdote, and that it has something to do with Plato's conception of political order in opposition to individual autarky, there is perhaps more behind it. The autarky of Hippias is peculiar; it certainly is not the autarky of a cynic sage who achieves apolitic independence by ascetic reduction of his wants. The ring, the seal, and the girdle look elegant; and from anecdotal tradition about Hippias we know that his gift for collecting money was far above average. Moreover, the anecdote about the self-made outfit appears in the context of a general survey of the sophist's polyhistory. On the nature of this "much-knowing" we have a piece of direct information through the only fragment that renders Hippias' own words: "Of these things some may be found in Orpheus, some in Musaeus, others in Homer and Hesiod, or in other poets, some in the writings of Hellenes, others in those of barbarians. From these all I have assembled the most important and the most related [*homophyla*] ones in order to make this new and variegated book." [8] The fragment is usually understood as symptomatic of a superficial eclecticism. It may, however, be a valuable clue to an encyclopedic interest which draws on Hellenic as well as barbarian sources for the purpose of extracting a body of relevant and true information,

[7] I am following the suggestion of Gigon, *Sokrates*, 264ff.
[8] Diels-Kranz, Hippias B 6, preserved by Clement of Alexandria.

the truth and relevance being guaranteed by the "homophylic" character of the items. And "homophylic" may mean a widespread agreement of the sources which is taken as proof of a common origin of the information. The fragment may be the program of an encyclopedist who sifts his sources in order to find a common wisdom of humanity that speaks through various authors and various nations.

The assumption gains probability in the light of a conversation between Socrates and Hippias on the nature of law, as reported by Xenophon in the *Memorabilia*. Socrates maintains that just (*dikaion*) and lawful (*nomimon*) are the same. Hippias at first has misgivings about the identification; laws do not seem to be such a serious business considering that the same men who make them quite frequently change them. Socrates ultimately wins him over by raising the problem of "unwritten laws" (*agraphoi nomoi*). Unwritten laws are defined by Hippias as those which are uniformly observed in all countries; and since such uniformity was not produced by an agreement of mankind, the gods must have made these laws for men. The term "law" in this conversation does not necessarily refer to positive, enacted law, as it includes such customs as gratitude for benefits; the nonobservance of such rules entails unpleasant consequences without legal sanction, and this self-enforcing character of the "unwritten law" is taken as proof of its divine origin. Since the gods do not order what is unjust, the interlocutors agree on the identification of just and lawful.[9] Back of this conception of the "unwritten laws" there must again lie a polyhistoric study of institutions resulting in the observation of uniformities. Scanty as the evidence is, it points to an attempt on the part of Hippias to create an empirical theory of human nature by extracting a common denominator from a comparative study

---

[9] Xenophon, *Memorabilia* IV, 4. I have rendered the argument as far as it concerns the problem of law with special care, because such care is usually missing in the accounts given of this Xenophontic chapter. Since it is used as the favorite source of Hippias' idea of natural law, one should be aware that the term "nature" does not occur in it. Moreover, the use of the conversation as a source of Hippian ideas rests on the assumption that Socrates (who leads the dialogue) introduced the argument of the "unwritten laws" because it would appeal to Hippias and force his consent to the identification of just and lawful of which Hippias otherwise was not convinced at all. The assumption seems to be justified because the idea of "unwritten laws" does not look very Socratic. The whole chapter, as a theoretical argument, is a rather poor piece of work. Unfortunately we do not know the Socratic dialogue on which Xenophon drew and, hence, we do not know how far he has mutilated or garbled the original. The break in the argument between IV, 4, 18, and 19 suggests that a good deal of subject matter must have disappeared under the hands of the suave editor.

of civilizations and literary sources. The *polymathie,* the much-knowing, which Heraclitus had berated, tries to become philosophical by substituting empirical generality for the universality of transcendence.

Such antiphilosophical philosophy could hardly be to the taste of Plato. The attempt to found the order of man in society on comparative study can only arouse the irony of a philosopher, as we see it displayed by Socrates in the *Hippias Minor.* The soul as the organ which experiences the unseen measure and through such experience creates its own order would be abandoned. The true order would have to be found through far-flung empirical studies; for the knowledge of this order, a society would be at the mercy of polyhistoric intellectuals; these "experts" would become the authoritative nucleus of a society; and the order that has grown historically would be devaluated by the argument that the people change their laws, thereby admitting their injustice. The immediacy and concreteness of order in the soul would be replaced by learned information. In brief: Man would abdicate before the sophistic intellectual. The sophist, by virtue of his comprehensive mastery of all things human, would be an epitome of humanity—but he would be such an epitome by the omniversality of his skills, not by the universality of his essence. The anecdote that we are discussing may well be a caricaturistic invention aimed at this externalized, surrogate humanity of the sophist.

The famous intervention of Hippias in Plato's *Protagoras,* finally, seems to fit into the interpretation suggested. Socrates and Protagoras have reached an impasse in the debate; Hippias counsels agreement with the following admonition:

> All of us present here I reckon to be of one kin, household and polis —by nature [*physei*], not by law [*nomo*]. For, by nature like is akin to like, while law, the tyrant of men, forces many things through against nature. How disgraceful then would it be if we, who know the nature of things and are the wisest of the Hellenes, and as such have foregathered now in Hellas' capital of wisdom and, in this city, in its greatest and most glorious house—if we should have to show nothing worthy of such worth, but should quarrel with one another like the meanest of men! (337 c–e).

The passage renders its full meaning only if it is taken in its entirety. If we isolate the first part on *physis* and *nomos,* the meaning of the terms becomes indeterminate, and we may arrive at erroneous conclusions.[10] Tempting as it may be to find in the opposition of *physis* and *nomos* the first stirrings of a theory of natural law, or the idea of natural equality of all men, or perhaps even of a brotherhood of mankind, such interpretations would either go too far or not far enough. As far as the essence of man is concerned—the essence that constitutes the equal humanity of all men—it had been discovered two or three generations earlier by the mystic-philosophers, in particular by Xenophanes and Heraclitus. As far as a higher law, in opposition to positive, enacted law is concerned, the idea was present wherever Dike was opposed to Nomos, and the conflict between the two was, in particular, the central problem of Aeschylean tragedy. What is new in the sophistic period is, first, the use of the term *physis* in a discussion of essential humanity, instead of such terms as *logos*, or *nous*; and, second, the direction in which essential humanity is sought. The first of these innovations, the use of the term *physis*, we shall explore later in the present chapter; the second innovation, the new direction, comes into view in the Hippias passage under discussion. "Nature" in this passage does not refer to an essence that is common to all men and makes them equal in the Heraclitean sense. Hippias expressly says that "like is akin to like by nature"; the kinship by nature prevails only among men who are "like"; and men are by far not all "like." In fact, the likeness which makes for kinship by nature is confined to "those present"; those present are kin by nature because they are the wisest of all Hellenes, and they are wisest because they "know the nature of things." It even looks as if it were precisely the like knowledge of the "nature of things" that made them "kin by nature," while likeness between men in other respects would not have this effect. The select group of the "wisest" is, furthermore, reckoned of "one kin, household, and polis" by nature. The enumeration of the three types of relationship which constitute *koinonia,* comunity in the Aristotelian sense, is probably meant to be exhaustive; the whole range of human relationships which ordinarily is covered by *nomos,* is for the wisest covered by *physis;* and since in fact they do *not* belong to the same kin, household, and polis, their relationship by nature is supposed to bind them as exhaustively as other men are bound by the ordinary human types of com-

---

[10] The first part is treated out of context quite frequently. See, for instance, Sir Ernest Barker, *Greek Political Theory. Plato and His Predecessors* (London, 1918), 64, and Jaeger, *Paideia* I, 326ff.

munity. Ordinary men, and in particular the "meanest," belong to the
sphere of *nomos* with its three types of community; the wisest belong
to the sphere of *physis* by virtue of their association in the knowledge of
the nature of things. The admonition of Hippias, far from being a declaration of the community of mankind, is the declaration of a *république
de savants*.

Hippias' evocation has its place in the history of order as the attempt
to transfer the idea of a community of mankind from the level of the
mystic-philosophers to the level of the encyclopedic intellectuals. A
Xenophantic movement toward the realissimum, or a Heraclitean exploration of the deep logos, is an event in the soul of the solitary thinker.
It results in the insight into the existence of community among men
through the universal spirit that is living in them all. The mystic-
philosopher has no information to tender; he can only communicate
the discovery which he has made in his own soul, hoping that such communication will stir up parallel discoveries in the souls of others. If he
has this effect on others, he will have actualized the existing community
to the extent of his effects. Nothing follows from this adventure with
regard to social organization directly, though indirectly the differentiation of the life of the soul in a great number of men in a community may
have the effect of changing the mores, and ultimately the institutions of
a society, because the hierarchy of purposes for individual action has
changed. In the case of Hippias, to be sure, a sense of the community of
mankind is present. The sophist, however, cannot come to grips with it
at the point of its concrete presence, that is, in his own soul. He must
search for it in its cultural objectivations in time and space, among the
manifold of peoples, among Hellenes and barbarians. The result is not
at all negligible, extending as it does to the arts and sciences, to a digest
of the common wisdom of mankind, and to the "unwritten laws." Nevertheless, the nature of things is a register of opaque, external manifestations; the search does not go into the depth of the psyche. Teaching,
therefore, must become information about things and training in skills;
learning cannot be the intimate movement in which a slumbering soul
awakens and opens to a differentiated, mature soul. The result of such
teaching is not spiritual growth within a concrete community but the
peculiar formation of a new supercommunity "by nature" beyond the
historically concrete societies of the *nomos*. The community "by nature"
of the encyclopedic sages is a figuration of the community of mankind

but it is not this community itself. The obvious danger of such a development, if the community of intellectuals should become socially effective, is the destruction of spiritual substance and its replacement by external information which cannot build the order of the soul and society.

This is as far as we can go in an interpretation of Platonic and related sources concerning Hippias of Elis. And now we must face the question: How much of all this is true in the sense that the ideas can, indeed, be attributed to a historical person named Hippias? The only answer can be that we do not know. We have one direct quotation in which the word "homophylic" appears—but with regard to its meaning we cannot form more than a reasonable guess. The Xenophontic chapter renders the term "unwritten laws"—but the source is in theoretical matters so dilettantic and superficial that again we gain no clear meaning. The anecdote in the *Hippias Minor* is highly suspicious; it may be an invention to illustrate Hippian ideas about self-sufficiency—about which unfortunately we have no independent information. The admonition put in the mouth of Hippias in the *Protagoras* is the most precise bit of information—but the passage is determined by its function in the dialogue: It is supposed to illustrate the attitude of a "foreigner," of an intellectual without a country, in contrast with a Socrates who is firmly rooted in the society of his polis and will die in obedience to the *nomos* which Hippias despises. The passage as a whole is suspect; it cannot be used as direct information about Hippias, and certainly we have no right to tear the sentence about nature and law out of context and quote it as a saying of the sophist—setting aside the fact that we would not gain much by the procedure because the removal from the context deprives the term "nature" of its meaning. We arrive at the conclusion that, with rare exceptions, the task of separating direct historical information from the form which it has received at the hands of Plato is hopeless. That does not mean, however, that the dialogues cannot be used as sources. On the contrary, a superbly competent critic has preserved the essence of ideas of which otherwise we would have no knowledge at all. Hence the dialogue can be used if the information that can be gained from them is recognized as the essence of sophistic ideas as seen by Plato.

This situation raises serious technical problems of presentation. On the one hand, the Platonic dialogues must not be neglected in an appraisal of sophistic ideas; on the other hand, the ideas are so firmly a structural part of the dialogue that their meaning cannot be determined without analyzing the dialogues as a whole. A study of sophistic ideas as related by Plato, if it has any value at all, would grow into an analysis of the respective dialogues, with the ludicrous result that a substantial sector of Plato's ideas would be treated as an appendix to sophistic ideas. The following compromise seemed to be expedient. Plato's information on sophistic ideas will on the whole remain in its context and be treated in Volume III of this study. An exception was made only for the case of the *Protagoras*. In this instance the information on the great sophist preponderates so strongly in the dialogue that it seemed justified to treat the opposition voiced through Socrates as incidental to the ideas of Protagoras.

§ 3. Plato's *Protagoras*

Can virtue be taught? This is the issue of Plato's *Protagoras*. The sophists are teachers; and Protagoras in particular teaches the *techne politike,* the art of politics, which will instill in young men the prudence (*euboulia*) necessary for public and private affairs. Socrates doubts that the art and virtue of politics can be taught; and he supports his doubt by the example of Athenian statesmen who certainly did not neglect the education of their sons and nevertheless were not able to transmit their virtue to their offspring. The ensuing debate develops the difference between Sophistic and Socratic conceptions of virtue as well as of the methods of teaching. Protagoras sets forth his position by telling the myth of Prometheus:

Once there was a time when only the gods existed, and not yet any mortal creatures. When the time for their creation had come, the gods fashioned them in various mixtures out of earth and fire. Before the creatures were released from the interior of the earth to the light of day, the gods ordered Prometheus and Epimetheus to equip them with suitable qualities. Epimetheus distributed the qualities and when he had equipped the various living creatures appropriately, Prometheus inspected the work and found that his brother had exhausted all the qualities at his disposition but had forgotten man—who was naked, shoeless, without bedding and arms. Prometheus, not knowing how he could otherwise provide for the helpless creatures, stole the inventive skill (*ten entechnon sophian*), together with fire, from Hephaestus and Athena. Thus man had the skills (*sophia*) necessary for the preservation of life but not for existence in community, for political wisdom was in the keeping of Zeus in his citadel where Prometheus could not penetrate. Released with their equipment to the light, men were the only living creatures to have gods; for through the Promethean gifts man participated in their attributes; he alone was their kindred. Nor was he slow in creating speech and names with his skill, in constructing shelter and clothing, and drawing sustenance from the earth. While thus provided for mere life, men lived scattered, without poleis, and were an easy prey to wild animals, for they did not have the political art of common action of which the art of warfare (*polemike*) is a part.[11] In order to prevent the extermination of the race Zeus sent Hermes to equip men with reverence (*aidos*) and justice (*dike*) as the ordering and binding principles of friendship. Moreover, these qualities should not be distributed in the manner of other skills where one man is gifted for others, but all men should equally share in them since otherwise poleis cannot exist.

We have explained why there is no sense in speculating whether Protagoras or any other sophist ever told a myth of this kind. We must accept the myth as a rendering of the essence of sophistic ideas about political virtue. Above all it appears that the sophists not only talked about the nature of man but made a serious theoretical effort at determining it more closely. Man belongs to the genus of mortal creatures; he is distinguished from them by the *differentia specifica* of inventive skills; he is defined as *homo faber*. Moreover, the skills are not on the same level as the natural equipment of other creatures but are divine attributes; through their possession man partakes of divinity and becomes of one kin with the gods—a quality which manifests itself in the "having" of gods and the institution of their cults. The inventive skill, furthermore, is a creative faculty. The Protagorean Prometheus does not, like the Aeschylean, endow man with the single arts but with the general faculty to invent them for himself. Civilizational progress, thus, becomes a specifically human achievement; we see in formation the conception of a human history of civilization. And then the Jovian Dike, in the Aeschylean sense, is introduced as the source of "reverence and justice," the virtues that make political order possible, distributed to all men alike. On the surface it seems that the sophistic theory of politics

[11] The association between a *techne politike* and *polemike* is still to be found in Aristotle's *Politics* where the term *politeia* is associated with the soldier-citizens who are its members.

and history has absorbed the problems at the stage at which they were left by Aeschylus.

The myth is told by Protagoras in support of his thesis that virtue is teachable. All men are equally equipped with the gifts of Zeus. This is the really decisive point for Protagoras—that no polis can exist unless all its members participate in the specifically political virtues, that is, in justice (*dikaiosyne*), temperance (*sophrosyne*), piety (*hosiotes*), courage (*andreia*), and wisdom (*sophia*) (324e–325a). Socrates' doubt is absurd because the whole life of a polis with its education from childhood is built on this assumption, and on the whole is built on it successfully (325c–326e). The argument that great statesmen have dubious sons is worthless because Socrates has overlooked the fact that in every skill besides the general human faculty there must also be present a natural ability; and there is no guaranty that the sons of great fathers inherit their natural talent. The teaching of virtue, thus, is possible; and he, Protagoras, professes to be such a teacher of men. He has the knowledge with which to make men "noble and good" (*kalos k'agathos*). He freely admits to being a Sophist, that is, a teacher of men, continuing a noble tradition; for the same profession was formerly pursued under the names of poets, hierophants, and prophets by such men as Homer, Hesiod, Simonides, Orpheus, and Musaeus.

Socrates, however, is not satisfied. He wants to know whether the list of virtues enumerated by Protagoras is meant to be a list of parts to be distinguished in a whole, or whether virtue is only one so that the Protagorean enumeration would be a list of synonyms. There is more behind this question than appears at first sight; in fact, though important in itself, the question becomes in the hands of Socrates the instrument for drawing Protagoras himself into question—as a teacher, as a foreigner, and as a gentleman.

The insistence on the precise, pointed question opens the Socratic attack on the sophistic method of teaching through speeches. The splendid discourse, he reminds Protagoras, is also at the disposition of Pericles and other Athenian speakers; but when these orators have made a speech, they are like books which you cannot ask questions; if you challenge the least part of their speech, they will answer you by a new speech, and you never can nail them down on a problem (329a). He now challenges Pro-

tagoras to be better than his Athenian speechmaking colleagues and to
show his wisdom by his ability to enter into a close argument. Protagoras
obliges; but when the argument turns against him he tries to break into
speechmaking again, with the result that Socrates threatens to leave. It
is the typical conflict between sophistic rhetoric and Socratic inquiry that
also occurs in the *Gorgias,* and there again leads to the Socratic threat of
a walkout. The reluctant Protagoras is at last persuaded to continue, but
not before he has betrayed his weakness through the bland assertion that
he would not have acquired his fame as the great sophist among the Hellenes if he had always submitted to the conditions of debate imposed by
his interlocutor (335a).

The ensuing discussion of a poem by Simonides, then, gives Socrates
the opportunity to attack Protagoras indirectly through the account of
Lacedaemonian archaic philosophy. Socrates contends that the ascendancy
of the Lacedaemonians in Hellas is due to their superior philosophy. This
is a great secret which they guard jealously. They let their imitators believe that gymnastic exercises and skill in arms are the sources of their
success, while indeed the source must be sought in the philosophical
training which enables them to utter the famous Laconian answers. When
they want to indulge in their debates freely, they first drive out all
laconizers and foreigners and then meet with their own sages (sophists);
from the training in such debates emerges the perfectly educated man
who is capable of brief utterances—like the Seven Sages of whom the
seventh was the Lacedaemonian Chilo. The first fruit of their wisdom
they dedicated to the Apollo at Delphi: the far-famed inscriptions "Know
thyself!" and "Nothing too much!" (342a–343c). Protagoras, thus, is
reminded roundly that he is a foreigner who should be thrown out before a serious philosophical debate will be undertaken, that his own education should begin with the Delphic self-knowledge of his humble stature as a man, and that his speechmaking is entirely "too much."

The debate about the poem which Protagoras had started, finally,
gives Socrates occasion to insist that the discussion should not be further
wasted on poems and their meanings. This is like entertainment for vulgar people who meet at a symposion and must hire flute-girls because
they are too stupid to entertain each other with their own conversation.
Gentlemen decline such entertainment; they prefer to talk with one
another, and to arrive at truth by testing each other in conversation
(347b–348a).

By means of such persistent prodding, urbane in form but hard in substance, Protagoras is pressured through the Socratic questions and answers on the issue of the one virtue. The result of the inquiry is the Socratic thesis that no human being errs voluntarily, or will voluntarily commit evil and dishonorable actions (345e). If he commits evil deeds he does so from ignorance of what is truly pleasant and good. The wrong things are preferred because their consequences are misjudged. Imminent evils loom larger than distant consequences, and present pleasures are overrated because of the same distortion of perspective through time. Just as in spatial perspective one cannot judge true dimensions by appearances but must apply the measuring rod directly, so in the temporal distortions of goods and evils an art of measurement is required in order to recognize the true proportions. The art of measurement (*metretike techne*) would do away with appearances and let the soul find rest in truth, saving our life (356d–e). To be overcome by pleasure, thus, truly means to be overcome by one's ignorance (357e). To be inferior to oneself is ignorance, to be superior to oneself is wisdom (358c). Virtue ultimately is one, the wisdom of measurement.

At this point the argument breaks off. The structure of the dialogue is completed because all its motifs are now gathered together in the Socratic conclusion. Protagoras started with the thesis that virtue can be taught; Socrates doubted the thesis—and he was right because virtue cannot be taught on Protagoras' assumption that the virtues differ from each other and are not reducible to wisdom which alone can be "taught." Moreover, the sophistic method of teaching by discourse is unfit for teaching virtue, even if it can be taught, because his very oratory prevents Protagoras from ever finding out what the virtue is that supposedly he can teach. Then, in the course of the argument, Socrates shifts to the position that virtue can be taught—and again he is right, under the condition that the different virtues are varieties of knowledge about the good. "Knowledge [*episteme*] is a noble and ruling thing"; it cannot be overcome by pleasures; wisdom (*sophia*) founded on knowledge (*episteme*) is the substance of all virtue (352c–d). If virtue is the art of measurement, then, and only then, is it teachable. The conclusion is hypothetical. Virtue is teachable *if* it is knowledge; but *is* it knowledge? The question remains in suspense. Socrates professes his desire (*prothymia*) to clear up this further question; and he desires such ultimate clarity because he prefers Prometheus to Epimetheus, in forethinking care (*prometheia*) about the business of his life (361c–d). The Prometheus-symbol of Protagoras is taken over in the end by Socrates. The sophist becomes the slow-witted Epimetheus who creates confusion because he cannot think ahead toward the most important part of his task; and Socrates, through his art of measurement, becomes the Promethean caretaker of man.

The Platonic Protagoras is inseparable from his Socrates. The opposition between the two types becomes fully intelligible only if we see the Protagorean insufficiency in the light of the Socratic position. The dialogue, however, does not give us such full insight explicitly because, as we have seen, it breaks off before the decisive point of Socrates' position is clarified. Nevertheless, while the answer is not given in the dialogue explicitly, it can be extrapolated, in our opinion, with absolute certainty. Such extrapolation requires a brief reminder of the methodical principle that is our guide, the principle that we must not search in the dialogue for direct historical information but only for information on the essence of ideas as seen by Plato. What we had to say with regard to the use of Platonic sources for the understanding of Sophistic ideas, is also valid for their use with regard to the ideas of Socrates. Since Socrates did not write, we have in his case no primary sources at all; the essence of his ideas, as mediated by Plato and the other Socratics, is our only source of knowledge. This state of things must be clearly realized now when we try to decide what Socrates meant by his identification of virtue and knowledge, as well as by his characterization of wisdom as the "art of measurement." Any attempt at reconstructing the opinions of the "historical" Socrates on this point can lead nowhere except into the well-known contradictions between the "utilitarian" Socrates who gives commonsense counsels about honest and law-abiding conduct, and the Socrates who is concerned about the health and salvation of the soul. The meaning of the identification of virtue and knowledge must be ascertained as a meaning intended by the "essential" Socrates, to be extrapolated from the text of the *Protagoras,* and from nothing else.

The *techne metretike* is carefully defined as the art that enables man to discount the distortions of judgment which stem from the perspective of time. Obviously, such perspectives may be of a longer or shorter range; and according to the range and the predictability of consequences the *metretike techne* will be a highly diversified field of knowledge. It will not require much training and persuasion to understand that lies will frequently be found out after a short while, that dishonest conduct in business matters will ruin your credit, that discourtesy will make no friends, that overindulgence of sensual pleasures will ruin your health or make you fat, that cowardice in battle will bring no honors, and that widespread disobedience to laws will disorganize a country. If reflections of this type were the sum of the Socratic wisdom, however, the impact of Socrates on his contemporaries would hardly be intelligible—though it is highly probable that a good deal of his conversation in fact dealt with distortions of judgment through such short-range perspectives. We are inclined to put it beyond doubt that the real importance of the "art of measurement" must have consisted in its application to the long-range perspectives, and especially to the longest of all, that is, to the whole of life that ends in death. In the Promethean wisdom that affects the whole of life all distortions of perspective through time will be corrected by the perspective of death and eternity. It certainly is no accident that the conception of wisdom as the art of measurement is developed in a dialogue with Protagoras, the Protagoras who opened his *Aletheia* with the affirmation that "of all things the measure is man." [12] We feel justified in extrapolating the Socratic art of measurement into the Platonic counterformula of God as the Measure. Whatever the formulations of the "historic" Socrates may have been, the "essence" of his identification of virtue with knowledge, as a principle in opposition to the Sophists, makes sense only if the distortions of time were meant to be corrected by the love of the measure that is out of time.

§ 4. THE FRAGMENTS OF PRIMARY SOURCES

The sophistic literature as a whole has perished. The extant primary sources consist of fragments, for the most part too small to allow reconstruction of the context of ideas from which they are torn; and frequently even so small that their own meaning cannot be determined with precision. If such fragments are treated in isolation, fanciful interpretations are difficult to avoid. The following survey of such fragments will, therefore, adopt a procedure that is likely to minimize the dangers of misinterpretation. Since the literary context that would illuminate their meaning is lost, they will be placed into a context of theoretical issues. This procedure is based on the assumption that there exists an historical

[12] Diels-Kranz, Protagoras B 1.

continuum of problems between the mystic-philosophers at the turn
from the sixth to the fifth centuries, about whom we are better informed,
and Plato, whose work is preserved. With our knowledge of the *termini
a quo* and *ad quem* of the problems, it will be possible to draw probable
lines of their development; and the attempt can be made to place the
fragments on these lines.

1. From Parmenides to Protagoras

The analysis will appropriately begin by recalling the origin of certain sophistic theorems in Parmenides' philosophy of Being. The Parmenidean "way," the mystical transport, led to a vision of Being, expressing
itself in the exclamatory *Is!* The organ of cognition for this Being beyond
the Night of appearances was the Nous; and the instrument for discursive articulation of the seen was the Logos. Moreover, the truth achieved
by the Logos was characterized as "immovable" and "well-rounded,"
that is, by the predicates of Being itself; the truth of the Logos participated in the nature of Being. Through logical speculation on the experience of the Nous, the mind of man had created a sphere of autonomous
truth beyond the delusionary knowledge of appearances, of the same type
as autonomous Being itself.

In the complex of Parmenidean speculation three ideas can be distinguished from which lines of meaning run through the sophistic age
into the fourth century. The first is the idea of the "knowing man," an
existential category denoting the type of man who is capable of insights
concerning Being. The second is the idea of the autonomous Logos that
will arrive at truth about Being independent of the manifold of decep-
tive appearances. The third is the idea of correlation between thinking
and being, identifying that which is with what can be thought. With
the first of the ideas we shall not deal specifically in the present context
because the emergence of the philosopher as a new existential type is
the general problem of the age, from the generation of the mystic-
philosophers, through the variety of sophistic types, to the climax in
Socrates and the founders of schools in his wake. Only the lines that start
from the second and third of the Parmenidean ideas will be traced.[13]

---

[13] The analysis closely follows the survey of the problem given in Gigon, *Sokrates*. Throughout this section on the fragments the numbers in parentheses (A 1, B 1) refer to Diels-Kranz,
Die Fragmente der Vorsokratiker (7th ed., Berlin, 1954). For an English translation of the B-
Fragments cf. Freeman, *Ancilla to the Pre-Socratic Philosophers*. The translations in the text,
however, are mostly our own.

Among the fragments of Anaxagoras there is preserved a sentence that can be considered the declaration of independence of the mind from the rest of being:

> The other things contain of all a part; the Nous, however, is something unlimited [*apeiron*] and self-ruling [*autokrates*], and is mixed with no other thing, but is alone for itself (B 12).

The autonomy of the Nous is asserted in this sentence even more forcefully than by Parmenides. The earlier thinker's predicates of Being and Truth, "well-rounded" and "eternal," indicated a self-contained remoteness, a resting within itself; Anaxagoras, while preserving these shades of meaning, adds a quality of action, of dynamism, through the predicate "self-ruling." This increased volume of sovereignty is due to a decisive change in the ontological status of the Nous. The Parmenidean Nous was the organ of cognition for Being; the Nous of Anaxagoras has become a part of being, though its highest ranking, sovereign part. And this "finest" and "purest" among things is, furthermore, the ordering force for all other things from the universal revolution and the celestial bodies to the qualitatively differentiated manifold of all things; it is especially the ruler of everything that has *psyche*, the greater as well as the smaller beings; and it can exert this ordering and ruling function because it has complete knowledge (*gnome*) of everything, and of all things has the greatest power (B 12).

The fragments of Anaxagoras fortunately are large enough to grant an understanding of his theoretical motivations. In his didactic poem Parmenides had left open the question how the gap between the Being discovered in mystical transport and the world of Delusion could be bridged; there was no answer to the question in what manner the Being revealed to the Nous and the world of appearances could be understood as parts of one universe. Anaxagoras wanted to solve the great problem by combining the Parmenidean philosophy of the Nous with an ontology of the Milesian type. In order to achieve his purpose he, first, preserved the Nous as an autonomous organ of knowledge and, second, made it a being that by virtue of its autocratic knowledge and power organized all other things into an ordered universe.

As a feat of metaphysical construction the attempt deserves respect —but the success was purchased at the price of a serious destruction of the insights gained by Parmenides. For, when the Nous becomes the sovereign organizer of being, its function as the revealer of Being is lost, and with it Being itself. The Parmenidean Nous and Being have their meaning as symbols in explicating an experience of transcendence; if they are torn out of their experiential context they become opaque terms of metaphysical construction from an immanentist position. The gap between the Truth of Being and the world of Doxa cannot be bridged by speculation, as we have pointed out in the chapter on Parmenides, but only by a myth of the type created by Plato in the *Timaeus*. And such merit as there can be found in the speculation of Anaxagoras on the Nous will have to be sought, therefore, in its nature as a myth that comes rather close to the Platonic Demiurge.

The procedure of Anaxagoras in solving his problem is characteristic of what may be called sophistic thinking in a technical sense. The problem of the mystic-philosopher, as well as his symbols (Nous and Being) are accepted, while the experience of transcendence, which lies at the root of the problem and motivates the creation of the symbols for its expression, is abandoned. As a consequence, the symbols of transcendence will now be used, or rather misused, in the speculation on immanent problems. A peculiar style of thinking develops that permits men who are no philosophers in the existential sense to express their opinions on problems involving the experience of transcendence with the usurped authority of the existential philosopher. This is the style of the sophistic intellectual. Whether Anaxagoras himself was guilty of such usurpation is doubtful because (1) as we shall see presently, he developed an epistemology of immanent knowledge, not relying on the Nous, and (2) the state of the fragments makes it impossible to see how the two parts of his philosophy were linked with each other.

In the case of his younger contemporary Protagoras, however, the new attitude is fully developed. Of his work *On Truth* the famous opening sentence is preserved:

> Of all things the measure is man, of the being that they are, of the not being that they are not (B 1).

The Parmenidean correlation between Nous-Logos and Being has become the correlation between man and immanent things; the autonomy of the Logos in exploring the Truth about transcendent Being has become the autonomy of man in exploring his surrounding world. The consequences of this radical immanentism, as far as problems of transcendence are concerned, become tangible in the opening sentence of Protagoras' work *On the Gods:*

> About the gods I am not able to know either that they are, or that they not are, or what they are like in shape, the things preventing knowledge being many, such as the obscurity of the subject and that the life of man is short (B 4).

The sentence does not express dogmatic atheism but rather a suspense of judgment concerning the existence of gods. This is the form in which the problem of transcendence will present itself to an immanentist who has no experience of transcendence, provided that his intellectual discipline will prevent him from falling into dogmatic negation of divine existence. Nevertheless, the line of dogmatic derailment is indicated by the odd conclusion of the sentence which seems to assume that certainty in this obscure matter could be reached, presumably by immanent means, if life were longer. More impetuous sophists will find sooner or later that their life is long enough to arrive at a judgment, and it will be negative.

In the Parmenidean experience of transcendence the Nous as its subjective, can be distinguished from the Being as its objective term. We have traced the line of immanentization from the subjective term to the Protagorean Man-the-Measure. We shall now trace the line of immanentization that runs from the objective term into sophistic thought.

Parmenides had formulated three propositions about being: (1) That only Being exists; (2) that only Non-Being exists; (3) that both Being and Non-Being exist. He decided that the first proposition was the Truth, the second proposition was unthinkable, and the third proposition was the opinion of men who were fascinated by the manifold of the changing world. The Parmenidean decision must have aroused resistance because it violated the common-sense experience of the world in which we live. The resistance is presupposed in the work of Zeno of Elea since it has the form of a demonstration that the thinker will involve himself in contradictions if he assumes that Being is not One but Many. The *Attacks* of Zeno consist of a series of demonstrations that, under the assumption of Being as Many, it will have to be at the same time large and small, homogeneous and heterogeneous, finite and infinite, moved and unmoved, and so forth. The brief B 4 may illustrate the type of argument: "That which moves, neither moves in the place in which it is, nor in the place in which it is not." This is probably the demonstration to which later were attached the famous Eleatic paradoxa, as, for instance, the one of Achilles and the Tortoise, or of the arrow which cannot move.

The Zenonic demonstrations imply a metaphysical misconstruction similar to that of Anaxagoras. The latter had made the Nous a being thing; Zeno construed the manifold of being (*ta onta*) as a Being (*to On*) that is Many, inevitably involving himself in the paradoxa of the infinite. The Being revealed to the Nous in the Parmenidean transport is not the being of immanent experience; and, hence, Parmenides was quite right when he categorized immanent being as Not-Being. The problem of immanent being cannot be solved by construing it as a Being that is Many; the quest for its nature will rather lead toward the discovery of form, of essence, in being, as it finally did with Plato and Aristotle. Once this misconstruction had happened, however, a style of dialectical demonstration was established that could extend beyond the Zenonic range of subject matter (time, space, motion, quantity, and so forth) to ethical questions. It seems that Protagoras was the first thinker to apply antilogical reasoning to problems of justice. A tradition has it that he was the first to say that there were two contradictory arguments about everything (B 6a); and, specifically, he had the reputation of being able to make the weaker cause the stronger (B 6b). In the extant form, this specific information probably has a slanderous intention; nevertheless, it indicates the use to which the antilogical technique could be put in public pleading.

The Protagorean antilogies concerning ethical questions are lost. Fortunately we can form an opinion of what they must have looked like from the anonymous *Dissoi Logoi,* probably written shortly after the Peloponnesian War. Under the chapter headings "On Good and Evil," "On Honorable and Dishonorable" (or "Decent and Indecent"), "On Just and Unjust," lengthy catalogs of contradictory opinions concerning the same event or action are given. A few examples from each of the chapters will illustrate the treatment of the problem:

> Satisfaction of wants with regard to food, drink and sex is good for the healthy, but bad for the ill man. Immoderate consumption of food and drink is bad for the immoderate consumer, but good for the tradesman. Victory at the games is good for the victor, but bad for the defeated. The issue of the Peloponnesian War was good for the Lacedaemonians, but bad for the Athenians.

> To put on finery and cosmetics is indecent for a man, but decent for
> a woman. In Macedonia it is decent for a girl to have premarital re-
> lations, in Hellas it is not.

> To deceive an enemy is just, to deceive a friend is unjust. Murder
> of relatives is unjust, but sometimes, as in the case of Orestes, it is
> just. Templerobbery is unjust, but to take the treasure of Delphi
> when Hellas is threatened by the barbarians is just.

The Twofold Arguments, thus, consists of a catalog of typical actions
and events that will receive contradictory value predicates according to
the situation in which they occur, or according to the position of the
evaluating person. The types range from household occurrences, such as
the breaking of a pot that is a loss to the owner and a gain to the potter,
through competitive situations in public games, to warfare; they show
an important influence of medical literature with its knowledge that
the same diet is not good for healthy and sick people; and of ethnographic information concerning the difference of mores in various civilizations. Common sense, medical, and comparative ethnographic knowledge seem to have been, in the sophistic age, the main sources for examples
of contradictory valuations. And the assembling of such catalogs could
imply, though it did not always have the purpose of proving, that one
truth about moral phenomena did not exist.

Finally, Anaxagoras' theory of sense perception must be considered,
as a mediating link between Parmenides' philosophy of Being and Protagoras' Man-the-Measure. Immanentizing the Parmenidean Being, Anaxagoras denied the manifold of changing things:

> Of coming-into-being and passing-away the Hellenes have no correct
> opinion. No thing comes into being or passes away, but out of ex-
> isting things does it mix itself together and into them it falls apart
> again (B 17).

Being is one and the same at all times, consisting of an infinity of un-
changeable, qualitatively differentiated things, agglomerating and mix-
ing in composite products and unmixing again. One such composite
product among others is Man (B 4). All kinds of things are mixed in the
composite products, though in different proportions, so that the com-
posites are indeed parts of the one constituting being:

> It is not possible to exist apart, but all things contain a portion of
> everything (B 6). Not separated from each other are the things in

the one cosmos, and not hacked off from each other with an axe,
neither the hot from the cold, nor the cold from the hot (B 8).

Hence, man is composed of the same being as all other parts of the surrounding world; and sense perception is a participation of being in being.
It occurs through the meeting of the component parts in the things with
their opposites in man. For instance, we receive the sensation of warm or
cold from what is warmer or colder than our body. The Parmenidean
correlation of Nous and transcendent Being is translated into the immanent correlation between man and things perceived (A 92, A 94, A
106).

Through Anaxagoras' speculation on being we again arrive at Protagoras' principle of *Homomensura*, which now becomes intelligible with
regard to its ontological foundation. As far as the implications of the
principle are concerned, the opinions of scholars differ widely. This is
not the occasion for a detailed discussion of the issue; we shall only
indicate our preference for the ancient tradition. According to the ancients, especially according to Plato's explanation in *Theaetetus* 152ff.,
the principle means that things are to every man as what they appear to
him, and that no truth about things can be reached independent of their
relation with the perceiving subject.

2. Democritus

The problems left by Parmenides were further developed in the work
of Democritus of Abdera. His speculation, like that of Anaxagoras, attempted to reconcile the experienced manifold of things with Parmenides' propositions that Being is One, and that Non-Being does not exist.
In order to make being one he assumed all appearing bodies to be composed of an "original being" (*archai*), consisting of invisibly small, indivisible units, the "atoms." The construction of being as an infinity of
atoms shows a speculative refinement, since it takes into account the
Zenonic arguments concerning infinite divisibility of things which leads
to the border of non-being. In order to have finite atoms compose the
visible things, Democritus furthermore assumed a void (*kenon*) in which
they could move; the divisibility of visible things could then be explained by their composition of atoms and the void. By the speculative
symbol of the "void" Democritus had invented a Non-Being that did
not exist in the manner of the Being, and nevertheless was something,
whatever it was. He expressed the peculiar ontological status of the void

in relation to the atoms in the compact formula: "No more [or higher, stronger, *mallon*] the Aught than the Naught" (B 156)—avoiding a predicate of being, which therefore should also be avoided in the translation.[14]

The details of Democritean physics are not the present concern. The analysis must concentrate on certain epistemological consequences which affect the theory of ethics and politics. Under the surface of appearances there lies the true reality of atomic Being. Man must learn that he "is removed from reality" (B 6). "In reality [*etee*] we know nothing; in the depth [*bytho*] lies the truth" (B 117)—a sentence with a Heraclitean touch. "Of knowledge there are two forms [*ideai*], the true one and the dark one; to the dark one belong all the following: sight, hearing, smell, taste, touch" (B 11). The dark knowledge is the one that conventionally is called knowledge: "By convention [*nomo*] exist color, sweet and bitter"; "in reality" (*etee*) there exist only the atoms and the void (B 125, B 9).

With regard to the interpretation of these fragments, opinions differ. The temptation is great to recognize in them something like the Lockean theory of primary and secondary qualities; others oppose this interpretation. We agree with the opponents because interpretation by means of modernist analogies is a methodological mistake on principle. The meaning must be found by placing the fragments into the context of their own problems; and about the Parmenidean character of the context there can be no doubt. Even though Democritus attributes to his invisible atoms extension, substance, infinite variety of shape, and variety of specific weight, these are no primary qualities of appearing things but the speculative hypotheses that must be made in order to explain the manifold of things in terms of the Parmenidean One Being. The metaphors by which Democritus expresses the relation between appearance and underlying reality, furthermore, do not point forward to Locke but hark back to Heraclitus. We noted the Heraclitean touch in the fragment on the depth (*bythos*) in which lies the truth; and other fragments bear out this ancestry: "Many much-knowing men [*polymathees*] do not have much insight [*nous*]" (B 64); "One should practice much-insight [*polynoien*], not much-knowing [*polymathien*]" (B 65); "Do not strive to know everything, lest you become ignorant of everything"

[14] The best study of Democritean problems is still Eduard Zeller, *Die Philosophie der Griechen* I/2 (6th ed., Leipzig, 1920).

(B 169). The immanentization of Parmenidean Being has led to a structure of reality in depth, expressed in the metaphors which Heraclitus developed for the depth of the soul. And, finally, one should be aware that Democritus' opposition of a knowledge of appearance "by convention" (*nomo*) to a knowledge "in reality" (*etee*) could be rendered by Diogenes Laertius (IX, 45) as: "The qualities are by convention [*nomo*], by nature [*physei*] are the atoms and the void." While the substitution of "by nature" for "in reality" can hardly have lain in the intention of Democritus, it shows the direction in which the problem was moving: the immanentization of the Parmenidean Being will end in the recognition of nature, of essence in reality.

In the physics of Democritus the movement toward the discovery of essence is still overlaid by the conditions of the Parmenidean problem. In his ethics the tendency becomes clearly visible. Moral phenomena are phenomena of the soul; the discovery of the soul is accepted, and the tradition of the mystic-philosophers and tragedians continued:

> Happiness [*eudaimonie*] is a property of the soul [*psyches*], as is unhappiness [*kakodaimonie*] (B 170).

The sentence is directed against the belief that eudaimonia could be found in external possessions, "in herds of cattle or gold"; this opinion is rejected by recalling the etymology of eudaimonia:

> The psyche is the residence of the daimon (B 171).

The location of happiness in the soul, however, does not determine by itself wherein happiness consists. At this point Democritus goes beyond the tradition by introducing definitions:

> The criterion [*houros*] of the advantageous and disadvantageous is pleasure and displeasure (B 4, B 188).

With the introduction of pleasure (*terpsis*) and displeasure (*aterpie*) as the criterion of preference one may justly say a science of ethics begins. But it does no more than begin; obviously, the criteria as well as the "advantageous" (*sympheron*) require further determination:

> It is best for man to lead life as serenely as possible, and as little discontented as possible; this could happen if one does not find one's pleasures in mortal things (B 189). Hence: Not every pleasure, but only that in the morally-beautiful [*to kalon*] should be chosen

(B 207). The great joys come from contemplating works [or actions] that are noble (B 194). [Happy is] the intellect [*logos*] that is accustomed to derive its joys [*terpsias*] from itself (B 146).

These fragments seem to reflect a study of moral phenomena, critically much more carefully considered than is usually assumed in interpretations of Democritus. He clearly distinguishes between good and bad pleasures, the problem of Plato in the *Philebus* and the *Laws*. And the fragments even indicate a conscious terminological differentiation between pleasure in general (*hedone*, B 189, B 207), and the pleasure that becomes the criterion of what is advantageous (*terpsis*, B 198, B 194, B 146). Only the specific pleasure, the joy (*terpsis*) defines the *sympheron*, not pleasure (*hedone*) at large. The difference between pleasure and joy is suggested by B 174:

> The serene man [*euthymos*], impelled towards just and lawful works [or actions, *erga*], is joyful, stronghearted and free from care; but who neglects justice, and does not what he ought, to him all this is discontent when he remembers it, and he is in fear and torments himself.

The eudaimonia of the soul is in this fragment more closely characterized as *euthymia*, serenity. And such serenity is the consequence of just action. The ethics of Democritus has absorbed the Aeschylean idea of action. "Justice [*dike*] is to do what should be done; injustice [*adikia*] is not to do what should be done but to evade it" (B 256). Only actions in conformity with Dike can properly be considered actions, while attitudes in neglect of justice, evading the issue and taking the easy way out, are the source of a lower tonality of the soul, of the discontent that leads to fear and self-abasement. Diogenes Laertius (IX, 45) apparently was right when he reported the central idea of Democritean ethics, guarding it against misunderstandings: "The end of action is *euthymia*, which is not the same as *hedone*, as some have falsely understood, but a continuously calm and strong state of the soul, undisturbed by any fear or superstition or any other emotion."

Serenity as a continuous state of the soul is dependent on right action. A continuous course of right action, with the effect of serenity, however, does not ordinarily flow by itself. It requires knowledge and practice. "The cause of wrong action [*hamartia*] is ignorance [*amathia*] of the better" (B 83); and "More men become good by training [*askesis*] than by nature [*physis*]" (B 242). At this point the ethics of Democritus closely approaches Protagoras, and probably other sophists as well. It was Protagoras who said: "The art of the teacher must rely on nature [*physis*] and training [*askesis*]" (B 3). And Democritus spins the thought further in the fragment: "Nature and instruction are similar. For instruction transforms the man, and in transforming creates his nature" (B 33). Intelligent habituation through knowledge and training, thus, will be the condition of true *epithymia,* not merely external conformity to rules, perhaps under compulsion; hence:

> A more effective guide toward virtue [*arete*] will prove to be he who uses exhortation and persuasive speech than he who uses law and compulsion. For in secret he will probably do wrong who is held back from wrongdoing by law; but he who is led toward duty by persuasion will probably neither secretly nor openly commit a misdemeanor (B 181).

The purpose of education is the building of a center of resistance to misconduct in the soul, of a moral personality that will function autonomously, without regard for external pressure:

> Not more should one be ashamed before other men than before oneself; and not more should one do evil if nobody will know than if all mankind will know. Rather before oneself should one have most shame. And that must stand as law before the soul: to do nothing that is improper (B 264, see also B 84, B 179, B 244).

A wealth of gnomic sayings and other fragments elaborates the principles in detail. Some of them deserve special attention as forming a step toward the ethics of Plato:

> A man who wishes to live in serenity should not engage in many activities, either in personal or in common life; and whatever he does, he should not burden himself beyond his own strength and nature. But he should carefully keep guard that, even when fortune strikes and leads him on to excess by its delusion, he will rate it low and not undertake things beyond his powers. For right weight is safer than overweight (B 3). Serenity will accrue to men through moderation of enjoyment [*terpsis*] and balance [*symmetrie*] of life. Want and excess of things is apt to turn into its opposite and cause great motions in the soul. And the souls that move in great amplitudes are neither stable nor serene. (B 191).

These fragments deal, in a compact form, with two aspects of excess in action that were later differentiated more clearly by Plato. The serenity of the soul will be disturbed, in the first place, by multifarious activities, in personal or communal affairs, beyond the limited powers of an individual. It is the excess which Plato has stigmatized as the *polypragmosyne* of the sophists, as he did in the caricature of Hippias and, with more conceptual elaboration, in the *Republic*. A man can lead a just life only if he adjusts his range of action to his powers so that the multitude of obligations will not compel him to fail in the adequate discharge of duties. Second, even if serenity does not sink under the overweight of multifariousness, the balance may be badly disturbed by excess in one direction to the detriment of other sectors of normally required action. And such excess would disturb the "symmetry" of life even if it were an excess of *terpsis,* of enjoyment, and not perhaps an indulgence in a lower type of *hedone*. In order to understand the theoretical importance of this point it will be necessary to recall a passage from Alcmeon of Croton, the physician who flourished in the early fifth century:

> According to Alcmeon what constitutes health is the balance [*isonomia*] of forces, wet-dry, cold-hot, bitter-sweet, and the rest; but single rule [*monarchia*] among them works disease. . . . Health is the harmonious [*symmetros*] mixture of the qualities (B 4).

Here we touch the origin of the conception of a balanced life in the medical idea of health; and this medical idea in its turn is couched in political terminology. At the beginning of the fifth century *isonomia* meant the constitutional balance between the old aristocracy and the rising forces of the people, a political equipoise of forces. Health was defined by Alcmeon as such an equipoise of the forces in the body, while disease would be caused by predominance of one of the forces, a *monarchia*. The fragments of Democritus are of importance as the mediating link between the medical conception of health and disease and the later Platonic conception of a "true politeia," characterized by the balanced mixture of component forces, and the "no-constitutions," as democracy, oligarchy, and tyranny, characterized by the domination of one of their component parts.

The physician's conception of health and disease may be said to be for Democritus the governing idea in judging human affairs. "Disease of the household and the life comes about in the same way as disease of the body" (B 288). And this principle he extends from the individual life (*bios*) and the household (*oikos*) to the polis:

> The affairs of the polis must be considered the greatest of all, that it may be well governed; neither must one strive in rivalry beyond equity, nor arrogate to oneself power beyond what is good for the community [*xynon*]. For a well-governed polis is the greatest supporting structure, and all is contained in it. As long as that is well preserved, all will be well preserved; and when that perishes, all will perish (B 252).

The means to preserve the polis in the balance of its health is the law. "The law wants to bestow weal on the life of men, but it can do it only if they want to receive weal; for only to the obedient does it reveal its proper virtue" (B 248). The restraint of the law is necessary because human beings are inclined to do harm to each other out of rivalry and envy; and such envy is the beginning of strife in the community (B 245). And if such strife (*stasis*) breaks out it is equally evil for both parties; both conquerors and conquered suffer the same destruction of the balanced life of the community (B 249). Only under the condition of concord (*homonoie*) can the great works of peace as well as of war be undertaken (B 250); for likemindedness (*homophrosyne*) makes for friendship among the members of the commonwealth (B 186).

As far as the state of the fragments permits a judgment, Democritus' theoretization of ethics, while not going far into the ramification of problems, has touched at least the essential issues. It has introduced the medical idea of health as a balanced constitution of the organism into the discussion of order, an idea that further determined the course of Greek ethics, especially in Plato's conception of justice and the mixed form of government. By means of this idea he, furthermore, arrived at criteria for healthy preservation and unhealthy disturbance, criteria which again make their influence felt in the Platonic and Aristotelian conception of *philia* and *homonoia* as the specifically political virtues, as well as in the later debate on the "advantageous," the *sympheron,* in moral conduct. And, finally, he has developed the conception of serenity, of *euthymia,* as the highest good to be achieved by proper conduct, and thereby has opened the great philosophical debate on conduct conducive to happiness that fills the fourth century. Beyond these special problems the ethics of Democritus should be a general reminder that the age of the sophists was not an age of moral relativism only. The fragments of other sophists which betray a relativistic touch were perhaps preserved because of the sensational novelty of their approach, while whole blocks of writings that may have been rather close to the position of Democritus are lost, perhaps because their literary quality was low compared with the dicta of Democritus who apparently was the greatest prose artist between Heraclitus and Plato. The ideas attributed by Plato to Protagoras, for instance, would indicate that the latter's substantive ethics (as distinguished from his antilogical theory) cannot have differed much from Democritus.

3. *Nomos and Physis*

One of the most intricate problems in the history of sophistic thought is the genesis of the idea of a Physis, a nature, in opposition to the Nomos, the convention, as it is usually translated. The revolutionary, disintegrating effectiveness of the sophists is concentrated in this attack on political order, civilizational traditions, mores, and religious beliefs in the name of a true nature of man that will assert itself. The effect is clear; and it has become so clear through the Platonic portrait of the sophists that the issue Physis-Nomos has become a historiographic cliché which obscures a rather differentiated problem. The method of reconstructing the meaning of the scanty fragments by placing them in the context of problems is especially important in this case.[15]

The search for the essence of man and social order under the title of Physis presupposes certain changes in the original meaning of Nomos. These changes originate historically in the transition from mythical to speculative symbolization of order. Pindar, in Fragment 169, speaks of the Nomos as "the king of all, of the mortals as well as of the immortals"; and Heraclitus, in B 53, says: *"Polemos* [War] is the father of all, and of all the king; and some he reveals as gods and some as men; and some he has made slaves and some free." These fragments of the early fifth century show the transfer of the attributes of Zeus (king, father) to speculative symbols, in the case of Pindar still with the full weight of his Jovian religiousness, in the case of Heraclitus with a touch of irony directed against anthropomorphic symbolization of divinity. An order of gods and men that hitherto had been accepted in its mythical com-

---

[15] For the lines of development, as well as for the materials, this section on "Nomos and Physis" relies on Felix Heinimann, *Nomos und Physis* (Basel, 1945).

pactness as willed by Zeus, including its historical varieties in the manifold of political communities, now became the object of speculative exploration with regard to its nature and the source of its validity.

In the new medium of speculation the problem of Nomos reveals a
complexity that becomes tangible in Heraclitus' fragment B 114:

> Those who speak with the intellect [*xyn nooi*] must strengthen them-
> selves with that which is common [*xynoi*] to all, as the polis does
> with the law [*nomo*], and more strongly so. For all human laws
> [*anthropeioi nomoi*] nourish themselves from the one divine law
> [*theios nomos*] which governs as far as it will, and suffices for all
> things, and more than suffices.

The fragment distinguishes between a divine Nomos and a plurality of
human Nomoi; moreover, the divine law must be assumed to be identical
with the common, the *xynon*, which in turn is identical with the Nous.
Hence, the fragment in its terseness is fraught with a whole series of ideas
that can perhaps be explicated in the following manner: First, there is a
common transcendent Nous which must nourish both the individual man
who thinks with his nous as well as the law of the community. Second,
the human law is a right law in so far as it truly nourishes itself from
the divine law; but obviously it may fail to do so. Third, therefore, it
may become Nomos to obey the will of one man, provided that he is a
man who nourishes himself from the divine Nomos (B 33). Fourth, there
is more than one polis with one human Nomos; the "human laws" exist
in the plurality of the historical manifold.

In this series of ideas are contained the following meanings of the
term Nomos: (1) Nomos as the transcendent divine order; (2) Nomos
as the constitutional and legal order of a polis in conformity with transcendent order—the Nomos for which a people should fight as if it were
their wall (B 44); (3) Nomoi in the plural, meaning the multitude of
orders of the historically existing poleis; (4) Nomos as the historical
order of a polis, regardless of its conformity with the divine Nomos; (5)
Nomos as the order that may live in one man, a *nomos empsychos*—as it
may appear in a *nomothetes*, or the Platonic philosopher-king; and (6)
Nomoi in the plural, which quite possibly carries the association of *nomoi*
in the sense of statutes, as it had come into use since the reform of Cleisthenes, replacing the earlier *thesmoi*.

With the differentiation of meanings the stage is set for the inevitable
problems (1) of reconciling the manifold of historically different Nomoi

with the oneness of the divine Nomos, (2) of interpreting the historical Nomoi in the light of their conformance with, or deviation from, the divine Nomos, and (3) of the tension between the Nomos that lives in the philosopher and the Nomos of the surrounding society.

In the complex of meanings determined by Heraclitean speculation there is no room for an idea of Physis in opposition to Nomos. The source of order is the divine Nomos; and the human Nomos is essentially right order in the measure in which it participates in divine Nomos. Hence, when the term *physis* occurs in Heraclitean fragments it has no bearing on the later sophistic distinction; it rather has the meaning of the nature of a thing or a problem. The idea of Physis, of Nature as an autonomous source of order in competition with Nomos can be formed only when the idea of a transcendent divine Nomos as the source of order has atrophied; and that can happen in a theoretical context only when philosophizing in the existential sense is abandoned.

This further stage of theorizing was reached by the middle of the fifth century, in the person of Protagoras, though Protagoras himself did not yet introduce the idea of Physis. The great sophist, as presented by Plato, professed to be a teacher of the art of politics. In order to discharge the duties of his profession effectively he had to accept the Nomos of the polis as it existed historically and to teach his pupils how to move with success in the concrete environment. His substantive ethics, as previously noted, probably did not differ much from that of Democritus, or from prevailing traditions in general. With such conservative conventionalism, however, he combined his immanentist relativism with regard to theory of knowledge. As a skeptic and agnostic, therefore, he rejected all speculation on the basis of experiences of transcendence; and, in particular, he could not allow speculation on the source of order and its validity in a transcendent divine law. The keystone of Heraclitean speculation on the Nomos, the *theios nomos*, was eliminated by Protagoras. The obvious theoretical gap left by this elimination, however, was not filled by him; he did not replace the transcendent source of order by an immanent source, the Physis of his sophistic successors, but left the problem wide open by simply accepting as valid order whatever (in any political civilization) men believed to be valid.

It would be rash, however, to see in the peculiar attitude of Protagoras nothing but a theoretical insufficiency. To be sure, he was unable to solve the problem. But when he accepted as valid what men believed he

was perhaps motivated by a profound respect for belief as the manifestation of a hidden order, if not as its source, a respect that perhaps did not
differ far from the prespeculative acceptance of order as the will of Zeus.
A motivation of this kind is suggested as possible by a reflection of Herodotus (III, 38) on the madness of Cambyses in violating and ridiculing
the customs of Persians and foreign peoples:

> It is clear to me beyond a doubt that Cambyses was very mad, or
> he would never have set himself to deride cults and customs. For
> if it were allowed to all men to choose from all nomoi the ones they
> considered the best, they would, after due examination, rank their
> own first; so firmly do they believe that their own nomoi are the
> best of all.

If the assumption of philologists that this passage is influenced by Protagoras be accepted, it would indeed be a key to the Protagorean attitude;
for the chapter closes with the line from Pindar that Nomos is the king
of all. The theoretical gap was perhaps not experienced too sharply because for Protagoras Nomos was still the king of human beliefs, rather
than human belief the king of Nomos.

In Protagoras appears, for the first time, the type of thinker who is
a skeptic, or agnostic, with regard to transcendent reality and, at the
same time, a conservative with regard to historical order. Since the combination of the two attitudes has caused, and is still causing, difficulties
in understanding the thinker, it may be well to recall that his case is not
singular. The type of the conservative skeptic recurs, toward the end of
the fourth century, in the person of Pyrrho and is continued by his
skeptic successors. In Western civilization it recurs, after the upheaval
of the Reformation, in Montaigne, Bayle, and Hume. The difficulty of
understanding the hybrid position is caused by its theoretical insufficiency; it seems unbelievable that an otherwise astute thinker should be
blind to the previously characterized theoretical gap. It is all the more
necessary to be clear about the strand of archaic wisdom in the conservative mind, preserving it in a time of rapid intellectual movement from
derailment into revolutionary dogmatism. While such balance can be
preserved in the individual case, the attitude of conservative skepticism
is unstable on principle; it can be preserved only under the condition
that the theoretical question of validity and its source will not be raised.
A more inquisitive mind will not be satisfied with such abstinence. And
as soon as the question is raised the position will dissolve either into the

immanentist dogmatism of the sophists of the second generation, making Physis the new source of authority, or into the restoration of the problems of transcendence as we have seen it in the opposition of Socrates to the sophist in Plato's *Protagoras*.

Protagoras himself maintained his thought in the skeptic suspense. His intellectual discipline was strong enough to preserve him from substituting an immanent Physis for the essence of order, unacceptable to him, that reveals itself in experiences of transcendence. Nevertheless, the term "Physis" appears in his work; and while it is not opposed to Nomos, it has an important function as a mediating link between the older aristocratic ethic and its later use in the revolutionary ethic of the sophists. We remember the fragment B 3: "The art of teaching must rely on nature [*physis*] and training [*askesis*]." This nature on which the art of teaching must rely is a generalization of the traditional Greek idea, advanced by the older poets in the paraenetic sections of their work, that the qualities of a man are not acquired but a gift of birth, and in particular of noble descent. Education can develop these gifts of nature, but no educational art can graft them on a man who lacks them from birth. In the fifth century, overlapping with the lifetime of Protagoras, the aristocratic conception of Physis has its great representative in Pindar, whose Odes are rich in praise of the natural equipment, the *phya*, of the scions of noble families who proved their worth as victors in the games. But this same Pindar who sings the praise of the nobility and its virtues enlarges the meaning of *phya* beyond the inherited nature of the aristocrat and includes other types of natural gifts, especially his own gift of poetry; and he turns against rivals who have acquired their art through learning and believe they can practice it without *phya*, that is, without the gift of the gods. The natural endowment in this generalized form is Protagoras' condition of education. It is definitely no longer an appurtenance of noble ancestry for, in Plato's dialogue, the sophist makes a special point that the sons of the great Athenian statesmen are singularly lacking in the gifts of their fathers and, therefore, unpromising material for his educational art. While removing the natural endowment from its context of aristocratic ethics, Protagoras, however, did not "democratize" it into a general "nature of man." His *physis* retained a positive value accent in so far as it fitted its owner for training in the art of politics. It is not a *physis* in opposition to Nomos, but clearly a natural gift that enables a man to lead a successful life within the Nomos. And since not everybody by far has this gift, one may speak of a Protagorean conception of a "natural aristocracy," capable of developing into the leaders of their polis and the preservers of its Nomos. Only when the orientation of the Physis toward the Nomos is lost, can Physis become an autonomous source of authoritative order, as in the Platonic Callicles. But even in such derailment the ethics of the "strong man" still bears the marks of the aristocratic tradition of which it is the caricature.

On several occasions a further meaning of "physis" was touched, that is, its meaning as "nature" or "essence" of things. In the sophistic opposition of Physis to Nomos this meaning became all-important because it carried the authority of a true nature of things against what uninformed people only believe (*nomizein*) they are. The origin of the meaning must be sought in the environment of Ionian speculation. Xenophanes, speaking of the rainbow, says: "And what they call [*kalein*] Iris is by its nature [*pephyke*] a cloud" (B 32). Heraclitus, in fragment B 1, proposes to expound words and things, analyzing each "according to its nature" (*kata physin*); and in B 112 he defines wisdom as "saying what is true and acting according to the nature [of things] observingly." Both philosophers use the term "physis" with a polemical tone that is of importance for our problem. They expound or insist on the "nature" of things because they are in search of truth; and the truth about things is different from what people ordinarily believe. In this compact archaic language "believing wrongly" is still the same as "calling things by a wrong name"; the philosophical search for truth, in its beginnings, is a struggle for a new vocabulary in opposition to mythical language; hence, the uninformed "call" (*kalein*) the rainbow Iris. This point is well illuminated by a line from Empedocles: "Not what is right [*themis*] do they say [*kalein*], but following custom [*nomo*] I use the same language" (B 9, 5). With Empedocles, whose prime lies about 450, *nomos* already has a derogatory connotation as the custom of the people who call (*kalein*) things by wrong names. And in the previously quoted B 17 of Anaxagoras (that the Hellenes do not opine, *nomizousin*, rightly concerning certain questions) the verb *nomizein*, substituting for the older *kalein*, has acquired the meaning of uninformed believing or thinking. The philosophers' search for the true nature of things, their *physis*, thus forces *nomos*, the unreflected body of civilizational traditions in the widest sense, into the position of erroneous beliefs of the unenlightened common people.

The lines along which the terms Physis and Nomos change their meaning have been traced independently of each other to the point where they converge toward the late-sophistic pair of opposites. There remains to be considered the historical situation in which they began to form a pair at all. As far as the sources allow a judgment on this question, the pair seems to have formed in the wake of the Persian Wars with their surprising victory of the weaker Greek power over the Persians. In search of an explanation for the victory the idea suggested itself that the numerical superiority of an army was in itself no guaranty of victory; an important factor will be the spirit in which the army fights, and this spirit is formed by the institutions, by the Nomos. This idea can be gathered from the Hippocratic treatise on *Airs, Waters, Places* which must be dated shortly before 430 B.C. In the second, ethnographic part of the treatise (Chapters XII–XXIV) the unknown author compares Asia and Europe, surveying their climatic, hydrographic, and topographic differences, as well as the differences of their peoples with regard to physical appearance and select character traits. In describing the differences now the author carefully distinguishes between characteristics due to "nature," caused by the climatic and topographic factors of the landscape, and characteristics that are caused by customs and political institutions, the Nomos. In particular, he reflects on the warlike character of Europeans and the more feeble, peaceable temper of Asiatics, finding in the Nomos an important factor determining the difference: "Europeans are more warlike because of their *nomoi*, not being under kings as are the Asiatics. For those who live under kings are by necessity the most cowardly men. For men's souls become slavish and unwilling to run dangers readily to increase somebody else's power. But independent men [*autonomoi*]—taking risks for themselves and not for others—are willing and eager to meet danger, for they gain the prize of victory for themselves. The *nomoi*, thus, have an especially strong share in forming courageousness" (XXIII).[16]

The same argument, elaborated more dramatically, is to be found in Herodotus VII, 101–104. The occasion is a review and census of his army and navy by Xerxes. Impressed by the result, Xerxes requests the opinion of Demaratus, the exiled king of Sparta who resides at his court, whether against such overwhelming strength the Greeks will dare to make a stand at all. Demaratus explains to the king that poverty is truly

[16] *Hippocrates* I (Loeb Classical Library), 132.

inborn (*syntrophos*) in Hellas while excellence (*arete*) is acquired (*hepaktos*), as the result of wisdom and strong Nomos. Because of their *arete* they will not submit to the king who brings slavery to Hellas. Xerxes smiles at such fancy and answers with his own idea of the nature of man. How should a small number of men, all free and not under the rule of one man, resist his strength? If they were under the rule of one, they might be in fear of him and prove themselves valorous beyond their nature (*physis*), and under compulsion of the lash they would fight against odds. But this they would not do if they were free. In his reply Demaratus enters into the argument of the king. The Lacedaemonians "are free, yet not wholly free; for *nomos* is their master, and they fear him much more than your men fear you." What their Nomos orders them to do, that they will do; and it orders them never to flee from battle, but to stay at their place in the rank until victory or death.

The *History* of Herodotus is contemporary with *Airs, Waters, Places*. Since no influence of the one on the other can be convincingly shown, the parallel use of the pair Physis-Nomos in both works probably goes back to common sources. But this older literature, the existence of which must be assumed, is not preserved.

4. Antiphon

To Antiphon the Sophist (as distinguished from Antiphon the orator and Antiphon the tragedian) is ascribed a group of fragments, contained in the Oxyrhynchus papyri, which were parts of a work on *Truth*. The work, as the title indicates, must have been a treatise on theory of knowledge, continuing the tradition of treatises on Aletheia in the wake of Parmenides. That the preserved fragments deal with the subject of justice is, therefore, probably an accident and does not justify the assumption that the whole work was a treatise on politics. The fragments must, rather, be considered a section of the work in which the general principles of ontology and epistemology were applied to the specific topic of justice. Hence, we shall proceed by first isolating the general principles, as far as they are discernible in the fragments, and only then deal with their application.[17]

In setting forth the principles of Antiphon, it is necessary to settle on definite terms in the translation, for the sophist developed a technical

---

[17] The analysis of principles closely follows the section on Antiphon in Heinimann, *Nomos und Physis*, 133–42.

vocabulary and used it consistently. He attempted a theory of the laws which govern the life of man, using for them the term *ta nomima*. In order to avoid confusion, we shall render this term as "rules." The rules originate either in nature (*physis*) or in human institution (*nomos*). The rules of nature are necessary (*anankaia*); the rules of human origin are adventitious (or fictitious, *epitheta*). The rules of nature, furthermore, are grown (*phynta*); the rules of the *nomos* are agreed or covenanted (*homologethenta*). In the environment of rules man has to find his way by orienting his conduct toward what is advantageous or profitable (*sympheron*) for him.

Conduct in pursuit of the *sympheron* requires examination of the two types of rules; for it is not *a priori* certain whether they are both advantageous, or whether only one of the types is advantageous, or whether they are partially advantageous and partially disadvantageous. For guidance in this matter Antiphon lays down two principles. The first principle concerns nature: A man who tries, against possibility, to violate one of the rules implanted by nature in us will do damage to himself; and the damage will not be a matter of opinion (*doxa*) only, but a damage in truth (*aletheia*). The second principle concerns the *nomos*: Most of what is considered just according to rules of law is inimical to nature. The principle is less demonstrated than oratorically enhanced by the passage: "There are laws made for the eyes, what they should see and what not; for the ears, what they should hear and what not; for the tongue, what it should say and what not; for the hands, what they should do and what not; for the feet, where they should go and where not; and for the mind, what it should desire and what not. And what the laws prohibit and enjoin to men, is equally little friendly and agreeable to nature." The law, thus, on the whole is a "chain on nature."

Equipped with the two principles one may approach the question of the *sympheron*. Antiphon's argument goes through the following steps:

(1) To nature belong both living and dying. Men draw life from things that are advantageous (*sympheronta*); they incur death from things disadvantageous. Things conducive to death, therefore, can be excluded from further discussion; we are interested only in things that enhance life. (It should be noted that *physis* is far from being the source of the advantageous only; in so far as nature entails death it is disadvantageous.)

(2) *Sympheronta* are laid down both by nature (*physis*) and by law (*nomos*). But the *sympheronta* of nature rise spontaneously, freely, while those of the laws are restraints imposed on nature.

(3) Now, things which cause pain (*algynonta*) cannot be rightly considered to benefit nature (because they are akin to death) as do the things which give delight (*euphrainonta*). Hence, things which cause impairment, restraint, annoyance (*lypounta*) cannot be advantageous as are those which give pleasure (*hedonta*).

(4) Hence, only the *sympheronta* of nature can be considered truly (*to alethei*) advantageous, while those of the law are in reality disadvantageous. Hence, a man who follows the *nomoi* will suffer damage.

The principles and the closer definition of the *sympheronta* then must be applied to the problem of justice. The application itself is brief and simple. Justice in the common view consists in not trangressing the rules of the polis in which one is a citizen. A man will, therefore, use justice to the most advantage for himself if, in the presence of witnesses, he upholds the rules of the laws but, when he is without witnesses, he upholds the rules of nature. If the man who transgresses the rules of law is unobserved by those who have agreed to them, he escapes punishment and disgrace; and only if the transgression does not remain hidden will he incur sanctions. If, however, he trangresses a rule of nature, the damage to him will be none the less if the trespass remains hidden, and none the greater if it is observed by all men.

An evaluation of these fragments is not easy. We know nothing about the larger context from which they are torn; and other parts of the work may have illuminated some of the puzzling points. One can do no more than, with due caution, suggest a few probabilities.

Clearly, in the exposition of his problem, Antiphon has a method. His argument is antithetical; it proceeds, in clarifying the *sympheronta*, by developing dichotomies and then systematically excluding one term of the dichotomy from further consideration. Rules are of nature or of law; to nature belong living and dying; therefore, the nature of man is faced with *sympheronta* and *me sympheronta*; *sympheronta* are established by nature or by law. From these dichotomies are dropped dying, the *me sympheronta* of nature conducive to dying, and the doxic *sympheronta* of law, so that in the end are left the *sympheronta* of nature which enhance living. It is reasonable to assume that this method of exposition was not invented by Antiphon, but generally used by sophists; it would lend an orderly appearance to the argument and make the classification convincing—especially in oral delivery when the listener would not have time to reflect on the complications of the problem.

The relation of the method to the subject matter presented is the second point to be considered. From the account of Antiphon's theory it will have become clear that the method is a mechanism rattling badly. The sophist wants to arrive at the proposition that the *sympheronta* of nature should be the guide of conduct. The structure of reality, however, is discourteous enough not to correspond to the method of dichotomies but to be more complex. Hence, the result cannot be achieved by consistently subdividing the positive term of each dichotomy but only by crossing several unrelated dichotomies. Moreover, the dichotomies do not sit too well on their objects. The dichotomy nature-law does not result from the dichotomy living-dying; and the dichotomy advantageous-disadvantageous (1) subdivides nature, (2) corresponds to nature-law, and (3) even subdivides law, a fact which Antiphon tries to cover up, apparently with a bad conscience, by the rhetorical passage that all laws are a restraint on nature, which is not so certain at all. In the aggregate, therefore, the argumentation is a clumsy piece of work, hiding the real issues rather than revealing them. The "theory" of Antiphon cannot be rendered adequately in the terms of his dichotomies. It would be incorrect, for instance, to say he opposes Physis to Nomos as the guide to right conduct, as one can frequently read in histories of ideas; for the dichotomy nature-law is part of the whole system of dichotomies; and the dichotomy living-dying reveals that one half of nature should not be followed at all in the pursuit of the *sympheron*. Hence, it will be necessary to extricate the substantive theory of Antiphon from the dichotomic form.

Since Antiphon's true *sympheronta* are those of nature it will be appropriate to begin with his idea of nature. To this nature belong living and dying. The conception of nature as divided into the two compartments of life and death is in itself rather odd. It is not rooted in the great tradition of tragedy or, farther back, of the mystic-philosophers, or ultimately of Homer, with its understanding of the immanence of death in life, of the tradition which in Plato blossoms into the idea of life as the practice of dying. The notion of dividing things into those which are profitable for life in the physiological sense, and others which precipitate death is peculiarly flat, beyond the pale of spiritual culture. Moreover, one cannot even say that such flatness is characteristic for the speculation on the necessities, the *anankaia*, of nature in general at the time. Democritus, for instance, who also reflected on the problem of Physis, treated it rather differently. He seems to hold practically the same position as Antiphon when he says: "It is unreasonable not to submit to the necessities of life" (B 289); but then he considers carefully what these necessities really are. In a specific instance he says: "To men it appears a necessity, arising from nature and the primaeval order of being, to have children. And so obviously it is with other animals too, for they all have offspring, according to nature, and not for the sake of any profit" (B 278); but then he reflects: "It does not seem to me that one should have children" (B 276)—asserting the freedom of the sage to reject for reason what "to men appears" a necessity of nature. And in general he formulates the principle: "To fight against desire is hard; but to dominate it is the characteristic of the eminently reasonable man" (B 236). Democritus, thus, recognizes necessities of nature, its urges and desires, as does Antiphon, but he sees them in relation to the rationally organizing center of man, to his Logos; and the Logos will frequently decide that it is better for man not to follow the necessities of nature but to frustrate them. Hence, the peculiar flatness of Antiphon's idea can be more precisely defined as his blindness for spiritual and intellectual sources of order; nature has become to him, indeed, an autonomous guide beyond criticism. This oddity now can be traced to his reliance on the medical conception of *physis* and that which is advantageous (*sympheron*) to the nature of man in the physiological sense. A sentence from *Ancient Medicine* VI will illustrate the point: "It must be well understood that slops will not benefit [*sympherei*] some men in disease; for, when they take them, their fever and pain grow noticeably worse; and it is plain that what is taken proves nourishment and increase to the disease, but wears away and enfeebles the body." [18] Here, in a therapeutic reflection, we find the dichotomy of advantageous and disadvantageous with regard to disease and health, ultimately of dying and living, in its original environment. And through a transfer of the medical idea to the quite different problems of ethics and politics the odd conception of Antiphon must be explained.

The medical dichotomy, once it is established for the realm of

[18] *Hippocrates* I (Loeb Classical Library), 22.

Physis, is then put to duty as the carrier of a corresponding dichotomy with regard to Nomos. To the pair painful-delightful (*algynonta-euphrainonta*), as we have seen, corresponds the pair restraining-pleasurable (*lypounta-hedonta*). The rules of law are restraining, not pleasurable; that the order of the Nomos has a meaning of its own does not become an issue; the rules of law have meaning only in so far as they affect Physis; and by analogy, sliding on a line of synonyms from painful to restraining and from delightful to pleasurable, the medical dichotomy is extended into the dichotomy concerning rules of law. It is a rhetorical trick, relying on a dubious syllogism by analogy. Even if one accepts Antiphon's disregard for the Nomos as an independent source of order as well as his faith in the Physis as a guide to the *sympheron,* still there would be required some proof that the *sympheronta* of the Nomos are actually harmful to Physis. And at this point, as we have seen, there is to be found nothing but the bland assertion that this is the case.

The "theoretical" treatment of the Nomos is so unconvincing that it must be assumed to be no more than a rhetorical mechanism covering a deeper issue. Even a not very astute thinker must have seen that very little "living" will accrue to anybody's Physis if everybody disregards the restraints of the law and acts according to the "necessities of nature." And Antiphon, to be sure, saw this point quite well. A further section of the fragment must be considered the key to his otherwise incomprehensible conception of the truly advantageous. In this section Antiphon explains that obedience to the laws would, indeed, not be without benefit if those who obeyed them received help from the laws, while those who violated them suffered evil effects. In actual court practice, however, the victim is not sure at all of finding redress; and the criminal through superior skills in pleading may easily sway the people's court in his favor. The Nomos of Antiphon, thus, turns out to be not the law in the philosophical sense at all, but the mores and courthouse practice of a corrupt society. In this jungle of blackmailing informers, perjurors, emotional and bribed judges, the man who abides by the rules of the law may indeed go under. And in this situation the introductory sentence of the fragment makes sense as a rule of survival: A man will use justice to his best advantage if he upholds the law in the presence of witnesses, but without witnesses follows the natural interest. Hence, even for Antiphon it will be *sympheron* to obey the law if the presence of witnesses makes transgression hazardous; for the law and its enforcing institutions are a part of the environment in which man moves with his Physis.

Whether the Antiphonian body of reflections can be characterized as a "theory of natural law," or as a "theory of the social contract," as is usually done by historians, seems to us highly doubtful. This jumble of ill-considered and poorly formalized (one can hardly say theorized) ideas looks rather like a counsel of *sauve qui peut* in a period of disintegration. To be sure, the laws in the widest sense, including the mores, are derived from "agreement"; but, at least in the extant fragments, there is no indication of the purpose which such agreement should serve. The existence of the agreed law is merely registered as a social fact, as a sort of nuisance; and certainly no obligation arises from this agreement. The basic theorems that would constitute a theory of law by contract, thus, are missing. The characterization of the law as "agreed" has, rather, the purpose of showing its doxic quality, its character as an erroneous "belief" in opposition to truth, *aletheia,* in the sense of Parmenides. The "rules of nature," on the other hand, are not elaborated into a theory of natural law. That part of Antiphon's ideas remains on the level of a physiological conception of the "necessities of nature" and of things advantageous to "living"; again the basic theorems that would build on this conception a viable order of life in society are missing.

Moreover, there is a further scrap of text extant which puts the nature of Antiphon's conception beyond doubt. He complains that we revere and venerate those who are of noble descent but not those who are humbly born. In this respect the Hellenes treat each other like barbarians. For by nature we are all endowed equally, Hellenes and barbarians, for all equally have the things which are necessary to all men by nature. We all breathe the air through mouth and nostrils, and eat with our hands. At this point the fragment breaks off. Again we consider it exaggerated to hail this passage as revealing a "theory" of the equality of men, perhaps attaining a new level of moral insight. For probably nobody had ever doubted that all men are equal with regard to their possession of a respiratory apparatus or of hands; but nobody had ever conceived the idea of making this observation an argument for the equality of men. The attempt at reducing the essence of man to his anatomy reveals that the pathos of Hellas, the pride in its Nomos, in its civilizational tradition, is dissolving.

The fragments of Antiphon, far from containing important new theories, look, rather, like an emergency structure erected by a third-rate intellectual in the ruins of Hellenic culture. That does not mean that the fragments are without interest. The fact of their preservation suggests they were considered a representative piece of writing and, therefore, worth preserving. If they are indeed representative for sophistic debate of the problems at the time (they probably have to be placed in the 420's), they furnish valuable insights into the rapid disintegration of Athens in the last quarter of the fifth century, as as well as into the decay of intellectual culture. The polis must have appeared so rotten to a sophist like Antiphon, who probably was an Athenian, that its Nomos had become devoid of obligatory substance and legitimated the withdrawal into the apolitism of Physis. The sophistic response to the state of disintegration must, in its turn, have aggravated the situation. When we read Antiphon we can understand the wrath which a conservative like Aristophanes displays in the *Clouds* against the sophists, especially in the contest between the allegoric figures of Dikaios Logos and Adikaios Logos (889–1104); and if Antiphon is typical for a class of literature, one must admit that the great comedian had hardly any room left for satirical exaggeration. The situation must have resembled our own in which Karl Kraus despaired of writing satire because he could not outdo the satire performed by reality on the truth of order. It is difficult to see, however, what thinkers of mediocre stature could have done under the circumstances of progressive disintegration, unless they should have kept quiet. It required men of a different caliber, a Socrates and a Plato, to restore the problems of order and to elaborate them further. And here again, in relation to Plato, the Antiphon fragments are of historical importance because they prove that Plato, in his polemic against the sophists, did not draw caricatures; if anything they were worse than they appear in the Platonic portraits of a Thrasymachus or a Polus.

5. Critias

Under the impact of the Peloponnesian War, in the last third of the fifth century, the Nomos of Athens disintegrated and parallel with it the idea of the Nomos. The antilogies of ethical speculation and the substitution of Physis as a criterion of order for Nomos were expressions of this process. A further such expression is the conception of Nomos as a product of evolution, as it is to be found in the *Sisyphus* fragment of Critias.

The conception has a venerable ancestry. The older generation of sophists must have developed it by the middle of the fifth century or shortly thereafter, if we rely on Plato, who attributed it to Protagoras. In the Protagorean form, as related by Plato, the idea of civilizational evolution was expressed in the myth of Prometheus. Since the figure of Prometheus had been created by Aeschylus, the sophistic must be considered as derived from the Aeschylean myth; and the myth of Aeschylus, in its turn, nourished itself from the theogonic and anthropogonic ideas of Hesiod. Into this genealogy there seems to have blended, at the time of Protagoras, a strand of Ionian speculation through the cosmogony of Archelaus. Unfortunately we know almost nothing about the aspect of his work that is revelant to our problem except that he extended his cosmogony beyond the genesis of animals and man into the origin of civilization and governmental order. A late source attributes to him the opinion that "just and unjust [*aischron*] are not by nature [*physei*] but by institution [*nomo*]" (A 1 and 2). In this form the report certainly is both incorrect and anachronistic. Neither were the forms *physei* and *nomo* in use at the time, nor is it probable that he opposed Physis to Nomos at all. Most probably, however, the report indicates that Archelaus had absorbed the Ionian ethnographic accounts since Hecataeus and explained the differences of mores among various peoples by their creation through Nomos in the sense of convention or belief.[19]

These antecedents must be presupposed in the story of civilizational evolution as told by the *Sisyphus* of Critias (B 25). The following is a translation, as literal as possible, omitting only a few minor embellishments not pertinent to our purpose:

> There was a time when the life of man was unordered, bestial and subjected to force; there was no reward for the excellent, and no punishment for the wicked. And then, so it seems to me, men established laws as the taskmasters that justice should be tyrant of all and hybris its slave; and punished was every transgressor. This regime of the laws, however, prevented open violence only, not crimes committed in secret. Then, so it seems to me, a wise and knowing man invented fear of the gods for the mortals that there would be

[19] For the ideas of Archelaus cf. Heinimann, *Nomos und Physis*, 110–15.

a terror to the wicked, even if they did, said, or thought anything in secret. For this reason he introduced the Divine [*to theion*]: "It is a Daimon, flourishing with inexhaustible life, hearing and seeing with his mind, knowing beyond measure and watching the world, being of divine nature, who will hear all that is said and all that is done among mortals; and even your planning of evil in silence will not remain hidden to the gods." Thus he introduced the most alluring of legends veiling the truth with a false tale [*pseudos logos*]. And in order to make his tale effective he let the gods reside in the place whose naming would frighten men most, in the revolving vault whence fears and rewards come to the hard life of man, where he perceives lightning and thunder, in the starglittering heaven, the beautiful tapestry of Chronos, the skilful craftsman. Thus he surrounded men with fears, establishing the Daimon by his story, giving it a proper habitat, and at the same time quenching lawlessness [*anomia*] through the laws [*nomoi*]. In this manner, I think, has someone persuaded the mortals to believe [*nomizein*] in the existence of a race of gods.

As in the case of Antiphon, it is not easy to determine the precise meaning of the story. Critias no more than Antiphon is a theorist capable of penetrating to the core of a problem of this type. His story is not a theory but what Plato later called a *doxa,* an uncritical opining, floundering in the complexities of the issues. Hence it would be an impermissible superficiality to summarize the story as a sophistic theory that the laws and gods were invented by man. To be sure, in comparison with the Prometheus myth of Protagoras a more radical tone of agnosticism is undeniable. In the Protagorean myth the gods create the mortal beings, Epimetheus equips them with their faculties, forgetting man, Prometheus provides the characteristics of the *homo faber,* and Zeus the gifts of ordered life in political community. In the story of Critias the creative gods have disappeared, the laws are devised by men at large, and the fear of the gods is the invention of a particularly "wise and knowing man." This change of the creative agents shows with certainty, however, only that the myth of the old style had lost for Critias the authority of "truly" symbolizing the mystery of order, both political and spiritual. It does not show that Critias seriously maintained a "theory" of human invention. On the contrary, he expressed his idea in the very form of the old myth; for the story opens with the same mythical "there once was a time" (*hen chronos*) that opens the myth of Prometheus in Plato's *Protagoras.* Moreover, the regularly interspersed "it seems to me" and "I think" deprecate any theoretical truth and insist on the role of the speaker as a mythmaker. It would be more appropriate, therefore, to characterize the story as a "sophistic myth" of human invention which tends to replace the older polytheistic symbolism. It is a form of symbolization halfway between the older myth, which no longer could be naively accepted, and the new myth of the soul, which required a Plato for its creation.

The myth of Critias, furthermore, does not intend to invalidate civilizational order. The life of man, before the inventions, was really unordered and bestial; the establishment of laws really made justice the tyrant of all; and the invention of the gods put a fear into men which really improved their moral conduct. The achievements are considered real, and Critias is the last man who would want to undermine the order of justice and morality. He does not offer an order of Physis as an alternative to Nomos. On the contrary, he insists that "more men are good through habituation than through *physis*" (B 9); and he complains bitterly that "nothing is just in the present generation" (B 12). In his *Constitutions* in verse and prose he praises highly the stern customs of the Lacedaemonians. And in a passage from his *Rhadamantys* he confesses to desire nothing for himself but a reputation of fair fame, as compared with others who desire to be noblemen, or to be masters of great possessions, or who are attracted by shameful gain rather than honor (B 15).

The key to the intention of Critias, if there is a key to be found at all in his fabulation, must be sought in the terse, enigmatic line that the wise and knowing man who invented the gods veiled the truth (*aletheia*) by his false story (*pseudos logos*). What is this truth veiled by the false Logos? Could it be the truth, now revealed by the speaker Sisyphus in the drama, that the Logos is false? Hardly; for that would be an imbecility not to be assumed lightly. The truth veiled by the story can only be the insight that man himself, from the resources of his soul, is the creator of justice and morality. Not every man, however. There are "excellent" men who suffer under lawlessness, and the devising of laws protects them against the wicked; and the invention of the gods is due to the "wise and knowing man" who apparently must be in possession of morality and who invents the Logos in order to induce moral conduct through fear of the gods in other men who cannot achieve it spontaneously without such support. The truth now unveiled is the creation of civilizational order by the excellent, the natural aristocrats, and its imposition on the mass of the people. If this interpretation be tenable, the Logos of Critias would have a special historical interest, for the same problem recurs in the work of Critias' greater nephew, in the *Republic*, where Plato introduces the *pseudos mythos* for the mass of the people, veiling the truth, because they are unable spontaneously to live in conformity with unveiled truth.

6. Equality, Inequality, Harmony

If the fragments of Antiphon and Critias be assumed to represent sophistic theorizing toward the end of the fifth century, the level of theoretical accomplishment cannot have been high. It is necessary to stress this point because of a still persistent historiographic habit of attributing to the thinkers of this period theories of natural law and of the social contract—a generosity which is not justified by the actual content of the extant fragments. Nevertheless, in such attributions there is a core of truth in so far as these thinkers, though no great theorists, created a new theoretical situation and found the symbols for expressing it. One cannot extract from Antiphon, for instance, a theory of the origin of law through contract, for the Nomos on which his men "agree" is not law in the technical sense but includes mores and customs whose transgression would be a "disgrace"; moreover, the "agreement" does not create an obligation but, on the contrary, invalidates the obligatory force of law and custom, as we have indicated. Nevertheless, Antiphon had seen that, under the concrete conditions of Athenian democracy, the Nomos on which men were in "agreement" did not have much substance and, hence, a search for substance had become necessary. Odd as it may sound at first hearing, the attitude of Antiphon was substantially the same as Plato's; and his characterization of the Nomos as "agreed" in a derogatory sense had the same intention as Plato's characterization of current opinions about justice as *doxa*. The attempt to find this substance in Physis in the medical or physiological sense, to be sure, was an abortive mistake and led to the idea of basing the equality of men on their anatomy. But here again, setting aside the philosophical inadequacy, there was the idea of equality itself. From the disintegration of the Athenian Nomos emerged the vision of a human community embracing Hellenes and barbarians. It was the forerunner of the ideas of the fourth century which transcended the polis as the ultimate unit of social existence, of the Panhellenism of Isocrates, of the Cynic and Stoic idea of a cosmopolis, and of Alexander's attempt to blend Persians and Hellenes in the harmony, the *homonoia*, of his empire.

Similar reflections are suggested by the *Sisyphus* fragment of Critias. The idea that laws are "devised" and the gods "invented" by somebody was a rationalization of the phenomena of order which can be dismissed as the fancy of an aristocratic dilettante bewildered by such problems. Nevertheless, the fancy was based on the experience of declining Athens, on the observation of an emotional populace, ready for any dishonesty and crime, and even for self-destructive, stupid political actions. Civilizational order could be wasted and destroyed by this free and sovereign rabble, but certainly not created. In such a crisis it became pellucid that not all men were equal, that the creation and maintenance of civilizational order was the work of minorities, of the excellent, and in emergencies had to rely perhaps on a single "wise and knowing man." Again, setting aside the inadequate rationalization, this was the insight on which Plato based his conceptions of the philosopher-king and of the royal ruler, and Aristotle his conception of the mature man, the *spoudaios,* who was the carrier of moral excellence as well as order in the polis.

From the disintegration of the polis and its Nomos the great problems of the fourth century begin to emerge: The quest for the nature of man that is the same for all human beings, the problem of the inequality of men within the amplitude of their equal nature, the search for a common order that will harmoniously hold together the unequals without destroying excellence, and the historical diversification of national civilizations. The sophists see these problems, even though their solutions are clumsy and inadequate. However fallacious their reasoning may be, they are, as we have seen with Antiphon and Critias, in search of truth, *aletheia.* The search for the truth of being goes in unbroken continuity from Parmenides to Plato. The fact must neither be obscured by the odd forms which the search assumes in the hands of the late sophists, nor by Plato's protest against the immanentist perversion of the search.

The late-sophistic fragments are not primarily important because of their reasoning or their theoretical content; their value must, rather, be sought in their motivations, in their character of symptoms of disintegration of an older order as well as their function as signposts pointing toward a new one. Under this aspect a number of brief fragments must be listed which in spite of their brevity illuminate the intellectual setting of the fragments of Antiphon and Critias.

There is preserved a passage from Prodicus of Ceos:

> He said: "Sun and moon, rivers and sources, and in general every-thing that is of use to our life, the ancients have believed to be gods because of their usefulness, such as the Egyptians the Nile," and that is why bread was believed to be Demeter, wine to be Dionysus, water to be Poseidon, fire to be Hephaestus, and so everything that could be put to good use (B 5).

The utilitarian explanation of the belief in gods shows that the ra-tionalization of Critias was not isolated in its time. Prodicus seems to have shared with Critias a dogmatic agnosticism as it would arise in the wake of the Protagorean critical agnosticism. There is no indication that either Prodicus or Critias used their criticism of polytheistic symbols as a first step in arriving at the idea of a greatest god as did Xenophanes.

There are extant two references by Aristotle to the political ideas of Lycophron. In *Politics* 1280b Aristotle speaks of the true polis as concerned with the excellence of its citizens; without such concern it would sink to the level of a mere contractual relationship, as in the case of an alliance between poleis. In this case the law would be a covenant (*syntheke*) or, "in the phrase of the sophist Lycophron, a guarantor of men's rights against one another"; it would not be designed to make the citizens good and just. The term "covenant" or "contract" in this passage, it should be noted, is Aristotle's, not Lycophron's, as is some-times erroneously assumed. As far as Lycophron is concerned one can say only that he conceived law as a guarantor (*engyetes*) of men's rights—apparently without displaying any interest in the moral sub-stance of a community. An Aristotelian fragment, furthermore, at-tributes to Lycophron the sentence: "The splendor of noble birth is spurious, it rests on talk only." [20] The Lycophron fragments betray af-finity with the intellectual environment of Antiphon and, since Lyco-phron was probably a pupil of Gorgias, perhaps also the wider ancestry of Antiphon's ideas.

The most radical expressions of the idea of equality, extending it beyond nobility, Hellenes and barbarians, to include slaves, already ap-

[20] Diels-Kranz, Lycophron 4.

pear in the fourth century. They are contained in a few fragments of
Alcidamas, the pupil of Gorgias and his successor in the direction of his
school of rhetoric. In *Politics* 1253 b 20–22, on the subject of slavery,
Aristotle reports that some authors maintain "it is against nature to be
another man's master, for only by law [*nomo*] is one man a slave, another a freeman; by nature [*physei*] they do not differ; the rule of
master over slave is based on force and, therefore, not just." On this
occasion Aristotle does not specify who "they" are who maintain this
principle. But one of them must have been Alcidamas, for in his *Rhetoric*
Aristotle refers to a passage from Alcidamas' *Messeniakos:* "God has
released all men into freedom; nature has made nobody a slave." [21]
Nomos is the tyrant who deprives men of the freedom given to them
by God and nature. Another passage of the *Rhetoric* (1406 a 22) lets
Alcidamas contemptuously refer to "the laws: these kings of the poleis
by tradition"—a devaluating allusion to Pindar's verse. But against these
kings, Alcidamas assures mankind, a protector has arisen: "Philosophy:
this bulwark against the *nomoi.*" [22]

Finally, there must be considered a number of longer, discursive
fragments of unknown authorship which indicate a conservative trend,
in opposition to the disintegrating sophistic ideas, at the end of the fifth
century. One group of these fragments stems from a treatise on *Harmony*
(*Homonoia*), attributed to Antiphon and printed under his name in
Diels-Kranz. If they are really by the man who wrote the previously
discussed fragments on *Truth*, Antiphon must have experienced an interesting change of heart sometime in his life. More probably they are
by somebody else. A second group stems from the *Protrepticus* of
Iamblichus. It was recognized as excerpts from an author of the late
fifth century, and goes under the title of *Anonymus Iamblichi.*

The author of the tract *On Harmony* is a subtle moralist, a man of
considerable stature and literary gifts. The life of man he experiences
as a night watch, to be passed on, when day breaks, to the next generation (B 50). Life, even when it is happy, has nothing remarkable, great,
or noble, but in reality is petty, feeble, short-lived, and mixed with
sorrow (B 51). Still, it is the only life that man has. But oddly enough
there are people who do not live their present life, but are wondrously
active as if they had another life to live; and meanwhile time runs out

[21] *Rhetoric* 1373 b 18 Scholion.   [22] *Rhetoric* 1406 b 11.

(B 53a). The time of life cannot be recaptured; it is not possible to re-arrange the past as if it were a draught on the board (B 52). In some of the sentences we hear a faint echo of Aeschylus' theory of action, as when the author speaks of men who hesitate where there is no place for hesitation (B 55), or of men to whom illness is a holiday for then they do not have to face action (B 57). And such scattered reflections are chained into a longer meditation on the man who is going out to do some harm to his neighbor. On the way he may become afraid that he will not realize his intention but reap an unexpected consequence. This is a beginning of wisdom; for, while he fears, he hesitates; and while he hesitates, time lapses and his mind may change. What has been done cannot be taken back; but hesitation is fraught with the possibility that the deed will not be done. For, he who believes he can do harm to his neighbor and not suffer harm himself, is unwise (B 58). Such temptation and resistance to it is essential for moral discipline; for a man who has not desired or touched evil is not self-restrained, there being nothing over which he could gain control and thereby prove his true decency (B 59). And of the prudence in another man no one will be a better judge than the man who is capable of repressing the desire of the moment and of conquering himself (B 58).

The sensitive spiritual culture of these fragments stands in sharp contrast against the brittle intellectualism and the brashness of other sophists. One almost could doubt that the author of the tract was a contemporary of Antiphon, unless one remembered that he also was a contemporary of Democritus and Socrates. His ideas, however, were not isolated in their time as is shown by the fragments of the *Anonymus Iamblichi*. These fragments do not have the literary quality of the tract *On Harmony* but they, too, betray the revulsion against extreme indi-vidualism, its unrealistic nonsense and its consequences. The unknown author is bitter about men who indulge their pleonexy, consider unre-strained force the virtue of man, and obedience to the laws a weakness. That is a reprehensible attitude because men are by nature unable to live as individuals; they have united under the pressure of necessity and invented the skills for maintaining life. And once they are in com-munity they cannot live in a state of lawlessness for that would be even worse than separate existence. Hence, law and justice rule by necessity among men; and that order of things cannot be changed, for it is estab-lished by nature (6).

While the sentences sound like a polemic against Antiphon, the immediately following passage seems to ridicule an idea of the "strong man" as it is advocated by Plato's Callicles in the *Gorgias*. Even if there should exist a man with an extraordinary natural constitution, the *Anonymus* continues, immune from wounds and disease, insensitive, supernatural (*hyperphyes*), and adamantine in body and soul, he would not be able to establish a rule of force beyond the law; for the multitude of the other men, by virtue of their legal order, would overcome such a character and subjugate him by stealth and stronger force (6). If a strong man, however, establishes a tyranny, it should be understood that he could gain his position only because of the general state of lawlessness (*anomia*). Some men, to be sure, are of the erroneous opinion that a people can be deprived of its freedom by a tyrant without its being at fault. But this is not so. Only when the mass of the people has turned toward evil can such things happen. For a community cannot exist without law and justice; and only when the people turn away from them, will their administration pass into the hands of one man. The man would have to be made of iron who could rob the law, the common advantage of all, from the multitude; since he is a being of flesh and blood, he can gain his rule only after he has debased the people into *anomia* (7).

Even our summarizing contractions have not quite eliminated the repetitious clumsiness of the text. Nevertheless, in substance it is a shrewd analysis of the origin of tyranny, and in general of the sophistic idea of the "strong man," in the lawlessness of the people. Moreover, in reflections of this type is prefigured Plato's idea that the order of a society writes large the order living in the men who compose it, and in particular his insight that the Athenian social order is the sophist written large.

7. *Hippodamus and Phaleas*

It would be strange if the rapid constitutional development of the fifth century, as well as the frequent civil wars and changes of regimes in the various poleis, had not given rise to a literature on constitutional devices for creating a comparatively stable political order. Attempts of this kind would have suggested themselves all the more since the practice of colonization, even though the great age of expansion through colonies had passed, offered the occasion for putting new devices to the test. Regrettably, however, this whole branch of literature which must have existed has perished. We know nothing about it except what Aristotle chooses to tell in Book II of his *Politics*. On one occasion, having concluded his analysis and criticism of the constitutions proposed by Plato in *Republic* and *Laws,* he says: "There are other constitutions, some proposed by private persons, others by philosophers and statesmen, all of them coming nearer to the established and actually existing constitutions" than the Platonic proposals (1266 a 30–33). The passage indicates a considerable body of literature as well as a certain range of authors. In the earlier period, the writing on constitutions apparently was an occupation for statesmen. One of them he mentions on occasion, "Pheidon the Corinthian, one of the most ancient lawgivers" (1265 b 13); and he makes it a point that Hippodamus of Miletus was the first man not engaged in politics to make inquiries about the "best constitution" (1267 b 29–31). Since, however, we know nothing at all about Pheidon the Corinthian, while Hippodamus had a long life probably extending from 480 to 400, this information does not permit one to fix the date when "private persons" began to write on constitutions. All one can say is that the extension of the constitutional debate beyond professional circles must have occurred sometime in the second half of the fifth century. With regard to the content of the debate, again Aristotle's information is only incidental. The Spartan constitution must have attracted favorable attention because of its stability, for there are "some" who say that "the best constitution is mixed of all constitutions" and, therefore, praise the constitution of the Lacedaemonians. "They say" it consists of oligarchy, monarchy, and democracy, these forms being represented by the council of elders, the king and the ephors (1265 b 33–1266 a 1). Others, however, concentrate on the question of property; for the distribution of property is the point on which all revolutions turn and an equitable distribution would, therefore, be the key to constitutional stability (1266 a 37–38). No more can be extracted by way of general information on this class of literature.

Aristotle deals specifically with two such proposals for a stable constitution. They are the projects of Phaleas of Chalcedon and of Hippodamus of Miletus. About Phaleas we know nothing beyond his appearance in this context. He probably lived toward the end of the fifth, or perhaps in the early years of the fourth century. Hippodamus is the well-known architect who, under Pericles, planned the new Piraeus with its rectangular city blocks.

Phaleas' claim to the honor of being mentioned was his proposal, made for the first time, that all citizens should have equal possessions and equal education. He thought that such a scheme could be easily introduced when a polis was newly founded, while in an already established polis it could be gradually realized by letting the rich give marriage portions and letting the poor receive them. He, furthermore, suggested that all artisans should be public slaves. This latter device indicates perhaps that he wanted to remove all sources of income other than from farming on equal lots. His polis would then have been a peasant community, without trade or commerce, using skilled workers only as slaves. It sounds like a nostalgic project for curing the evils of the time by a return to the simple life, resembling the ideas of contemporary intellectuals who want to abolish the evils of capitalism by a return to agricultural modes of production. Aristotle has no difficulty in demonstrating the insufficiencies of the scheme.

Hippodamus of Miletus apparently devised a more elaborate project. He assumed a polis of ten thousand citizens. The citizenry was divided into three classes: artisans, peasants, and armed defenders of the polis. The land was divided into three parts: sacred, public, and private. The revenue of the sacred land should provide for the customary worship of the gods, the public land for the sustenance of the warriors, and the private land should be in the hands of the farmers. The three classes should form the assembly of the people whose chief function would be the election of the magistrates. The jurisdiction of the magistrates extended to three subject matters: common affairs, matters relating to resident aliens, and orphans. There should be three divisions of the law, according to the main types of grievances: insults to honor, damages, and homicide. The project, then, provided for a reform of court procedure and the institution of a supreme court of appeals, honors for those who discovered something of advantage for the polis, and public support of war orphans.

Aristotle points out the questions left open by this project (as, for instance, who would work the sacred and public lands), but he says nothing about its motivations. The recurrence of the number three suggests Pythagorean affinities and quite possibly the constitution of Hippodamus relied strongly on a symbolic play of order as did the constitutions of Plato to which they bear some resemblance. In that case the criticism of Aristotle, which pretends that Hippodamus offered a solution on the level of utilitarian motivations, would have missed the point quite as much as did his criticisms of Plato's *Republic* and *Laws*. The meaning of the Hippodamian project is probably lost.

CHAPTER 12

Power and History

Our study of *The World of the Polis* opened with reflections on the delimitation of Greek history through the memory of the classic period. We have measured the range of the memory, from the Aegean beginnings down to the end of the fifth century, and have arrived at the present of its formation. The earlier reflections on Herodotus and Thucydides, limited to the translation of Minoan and Mycenaean traditions into Greek history, must now be expanded by an inquiry into the genesis of historical consciousness as well as of its categories.

The situation in which the consciousness of history formed resembled in many respects the Homeric. Again the societies of the Aegean area were engaged in a great war; and again they came into view as a whole when their allotted time was running out and the visible decline provided the incentive for its exploration. Hellas and Persia, to be sure, had taken the place of Achaeans and Trojans, but the persons of the drama were still the powers surrounding the Aegean. Moreover, the historians of the fifth century were as much aware of the drama of mankind enacted on the scene as had been the poet of the *Iliad*. The pathos of Hellenism, proudly setting itself off by its Nomos against the barbarians, had impaired but not extinguished the sense of common destiny. And toward the end of the fifth century the sense of a common humanity broke through the pathos of the tottering Nomos and dared to insist on the equal nature of Hellenes and barbarians. Even at the height of the tension, however, shortly after the Persian Wars, the tragic sentiment was strong enough to assert itself in a manner hardly conceivable in the plebeian, moralizing morass of our own time, when Aeschylus in his *Persians* celebrated the victory by dramatizing the tragedy of the defeated enemy. Within a decade of the struggle for survival, when the city was still in ruins, there was written and performed in Athens the drama that mirrored triumph in the tragic fall of the great enemy through the hybris of his rulers.

The sense for the dramatic unity of mankind must be stressed, because in the symbolism of history its presence is not as tangibly manifest as in the myth. In the Homeric epic there can be no doubt about the common fate engulfing Trojans and Achaeans in the breakdown of Mycenaean civilization, for the Olympian gods are, in the most literal sense, the poets of the tragedy; nor can there be any doubt in the *Troiades* of Euripides, for the Olympian symbolism marks the Athenian disaster in the Peloponnesian War, caused by the hybris after the victory over Persia, as the mythical repetition of the Achaean disaster after the victory over Troy; and the same clearness about the interlocking fates of East and West pervades the Platonic myth of Athens and Atlantis. The symbolism of the historians does not always allow such clarity of expression. The Olympian world government, holding mankind in its universal grasp, is gone. The world of the historian is an open field of experience for the inquirer, a manifold of peoples and civilizations with different Nomoi, and especially with different gods; and in this world a struggle for power is going on, between man and man, ruler and subject, nation and nation, motivated by fear and greed, by passion and hope. Such a world threatens to fall apart into individual and national centers of power, rising and falling without a discernible meaning. We shall see how the historians try to preserve the sense of common drama in a world without gods by expressing it in philosophical categories, and how the task becomes increasingly difficult when the scene of significant action narrows from the European-Asiatic conflict described by Herodotus to the eruption of Periclean Athens and its subsequent disaster described by Thucydides.

The following sections deal, first, with the *Histories* of Herodotus; second, with the Pseudo-Xenophontic *Constitution of Athens*, a speech by an unknown author, conventionally referred to as the Old Oligarch; and, third, with the *History* of Thucydides.

§ 1. HERODOTUS

Herodotus of Halicarnassus was born *c.*485 and died *c.*425. His life extended from the Persian Wars into the early years of the Peloponnesian War. At the time of his birth the city of Halicarnassus was a dependency of Persia, organized as a tyranny under a Greek dynasty. The status of Herodotus as a subject of Persia as well as of a local tyranny made it impossible for him to embark on a political career as it would have been normal for a young man from a wealthy upper-class family in a free Greek city to do, and it probably was a factor in his early devotion to a literary life, to the purposeful travelling, and the collecting of the materials which entered into the *Histories*. Geographically, the world he knew extended from Susa to Carthage, and from the Black Sea to Egypt. Politically, his world was the upheaval of power since Cyrus the Great. In the half century before his birth Cyrus revolted against the Medes, conquered Lydia (546) and Babylonia (538), and established the Persian Empire; Cambyses conquered Egypt (525); Darius I extended the Empire beyond the Indus and reorganized it, subdued the Ionian revolt, and experienced the first Persian check at Marathon (490). In his lifetime fall the naval policy of Themistocles; the expedition of Xerxes; the battle of Salamis (480) in which Artemisia, the queen of Halicarnassus and Cos, had a distinguished share on the Persian side; the formation of the Delian League and its transformation into the Athenian Empire; the Athenian adventure in Egypt; and the Periclean Golden Age. In his later life he participated in the Panhellenic colonization of Thurium, where he became a citizen. He had outlived Pericles when he died in 425. Intellectually, his was the world of the epic literature, of Ionian lyric, of Aeschylus and Pindar, and of the Ionian philosophers from Thales to Heraclitus. These variegated influences he blended in the worldly-wise rationalism, as it was engendered on the Ionian frontier between Asia and Europe by a comparative knowledge of civilizations. He was well acquainted with the work of his great predecessor Hecataeus of Miletus and probably other ethnographic literature that has not survived; and by his own inquiries he assembled the knowledge of geographic, historical, social, and economic facts, of traditions and folklore covering the world of his time, which makes the *Histories* both a romantic fairy-garden and a universe not paralleled since Homer.

Herodotus has set forth his theory of history, not discursively, but in brief formulations of principles scattered through the work. His theoretical intentions must be derived from these formulations in juxtaposition with content and form of the historical relation. Some of the principles are delivered as programmatic declarations by the historian himself, others are pronounced by persons of the story, closely interwoven with the narrative. Some are placed at the main incisions of the work, others at high points of action, still others appear to be incidental.

The *Histories* opens with the sentence:

> This is the record of an inquiry [*historie*] by Herodotus of Hali-
> carnassus, set forth in order that what is remembered [*genomena*]
> by men may not be obliterated by the lapse of time, that great and
> wonderful deeds performed by Hellenes and barbarians may not
> become unrenowned, and in particular the reason [*aitie*] why they
> made war against each other.

The program, in order to render its full meaning, must be read in the
light of its execution. The work of Herodotus has a clear major incision:
Books I–VI deal with the European-Asiatic conflict from its beginnings
to its culmination in the expedition of Xerxes; Books VII–IX deal with
the campaign of Xerxes, its preparation, course, and issue. Frequently the
division is interpreted as revealing the author's intention of writing
the history of the War of 480/79, so that Books VII–IX would be the
work proper, while Books I–VI were in the nature of an introduction.
This interpretation must arouse misgivings, for it imputes to a Greek
author with a sense of proportions the guilt of writing a monstrous introduction filling two thirds of the whole work. It is preferable, therefore, to accept Herodotus' own opinion about what he was doing. The
above-quoted programmatic declaration is immediately followed by the
beginning of the story itself: that the Phoenicians were the cause (*aitioi*)
of the conflict (*diaphore*) since they abducted Io from Argos. The war
explored by Herodotus is not the campaign of Xerxes but the war between Europeans and Asiatics, going as far back as the memory of mankind and only reaching a climax in the campaign of 480. The three
parts of the programmatic declaration, thus, have a clear connection.
The remembrances of men should not be obliterated by the lapse of
time because in the traditions are preserved the great and wonderful
deeds of Hellenes and barbarians; and these deeds are great and wonderful in as much as they are the deeds of the war between Europeans
and Asiatics, who together are mankind. But why are the deeds so great
and wonderful that their lapse from the memory of mankind should be
prevented? That question will be answered by the description of the
war itself as well as by the exploration of its causes.

The war in its single phases consists of typical actions and reactions,
the war as a whole of a chain of such typical phases. Io is abducted
by the Phoenicians, Europa by the Greeks. That is such a phase of ac-

tion and reaction, and "the account was balanced" (*isa pros isa*). On occasion of the next phase Herodotus further elaborates the problem. Medea is abducted by Greeks, but the king of Colchis demands restitution and reparation; the Greeks refuse because they had been refused reparation for the abduction of Io. The action of the second phase, thus, is chained to the first phase and the matter rests for the moment. Two generations later Paris abducts Helen, convinced that he will not have to make reparation because none was made for Medea; and the Greek demand consistently is refused. The Greeks respond with their expedition resulting in the destruction of Troy; and now the conflict has reached the stage of world wars in which the next move is up to the Asiatics. The conflict is snowballing up to the division of the world between Persia as the representative of Asia, and Greece as the representative of Europe (I, 4). Within this great conflict of the world, however, there are running the lines of numerous subconflicts. The story of the war of mankind, therefore, cannot be confined to the Greeks and Persians but must embrace the whole network of minor clashes chained at some point to the struggle of the great protagonists in the time of Herodotus. The narrative will extend to the whole known world and deal with "small and great settlements of men alike." "For many that were great of old have now become small; and those that are great in my time were small formerly." "Human happiness [or prosperity, ascendancy, *eudaimonie*] never lasts long" (I, 5). The description of the world in concrete detail, geographic and ethnographic, forms a necessary part of the story, because the earth in its spatial extension is the scene on which human societies as the actors perform the drama of the war in time.

The names of Anaximander and Heraclitus are never mentioned by Herodotus. Nevertheless, it will be appropriate to recall them now, for the conception of historical dynamics emerging from Herodotus clearly continues the conception of cosmic dynamics developed by the Ionian philosophers. Anaximander pronounced the principle: "From whatever is the genesis of the things that are, into that will be their perishing as a debt of necessity [*chreon*]; for they pay penalty [*dike*] and reparation [*tisis*] to one another for their transgression [*adikia*] according to the decree of time" (B 1). And Heraclitus said: "One must know that war is the common [*xynon*, the reality of order] and right [*dike*] is strife, and everything happens according to strife and atonement [*chreon*]" (B 80). Whatever is done is action in the general strife, and for success must be paid the price of defeat at the hands of the next victor who in his turn will go down in the chain of rise and fall. That is the principle transferred by Herodotus to the process of history. In its most succinct form it is pronounced by Croesus, giving advice to Cyrus. The former king of Lydia reflects with an Aeschylean touch: "My sufferings [*pathemata*] have turned to wisdom [*mathemata*]." And spinning out the theme of transformation he continues: "If you deem yourself immortal, as well as the army that you lead, it is not for me to give advice to you. But if you know yourself man, as well as those whom you rule, know this above all: There is a wheel [*kyklos*] of human affairs which, turning, does not suffer the same men to prosper always" (I, 207).

A few examples will illustrate the shades of meaning which the principle of the turning wheel assumes in the hands of Herodotus. Amasis, the king of Egypt, warns his friend Polycrates, the too-successful tyrant of Samos, that the divine (*to theion*) is jealous. He would prefer a mingling of successes and mishaps to unbroken good fortune; for never had he heard of a man whose continuous prosperity had not ended in evil and utter destruction (III, 40). The advice of Amasis to break the sinister threat of success by a voluntary sacrifice, however, proves to be vain; the wheel moves by its own law and cannot be cheated by human tricks. More complex is the occasion of Darius' campaign against the Scythians. After the fall of Babylon, Darius decides on the war against the Scythians as his next enterprise. Two factors determine the decision. The new wealth and manpower of the realm arouse the "desire" in the king to put them to use in action; and the Scythians are a suitable target because two hundred years ago they attacked the Medes and this wrong must now receive its "balancing punishment" (IV, 1). The Scythians, when they learn of the impending attack, appeal to the neighboring tribes for help. But the neighbors refuse, pleading that the Scythians had without provocation attacked the land of the Persians and held it "for such time as the god permitted; and the same god now urges the Persians on to requite them in like manner" (IV, 119). Their virtuous abstinence, however, does not help the neighbors any more than the voluntary sacrifice did Polycrates, and they come to bitter grief in the course of events. In the turning of the wheel the forces that keep it moving become visible—wealth and great military power in the hands of a man who is desirous for expansive action. The Scythian success of two centuries ago is rather a pretext barely veiling the royal desire as the real motive of action. And this factor, shorn even of wealth and power, is isolated as the moving force by Herodotus in the case of Deioces, the Mede, who is possessed by the "desire for lordship" (*erastheis tyrannidos*) and by sheer wits manoeuvres himself to the place where wealth and power are at his disposition for further action (I, 96).

The drive in its nakedness is more discursively characterized in the speech of Atossa to Darius. The queen wants to incite the king to the expedition against Hellas. Why, she asks, does a mighty king sit idle instead of gaining more subjects and more power for the Persians? A man who is young and lord of great wealth should let his qualities shine so that the Persians will know they are ruled by a man—and besides, the stress of war will prevent the breeding of revolt. Youth is the time for great deeds. For as the mind grows in strength with the body, so it ages with the aging body and declines to dullness and inaction (III, 134). The expansionist drive, thus, is of the essence of man. There is war because it is human nature to expand from youth to maturity, blind to consequences; to be a man means to participate in the drama of warlike action and retaliation; to sit idle means decline and death, for as soon as the tension of the drive relaxes, the drive of others will assert itself in revolt. This indefiniteness of expansion raises the question whether the power drive of a nation, if maintained by successive rulers, cannot swallow up all human societies, weld them into one empire, and thereby make an end to strife? The answer of Herodotus is negative. The drive will not become the stone that fills the world and makes an end to all empires; it will be checked in due course, and the war will go on. After the battle of Salamis, Themistocles tells the Athenians: "It is not we that have achieved this victory, but the gods and heroes who were envious that one man should be king of Asia and Europe" (VIII, 109). And not only the Greeks know it as a piece of hindsight, but the Persians themselves go knowingly toward disaster. On the eve of Plataea a Persian lord tells his Theban friend at the banquet that soon few of them will be left. But nothing can be done about it: "What shall come to pass by the will of God cannot be averted by man, for nobody will believe what is most certainly true. Many of the Persians know it, but we follow in the bond of necessity. It is the most hateful of sorrows afflicting mankind to have knowledge of so much and power over nothing" (IX, 16). This is one of the rare occasions where the undercurrent of pessimism and bitterness in Herodotus breaks through the narrative of great and wonderful deeds. Man is bound by a purposeless necessity to the game of expansion and defeat without hope of escape; he knows how it all happens but the why remains a mystery. This bitterness, heavily overlaid in Herodotus by the joy in the wonder and grandeur of the spectacle, will come near its breaking point in Thucydides' icy pathos of despair and pride.

The course of events illuminates the principles and the principles illuminate the meaning of the story. This technique of mutual illumination is the method of historiography invented by Herodotus. It is admirably suited to his style of chaining episodes and, in general, he uses it with the same freedom as Homer does with his interventions of the gods. The principles can appear, as we have seen, in reflections of the author, in traditions related by him, in public speeches, in conversations between husband and wife, in diplomatic exchanges, in confidences at the dinner table, and in letters.

Herodotus, however, can also tighten his method, so pleasantly pliable to the contingencies of the meandering story, and develop it into a more formal instrument for writing history. Two instances occur in which these further potentialities of the method become visible. The great expedition of Xerxes against Hellas opens with a debate in the royal council, the intentions of the king as well as the arguments for and against the enterprise being set forth in a series of speeches (VII, 8–11). And the same opening is used on occasion of the revolt of Darius and his friends against the false Smerdis. After successful conclusion of the revolt the seven lords meet in council in order to determine the future form of government for Persia, the arguments for and against the various forms again being set forth in a series of speeches (III, 80–82). The method of placing a group of speeches, each illuminating another aspect of the problem, at critical junctures before a great decision offers the opportunity of casting a light of meaning over long courses of events. Such a course, set by the decision, may take unexpected turns and have results at variance with the original intention; the arguments of the speeches can systematically present the forces which determine the actual configuration of the course and its issue. The method has historical importance beyond its use by Herodotus because there can hardly be a doubt that it influenced Thucydides in using pairs of speeches for bringing out in relief the meaning of the events.

The debate preceding the expedition against Hellas consists of four speeches: the two speeches of assent and dissent, framed by the opening and concluding speeches of the king. Xerxes informs his council of nobles of his intention to bridge the Hellespont and to punish the Athenians for the unprovoked wrong they have inflicted on his father. The motive of punishment, however, is subordinate to the ulterior aim that will be reached by the subjugation of the Hellenes. For, when the Athenians and Peloponnesians are subdued, the territory of the Persian empire will extend as far as the aether of Zeus; no land under the sun will lie beyond its borders; they all will form one country since, as the king is informed, no nations will be left that could offer battle once the Hellenes are out of the way. After the king Mardonius speaks, assenting to the royal purpose. The Persians have extended their sway over Sacae, Indians, Ethiopians, Assyrians, and many other great nations who had never done any wrong to the Persians, only because they desired to increase their power; it would be strange indeed if the Hellenes should be excepted since they after all had furnished some cause for war. Besides they are poor, badly organized, and foolish in their military tactics, so that the task should not prove too difficult. In any case, one should be venturesome: "For nothing comes by itself but all that men love to possess comes by venture." The rest of the nobles do not like the plan at all; the embarrassed silence that follows is broken by Artabanus, the king's uncle, with a speech in opposition. He refers to his previous experience with ill-considered expeditions, such as the campaign of Darius against the Scythians and the near-disaster in which it ended. And then he discreetly reflects on the hybris of Xerxes. "You see how the God with his thunderbolt smites the overgrown creatures, not suffering their arrogant appearance, but is not aroused by the little ones. . . . He loves to bring low that which rises too high. . . . For the God suffers great-mindedness in none but himself." Caution, therefore, will be in place. The king is incensed by the speech; if Artabanus were not his uncle, unpleasant things would happen to him for his lack of spirit; he insists on the expedition as inevitable, because the Hellenes will take the initiative even if the Persians remain at peace.

In the four speeches the problem of the expedition comes into view as a whole: the dream of world dominion and the fear of such hybris, the drive of the king and the hesitation of the nobles, the facile assent of the general who underrates the enemy's military strength and the warning against such irresponsible assumptions, the technical problem of bridging the Hellespont and the weakness of this link that may be cut by a surprise attack with subsequent disaster, and above all the candid admission that the pursuit of power is a purpose in itself without relation to any wrongs committed by the victims of the attack. With the adjournment of the council the analysis of an imperialistic adventure is closed and the stage seems to be set for action.

Action, however, does not immediately ensue. The debate is followed by an episode of profound meaning. The arguments of Artabanus begin to sink in and Xerxes reconsiders his decision; on the next morning he calls the expedition off, to the unrestrained joy of the nobles. But this again is not the end. The night before rescinding his decision the king had had a vision which he disregarded, and the vision comes back the next night. An impressive man appears in the dream and threatens the king with his downfall unless he reverses himself and throws himself into the adventure. The frightened king implores his uncle to don the royal robes and sleep in his bed, in order to see whether the same vision will come to him; and the vision indeed threatens the uncle, too. The divine sign finally determines both in favor of the campaign. The decision, thus, ultimately does not spring from a rational debate but from the dream that comes to a man when he wears the mantle of a king. Herodotus does no more than tell the story, but it would be difficult not to recognize Heraclitean ideas of the sleepwalkers who live in their private worlds cut off from the *xynon*. The debate in council, the *xynon,* turns against the adventure; it requires a dream to throw a nation into the disaster. One is, furthermore, reminded of Plato's insight that a tyrant realizes in action what other men only dream. And, finally, the construction of the episode of the council and the dream recalls that other episode of dream and council before the disastrous battle of the Achaeans, in *Iliad* II. By its literary form, the Herodotean transposes the Homeric episode into the medium of history; by its psychology it forms an important link between Heraclitus and Plato.

The second group of speeches has a special place in the history of order because it is the earliest preserved argument on the best form of

government. After their successful *coup d'état* Darius and the other conspirators meet in order to decide whether Persia shall be a monarchy,
oligarchy, or democracy. The idea of such a debate is not as anachronistic
as it sounds at first hearing. While we may safely assume that such a
debate was not conducted on the occasion, it must be considered that the
Peisistratide refugees living at the court of Darius had a few words to
say about Athenian oligarchs and democrats as well as about the superiority of their tyrannis. Debates of this kind must have occurred
on the Greek-Persian frontier even in the sixth century, though in the
details of their Herodotean form they belong, rather, in the sophistic
period. It was a topic that suggested itself in the conflict between kings
and tyrants on the one side, and democrats and oligarchs on the other
side.

Otanes delivers the first speech in favor of democracy (*isonomia*).
The hybris of Cambyses has bred the hybris of the Magians. On right
consideration, no good can be found in monarchy. The best man, when
given such power without restraint, will fall into insolence and jealousy,
commit wicked deeds, and turn the law upside down. The rule of the
multitude (*plethos*), on the other hand, is the best as suggested by its
name *isonomia*, equality of law. The offices are assigned by lot, their
incumbents are answerable for what they do, and the counsels are taken
by the common assembly. All good lies with the multitude and, therefore, its power should be increased (III, 80). Megabyzus, in the second
speech, agrees that monarchy is no good; but a mob, if anything, is
worse. To change the hybris of a despot for the hybris of a demos would
be unbearable. It would be preferable to vest power in a group of the
best men among whom they themselves belong (III, 81). Darius, in the
third speech, agrees with Megabyzus' appraisal of democracy but not
of oligarchy. He favors monarchy. No better rule can be found than
that of the one best man whose judgment is like to himself. Moreover,
the other forms are unstable. Oligarchy engenders jealousy, enmity, and
factionism among the members of the ruling group, resulting in violence
and bloodshed; and from the disorder (*stasis*) rises monarchy which
thereby is proved the best. Again, the rule of the demos engenders evil-
mindedness and conspiracies against the common good. This will continue until there rises a leader (*prostas*) of the people as its protector
who will become the monarch. And in conclusion he reminds the friends
that the freedom of the Persians came neither from the people nor from

an oligarchy but from a monarch; they should not reject their ancient institutions (*patrious nomous*) (III, 82).

The three speeches in their aggregate have an intricate structure. They argue in succession that monarchy, democracy, and oligarchy are bad forms of government in so far as they all are potentially vitiated by the hybris of the rulers. In the same succession they argue that democracy, oligarchy, and monarchy are the best forms of government in so far as the rulers are the best men and intelligently pursue the common good. Neither of the two lines of argument invalidates the other one; we move in a cycle and the result is a draw. Herodotus breaks this cycle of antilogical reasoning by penetrating to the deeper cycle of historical reality. The goodness of each form is transitory at best; and when the form in reality is corrupted by hybris the situation must be remedied by action of a leader. The good monarch is the cure for despotism, tyranny is the cure for oligarchy, and prostasia the cure for democracy. The rule of one man restores order to its goodness; and monarchy in this dynamic sense is the stabilizing constant lasting through the cycle of static forms. The empirical observation, however, cannot become an argument for monarchy as a static form which as such is exposed to the same corruption as the others; on this level the question of the preferable form must be settled by recourse to the concrete historical situation. And to the historical situation Darius appeals in fact when he supports his preference by praising the freedom gained for the Persians by Cyrus, as well as the venerable antiquity of the monarchial institution in Persia. Nevertheless, this appeal still leaves open the question whether in the concrete revolutionary situation there is a best man to be found who can dynamically fill the static form of monarchy. This ultimate question lies beyond argument; it must be solved by action in the concrete. As in the Xerxes debate, the historical decision does not spring from rational argument but from the forces of reality itself. Darius becomes the monarch because he outwits his competitors by a trick (III, 83–87). The debate, thus, issues into the course of history itself and the wheel of human affairs turns on.

The turning of the wheel is inexorable. The pessimism of Herodotus expresses itself unreservedly in the story of the Scythian advance into the land of the Cimmerians, a story which he prefers to alternative versions of the event (IV, 11). At the approach of the Scythians who outnumber the Cimmerians hopelessly the threatened nation takes counsel. The royal clan wants to defend the country; the demos wants to depart without a fight and settle elsewhere; neither side can persuade the other. The princes will rather die and be buried in their native land where they have been happy. Being thus resolved they draw apart into two groups and fight each other until the last man is slain. The demos then buries them and departs; the Scythians take possession of the deserted country.

§ 2. THE OLD OLIGARCH

As part of the works of Xenophon there has survived a brief tract called the *Constitution of Athens,* written in the literary form of a speech. About the time of its composition the philologists disagree. The older opinion favors a date between 431 and 424 B.C., the more recent opinion very convincingly argues for a date preceding the outbreak of the Peloponnesian War. If the more recent opinion, especially the careful argument of Fritsch,[1] should be tenable (as we believe it is), the tract would gain in importance, since in that case its presentation of Periclean policy would not be influenced by the hindsight of the war. As far as the unknown author is concerned certain details of the tract suggest that he was an Athenian, perhaps a man of high rank in the navy, a member of the oligarchic upper class, living as a political emigrant in an environment of refugees and other Hellenes who heartily disliked Athens. As to its content the fictitious speech is a cold-blooded exposition of the merits of Athenian democracy to an audience which, like the author himself, detests the democratic order. It is a warning that personal likes and dislikes in political matters do not in the least affect the course of history, and that the order of Athens is superbly tailored for democratic success, however immoral and vulgar the spectacle may be.

The ambiguous attitude of the author, the schism that runs through his valuations, is the point of interest for the origin of historical consciousness in general, as well as of the special form which it assumes in the second half of the fifth century. The peculiar problems of the process of history come into view when a concrete political unit, while preserving its identity, rapidly changes its social structure, its policies, and values. The Periclean city is still Athens but it is no longer ruled by

[1] Hartvig Fritsch, *The Constitution of the Athenians* (Copenhagen, 1942).

the aristocrats who gave it birth and formed it; there still exists an Athenian people, more powerful than ever, but it no longer accepts the ethos of Homer and Pindar; it is still the defender of Hellas, but no longer the city of the hoplites who were victorious at Marathon; the pathos of Athens lives strongly in Pericles, but is no longer the pathos of Attica and is dangerously close to becoming the pathos of the Piraeus. When history, thus, runs away with the essence of a city, some will no longer even recognize its identity; a strange monster has taken the place of the polis they loved. Against such romantic resentment the author of the tract asserts the vitality, intelligent policy, and victorious viability of democratic Athens; the end of the world has not yet come, it is only that history is moving on. He can only hold this position, however, because he transfers the identity of the polis from its aristocratic ethos of the past to its existence as a power unit in history which, as in the past, it is also at present. The essential shift from ethos to power creates the idea of history as the medium in which power units remain identical while undergoing changes of ethos, as well as the idea of political entities which have history in so far as their ethos changes. In dealing with this formidable problem the unknown author has neither the insight nor the discipline of a Thucydides who never let his own valuations intrude when he described the breakdown of ethos; and still less so does he have the range and vision of a Plato who understood the process as a decline of civilization. His tract displays the ethos of the oligarch in stark contrast with the reality of democracy. And the same rift runs through his language when side by side he uses the vocabulary of the old ethos since Homer with that of the new sophistic era. Sometimes he even uses the same words in the old and new meanings as, for instance, in the case of *poneroi* which regularly occurs as the technical term for "the lower classes," "the proletarians," and then without a warning appears with the old meaning of "bad." [2]

The tract as a whole is an extended argument against the misconception that the merits of Athenian democracy can be appraised in terms of oligarchic ethos. Not that the judgment of the oligarchs was unsound; on the contrary, the author assures his audience that he disapproves of the Athenian constitution just as much as they do, because it favors the vulgar people at the expense of the good (or: righteous, best).

[2] For the linguistic problems cf. the chapter "Sophistics and Sociology" in Fritsch, *Constitution of the Athenians.*

But such disapproval should not obscure the fact that the political practice of Athens, which arouses the severe criticism of oligarchs, is excellently calculated to strengthen democracy internally and to increase the power of the polis in foreign relations.

A first group of criticisms and counterarguments is concerned with the supremacy of the lower classes in Athens and her empire. "The vulgar, the poor, and the people" are "justly" preferred to the "distinguished and the rich" for the good reason that the people are the motive power of the navy on which, rather than on the heavy-armed infantry, rests the strength of Athens. Therefore they are rightly admitted to the offices by lot and election and allowed to speak up in the assembly (I, 2). To favor and enrich the lower at the expense of the upper classes is a sensible thing to do; for, when the vulgar and poor prosper, democracy will be strengthened (I, 4). For in every country there is the tension between aristocrats and the common men; the best people are the least licentious and iniquitous, and have an eye for morals; in the common people there is a high degree of ignorance, disorder, and roguery (*poneria*) (I, 5). Hence, if only the best people were allowed to speak in assembly and determine the conduct of affairs, they would do what is good for them but not for the proletarians (*anthropos poneros*) (I, 6). The common men know that one of their own ilk will say what is "useful" to them (I, 7). Such a polis will not be the best, but democracy will be well maintained. For the people do not want to be slaves under a well ordered (*eunomia*) constitution; they want to be free and powerful whether the constitution is good or bad (*kakonomia*). "For what *you* think is no good order, is just the condition under which the people is powerful and free" (I, 8). The reader will note that the argument relies on the previously discussed shift from the old ethos to the new utilitarianism of power.

The same considerations apply to the treatment of the tributary poleis of the empire. The Athenians try to ruin the upper classes in the cities of the empire, if necessary by trumped-up charges. The oligarch will certainly frown on such policies, but from the Athenian point of view this again is the right thing to do. For the oligarchs of the empire cities hate the lower classes of Athens, and the upper classes of Athens support the oligarchs in the empire. Hence, plundering, exiling, and killing the upper classes in the empire strengthens the democracy in Athens. To be sure, the wealth of the empire cities will thereby be

diminished but politically it is more profitable to drain their wealth
off to Athens and to leave the local rabble with just enough to live on
so that they have no time and means for starting revolutions (I, 14–15).
It is, furthermore, good policy to have legal conflicts decided in Athens
because by this method the verdicts can be safely rigged against the
oligarchs (I, 16). If the lawsuits were decided on the spot by Athenian
generals, admirals, and ambassadors, these personages might gain a position of power to the detriment of the demos of Athens (I, 18).

The second group of arguments is concerned with the position of
Athens as a sea power. The author does not mention any specific charges
against which he directs his argument; but he conducts it in such a manner that plainly the development of sea power as such must have been
a grievance of the oligarchs everywhere in Hellas. He takes pains, therefore, to point out the advantages of sea power over land power. First he
mollifies his audience by the assurance that Athenian infantry is nothing
to be proud of; it could not hold its own against a first class land power
but is deliberately kept at a strength sufficient only for use against the
tributary cities (II, 1). No more is necessary, because military superiority is secured through the navy. Rebellious subjects of the island empire
cannot hope to succeed because they cannot pool their forces as neighboring poleis on the continent could do; as long as the Athenians control the sea, they have to deal only with single, weak enemies. The larger
continental towns under Athenian rule are controlled by fear, the
smaller ones entirely by need; none of them could hold out if its im-
ports and exports were cut off (II, 2–3). In fighting a superior opponent
the Athenians can use their navy as transports and engage in raids under
conditions favorable to them (II, 5). Economically, they are largely
independent of bad harvests because such a misfortune will never strike
their far-flung empire as a whole; the luxuries of the whole world are at
their disposition through trade; from their rich revenue they beautify
their city and provide gymnasia and public baths for the masses; they
control international trade and thereby all the raw materials for maintaining their navy (II, 6–12). Their position has only one disadvantage
—Athens does not lie on an island. If the rulers of the sea were islanders
they could inflict damage on others without being in danger of retaliation. As it is, the farmers and the rich people of Athens who have their
holdings and properties in Attica must be afraid of devastation by an
enemy; this however is of little concern to the mass of the people who

live in the city and the Piraeus and have nothing to lose in a war. More-over, if they lived on an island their democracy would be completely safe against treachery of the upper classes because no help over land could come to them. This defect, however, is largely repaired by a deliberate policy of distributing property over the islands and leaving Attica to devastation in case of war (II, 14–16).

In conclusion the author returns to the question of ethos and power. He maintains that the Athenians know quite well which of their citizens are good and which are rogues; with full knowledge they prefer those who are devoted and useful to the demos, however roguish they are, and hate the good ones because they are convinced that inborn excellence does not benefit but, rather, harms the people. On the other hand, there are a few individuals who sincerely take the side of the people though by nature they are not of the mass type (*demotikoi*). The author is quite willing to forgive the demos its democracy, for everybody must be for-given for looking to his own interest; those, however, who choose to live under a democracy though they are not of the demos are on the road to immorality (*adikein*), well knowing that a bad character can slip through more easily in a democracy than in an oligarchy.

The tract can hardly be called distinguished either as a work of thought or of literature. Its unassuming character makes it valuable as a source of information on what an intelligent Athenian would know about the politics of his time and to what degree he would understand the social forces that were soon to break out in the great crisis. This knowledge is astonishingly clear and penetrating; it reveals the basis of common understanding on which Thucydides could build his masterful study. The main features of the Periclean imperial policy are well brought out: the deliberate preferment of the demos because it furnishes the man power of the navy; the defensive strategy against the Peloponnesian land power, which exposed Attica to devastation and concentrated on the Piraeus and the Long Walls that connected it with the fortifications of the city; the offensive strategy with regard to the island and coastal em-pire, based on the stronghold of the Piraeus; the degradation of the land-owners and farmers of Attica to second-class citizens in comparison with the urban masses; the relentless undermining and destruction of the up-per classes in the tributary poleis of the empire, transforming them into something like satellite cities with "people's democracies"; the enrichment of the Athenian demos through tributes, trade revenues, and legal fees;

and even, though only discreetly hinted at, the misuse of confederate funds for the architectural embellishment of the city. Furthermore, there emerges the picture of social classes, representing different ways of life, as well as the implacable hatred and the more or less open war between them. The category of the advantageous, the *sympheron*, is introduced in order to describe and understand the motivations of the demos who, after all, wants only to be free and to live after its own fashion; and the recognition that the masses want to be free and feel their power, unrestrained by aristocratic rules of conduct, makes it necessary to distinguish between different types of men, the natural aristocrats and the natural mass men (*demotikoi*). Types of order, thus, are related with the types of men who politically and socially predominate. One can recognize in these apparently casual classifications the foundations on which the politics of Plato and Aristotle is built, with its distinctions of several types of men who all must be accommodated in a stable, balanced constitutional order. And in the firm resolve of recognizing both the standards of value and the game of power, finally, one can see prefigured the attitude of the Aristotle who develops a paradigmatic constitution by the standards of his philosophical anthropology and, at the same time, recognizes that in the historical situation of his age the paradigm has no chance of realization.

§ 3. THUCYDIDES

Thucydides was born *c*.460 B.C. from one of the first families of Athens, related to Cimon and Miltiades. His public career was luckless and brief: In 424 he was elected strategos and entrusted with a relief expedition for Amphipolis; he failed in his task because the means put at his disposition were insufficient, and he was exiled. The following twenty years, to the end of the war, he lived in Thrace where apparently he had some property; in 404 he returned to Athens and there, probably not long after 399, he died. Not much more is known about his life; he was an inconspicuous figure in his age, for the great work on which his fame rests was an unpublished fragment at the time of his death.

1. *The* Syngraphe

In a critical study it cannot be accepted as an unquestioned fact that Thucydides wrote a "History of the Peloponnesian War." The work which in contemporary translations goes under this title was inscribed by its author, if at all, simply as "Syngraphe," a word that can best be translated by the slang "write-up"; and what he "wrote up" was "the war between Peloponnesians and Athenians" (*xynegraphe ton polemon*, etc.). In what sense of the word the result of his effort was a "history" is the question that must be explored.

This question is inseparably connected with the subject matter of the *Syngraphe*. Today, under the influence of Thucydides, it is accepted as a fact that there was such an event as the "Peloponnesian War" from 431 to 404, lasting for twenty-seven years. The contemporaries of Thucydides, however, were not aware of the fact. They only knew of an Archidamian or Ten Years War, lasting from 431 to 421, and of a Decelean or Ionian War, lasting from 414 to 404. The seven years in-between were not exactly peaceful but, in the eyes of the contemporaries at least, the desultory minor clashes did not exceed the habitual punctuations of what the Hellenes called peace among their poleis; and the great expedition of Athens against Sicily in 415–413 was not a war with the Peloponnesians. Even after 404, since the work of Thucydides was not yet published, the classification of war and peace did not change; throughout the first half of the fourth century, at least, nobody knew that there had been a great Peloponnesian War.

Moreover, it is uncertain at what time Thucydides himself discovered the subject matter of his work. The *Syngraphe* opens with the declaration of the author that he wrote "the war between the Peloponnesians and Athenians," an opening that would appear to cover the whole work. But in V, 26 there is a second opening sentence saying that "the same Thucydides" wrote the events from the Peace of Nicias to the end of the Athenian empire by which time "the war had lasted twenty-seven years all in all." This unexplained second opening suggests that Thucydides had written, and circulated, the Archidamian War, perhaps in a less elaborate form than the one now preserved. Like everybody else he had assumed the war had come to its close; and only sometime after the resumption of hostilities in 414 had he conceived the great unit of events overarching the two wars, the peace, and the Sicilian Expedition. The vision of this great unit and its peculiar significance, then, would be the achievement of his genius; in creating this unit—which did not exist on the pragmatic level of events, and escaped the contemporaries—he created "history."

The nature of the unit cannot be concentrated in a brief definition, unless one is satisfied with a summary reference to the "fall of the Athenian Empire." The new creation required not only a theory but also very serious efforts at methodological clarification. In the following sections we shall deal, first, with the method of Thucydides and, second, with his theory of the new historical unit itself.[3]

2. The Method

Thucydides gave the name *kinesis* to the type of unit created by him; the war he described was a movement, or upheaval. It was the greatest *kinesis* that had ever occurred, since it affected not only "the Hellenes but also part of the barbarians, one might almost say the majority of mankind." The greatness of the *kinesis* in a quantitative sense apparently was a strong motive in Thucydides' occupation with the events of the war. He embarked on his recording work right at the outbreak of hostilities, because the protagonists were at the height of their strength and the rest of the Greeks were supporting one side or the other. He could see that the war would be "greater and more important" than any that had preceded it (I, 1). The proof of this judgment he furnished by the *Archaeology*, a survey of Hellenic history from its earliest times to the present. It showed that at no previous time had the population, wealth, military equipment, and organization of power in Hellas come near the magnitude which it had at the outbreak of the war (I, 2–19). Moreover, the Peloponnesian War was without parallel both by its length and the misfortunes which it brought upon Hellas. Never were so many cities conquered, destroyed, and depopulated; never were so many killed in battle; never was there so much banishing and bloodshed by civil war within the cities (I, 23).

Thucydides takes a peculiar pride in the greatness of disaster. This sentiment is rare but not singular; it recurs in Italian writers of the fifteenth century who, by the pride in the upheavals of their age, assert their independence from a paradigmatic antiquity; the greatness of *kinesis* heightens a "modern" self-consciousness in opposition to the

---

[3] For this section were used Thucydides, *Historiae*, ed. Jones and Powell; A. W. Gomme, *Essays in Greek History and Literature* (Oxford, 1937); A. W. Gomme, *A Historical Commentary on Thucydides*, I (Oxford, 1945); the chapter on Thucydides in Jaeger, *Paideia* I; Finley, *Thucydides*; G. B. Grundy, *Thucydides and the History of His Age*, I (2d ed., Oxford, 1948); David Greene, *Man in His Pride. A Study in the Political Philosophy of Thucydides and Plato* (Chicago, 1950); also the translations by Jowett, Crawley, and Smith.

"ancients." In the case of Thucydides, too, insistence on greatness betrays a rejection of the past, an awareness of the specific problems of a new age. The Trojan War was a comparatively minor affair, hampered by insufficient supplies; and the Persian War, decisive but brief, was over with only four battles—two on the sea and two on land (I, 11 and 23). Such reflections not only minimize the importance of the past, but also suggest the perspective in which Thucydides wants his work to be seen in relation to Homer and Herodotus. Not that he wants to rival their particular achievements. On the contrary, he considers his own effort at recording a *kinesis* superior to the work of poets and logographers in so far as he has to offer a reliable description of events, based on critically sifted evidence, instead of their exaggerated embellishments and uncritical tales of hearsay (I, 21). His refusal to indulge in the legendary will make the work less enjoyable perhaps, but he will feel compensated if it is found useful by those who want to have an exact knowledge of things past as a guide to things future, which are the same or similar in accordance with human nature (*kata to anthropinon*). His work is not a performance craving for the applause of the moment but meant as "a possession for ever" (I, 22).

The rejection of the past for lack of greatness, thus, is closely connected with the consciousness of a new method that will render truth more exactly (*saphes*). While Thucydides only uses the method without pronouncing formally on its nature, there are sufficient indications in the work to relate it with methodological problems known from other contemporary sources. Especially revealing is the reflection on the comparative insignificance of the Persian War, with the implication that the work of the "logographer" who describes it is correspondingly unimportant. The "logographer" happens to be Herodotus. Now, the subject matter of Herodotus' work, as we have seen, is not the Persian War but the war of mankind, coeval with human memory, that reaches its climax in the expedition of Xerxes. Even a Thucydides would admit that the war of mankind as a whole is a "greater" course of events than any limited *kinesis* that forms only part of it. If he does not admit it, the reason must be sought in his refusal to recognize the "war of mankind" as a methodologically legitimate unit of events; he admits only the subdivisions of this war as genuinely kinetic units so that the Persian War, the largest of the subdivisions, will appear as the greatest previous instance.

The reasons for the methodological reinterpretation of Herodotus can be found explicitly stated in the contemporary medical literature. The Hippocratic treatise on the *Nature of Man* opens with the following passage:

> He who is accustomed to hearing speakers discuss the nature of man beyond its relations to medicine will not find the present account of any interest. For I do not say at all that a man is air, or fire, or water, or earth, or anything else that is not an obvious constituent of man; such accounts I leave to those who care to give them. Those, however, who give them have not in my opinion correct knowledge. For while they arrive all at the same insight they do not give the same account of it. To be sure, they all explain their insight by saying that "what is" is one, and that it is both the one and the all; yet they do not agree as to its name, respectively calling this One and All air, fire, water, or earth, each supporting his own account by evidence and proofs that amount to nothing.[4]

The author is in arms against the inroads of speculation into an empirical science. He has a clear understanding of a "nature of man," to be described in terms of constituents on which empirical observers can agree; and he is on the defensive against readers who apparently expect a medical disquisition on the nature of man to express itself in symbols of Ionian cosmology and Eleatic speculation on the One and All. This peculiar intellectual situation is further illuminated by the treatise on *Ancient Medicine*. The "ancient medicine" is not perhaps an obsolete phase of science to be replaced by a new method; on the contrary, it is the old empirical science of the practitioners which now is endangered by the novel fashion (*kainos tropos*) of abandoning the study of proximate causes (*aitioi*) of diseases in favor of a speculative hypothesis (*hypothesis*) concerning an ultimate cause. Such hypotheses, the author concedes, may be useful in exploring the things in the sky and under the earth, where propositions cannot be verified anyway, but they have no place in a well-developed science with a principle (*arche*) and a method (*hodos*).[5]

As far as the position of Thucydides is concerned, the parallel is clear. Although he does not say it explicitly, he rejects the "hypothesis" of Herodotus, derived from Anaximander and Heraclitus, that is, the hy-

---

[4] "Nature of Man" in *Hippocrates*, IV (Loeb Classical Library). I have changed the translation by W. H. S. Jones in minor points.
[5] "Ancient Medicine" i, ii, xiii (*Hippocrates* I).

pothesis of a compensatory rise and fall of all existing things as the
principle for explaining the course of human affairs. For Thucydides, as
for the Hippocratic authors, the Ionian hypothesis is useless in the study
of proximate causes of a phenomenon that is more or less clearly defined
as to its nature. The hypothesis not only detracts attention from the
causes, it also obscures the nature of the phenomenon, be it a movement
(*kinesis*) or a disease (*nosos*).

The difficulties in defining and maintaining this empirical position
arise from the lack of an adequate terminology for its expression. One
can discern no more than the direction in which the new methodological
consciousness is moving linguistically. There is an interesting attempt at
conceptual clarification in *Ancient Medicine* xv. The author criticizes
the advocates of hypotheses because they surely have not yet discovered
a "hot or cold, dry or moist" that would be "a thing in itself," not "participating in another form." The "thing in itself" (*auto eph heoutou*)
is an attempt to form the notion of an essence that is not an accident; hot
and cold, dry and moist, the various hypotheses mentioned, are accidents
participating in a form (*eidos*). But the usage of *eidos* is not yet consistent—in the context of *Ancient Medicine* xii the author suggests that
more than one *eidos* of medicine (meaning a "branch" of the science)
has achieved a high degree of exactness.[6] In Thucydides the usage tends
toward the meaning of essence and its component parts. On occasion of
the plague he speaks of the *eidos*, the nature of the disease which baffles
description (II, 50), and a bit later he calls the aggregate of symptoms
the *idea* of the disease (II, 51). In the same context, when stressing the
greatness of the epidemic, he uses for disease the term *metabole* (disturbance, revolution, upheaval), associating the meaning of disease closely
with the general *kinesis* under investigation (II, 48). Thucydides, we
may say, was strongly influenced by the methods of the Hippocratic
school. He used the medical conception of disease as a model in conceiving
his *kinesis;* he was in search of an *eidos* or *idea* of the *kinesis* as well as of
its causes; he wanted to explore and define this essence in order to furnish a basis for prediction (*prophasis*) in the future; and for this reason
he rejected the Ionian hypothesis by which Herodotus formed the unit
of his inquiry.

That Thucydides used the Hippocratic method as a model is rea-

---

[6] The same inconsistent use in Democritus. In B 167 *idea* has the meaning of form, in B 11
it has the meaning of a branch of knowledge.

sonably certain. There remains, however, the difficulty that he could oppose it as the new method to the older one of Herodotus, while the physicians opposed it as the old method to the new Ionian fashions. The methodological situation at the end of the fifth century apparently was more complex than is generally assumed, and it will be advisable to reconsider, and to qualify, certain historiographic conventions: (1) If the method of hypotheses was an obstacle to empirical science, one can hardly maintain without qualifications that the philosophers of the sixth and early fifth centuries were the forerunners of science; (2) if the physicians could speak of this philosophy as a new intrusion into their old science, there must have existed sources of science independent of Ionian speculation; (3) if Thucydides could insist on the novelty of his method in opposition to the logographers, the situation in the science of man in society must have substantially differed from the situation in medicine; and (4) if the method of Thucydides, which was intimately related to sophistic psychology, could lead to the search for the *eidos* or *idea* of social movements, the Platonic search for the Idea must have been more deeply indebted to sophistic empiricism than is usually acknowledged. The questions raised by these reflections, so formidable that they would require a monograph for an answer, cannot be treated incidentally to the present context. Only a few suggestions, summarizing what has emerged with regard to this problem in the course of our own study, can be offered.

The invasion of medicine by philosophical hypotheses, about which the physicians complained, was apparently part of the general process of immanentization that we analyzed in our study of sophistic fragments. Symbols, which had their good sense in explicating experiences of transcendence, were used in speculation on world-immanent phenomena; and such use led to hypothetical constructions which, from the point of view of empirical science, were impasses, as for instance the atomistic physics of Democritus. The expansion of immanentist speculation had various effects according to the realms of phenomena to which it extended. If an empirical science of the phenomena in question did not yet exist, the hypothetical construction did not encounter the resistance of empiricists; cosmological speculation from the Ionians to Anaxagoras and Democritus could expand freely because a science of physics was not in existence; resistance had, rather, to be feared from a conflict with popular beliefs concerning the gods and the structure of the universe. Up to a certain point, therefore, speculative physics was a genuine advance of knowledge; the results of empirical inquiry by the physicists had their value even if they were submitted to "hypothetical" misconstruction; and the advance would be genuine until the point of diminishing returns was reached at which the hypothetical construction prevented the digestion of facts and even their observation. If, however, hypothetical construction extended to an area of phenomena that was already occupied by an empirical science, as was the case of medicine, the resistance of the scientists would be aroused. Hence, hypothetical speculation appeared in different perspectives according to the maturity which an empirical science had reached at the time. To a physician with his old science, the hypotheses would be a new fashion. To a Thucydides, occupied with politics, the same hypotheses would be old and obsolete because a political science was just about to be created by his efforts and the efforts of his contemporaries.

Empirical science is an independent factor in intellectual history; and, in particular, its independence from the development of philosophy must be recognized. Unless one has preconceived ideas about the origin of science, the existence of this factor should not be too surprising; for a more or less extended knowledge of causes and effects in the surrounding world is an ineluctable condition of human survival even on primitive levels of civilization. And wherever this knowledge is intensified through specialization of crafts, the basis for systematic elaboration into an empirical science is present. In all civilizations, Western or Eastern, ancient or medieval, empirical science does not originate in philosophy but in the knowledge of craftsmen. When such a body of empirical knowledge falls into the hands of professional theorists, it may flower into a science if the methods (as, for instance, experimentation and mathematization) are suitable; but, obviously, it also may be ruined if the method is a fashion of fallacious speculation. That was the danger which a rather highly developed science like Greek medicine had to face. But the same fate might befall the empirical knowledge of politics as it was to be found in the art of the statesmen, the craftsmen of politics. A foretaste of what could happen in this respect was furnished by the cases of Hippodamus and Phaleas, of whom the former was singled out by Aristotle as the first private person, that is, the first non-craftsman who speculated on the best form of government, apparently using a Phythagorean "hypothesis." Thucydides has his place in this development as the first craftsman who tried to transform the empirical knowledge of politics into a science, using the science of medicine as his model for this purpose. The speeches in the *Syngraphe* gain a particular importance under this aspect, because in the speeches Thucydides let the political craftsmen, the leading statesmen, generals, and ambassadors, form and formulate the *eidos* of the *kinesis* which he as a scientist described.

Thucydides' feat of transforming the knowledge of the craftsmen into a science, however, inevitably raised grave problems for the future of political science. The *kinesis* was a "disease" of political order; the craftsmen who shaped and defined its *eidos* were the gravediggers of Hellas, as Plato characterized them in the *Gorgias;* and the political science of Thucydides was a model study of the suicide of a nation but hardly a study of successful political order. If Cimon, Militiades, and Pericles, according to the diagnosis of Plato, were poor statesmen who shaped a *kinesis* and thereby destroyed the order of the Athenian polis and its empire, where was the craftsman to be found, and what would he look like, who could shape a just order? Plato's answer to this question was the philosopher-king, the ruler who carried the right order in his soul and, as a craftsman, could shape the order of the polis in the image, the paradigm, of his soul, which in its turn was shaped after the paradigm that is laid up in heaven. The science of Thucydides explored the *idea* only of *kinesis*, of the disturbance of order; Plato explored the *idea* of order itself. This relation between Thucydides and Plato needs emphasis, because on occasion one can still hear voiced the nostalgic sentiment: How marvellously could political science have advanced if others had followed in the footsteps of Thucydides, and if this promising beginning of a science of politics had not been cut off by the influence of Plato's philosophy. This preconception of empiricists overlooks the fact that the two thinkers complement each other: Thucydides studied a political society in crisis, and created the empirical science of the lethal disease of order; Plato created the other half of politics, the empirical science of order. If Plato understood his task as a search for the ideas of virtue in general, and of justice in particular, and for his purpose used the same terms *eidos* and *idea* as the physicians and Thucydides, the usage should not be considered a philological curiosity but a clue to Plato's intentions. The understanding of this complicated phase of Greek intellectual history will certainly increase if one does not dispose of Plato by classifying him as a philosophical "idealist," but recognizes him as the empirical craftsman who tried to define and shape the *eidos* of order in society by linking immanent order with its transcendent origin in the Agathon.

3. The Theory

The contemporaries of Thucydides, as previously noted, did not share his opinion that a great Peloponnesian War had occurred. When they said war they meant a series of battles and campaigns that had a formal beginning with a declaration of war and a formal end with a treaty of peace. When Thucydides said war he meant a movement that was more than a series of diplomatic and military actions in so far as, beyond physical clashes and conflicts of passions, it had a dimension of meaning extending into the regions of moral breakdown and transfiguration. On the pragmatic level of political and military action, the empire of Athens first rose to greatness as a power and then went down in defeat; on the level of Thucydidean historiography, rise and fall did not follow one another in time but were interwoven in a texture of meaning out of time. It was an intricate weave, and sometimes the reader wonders whether the historian himself was always quite sure of the pattern he wove. The Athenian rise to power was physically and emotionally an outburst of forces, an aggrandizement of the hegemonic city at the expense of weaker allies and neighbors; while morally it was a ruthless indulgence in violations of justice and satisfactions of greed, a breakdown of ethos, a great fall containing the seeds of the subsequent political disaster.

This much is clear; but as Thucydides is not a moralizing intellectual reading a lecture to imperialists, it is not all. To be sure, aggressive expansion and disintegration of ethos were inseparably one; but it did not follow that aggressive expansion was bad. While the external rise was vitiated by the rotting of moral substance, it opened a field of great opportunities and released men into the freedom of proving their skills, inventiveness, and imagination; the Athenian rise to power was a splendid spectacle from the navies dominating the seas to the architectural adornment of the empire city; the vulgarity, brutality, atrocity, and general sordidness, which Thucydides recognized as clearly as the Old Oligarch, were the price that had to be paid for the Acropolis and the splendor of the Periclean golden age. Athens, as Thucydides saw it, was a progressive power in history, and her civilizational potentialities could not have been actualized without the imperial exploitation of her confederates and subjects. But again caution is indicated. Thucydides, while not a moralist, was also not a jingo who would justify imperial domination by the civilizational superiority of the aggressor. He clearly was on the side of Athenian enterprise and innovating activity, but he was appalled by the moral disintegration and physical destruction which, apparently of necessity, balanced the ephemeral splendor of Periclean Athens.

Further aspects of the *kinesis* came into view when the apparent necessity of this connection was more closely examined. The responsibility for the peculiar form which the political and civilizational expansion assumed did not rest on Athens alone. The defense of Hellas against the Persian threat required a strong navy, as Salamis had shown, and the Delian confederates were quite willing to let Athens carry the burden of energetic action. The concentration of naval power in Athens was largely due to the fact that the members of the Delian League preferred the payment of money contributions to the building, maintenance, and manning of their own fleets; they built the instrument of their subjugation out of their own treasure and had themselves no military strength to resist encroachments of the hegemonic city when it increased in power at their expense. When after the Peace of Callias the Persian danger had become less imminent, the social structure of Athens had changed from the semi-aristocratic, agricultural polis of Marathon to a bustling industrial and commercial democracy, a shipbuilding center for the confederacy, and a maritime power. No statesman could reverse the evolution against the interest and will of the people. Athens had adjusted herself to the exigencies of the new age; and now the former allies had to adjust themselves to the new Athens and submit to the transformation of the League into an Empire.

A similar problem arose in relation to the Peloponnesian League. The Peloponnesians certainly had reason to fear the new and still growing power of Athens. But they had to fear it because the Lacedaemonians and their allies chose to preserve their old pattern of existence. Willingness and imagination were missing to balance the Athenian transformation by adjustments of policy and constitutional order of the same radical character. The conditions of power were changing, and only Athens among the Hellenic poleis was pliable and venturous enough to meet them. The Peloponnesians, the islands, and the Asiatic Greeks were inclined to consider the new order a violation of justice and the revolutionary power an aggressor.

The frictions arising from the changes in the relative strength of forces, carefully detailed by Thucydides, furnished the historian with material for reflections on the causality of political action and its conflict with principles of justice. The expedition of Xerxes had been a brute fact of history, a cause that had set off a chain of effects. The first of these effects was the naval policy of Themistocles which saved the independence of Hellas. The success at Salamis became a further cause, determining the continued naval policy of the Delian League, which in its turn caused the transformation of Athens. By 450 the new order of Athens had become an accomplished fact; and its irreversibility became the initiating cause of the empire policy. The expedition of Xerxes, the battle of Salamis, the foundation of the League, and the transformation of Athens form a chain of cause and effect ending in the disturbing power of the hegemonic city; we are in the realm of the *aitiai* which have their effect with necessity. Causality, however, is no argument in the issues of justice and morality. Thucydides does not expect the Athenian masses to act against their interest, to surrender their profitable occupation and agreeable life, and to return to tilling the soil of Attica as modest peasants under cramped conditions, once the Persian danger is over; they are "compelled" to organize their empire. And once it is organized with brutality they cannot be expected to give it up and to abolish their navy as a gesture of appeasement, for their former subjects would ally among themselves or with Sparta and take their vengeance against the former oppressors; hence they are "compelled" to maintain it ruthlessly. Nevertheless, the "compulsion" to commit injustices and atrocities still is a moral breakdown; and never is it more evident than when the compulsion of interest is erected into the law of action which justifies transgressions of morals and justice.

The conflict between necessity and justice is further complicated by the dubious conduct of the enemies of Athens. The increasing difference of power between the empire city and its enemies is only in part caused by Athenian action; in another part it is caused by the inaction of the members of the symmachy and of the Peloponnesians. In the ethics of tragedy, however, inaction is evasion of Dike; the man who does not meet circumstance with decisive action is remiss in his duties. It is immoral to let oneself become weak through changing circumstance if remedial action could maintain or restore strength. A power that has become relatively weak through inaction cannot put all of the blame for its misfortunes on a stronger power that avails itself of its opportunities.

Thucydides was faced with the problem that the very genius, courage, and energy of Athens which saved Hellas, as well as the continued operation of the released forces which resulted in material benefits and cultural achievements, had disastrous consequences in a civilizational environment of less energetic partners. It is the perennial problem of the effects of a progressive power on the slower neighbors. Should it be considered a principle of justice in social relations in general, and in political relations in particular, that a man or society, willing to put their energies to good use, should restrain themselves and courteously keep step with the marginal stragglers and laggards? Especially when energetic action has a clear nucleus of service to the common interest, and the defenders of the *status quo* by their resistance endanger the safety of the community? Thucydides decides for the progressive side. The problem is well illuminated by the famous difference of opinion between Thucydides and Plato concerning the merits of Archelaus, the king of Macedonia. Thucydides sees him as the benefactor of his country who constructed the fortifications which for the first time made Macedonia safe against invasions, built a new road system, organized a military force, and increased the resources of defense more than the eight kings who preceded him (II, 100). In Plato's *Gorgias* the same Archelaus appears as the prototype of an unsavory politician who rises to power by murder and assorted crimes. The trouble is that probably both portraits are equally correct; there are situations where the nature of the opposition requires brutal means for the achievement of political ends desirable in themselves.

The tortuous boring into structure and meaning of the great movement, however, does not end in the flatness of intentionalist ethics. The means remain means to an end in the order of causality and do not rise to the dignity of morally justified action because the end is valuable; and if they are crimes they remain crimes in the order of morality. Only on one important occasion, in the Funeral Oration, does Thucydides present an argument that is meant to bridge the gulf between the orders of necessity and morality. This occurs when he lets Pericles plead: "No enemy will suffer indignity when he is defeated by such a city, and the subjects will not complain of being ruled by an unworthy master" (II, 41). If by the order of necessity there have to be conquerors and defeated, masters and subjects, this bleakness without sense will gain meaning by the worthiness of the conqueror or master. The necessity of power is something like a fate to be borne by mankind—the master is suffering

it just as much as the subject; and in the worthiness of the master the subject is experiencing (or supposed to experience) something like a common representation of human greatness. Obviously, the argument is thin;
Thucydides himself furnishes examples of prospective subjects who would
rather run the risk of extermination than experience a representation by
Athenian worthiness. Nevertheless, this very thinness is important in so
far as it reveals the desperateness of the dilemma. Not even the leading
Athenian statesman would, in the presentation of Thucydides, stoop so
low as to smear the slime of moral hypocrisy over the brutal reality. All
Thucydides can do is to fall back on the pride of Athens; and in his
pathos one can feel his suffering under the burden of a necessity which
needs Athens to atone for its shame.

There is no solution to the conflict. The deepest stratum that can be
touched in the theory of the *kinesis* is despair. Athens is moving on,
under compulsion of necessity, and each further step leads deeper into
the morass of injustice. The brilliant expansion is self-destructive in the
most literal sense of a destruction of moral personality. The process,
spreading from the public to the private sphere, begins with habituation
to unjust action in affairs of state and ends with the dissolution of hon-
esty, loyalty, and shame in personal relations. Thucydides describes the
process and its results with the passion of an anatomist dissecting a diseased organ; and with an eye trained by his description we can discern
the despair caused by the corrosion of personality in the sophistic fragments of the last quarter of the fifth century as well as in the sophists
portrayed by Plato. This advice to follow the *sympheron* in transgression
of the law, these truculent assertions that justice is what benefits the
stronger, these claims that the strong man rules by right because he is
the better man, these "theories" of law and justice as the invention of
the weak to keep the strong men down—all this desperate opining, never
approaching theoretical coherence, reflects the moral confusion of the
great *kinesis*. These various *doxai* illuminate aspects of the conflict between necessity and justice that shook the age.

Even the intellectual discipline of a Thucydides could not entirely
escape the profound confusion of the conflict. Here and there we find
reflections that, in spite of necessity, the actual course of events was not
inevitable. The war, to be sure, was inevitable but it was not necessary
that Athens lose it. The Periclean policy of cutting the losses of over-

expansion in the 460's and 450's, of abandoning Attica to invasion in case of war, and of holding the empire by the control of the sea would have assured victory. But after his death in 428, under the leadership of the emotional and ambitious Cleon, the best chances for a peace after the affair of Pylos were missed; and neither Cleon nor his successors had the integrity and personality that would keep the imperialist rabble in check and prevent disastrous adventures. Such failure of personal leadership that lost a war which by military calculation should have been won, Thucydides is inclined to consider accidental, an unpredictable misfortune playing havoc with the co-ordination of means and ends in the order of necessity in the same manner in which the plague disturbed the well-laid plans of Pericles.

Reflections of this kind show an unclearness in the mind of Thucydides concerning the connection between rationality and ethos. Apparently his sense was numbed, like that of his sophistic contemporaries, and he could not see that the sphere of power and pragmatic rationalism is not autonomous but part of human existence which as a whole includes the rationality of spiritual and moral order. If the controlling order of spirit and morality breaks down, the formation of ends in the pragmatic order will be controlled by the irrationality of passions; the co-ordination of means and ends may continue to be rational but action nevertheless will become irrational because the ends no longer make sense in terms of spiritual and moral order. When the corrosion of reason has reached a certain degree in depth and has befallen a sufficiently large proportion of the people, effective leadership in terms of reason becomes difficult and perhaps impossible, even if the man at the head under more favorable conditions could exert such leadership; in a further degree of corrosion a man of such qualities will, precisely because he possesses them, find it impossible to reach the position of leadership; and in a final degree the society by its corruption may prevent the formation of a man of such qualities even if by nature he should not be lacking in gifts. This connection between corruption of society and the impossibility of rational leadership Thucydides was unwilling to admit. He could not or did not want to see that a society and its political system was doomed if it could maintain itself in existence only by the miracle of a succession of Periclean personalities; nor would he admit that with progressive corrosion of ethos another Pericles could hardly emerge from Athenian society.

And the idea probably never occurred to him that a first rate man would not care to be the political leader of Athens and would turn to a less nauseating pursuit.

We have reached the end of Thucydides' theory of the *kinesis*, and can summarize the result. In the execution of his plan it appears that the limits of the *kinesis* in time had to be extended beyond the formal beginning of the war. The opening sentences named the "war" itself as the *kinesis;* but since Thucydides wanted to give more than a relation of military and diplomatic events, he had to extend the unit of meaning by including the aetiology of the crisis which reached its climax in actual warfare. For this purpose he inserted the *Fifty Years*, the history from Salamis to the outbreak of the war, in the First Book (I, 89–117). With this extension the movement became the great disturbance of the world of the poleis in the wake of the Persian Wars, lasting altogether from 480–404. The inquiry into the *eidos*, the nature of the movement, then, illuminated the various aspects of a complicated dilemmatic structure: of power and justice, necessity and morality, progress and backwardness, civilizational rise and breakdown of the ethos. The genius of Thucydides revealed itself in the discipline by which he resisted the temptation to obscure the dilemmatic structure of political existence by any attempt at rationalization. Because of this achievement he must be considered the true heir to the tragic tradition. But at the same time, because of its content, his work marks the formal end of tragedy in so far as it tells the story of the death of the hero who once represented the order of Zeus against the disordering hybris of power. The Dike of Zeus had disappeared from the order of Athens, and the tragic sentiment had withdrawn from the people into single individuals who as contemplators preserved the meaning of order in measuring the surrounding disorder by the memory of its standards.

At this point we touch the limit of Thucydides' achievement. It is worthwhile to compare his difficulty with the similar one of Machiavelli. Both thinkers were sensitive to the dilemma of power and morality, both were resigned to the necessity of criminal means for what they considered a desirable end. But Machiavelli was supremely conscious that the Prince could realize no more than external order, while genuine order had to be instilled into the community by a spiritual reformer. Thucydides, while moving on the same level of political action as Machiavelli, apparently had no conception of an alternative to his Periclean prince—for

which he can hardly be blamed since he did not have the experience of pro-
totypical saviors which Machiavelli had. This absence of a spiritual reform-
ing personality not only from the reality of Athens, but even from the
imagination of a Thucydides, shows clearly that an age of political culture had irrevocably come to its end. The time of the polis was running
out; a new epoch of order began with Socrates and Plato.

4. The Form

The *Syngraphe* is a fragment which breaks off in the twenty-first of
the twenty-seven years of the war. Moreover, the later books most probably are not in the form which their author would ultimately have given
them. A study of the literary form, therefore, must be based primarily
on the first four books. A brief consideration of this subject matter is
necessary, because the literary form of Thucydides is intimately connected with his theory.

Thucydides never presented his theory discursively, but suggested it
through the mutual illumination of events and speeches, only occasionally
interspersing direct reflections. The literary device, as we have seen, was
developed by Herodotus for the purpose of interpreting history by means
of an "hypothesis," but it gained a new meaning when Thucydides used
it for the purpose of exploring political reality. The question of what
Thucydides meant by reality, still much debated, is of crucial importance
for understanding the interrelation of his form with his theory. In our
contemporary intellectual climate, which is still strongly moved by the
winds of positivism, it tends to become the question of Thucydides' reliability as an historian in the modern sense. To twist it in this direction,
however, while not entirely improper, is sufficiently wrong to distort the
essence of the problem. If the *Syngraphe* were nothing but an account
of "historical facts" on the pragmatic level, it would never have been
written; for, as we have sufficiently detailed, on the pragmatic level there
was no such occurrence as a Peloponnesian War. The *kinesis* is a unit in
that it is the catastrophic drama of men who are caught in the bewilder-
ing dilemma of necessity and ethos; and this dramatic unit could not be
created by a mere narration of events but required the speeches which,
as a chorus in tragedy, raised the dilemma to lucid consciousness. The
reality of Thucydides, thus, is dramatic in the sense that actions are not
merely reported as events in time and space but are made transparent for
the drama of the soul through the device of the speeches. As a conse-

quence, the question of "historical reliability" in the modern sense cannot be answered with a plain Yes or No, but requires a distinction drawn by Thucydides himself. In I, 22 he distinguishes between speeches (*logoi*) and events (*erga*), and the degrees of exactness (*akribeia*) which he could achieve in reporting the two classes of historical materials. With regard to events he used the method of collecting reports of eyewitnesses, of comparing them, and of ascertaining the truth as far as possible when they were in conflict. With regard to the speeches he made no attempt at reporting them literally, since his own memory as well as that of others was too defective an instrument. Rather, he ascertained the situation in which the speech was made as well as the general purport of what actually was said, and then put into the mouth of his speakers the language that was "suitable" (*ta deonta*) to the occasion. The speeches, therefore, render neither the exact words nor the style of the speaker, but bring the "suitable" arguments uniformly transposed into the rhetorical style of Thucydides.

The speeches are inseparable from the events. It is not permissible to extract the events from the work and be satisfied with a harvest of reliable "facts" about Greek history; the events are true only as long as they remain parts of the whole that is constituted by the literary form. That raises a delicate problem. On the one hand, the speeches are themselves an integral part of reality, persuading and moving their audience toward specific action, the events; on the other hand, they are clearly a literary device, used with artistic circumspection, in order to create a unit of meaning. And in this latter function they shade off into the direct reflections of the author himself. Where, under these circumstances, does reality end, and where does the literary form begin? There seems to be only one answer possible: This peculiar structure can claim to be a description of reality only under the condition that reality itself contains the formal elements which can be heightened, without distortion, into the artistic form. Concretely: The Thucydidean use of the speeches presupposes a political culture in continuity with the culture that produced tragedy as its representative expression; government by argument and persuasion is the reality that can be heightened, without falsification, into well-defined courses of events through the meaning which radiates from strategically placed speeches. Moreover, the placing itself need not be in conflict with reality. We may safely assume that speeches were delivered on the occasions selected by Thucydides—for the good reason that the style of Hellenic politics required them on every occasion. Rather than doubt the three speeches of Pericles reported in the *Syngraphe*, one would assume that he made many more of a similar type. And with regard to their content, again there is no reason to doubt their substantially correct rendering; however, it is possible, and even probable, that Thucydides concentrated into his selected speeches a body of argument that actually was dispersed over several oratorical occasions. The speeches, in general, are probably composite pictures of an indefinite stream of debate that was going on among Greeks on these burning issues. Such preformation of reality through debate and persuasion could be raised to the dramatic form of representative speeches; and the dramatic luminosity of history thus gained could be further heightened to the great drama of the *kinesis* through the compositional art of the author as well as through the added touches of his personal reflections.

The Thucydidean form of historiography is unique in the sense that it was an efflorescence of Hellenic political culture in the fifth century; it could not be imitated as a literary model under different circumstances. Its artistic means, however, were not unique in their own time. The heightening of human reality into great types by an artist was generally possible in a culture with a high sense of form, with a gift and trained ability for discerning the typical in human situations, functions, and actions, and a willingness to stylize reality in the direction of the discerned types; and this willingness to form life into a drama of the typical could be fortified and facilitated by the creation of great paradigms on the part of the poets. As far back as the literary records go, Hellenic culture was pervaded by this mimetic interplay between the types of life and art. In the Homeric epics the paradigmatic myth was used for influencing the conduct of heroes, and the heroes were willing to form their actions in the image of paradigms. The epics themselves, then, became the great storehouse of paradigmatic wisdom and deeds down to the imitation of Achilles by Alexander. The cult of the tragedy, furthermore, rested on the mutual representation of the political decision for Dike by the tragic heroes and the heroic decision for Dike by the assembled citizenry of the polis. And this mutual formation of paradigm and reality, finally, reached its climax in the figure of Socrates who disappeared so completely behind the types created by the Socratic literature that we know next to nothing about him unless we assume that the reality of his life and thought conformed to the literary types. Toward the end of the fifth century new types arose in reality, and the formation of paradigms passed from the poets to the historians and philosophers; but the relationship between reality and types did not change on principle. In our study of the Sophists it became one of the great problems to discover to what extent the Platonic portraits could be used as an historical source; and the analysis of the fragments of primary sources suggested that the real sophists ran rather true to the types developed by Plato. And the climax again was the Platonic creation of the type of the philosopher out of the reality of Socratic existence. The peculiar achievement of Thucydides, in the context of this problem, was the creation of the type of *kinesis* out of a reality that was strongly preformed in the direction of the type.

5. *Formulations*

The development of theory as a subtle heightening of the typical in reality may be called the essence of classical culture. The profound realism of such theorizing, keeping so close to the object that its results are barely distinguishable from the object itself, causes, however, serious difficulties for the historian who wants to describe it adequately. The theory of Thucydides, presented in the preceding section, had to be extracted from the *Syngraphe* by relying on the suggestions of the story, especially of the speeches, rather than on the reflections of the author. Thucydides himself conveyed his theory of the *kinesis* by letting the object present itself through its self-articulation in speeches and debates. As a consequence, our extract neither rendered the words of Thucydides nor the language of the speeches. The theory, to be sure, could be extracted but the greatness of its expression was lost. No account, in fact, can substitute for reading the work itself. In order to remedy this loss at least in part, a selection of certain key passages will be given.[7]

The first of these selections will include passages from the speeches of the Corinthian and Athenian envoys at the first congress at Sparta which summarize the positions of the great protagonists in the war (I, 68ff.).

The Corinthian delegate presented the case of the Peloponnesian allies:

> The trust, Lacedaemonians, which you have in your constitution and social order, makes you distrustful of us when we bring charge against others. Hence springs your moderation, but also your ignorance of what is going on outside your own country.

[7] In the following selections I have used the translations of Jowett, Crawley, and Smith, with such changes as a more exact rendering of meaning seemed to require.

Having detailed the Athenian encroachments he continued:

> For all this you are responsible. For you have first allowed them
> to fortify their city, and then build their Long Walls. You are
> depriving of freedom not only those whom they have enslaved, but
> also those who as yet have been your allies. For he truly enslaves a
> people who has the power to prevent enslavement but does not use
> it. . . . And we know by what method and small steps the Athenians
> encroach upon their neighbors. They are confident even while they
> feel that you are too dull to observe them; but when they know that
> you do not want to interfere they will strike and not spare. Of all
> the Hellenes, you Lacedaemonians alone are inactive; you alone de-
> fend yourselves not by actions but by intentions, and try to crush
> an enemy not in the infancy but in the fulness of his strength . . .
> The Athenians are given to innovation, equally quick in the concep-
> tion and execution of every new plan; while you are careful only
> to keep what you have, originating nothing, and not acting even
> when action is most necessary . . . They are impetuous and you
> are dilatory; they are always abroad, and you are always at home
> . . . One might truly say, they were born into the world to take
> no rest themselves and to give none to others.
>
> You fail to see that peace stays longest with those who not only
> use their strength justly but show equal determination not to submit
> to injustice. It seems to be your idea of justice not to injure others
> so that you will run no risk even in self-defence. This policy would
> hardly have been successful even if your neighbors were like your-
> selves; but in the present case your habits are old-fashioned com-
> pared with theirs. And of necessity, in politics as in arts, the new
> will prevail over the old . . . The vast experience of Athens has
> carried her farther than you on the path of innovation.
>
> Let your procrastination end . . . Do not drive us in despair to
> some other alliance . . . The true breakers of treaties are not
> those who, when forsaken, turn to others, but those who forsake
> allies whom they have sworn to defend.

The Corinthian was followed by the Athenian envoy, speaking in
defense of the empire (*arche*):

> That empire was not acquired by force; but you would not stay
> and make an end of the barbarians, and the allies came of their own
> accord and asked us to be their leaders. From then on circumstance
> compelled us to advance our power: fear was our first motive; then
> it was honor; and finally interest. When we had incurred the hatred
> of most of our allies; when some of them had already revolted and
> been subdued; when you were no longer the friends you once had
> been, but had become suspicious and ill-disposed, our hold could

not be relaxed without risk, for the cities falling away from us would have gone over to you. And no one can be reproached when in greatest danger he does what is most advantageous [*ta sympheronta*]. If you, and not we, had persevered in the leadership of the allies long enough to be hated, you would have been quite as intolerable to them as we are now and you would have been compelled to choose between ruling forcefully or endangering yourselves. You have no reason to be astonished that, acting as it is the way of human nature, we accepted an empire that was offered to us and then refused to give it up, submitting to three all-powerful motives: honor, fear, and interest. Besides, we have not set an example without precedent, for always has it been held that the weaker should be subject to the stronger. And we think that we are worthy of our position, and so you thought until now, when calculating your interest [*ta sympheronta*] you talk about justice—a consideration which never deterred any one from taking by force as much as he could. Praised as worthy should be those who, while indulging their human nature to rule others, show themselves more just than they need be.

Thucydides closed the prelude of the speeches with a reflection of his own that the Lacedaemonians declared themselves for war, not because they were convinced by the arguments of their allies, but from fear of the growing power of Athens.

One of the most important factors in the *kinesis*, that is, the pathos of Athens, cannot be translated into theoretical propositions at all. In this case the speeches which express it are not primarily concerned with a marshalling of arguments but are a manifestation of pride in existence. A few passages from the Periclean speeches will convey this pathos. A first group will be selected from the Funeral Oration (II, 35ff.):

Before I praise the dead, I should like to point out by what methods we rose to power, by what constitution and what manner of life our empire became great . . . It is called by the name of democracy because it is administered for the many, not the few. But while the law secures equal justice to all alike in their private disputes, the claim of excellence is also recognized . . . There is no exclusiveness in our public life, and in our private intercourse we are not suspicious of one another, nor angry with our neighbor if he does what he likes . . . While we are thus unconstrained in our private intercourse, a spirit of reverence pervades our public acts; we are prevented from doing wrong by respect for authority and for the laws.

Our public men have, besides politics, their affairs to attend to; and our ordinary citizens, though occupied with their business, are still fair judges of public matters. We alone regard a man who takes no interest in public affairs, not as harmless, but as a useless character; and if few of us are originators, we are all sound judges of a policy. We do not consider discussion an impediment to action, but rather the indispensable preliminary to any wise action at all. To sum up: I say that Athens is the school of Hellas, and that the individual Athenian in his own person seems to have the power to adapt himself to the most varied forms of action with the utmost versatility and grace . . . No enemy who comes against her is indignant at the reverses which he sustains at the hands of such a city; no subject complains that his masters are unworthy of him . . . We shall not need the praises of Homer or of any other panegyrist whose poetry may please for the moment, although his representation of the facts will not bear the light of day. For we have compelled every land and every sea to open a path for our valor, and have everywhere planted eternal memorials of our friendship and of our enmity.

I would have you day by day fix your eyes upon the greatness of Athens, until you become filled with the love of her; and when you are impressed with the spectacle of her glory, reflect that this empire has been acquired by men who knew their duty and had the courage to do it, who in the hour of conflict had the fear of dishonor always present to them, and who, if ever they failed in an enterprise, would not allow their virtues to be lost to their country, but freely gave their lives to her as the fairest offering which they could present at her feast.

Even the Periclean pathos, however, comes near the breaking point under the stresses of the war, aggravated by the plague (II, 64):

You must realize that your city has the greatest name among all mankind because she has never yielded to misfortune, that she has spent more men's bodies and pains on war than any other, and that she has obtained the greatest power seen to this day. Even if some day we shall recede from it (for all that has grown must decline) the remembrance will remain that of all Hellenes we ruled more Hellenes than any other polis; that in the greatest wars we held our own against them all united and singly; and that our city was the most prosperous and abundant with regard to everything.

To be hateful and offensive has always been the fate of those who aspired to rule others . . . But hatred does not last long; the brilliance of the present, however, and the ensuing renown will remain in memory forever.

Nothing will remain but the memory of ephemeral brilliance and power. This pathos strongly resembles the archaic Tyrtaean faith in immortality through preservation in the grateful memory of a people. The people, to be sure, now has become mankind; still, there is a wintry anachronism about this consolation with remembrance of actions both glorious and corrupt. And, indeed, if Athens is remembered today it is not because once she ruled the sea.

The glory to be remembered was spreading thinner and thinner over the mounting horrors of the war. In a probably calculated counterpoint Thucydides balanced the pathos of Pericles with his own description of the atrocities into which the party struggle between oligarchs and democrats degenerated (III, 82):

> When troubles had once begun in the cities, those who followed carried the revolutionary spirit further and further, and determined to outdo the report of all who had preceded them by the ingenuity of their enterprises and the atrocity of their revenges. The meaning of words no longer had the same relation to things, but was changed by them as they thought proper. Reckless daring was held to be loyal courage; prudent delay was the excuse of a coward; moderation was the disguise of unmanly weakness; ability to see all sides of a question inaptness to act on any. . . . The lover of violence was always trusted, and his opponent suspected . . . The tie of party was stronger than the tie of blood, because a partisan was more ready to dare without asking why . . . The seal of good faith was not divine law, but fellowship in crime . . . Any agreements sworn to by either party, when they could do nothing else, were binding as long as both were powerless . . .

> The cause of all this was the desire to rule, originating in pleonexy and ambition, and the party spirit engendered by them when men are fairly embarked in a contest. For the leaders on either side used specious names, the one party professing to uphold "the political equality for the masses under the law," the other "a temperate aristocracy," while they made the public interest, to which in name they were devoted, in reality their prize . . . And the citizens who were of neither party fell a prey to both, either because they did not make common cause with them, or through mere jealousy that they should survive.

> An attitude of perfidious antagonism everywhere prevailed; for there was no word binding enough, nor oath terrible enough to reconcile enemies. Each man was strong only in the conviction that nothing was secure; he must look to his own safety, and could not afford to trust others . . . Inferior intellects generally succeeded best. For,

aware of their own deficiencies, and fearing the capacity of their opponents . . . they struck boldly and at once.

Shorn of pathos, and reduced to power in the raw, the breakdown of ethos, finally, manifested itself in the Melian Dialogue. The following two passages concern justice and the gods (V, 89 and 105):

> You know as well as we do that in human discussion justice enters only where the pressure of necessity is equal. For the rest, the powerful exact what they can and the weak grant what they must.

> Of the gods we believe, and of men we know, that by a necessity of nature they rule wherever they can. We neither made this law nor were the first to act on it; we found it to exist before us and shall leave it to exist forever after us; we only make use of it, knowing that you and everybody else, if you were as strong as we are, would act as we do.

The Melians did not submit; when their city was conquered all men were butchered, and the women and children were sold into slavery.

The Athenians had occasion to remember their misdeeds when at Aegospotami their last fleet was destroyed and the end had come. In his continuation of Thucydides' *Syngraphe*, in the *Hellenica*, Xenophon described the scene when the news of the disaster arrived: "It was at night that the *Paralus* [one of the fast dispatch-ships that had escaped] arrived at Athens with the tidings of the disaster, and a sound of wailing ran from the Piraeus through the long walls to the city, one man passing on the news to another; and during that night no one slept, all mourning, not for the lost alone, but far more for their own selves, thinking that they would suffer such treatment as they had visited upon the Melians." [8] The Corinthians and Thebans, indeed, were in the mood to destroy the city. Unless the Lacedaemonians had resisted the policy, in view of the services of Athens in the Persian War, that would have been the end of her history.

[8] Xenophon, *Hellenica*, trans. C. L. Brownson (Loeb Classical Library), II, ii, 3.

Greek Terms

achreios—Aristotle 140; Hesiod 140
agnoia—Plato 174
aidos—Aristotle 157; Hesiod 157 f.; Protagoras 272, 286
aitia, aition, aitios, 133; Herodotus 335; Hippocrates 353; Homer 107; Thucydides 360
akoe—Thucydides 42
alazoneia, 138
aletheia, 4; Antiphon 313 f.; Critias 321 f.; Hesiod 130; Parmenides 204, 209; etetyma (Hesiod) 130
amathia—Democritus 301
andreia—Plato 89, 158; Protagoras 287; Simonides 200
anomia—*Anonymus Iamblichi* 328; Critias 321
aoidos—Homer 72
apeiron—Anaxagoras 293; Anaximander 181 f.
apistia—Heraclitus 228
arche, 134 f.; Anaximander 183; Hippocrates 353; Thucydides 369; *arche kai peras* (Heraclitus) 235
arete, 170, 185; Democritus 302; Herodotus 312; Hesiod 139; Solon 196 f.; Tyrtaeus 188 f.
askesis—Democritus 302; Protagoras 309
asynetos—Heraclitus 228
ate—Homer 87 f., 105 f.
atomos—Democritus 212, 298; Parmenides 212
authadia—Aeschylus 258 f., 260 f.

bathys—Heraclitus 173
bios—Heraclitus 237
bythos—Democritus 299

charis—St. Paul 12
cholos—Homer 89 f., 91 f., 97ff., 108
chreon—Anaximander 336; Heraclitus 337
chros—Homer 102

daimon—Democritus 300; Empedocles 222 f.; Heraclitus 224 f.; Plato 205 ff.; Pythagoreans 224
demagogia—Aristotle 120
demos—Aeschylus 250; Heraclitus 239

demosion kakon—Solon 194
demotikoi—Old Oligarch 348, 349
dikaiosyne—Protagoras 287
dike—Aeschylus 243, 249, 253, 255–64, 286; Anaximander 234, 336; Democritus 301; Heraclitus 233, 336; Hesiod 132, 138 ff., 141 f., 144, 155 f., 158, 163; Parmenides 204 f.; Protagoras 272, 286; Solon 243; Thucydides 360
doxa, 247; 251; Antiphon 313; Parmenides 204, 214 f., 216, 220; Plato 321, 323; Solon 195 f., 202; *dokos* (Xenophanes) 173; *dokounta* (Parmenides) 205
dysnomia—Solon 194

eidolon—Homer 103
eidos—Hippocrates 354; Plato 355; Thucydides 354 f., 357
eikos mythos—Plato 26
eironeia, 138
ekpyrosis—Heraclitus 237; Hesiod 146
elpis—Heraclitus 228
entole—St. Paul 11
epiprepei—Xenophanes 172–74
episteme—Plato 289
epithymia—Plato 206
eris—Heraclitus 237; Hesiod 139; Homer 88, 92
eros, 96 f., 99; Heraclitus 233; Hesiod 134; Homer 96 f., 99; Parmenides 217; Plato 137
etee—Democritus 299 f.
etetyma—Hesiod 130, 138
ethos—Heraclitus 224 f., 227; Parmenides 209; *ethos anthropeion, theion* (Heraclitus) 224
euboulia—Protagoras 285
eudaimonia, eudaimon—Democritus 300; Herodotus 336; Plato 206
eukosmos—Solon 195
eunomia—Hesiod 132; Old Oligarch 346; Solon 118, 194, 197, 199, 243; Xenophanes 184 f., 186 ff.
euthymos, euthymia—Democritus 301, 304

genesis, 182; Heraclitus 237
geneto—Hesiod 134

Modern Authors

Subjects and Names

Abel-Remusat, J.-P., 19
Abraham, 29, 34
Academy, 168, 271
Achaeans, 31, 54 f., 67; occupation of Hellas, 54; Homer on Achaean kingdoms, 77–83
Action, 247–53, 263; Aeschylus, 104, 247–53, 301; decision in favor of Dike, 249 ff.; Democritus, 301 f., and dream, 80 f., 341 f.; Herodotus, 340–43; Homer, 80 f., 103 ff.; Pseudo-Antiphon, 327; Rational, 43; Thucydides, 359 ff.
Aeschylus, 51, 73, 104, 243–64, 282, 286 f., 301, 320, 334, 337; *Eumenides*, 264; *Oresteia*, 133, 252, 256 f.; *Persians*, 332; *Prometheus Bound*, 253–61, 264; *Prometheus Unbound*, 256, 262; *Suppliants*, 247–51, 253, 257
Aetiology of Disorder, 101–05, 107 f.
Agathon, 186, 193, 197
Age of the Bull, 150, 159
Age of the Ram, 150
Ages of the World, 144–54; Bronze, 33; Chinese, 151 ff., Golden Age, 10, 156; Heroic, 34; Hesiod, 144 f.; Iron, 33; Jainist, 145 f.; Ovidius, 147 f.; *see also* Metal Ages
Agnosticism—critical and dogmatic, 325
Agonal Culture, 187 f.
Aidos, 157 f.
Aion—Euripides, 236; Heraclitus, 235 f.
Akhenaton, 127
Alalakh, 61
Alcaeus, 35
Alcibiades, 138, 244
Alcidamas, 326
Alcinous, 74
Alcman, 35
Alcmeon, 303
Aletheia—search for from Parmenides to Plato, 324; *see* Truth
Alexander the Great, 61, 199, 231, 324 f., 367 f.
Alphabet, 34, 47

am Yahweh, 12
Amarna Age, 61
Amasis, 337
Amon Hymns, 127
analogia entis, 176 f., 210
Ananke—Aeschylus, 262; of Being and Logos, 214; Empedocles, 222
Anaxagoras, 35, 166, 182, 212, 268 f., 293 f., 297 f., 355
Anaximander, 35, 118, 167, 181 f., 183, 233 f., 235 f., 353
Angelology, 157
anima animi, 176
Animism, 177 f.
Anonymus Iamblichi, 326–28
Anthropogony, 148
Anthropomorphism, 5, 174–78, 254; Comte, 175; Hesiod, 176; Scientist Cliché, 176; Xenophanes, 174–78; *see also* Theomorphism
Antilogical reasoning, 296 f., 343
Antiphon the Sophist, 312–19, 323, 325 ff.
Antisthenes, 211
Anxiety—of annihilation, 156 f., 162, 164
Apeiron, 182 f.; Dialectics of, 182
Aphrodite, 136
Apocalypse, 154–64; dual symbolism, 155 f.; Hesiodian and Prophetic, 159–61; Homer, 162; of just and unjust cities, 156; and reality, 164
Appearance and Reality, 202; apocalyptic nightmare and true order, 163 f.; blindness and seeing, 72 f.; Doxa and Aletheia, 204 f.; Doxa and Unseen Measure, 197; nihilism and anxiety, 164; *see also* Existence (Polarity)
Archelaus (King), 361
Archelaus of Miletus, 320
Archilochus, 118, 201 f.
Areopagus, 256
Arete, 188, 190 f., 193, 196, 289; Homeric, 189; of the polis, 190; Solonic, 196 f.; Tyrtaean, 188–94; Xenophantic, 184–88
Arete (Catalogues)—Plato, 193 f.; Protagoras,

200, 207, 212, 214, 222, 227, 232, 234,
240 f., 252 f., 264, 267, 269, 271 f., 273 f.,
278 f., 281, 284 f., 292, 302 f., 304 f., 306 f.,
315, 319 f., 323 f., 328, 341, 345, 349,
355, 361 f., 365, 368
Plato (Works)—*Charmides*, 278 f.; *Critias*,
56 f., 230, 333; *Gorgias*, 8, 158, 164, 202,
223, 288, 310, 319, 357, 361; *Hippias
Major*, 278; *Hippias Minor*, 278 f., 281,
284; *Laws*, 43 ff., 47, 193, 236, 272, 301,
329, 331; *Parmenides*, 211; *Phaedo*, 133,
223; *Phaedrus*, 133, 220, 223, 225; *Philebus*,
301; *Protagoras*, 272, 278, 281, 284 f., 285–
91, 309, 321; *Republic*, 130, 171, 173 f.,
180, 183, 187, 193, 199, 207, 214, 222 f.,
271, 273 f.,,276 f., 279, 303, 323, 329, 331;
Statesman, 110, 264, 336; *Theaetetus*, 298;
Timaeus, 131, 199, 205 f., 216 f., 230, 253,
294
Playing Child, 235 f., — God, 236
Poet, 165; authority, 171; blindness and seeing, 72 f.; existence under God, 74 f.; holy
mouth of the Muse, 73; and the Muses,
72 ff.; philosophers' opposition, 171 f.;
prophet of Zeus, 73; revelation and proph-
ecy, 74; servant of the Muses, 73; singer of
the memorable, 74
Polis, 113–25, 203; burden of the, 169; Eunomia, 243; gentilitian structure, 115 f.; history, 117 f.; immortalizing pathos, 203;
leagues, 122–25; limitation of political philosophy, 170; origins, 113 f.; Platonic paradigm, 141; paradigm of the best, 46; pathos,
120 f., 243; savior, 44; split between pathos
and ethos, 190
Polis (Greek terms)—*anchisteia*, 115; *archon*,
115; *demos*, 116; *demotikon*, 116; *genos*,
115; *hetaireia*, 168; *nomos*, 306; *phratria*,
115; *phyle*, 114, 116; *politeia*, 286; *prostasia*,
119 f., 342 f.; *synodos*, 194; *thesmos*, 306
Polycrates, 337
Polyhistory, 271
Poseidonius, 8, 10
Power, 332–73
Prodicus, 268, 271, 325
praeparatio evangelica, 15
Preamble, 201
Predestination, 11
Prelogical mentality, 5
Prometheus—Aeschylus, 253–64, 286, 320;
Critias, 320 ff.; Goethe, 254; Hesiod, 142 f.,
254; Marx, 254; Plato, 290; Protagoras,
285–87, 320 f.; Shaftesbury, 254; Shelley,
254; Zosimos, 254

Prophets, 8 f., 13, 156, 162; dual symbolism,
155–62
Protagoras, 211, 214, 268 f., 272 f., 274–77,
285–91, 292–98, 302, 305, 307–10, 320;
Aletheia, 291, 294; *Antilogies*, 276; Myth
of Prometheus, 285 f., 321; *On the Gods*,
295
Pylos, 63
Pyrrho, 308
Pythagoras, 20, 35, 59, 173, 221 ff., 224 f.,
232
Pythagorean Movement, 165, 168, 170
Pythagoreanism, 59, 205

Ramses III, 62, 65
Rationalism—Herodotus, 40; of power, 41,
359; transition from ethos to power, 345 ff.,
373; Thucydides, 41
Religion, 179; higher, 21 f.; history as progress
of, 21; natural, 177
Remythization, 136
république de savants, 283
Revelation, 1, 3, 6, 8, 52, 126, 169, 218 f.,
225, 264
Rhea, 56
Rhodus, 62
Rome, 13 f.

Salamis, 244, 359 f.
Salvation, 8 f.; through work and faith, 12
Sappho, 35, 74, 118, 200–202, 210, 240
Scaevola (pontifex maximus), 13
Schelling, 136
Schools of philosophers, 166 ff.; Parmenides,
Pythagoras, 168; successions, 165
Science—empirical, medical, political, 357
Seemliness of Symbols, 171–74, 176, 178, 239;
criteria, 172 f.; Heraclitus, 173; Xenoph-
anes, 172 f.
Sefiroth, 135 f.
Shaftesbury, 254
Shelley, 254
Sheol, 4
Sicilian expedition—*see* War
Sicily, 35
Simonides, 200, 287 f.
Singer—*see* Poet
Skepticism, 308 f.
Sleepwalkers, 241
Smerdis, 339
Society—Achaean, 61–66, 76; attunement with
the order of being, 2; civilizational, 6; con-
crete, 1, 3; Cretan, 54–61; generic and
unique qualities, 2; Greek, 32, 34, 62; Hel-